LEGENDS
OF THE
NAHANNI VALLEY

LEGENDS
OF THE
NAHANNI VALLEY

BY
HAMMERSON PETERS

MYSTERIES
OF
CANADA

"The Northern Lights have seen queer sights..."

- Robert W. Service, *The Cremation of Sam McGee*, 1907.

Table of Contents

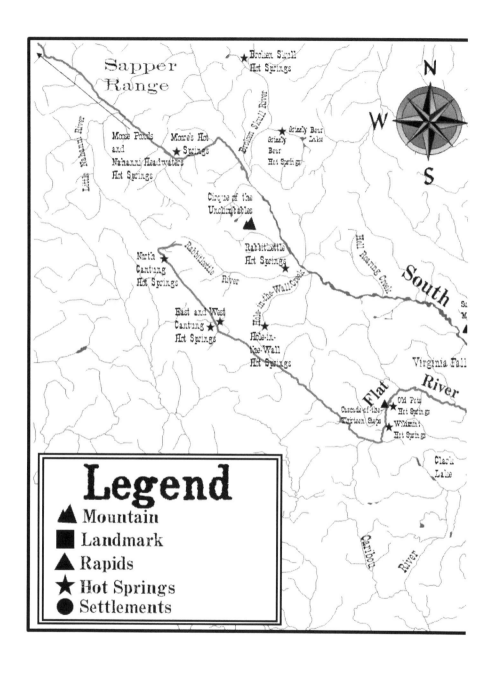

Legend
▲ Mountain
■ Landmark
▲ Rapids
★ Hot Springs
● Settlements

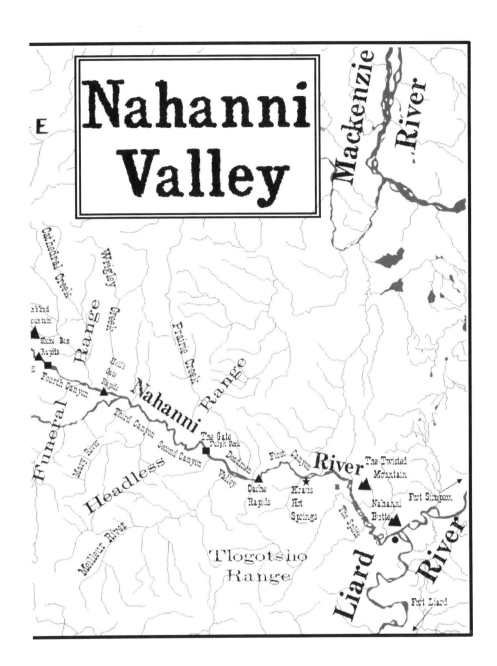

Acknowledgements

WHILE CONDUCTING RESEARCH for this book, I consulted professionals from a diversity of disciplines, from river guides, bush pilots, and First Nations chiefs to paleontologists, Mounties, and dog trainers. Representatives of each of these vocations provided me with some modicum of information, in one way or another, and I am grateful for every bit of help I received.

Of all the various experts from whom I sought assistance, three authorities in one particular field were especially accommodating. These excellent gentlemen, in the context of their contributions towards this book, can perhaps most accurately be described as 'Forteanologists'- specialists in the study of 'Fortean', or unexplained phenomena. In response to my request for information on the various stories and legends surrounding the watershed of the South Nahanni River, these Fortean scholars- Dr. Michael D. Swords, Mr. Will Matthews, and especially Mr. Gary S. Mangiacopra-graciously provided me with reams of rare and invaluable material from their personal files, without which this book could not have been written. I cannot thank them enough for their tremendous generosity.

Special thanks is due to author Lyn Hancock, a sourdough in her own right, for access to restricted files in her personal archive; to Dene language translator Allan Adam, for his interpretive services; to Gina Payzant of the Athabasca Archives, for permission to display certain rare and historic photographs in this book; and to Anthony Roche, a native of the Canadian North, for sharing his own strange experiences in the subarctic wilderness.

I would be remiss if I did not thank the following archivists and librarians for their considerable research assistance: Bev Bayzat of McMaster University; Doug E. Cass of the Glenbow Museum; Chelsea Shriver and Weiyan Yan of the University of British Columbia Library; Susan and Teresa Neamtz of the Canadian Museum of Nature; Cindy Preece of Wilfred Laurier University; Robin Weber of the NWT Archives; and especially Molly Wittenberg, Moira Marsh, and Carrie Schwier of Indiana University Bloomington. Their help is greatly appreciated.

Introduction

"The Nahanni River drains a vast land of fascinating beauty and splendor. The lure of gold has enticed many men through the canyons to this alluring land. Many have perished in its valley and mountains; some in search of gold. It is possible that most have died violent and unexplained deaths. Conjecture has given rise to all sorts of weird theories as to the cause of these misfortunes."

- Dick Turner, *Nahanni*, 1989.

FOR MANY CANADIANS today, the word 'Nahanni' is a foreign one. In some outdoor adventurers, it might evoke the South Nahanni River, a wild mountain waterway located in the southwest corner of the Northwest Territories; a subarctic Mecca for white water enthusiasts chock-full of world-class rapids, made famous by Raymond M. Patterson's 1954 adventure book *Dangerous River*. Others might know it as a breathtaking National Park and UNESCO World Heritage site through which the South Nahanni runs; a land of astounding geological and biological diversity, complete with dizzying canyons, enormous tufa mounds, and a waterfall nearly twice the height of the Niagara Falls. To a relative few, however, the Nahanni- this remote country hugging the junction of the British Columbia, Yukon, and Northwest Territories' borders- is land of myth and mystery, home to legends commemorated in the names of its landmarks, such as Deadmen Valley, Headless Creek, Broken Skull Hot Springs, and the Funeral Range. This book will explore these legends surrounding the watershed of the South Nahanni River, a land popularly referred to as the 'Nahanni Valley.'

In order to fully appreciate these legends, one must have a sense of the remoteness of the valley around which they revolve. Perhaps the best way to elicit that sense is to consider the general geography of the Canadian North, in the heart of which the Nahanni Valley resides.

For most Canadians, the North consists of Yukon, the Northwest Territories, and Nunavut, Canada's three federal territories. This vast region covers an area of nearly 3.9 million square kilometres (2.4 million square miles), most of it desolate wilderness. For all its size, the entire Canadian North houses a grand total of 120, 000 human residents, making it slightly less populous than the metropolitan of Lethbridge, Alberta. That's 8,000 acres per person, with room to spare.

Broadly speaking, the three territories that comprise the Canadian North can be divided into four main physiographic regions.

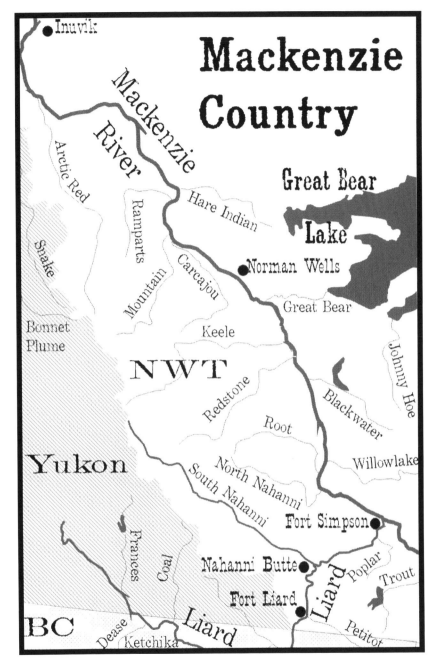

Far to the north, beyond the tree line, sits the high Arctic, land of the midnight sun, the polar bear, and the Inuit. North of the arctic mainland- a stretch of permafrozen tundra skirting the Arctic Sea- is the Arctic Archipelago, a maze of huge rock-strewn islands and shifting sea ice through which explorers Martin Frobisher and John Franklin once sailed in search of the Northwest Passage.

South of the Arctic and to the east lie the Keewatin Barrens, a sprawling expanse of subarctic prairie and Precambrian rock stretching from eastern Northwest Territories to the Atlantic coast of Nunavut. Populated by enormous aggregations of caribou, mosquitoes, and black flies (and little else!), the Barren Lands are almost completely devoid of human presence.

Far to the west, tucked between the soaring Saint Elias Mountains of the Pacific Coast and the more easterly Selwyn Range, is the Yukon, home of the historic Klondike. Replete with snow-capped mountains, taiga-covered hills, emerald lakes, and the great Yukon River, this land of gold is as beautiful as it is unforgiving.

And in the midst of the Canadian North, along the western edge of the Northwest Territories, between Yukon and Keewatin and south of the Arctic, lies the Mackenzie country. This fourth and final Northern region- the region in which the aforementioned legends are set- comprises the watershed of the mighty Mackenzie River, an immense northward-flowing watercourse which owes its name to the Scottish explorer who first paddled its length in 1789. A rugged, mountainous territory carpeted with boreal forest and interspersed with muskeg-bottomed lowland, the Mackenzie drainage basin consists of two massive lakes and five major tributaries: the Liard, Keele, Arctic Red, Peel, and Great Bear Rivers.

If you travel west up the Liard River from its confluence with the Mackenzie, past the little village of Fort Simpson and over the Beaverdam Rapids, you'll come to a lonely spruce-covered mountain called Nahanni Butte. At its foot, the Liard River is greeted by its main tributary, the South Nahanni River.

Up the South Nahanni and past the tiny Indian settlement of Nahanni Butte, located across the river from the mountain after which it was named, lies a section of river known as the Splits. This deadly labyrinth of gravelly islands and tangled log jams has claimed the lives of many a canoeist, both native and white, serving as an appropriate gateway to the sinister realm of mystery and menace beyond.

Past the Splits, the South Nahanni snakes out of the razor-ridged Mackenzie Mountains, carving its way through the limestone. The gloomy watershed of the river beyond, a series of mist-shrouded valleys fringed by rocky crags, is where our legends take place.

In the late 1940's, Canadian historian Pierre Berton, in reference to the Nahanni legends, said, "You know, we haven't got very much folklore in this country- country's too young, I guess. But it's a genuine piece of folklore and it's interesting to see how it grew and grew."

In fact, the two core Nahanni legends around which many of the others revolve- legends referred to in this book as the tale of the 'Lost McLeod Mine' and the 'Curse of the Nahanni Valley'- were born in the early 1900's, catalyzed by a string of mysterious deaths which took place in the valley during that time. Bolstered by native myth and prospector folklore, the legends grew throughout the 1920's and '30's, supplemented every time another prospector or trapper fell victim to the Nahanni country, perishing under mysterious circumstances or vanishing without a trace.

In the '40's and '50's, following the end of WWII, the Nahanni legends suddenly garnered international attention when celebrated authors and journalists began publishing often-exaggerated variations of them in books, newspapers, and magazines. The legends swelled in popularity throughout the sixties and seventies before finally fading from public consciousness throughout the 1980's. Today, these incredible tales are all but forgotten, preserved in the memories of a handful of baby boomers and members of the so-called 'Silent Generation,' and in countless magazine and newspaper articles languishing in the archives of various Canadian museums and universities.

The aim of this book is to bring the fantastic stories and legends of the Nahanni Valley back into Western awareness, if only for the purposes of education and entertainment. Perhaps, if the author might be bold as to suggest it, this book might even serve as a tool by which you, dear reader, will solve, once and for all, the mysteries of what magazines and newspapers of bygone days have styled 'The Headless Valley'.

A Word on the Dene

L IKE MOST GOOD CANADIAN frontier stories, the legends outlined in this book are inextricably intertwined with the history and mythology of the First Nations. As such, this book is filled with allusions to the various native tribes of Northern Canada and Alaska, necessitating a brief description of their tribal divisions.

Aside from the Inuit, who are considered a distinct aboriginal group based on their unique history and ethnicity, as are the Tlingit people of the Pacific Northwest, the natives of the Northland call themselves *"Dene"*, or some variation thereof, which translates to the "People". United by ancient blood ties and a common language family, the Dene people, also known as "Athabascans" or "Athapaskans", are comprised of roughly twenty one different tribes, sixteen of which will be alluded to in this book. These sixteen tribes include:

- **The Slavey** (a.k.a. Slave), whose traditional homeland includes Northwest Alberta, Northeast British

Columbia, and Southeastern Northwest Territories, from the Mackenzie River to Great Slave Lake.

- **The Kaska,** whose traditional homeland includes Northern British Columbia and Southeastern Yukon.

- **The Mountain Indians,** whose traditional homeland includes much of the Mackenzie Mountains in the Northwest Territories.

- **The Sahtu Dene** (a.k.a. Hare; and Bear Lake Indians), whose traditional homeland includes the Northwest Territories north of Great Bear Lake up to the Arctic Circle.

- **The Dogrib** (a.k.a. Tlicho), whose traditional homeland includes the area between Great Slave and Great Bear Lakes.

- **The Yellowknife,** whose traditional homeland includes land between Dogrib territory and the Arctic Circle.

- **The Chipewyan** (a.k.a. Denesoline), whose traditional territory includes the Keetwatin Barrenlands in Northern Manitoba, Northern Ontario, and much of the Nunavutian mainland south of the Arctic Circle.

- **The Gwich'in** (a.k.a. Kutchin), whose traditional homeland includes Northwestern Yukon and Northeastern Alaska, south of the Arctic Circle.

- **The Beaver** (a.k.a. Dunne-za), whose traditional homeland includes West-Central Alberta and East-Central British Columbia.

- **The Sekani,** whose traditional homeland includes North-Central British Columbia south of Kaska territory.

- **The Tahltan,** whose traditional homeland includes Northwest British Columbia east of the Pacific Coast.

- **The Tagish,** whose traditional homeland includes Southwest Yukon.

- **The Tutchone,** whose traditional homeland includes Southwest Yukon north of Tagish territory.

- **The Han,** whose traditional homeland includes West-Central Yukon.

- **The Tanana,** whose traditional homeland includes East-Central Alaska.

- **The Koyukon,** whose traditional homeland includes northern Alaska south of the Arctic Circle.

The Legends

"The Legend of the Headless Valley. It is, or was, one of the few pieces of bona fide folklore that we have in Canada. I think you will agree that it is a pretty good legend, too, for it has something of almost everything in it."

- Pierre Berton, circa 1947.

DEEP IN THE HEART of the Canadian North, in the southernmost reaches of the Mackenzie Mountains, lies the valley of the South Nahanni River, a mysterious area shrouded in legend. Long before the first white explorers paddled their canoes into the country in search of fur, local Dene Indians gave the place a wide berth. These natives believed that the valley was an evil area pervaded by bad medicine- a malevolent, supernatural presence which hung over the place perpetually like its ever-present fog.

Over the years, a number native hunters, spurred by bravery, foolishness, or desperation, wandered into the valley in search of game. The few who returned regaled their fellows with all manner of hair-raising tales. At night, while their compatriots crouched around the campfire, these survivors told of encounters with an evil spirit who haunted the valley, whose unearthly shrieks echoed throughout the canyons on windy nights. Others described a race of fearsome, hairy giants who dwelled in caves carved from the canyon walls. Led by a beautiful, pale-skinned chieftess, these primitive mountain men killed and ate anyone who trespassed on their territory.

According to Dene tradition, in ancient times, the Nahanni Valley was inhabited by a nomadic, warlike tribe known as the Naha. The Naha were ferocious warriors who frequently descended from their mountain homes to raid Dene settlements in the lowlands surrounding the Liard and Mackenzie Rivers. After suffering a number of devastating incursions, a party of Dene braves took to the warpath, travelling into Nahanni country with the intention of pillaging a Naha camp. In time, the warriors came upon a scattering of teepees and prepared to attack. Upon rushing into the camp with their weapons at hand, however, the Dene discovered that their enemies were nowhere to be found. It was as if they had vanished into thin air. With all the campfire tales of evil spirits and giant cannibals swiftly recalled to mind, the Dene warriors fled the country, beating a fearful retreat back to the lowlands. They never saw the Naha again.

In the early 1800's, fur traders of the North West Company established Fort Liard and Fort of the Forks (the latter later renamed Fort Simpson), two trading posts situated on the Liard River upriver and downriver of the mouth of the South Nahanni, respectively. In the trading room and on the trail, these tough frontiersmen learned of the horrors of the Nahanni from their Dene clients. In 1823, two years after the North West Company amalgamated into the Hudson's Bay Company, a valiant voyageur named John McLeod attempted to explore the remote valley, but did not make it far upriver on account of the rapids. He embarked upon a similar expedition the following year and met with similar results.

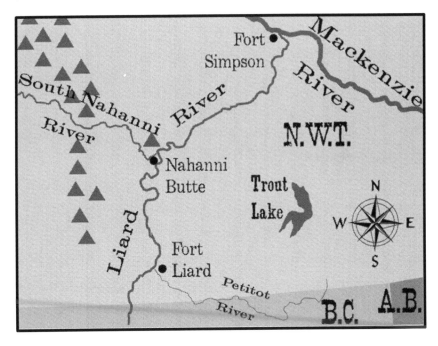

In the summer of 1897, word spread of a fabulous gold strike in the Klondike. In no time, men and women from all over the world were on their way to the northern diggings. These so-called 'Stampeders' approached the Yukon by a number of different trails. One of them was a gruelling 'all-Canadian' overland route which began in Edmonton, Alberta. Of the 766 Stampeders who attempted this treacherous trail, a handful opted to take an even more hazardous shortcut by way of the South Nahanni River. Although at least two of these men successfully reached their destination, many more disappeared in the misty valley long shunned by the natives.

In the aftermath of the Klondike Gold Rush, sourdoughs (as veterans of the Northland are sometimes referred to) who failed to strike it rich in the Yukon began to look elsewhere for gold. A number of these restless prospectors wandered into the Nahanni country and began to pan the myriad creeks which fed the South Nahanni and the Flat Rivers (the Flat being the South Nahanni's primary tributary). Some who returned from these remote diggings filled northern trading posts and saloons with strange tales of a paradisiacal valley hidden away somewhere in the mountains of the Mackenzie. This valley, they maintained, was snow-free all year round, its tropical climate attributable to the hundreds of bubbling hot springs which ran through it. Cloaked by heavy fog, the valley's soil was black and fertile, supporting a spectacular variety of lush and exotic greenery. This subarctic Eden was purportedly a hunter's paradise; due to the excellent grazing conditions, it teemed with wild game. One prospector said that the moose, caribou, and mountain sheep that lived in this lost world were so well-fed as to appear "almost square from fat."

Hand in hand with tales of a tropical valley were stories of mammoths, mastodons, and other prehistoric monsters said to still roam the most desolate recesses of the Nahanni. Indian trappers and white prospectors alike claimed to have observed fresh tracks of these Pleistocene relicts in the snow or the soft clay of creek beds, and many frontiersmen returned from the wilderness bearing priceless ivory tusks with hair and flesh still adhered to the bone. Rumour had it that some hunters had even encountered the antediluvian beasts deep within Mackenzie country and lived to tell the tale.

In spite of all the dreadful stories of bad medicine, evil spirits, hairy giants, and prehistoric monsters, a handful of enterprising prospectors continued to try their luck in the Nahanni Valley in the hopes of discovering gold. Two such men were Willie and Frank McLeod, Metis brothers whose father Murdock once served as Chief Factor at Fort Liard. Sometime in 1904 or 1905, the McLeod brothers, equipped with mining gear, disappeared up the South Nahanni and, according to some, further up the Flat River. They were never seen alive again.

Three years after the McLeod brothers' departure, Willie and Frank's younger brother Charlie, fearing the worst, mounted a search party. The ragtag band of trappers, aboriginals, and ex-Mounties he recruited headed up the

South Nahanni, warily scanning the wooded shore for anything out of the ordinary. After several days of tracking, paddling, and poling their canoes upriver, Charlie and his crew made a grisly discovery. On a flat stretch of riverbank, known thereafter as Deadmen Valley, sprawled the decapitated remains of Willy and Frank McLeod. Their heads were nowhere to be found.

Word of the macabre find spread like wildfire throughout the Canadian North. Over steaming mugs of sweetened tea- a staple of the northern frontier- trappers and traders speculated as to the nature of the McLeod brothers' gruesome fate. Had they been killed by one of the hairy, cave-dwelling giants of native lore? Had they been murdered by the Nahanni Indians- an elusive, mysterious tribe said to be fiercely protective of their hunting grounds? Perhaps they had been beheaded by a rival prospector or a trapper gone mad, his mind shattered by years of isolation in the bush.

Growing in conjunction with these conjectures were rumours that the Nahanni country was rich in gold, and that the McLeod brothers had made a massive strike on one of its creeks sometime prior to their untimely deaths. In no time, whispers of the Lost McLeod Mine- a subarctic El Dorado where gold nuggets the size of goose eggs littered the creek beds- rippled up and down the Mackenzie. One by one, veterans of the Fortymile, Klondike, Nome, and Fairbanks goldfields trickled into the Nahanni Valley, pans, picks, and whipsaws strapped to their dog sleds and canoes.

One of these prospectors lured by tales of lost gold was Martin Jorgenson, a Norwegian woodsman who entered Nahanni country in 1910. Five years later, his headless corpse was discovered about a mile above the mouth of the Flat River. Nearby stood the charred remains of his log cabin, which had mysteriously burned to the ground. Like the McLeod brothers, Jorgenson's head was never found.

In the wake of Jorgenson's death, dozens of prospectors similarly met with bizarre ends in various reaches of the Nahanni Valley. In the winter of 1922, for example, the body of a WWI veteran named John O'Brien was discovered on a mountainside not far from Deadmen Valley, hunched over a pile of tinder with a matchbook in his hand as if he had frozen to death while trying to light a fire. Legend has it that another man, an Ontario prospector named Ernest Savard, was found dead in his sleeping bag in 1945, his head severed from his shoulders. Other men who entered the country, like trappers Bill Epler and Joe Mulholland, simply vanished without a trace. Some sourdoughs saw these bizarre deaths and disappearances as affirmations of what they had long believed- that the Nahanni Valley is cursed, and that those who dare to search for its gold, or come close to finding it, invariably suffer some sort of ghastly fate.

As the years drew on, the remote wilds of the Nahanni began to appeal to geologists, naturalists, and other representatives of the scientific community. With the northern frontier ever shrinking under the onslaught of industrial exploration, these academics jumped at the opportunity to study this vast tract of virgin wilderness virtually unspoiled by man. Throughout the 1960's, some of the scholarly professionals who entered the Nahanni returned from their expeditions with experiences they could not explain. The accounts of these academics, coupled with local anecdotes, gave rise to a new Nahanni legend.

According to these witnesses, the Nahanni Valley is home to an enormous, solitary, wolf-like creature eerily reminiscent of a monster of Inuit myth. Dubbed the "waheela," this mysterious *caniform* is believed by some to be a relict *Amphicyon*- an ancient, carnivorous, bone-crushing mammal colloquially referred to as a "bear dog," supposed to have gone extinct about eight million years ago. Others maintain the waheela's physical description corresponds more closely with that of the dire wolf, a prehistoric relative of the modern day timber wolf. Whatever the case, some considered the waheela to be a likely suspect in many of the Nahanni's mysterious deaths and disappearances.

Around the same time as the waheela encounters, various sightings of a short, hairy, half-naked "sub-human" were reported in the vicinities of Fort Liard, Nahanni Butte, and Fort Simpson, respectively. Clad in a moose skin loincloth, carrying a stone club, and sporting a long, dark beard, this creature was given the name "Nuk-luk" by the local Dene. Its diminutive stature notwithstanding, this creature sharply evoked the old tales of the hairy, cave-dwelling cannibals first told around Dene campfires so long ago.

The Tropical Valley

"There are more . . . stories about the Nahanni River than any other place in Canada. The most famous of them is the story of the tropical valley, where 10,000 hot springs bubble out of the ground, ferns grow 30 feet high, and the temperature never goes below 50 degrees in midwinter."

- Colonel Harry Snyder; *Toronto Daily Star*; October 9, 1937.

ONE OF THE MOST ENDURING legends of the Nahanni Valley- one which transcends its sinister reputation as a land of murder, madness, Indian curses, and lost gold- has it that somewhere in that wild domain, perhaps surrounding one of the many tributaries of the South Nahanni River, lies a tropical valley free of snow and ice. This legend is but a piece of a much larger puzzle spanning the entire North Country- a puzzle which has its origins in a historic event that changed the face of the Canadian North forever.

THE KLONDIKE GOLD RUSH

On July 14, 1897, a steamship called the *Excelsior* slipped into the San Francisco harbour. To the stevedores working on the docks that day, this rusty little ship with two blackened smokestacks appeared to be nothing out of the ordinary. A few heads might have turned, however, when its passengers walked down the gangplank. The people who poured off the steamer were a gaunt, ragtag bunch clad in ragged work clothes and broad-brimmed hats. The men bore rough, unkempt beards, the women wore wild, tangled hair, and all had the sun-burned, wind-whipped faces of frontiersmen well accustomed to long days in the bush.

What really captured the attention of the men on the docks that day, however, was the mysterious cargo the passengers hauled from the ship. Some wrestled with extraordinarily heavy suitcases. Others lugged bulging buckskin sacks. Others still hauled heavy tin canisters with both hands, their cracked lips drawn back over tobacco-stained teeth in grimaces of exertion. The strange site piqued the curiosity and imaginations of nearby locals. Soon, a growing throng of city residents began to gather around the newcomers.

Some of the *Excelsior's* passengers immediately made their way to the Selby Smelting Works on Montgomery Street. There, on the establishment's counters, they revealed their identities and the contents of their cargo to the curious onlookers; they were prospectors from the north, and they had brought with them several metric tons of raw northern gold.

The news spread like wildfire throughout the streets of San Francisco: a spectacular gold strike had been made in an obscure region of northwestern Canada known as the Klondike. Immediately, gold fever swept throughout the Pacific Northwest like an epidemic, infecting men and women from all walks of life with a restless furor which some newspaper men dubbed *"Klondicitis"*. Rallying to the cry of "Klondike or bust," so-called Stampeders deserted their day jobs *en masse* and headed for the Yukon in search of fortune and adventure.

The Stampeders of 1898- men and women of all nationalities and occupations- approached Dawson City, the heart of the Klondike, by a number of different routes. Some purchased steamboat tickets in San Francisco or Seattle and travelled north up the Pacific Coast to the Lynn Canal, an Alaskan inlet. From there, they packed their gear over the Coast Mountains by way of the Chilkoot Trail or White Pass, hand-crafted their own canoes on the other side of the divide, and paddled up a series of lakes and rivers to the Klondike. Wealthier Stampeders travelled by steamer the whole way, heading to the old Russian fur trading settlement of St. Michael, Alaska, on the coast of the Bering Sea, before travelling up the Yukon River to Dawson. Some patriotic Americans, in an effort to circumvent Canadian customs, opted to take the "all-American route" to the Yukon- a suicidal trek over the crevasse-ridden Valdez and Malaspina Glaciers. Some poor prospectors attempted to reach the Klondike on horseback via the Ashcroft Trail, slogging through the sunny grasslands of the Cariboo Plateau, the misty jungles of the Great Bear Rainforest, and the dismal, mosquito-infested swamps of northern British Columbia. Others, prompted by encouraging articles in the *Edmonton Journal*, toiled over the "all-Canadian route", a long, arduous, overland journey starting in Edmonton, Alberta. A handful of those who took this latter route disappeared into the Nahanni Valley, hoping that the South Nahanni River might serve as a shortcut to the Klondike.

Throughout the course of the Klondike Gold Rush, more than 100,000 Stampeders from all over the world set out for the northern diggings. About 30-40 thousand of them actually reached their destination, and of those, only about 20,000 bothered to look for gold.

These 20,000 enterprising prospectors, throughout the last few years of the 19th Century and the first few of the 20th, panned the creeks just south of Dawson City. Those who found promising colours- trace amounts of gold dust, flakes, or nuggets- in their pans staked claims on the sites of their discoveries.

In the winter, those who staked claims exchanged the gold pan of the prospector for the pickaxe of the miner and set about sinking shafts to bedrock. In order to carve through the nigh-impermeable permafrost, they lit huge fires on top of their shafts and fed them constantly so that they burned throughout the night. In the mornings, with picks and shovels, they dug their way through the smoky ashes and the softened earth beneath. The gold-flecked rubble which they removed from their shafts was set aside in a massive 'dump' pile.

In the spring, when the ice began to melt, the Klondikers shoveled their gold-bearing pay dirt into sluice boxes- long, ribbed troughs oriented at a decline. That accomplished, they poured water into the top of the sluices and let gravity do its work; as gold is considerably heavier than sediment, it floated downwards during this process to collect in the sluice box's ribs, where it could be easily extracted, while the lighter gravel and sand simply washed away.

Of the 20,000 Stampeders who toiled for gold in this manner, only 4,000 found anything of significance. Of those 4,000, only a few hundred struck it rich. Dejected, many of the thousands of prospectors who failed to find their fortunes in the creek beds of the Klondike set out for home. Others, held in thrall of what British-Canadian poet Robert Service termed "The Spell of the Yukon", began to look elsewhere for the elusive yellow metal that had lured them into the North Country. Some made the long westward journey to the newly-established Nome mining district in Alaska, where another gold rush was underway. Others, travelling by dogsled or canoe, explored more remote reaches of the subarctic, only to return from these far-flung gold-seeking expeditions with tales that defied belief.

AN OASIS IN THE ARCTIC

Throughout the early 1900's, some of the prospectors who wandered throughout the boreal wilderness in the wake of the last great gold rush returned to civilization telling all manner of strange tales. Northern saloons, HBC trading rooms, Mountie outposts, and Mission rectories resounded with their stories of phantom lights, lost mines, woolly mammoths, and hairy wildmen. One of the tales told by these travelling prospectors spoke of a tropical valley hidden away somewhere in the northern wilds. This lost valley, the stories went, was a steamy paradise filled with luxuriant vegetation and an abundance of wild game, its peculiar climate owing to hot springs, volcanoes, or some other variety of subterranean thermal activity.

Russell and Lee's Account

The tale of the tropical valley circulated rapidly throughout the North Country by word of mouth. By the 1920's, it was finding its way into print. One of the first papers to run the story was the *Valdez Miner*, a weekly periodical based out of Valdez, Alaska. On Remembrance Day, 1922, it published an article entitled "An Oasis in the Arctic," describing a strange find made by prospectors Hank Russell and Jack Lee.

According to the article, one morning, while climbing a snow-covered "high arctic mountain pass," Russell and Lee spied a green valley far below, partially obscured by the mist. Determined to investigate this geological anomaly, they descended into the area.

Dressed as they were in heavy, fur-lined parkas, Russell and Lee found the valley uncomfortably warm. In some spots, the heat was so intense that it penetrated the thick moose hide soles of their moccasins. The two prospectors reasoned that the unusual temperature- along with the presence of powerful geysers and steamy fumaroles, the latter over which they allegedly cooked their food- was an indication that the valley was actually the crater of an enormous, ancient volcano.

Naturally, the valley attracted huge populations of wildlife. Herds of fat caribou grazed in fields of succulent, shoulder-high grass, eying the newcomers with lazy indifference. Thousands of birds, chiefly warblers and robins, flitted about in the canopies of the valley's thick-trunked trees. Huge flocks of geese and ducks congregated on a small lake in the middle of the valley, and enormous grizzlies and black bears prowled about the valley's edge, where many varieties of colourful flowers grew in abundance.

In addition to these faunal fixtures of the North, Russell and Lee observed signs of a more mysterious valley denizen; around the lake were strange, perfectly round tracks eighteen inches in diameter, which bore three toe-like depressions in the front. "Had they been living in a prehistoric age," the article went, "the prospectors would have sworn the tracks to be those of a mastodon or mammoth."

Captain Scotte's Account

Although Russell and Lee's account of the tropical valley was not particularly specific as to location, other stories placed the hidden paradise in a precise geographic region. One such story appeared in the July 25, 1924 issue of the *Alaska Weekly*, a newspaper based out of Seattle, Washington. Under the headline "Winter in Paradise," this story detailed the testimony of an American military man named Captain Samuel C. Scotte.

According to the article, Scotte alleged to have spent two winters in a tropical vale tucked away somewhere in the Cassiar Mountain Range of northern British Columbia. Accessible by both the Stikine River and Telegraph Creek- two waterways which cut across northern BC- this valley was purportedly 20 miles (32 km) long and 3-4 miles (5-6 km) wide. "The valley is swampy," said Scotte, "with many small lakes and timbered flats. The soil is a rich, black loam" well-suited to growing vegetables.

Captain Scotte believed that the valley owed its balmy climate to hot springs situated in the nearby foothills. These springs were warm in the winter, yet curiously ice cold in the summer. Following the captain's description of the hot springs, the author offered his own theory regarding the valley's tropical condition, suggesting that its unusual temperatures might have something to do with the fact "that it is 3,000 feet lower than the general contour of the surrounding country."

The article ended with a vague reference to various strange animals which Scotte observed in the valley, including a mysterious "white deer."

Perry's Account

The following year, on June 26, 1925, the *Alaska Weekly* published another, far more dramatic article on a tropical valley, entitled "The Valley of Eden." This narrative is, in many ways, eerily consistent with that of Russell and Lee. The source for this piece was Frank Perry, a mining engineer from Vancouver who, "for seventeen years, with only two pack dogs to carry his equipment... explored the unknown subarctic regions until, by chance... he came upon a vast paradise in the midst of the snow-covered mountains."

The article opens with a description of how Perry, while mushing over a remote mountain pass located somewhere between the Fort Nelson and Liard Rivers, on the eastern slopes of the Cassiar Mountains, stumbled upon a strange valley filled with heavy mist. Rivers of hot water "fed by hundreds of hot springs" ran directly through it, their steamy vapours colliding with the frigid subarctic air to condense into a thick layer of fog.

The tropical temperatures generated by the hot springs, in addition to keeping the valley free of snow and ice all year round, supported marvellously robust vegetation. This spectacular plant life included sixty-foot vines, nettles and ferns "higher than a man's head," trees three feet in diameter, and impenetrable patches of wild rosebushes with "stems as thick as a man's forearm." The lush flora, in turn, attracted "hundreds of mountain sheep, goats, caribou, and moose, with bears and other fur-bearing animals." Perry maintained that, "due to the exceptionally good grazing in the valley... the moose and caribou looked like the pictures of the old Norman horse- almost square from fat."

Perry learned that neighbouring Indians, in spite of its surfeit of game, gave the place a wide berth. This was on account of "imprints of huge three-toed prehistoric animals found in the sandstones and shales" – imprints strikingly evocative of the mysterious tracks reported by Russell and Lee. The natives believed that the monsters which made those tracks still roamed the area.

The piece ended with a brief description of the valley's abundant mineral formations, which included healthy veins of gold, silver, and copper; huge seams of coal; and large concentrates of iron ore.

Colonel Williams' Account

Three months after Perry's account was published in the *Alaska Weekly,* an Alaskan newspaper ran with a story that seemed to corroborate the engineer's claims. According to the article "Where the Waters Run Warm," published in the September 24, 1925 issue of the *Wrangell Sentinel,* a

Montreal-based Royal Canadian Air Force colonel named J. Scott Williams stumbled upon a tropical valley while conducting British Columbia's first aerial prospecting expedition. This valley contained "numerous hot springs, grass, and verdure of amazing growth due, it is thought, to the warmth generated by the springs." Other floral marvels included giant tulips and a fantastic profusion of currents and raspberries.

Colonel Williams claimed that he and his crew had prospected in the valley for three months, feasting on moose meat, mountain mutton, and vegetables which he and another prospector, whom he identified as "Smith," had planted. During their three-month stay, Williams and his crew observed a number of interesting animals, including an albino moose somewhat reminiscent of Captain Scotte's white deer and a "white bear similar to the Beacon Hill Park animal in Victoria." The "Beacon Hill Park animal" Williams was referring to was a Kermode or 'spirit' bear- a rare, often cream-coloured subspecies of the American black bear- which resided at that time in Victoria's Beacon Hill Park zoo.

Perhaps most interestingly, Colonel Williams placed his tropical valley in the Liard River country "beyond the Liard Trading Post," in the same general vicinity as Frank Perry's northern paradise. It seemed as if a tropical valley might indeed lie somewhere among the eastern slopes of the Cassiars.

THE EXPEDITIONS

Due in part to its proliferation by northern newspapers, the legend of a tropical valley nestled somewhere in the Cassiar Mountains of northern British Columbia began to spread south. By the early 1930's, the story was on the lips of nearly every Canadian woodsman to take an interest in the North Country. In the summer of 1930, one of these woodsman, a trapper from Jasper, Alberta, told the tale to an ecotourist visiting from Philadelphia. This tourist's name was Mary Gibson Henry.

The Mary Gibson Henry Expeditions

Sometimes erroneously referred to as America's first female botanist, yet a pioneer in her field nonetheless, Mary Gibson Henry was a woman naturally inclined to blaze trails, figuratively speaking. When she heard tell of a tropical valley in the Canadian subarctic, her pioneering spirit, coupled with her interest in horticulture, compelled her to search for this geological anomaly in the hope that she might study the exotic vegetation it was rumoured to support. By 1931, she- along with her husband, Dr. John Norman Henry of the Philadelphia Academy of Natural Sciences; her children, Howard, Norman, Josephine, and Mary; topographer Knox McCusker; friend and physician Dr. B.H. Chandler; outfitter Stan Clark; a number of cowboys; and sixty eight horses- was blazing physical trails through the eastern Cassiars in search of the fabled tropical valley.

The Tropical Valley

Henry's 1931 expedition in the Cassiars began in the small fur trading town of Fort St. John, BC. For the next forty days, Henry and her crew rode through five hundred miles of taiga, stopping periodically in order to collect plant specimens. Their route took them across British Columbia's Peace River, up the Halfway River (a tributary of the Peace), north up the eastern slopes of the Cassiar Mountains, and past the Sikanni Chief and Prophet Rivers, these last two comprising a river system which drains into the Fort Nelson River. On the Prophet River, the party happened upon the Prophet River Hot Springs. Although the area surrounding them was certainly no tropical valley, these springs bore a few curious characteristics, including a large tufa mound (hot spring-generated limestone) and hundreds strange, spherical stones arranged in a curious pattern which spoke of intelligent design.

The party continued on past the Muskwa, Gathto, and Tuchodi Rivers, these three being part of the same Fort Nelson River system to which the Sikanni Chief and Prophet belong. Eventually, the expedition came to the head of the Tetsa River. There, they encountered a band of Kaska Indians, who informed them that the tropical valley they sought was a close at hand.

Henry and her crew employed the services of the chief's son, a man named Charlie Macdonald, who guided them northwest through the watershed of the aptly-named Racing River. There, just one kilometre upriver of the

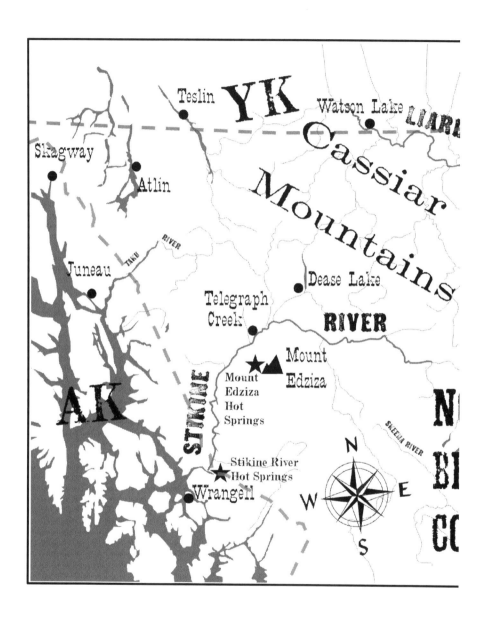

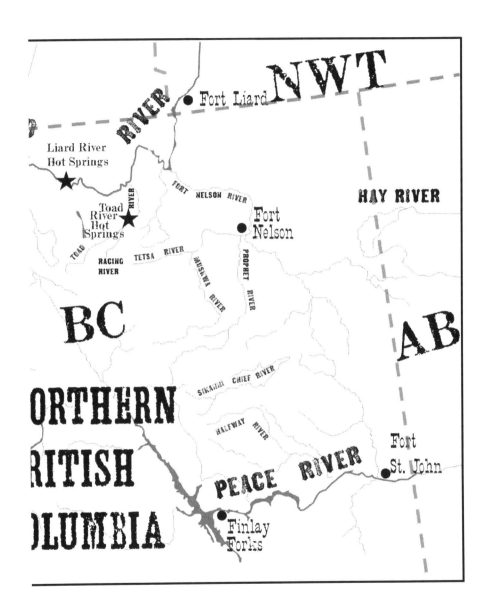

confluence of the Racing and Toad Rivers, Mary Gibson
Henry and her crew came upon the tropical valley of legend.

The Toad River Hot Springs

The location of this 'tropical valley' corresponded with
that of Frank Perry's, situated as it was on the eastern slopes
of the Cassiars, in the country between the Liard and Fort
Nelson Rivers. Far from being a steaming paradise filled with
trees three feet thick in diameter and gigantic caribou the size
of medieval Norman destriers, however, this "tropical valley"
was little more than a stretch of the Toad River Valley, on the
left bank of which bubbled a series of hot springs. Although
the heat generated from the springs did support a healthy
and diverse plant community in its immediate vicinity, it
seemed unlikely that it would preserve the entire valley from
the brutal, bone-chilling cold of the subarctic winter.

Although not exactly what she had hoped for, Mary
Gibson Henry was anything but disappointed. She described
the place thus:

*"The valley contained a rank growth of delphinium, often
over eight feet tall, and raspberries, roses and vetches growing in
the thickest, most luxuriant tangle I ever saw. They were very
difficult to penetrate. There were a number of hot springs. The
largest had formed a pool about nine feet in diameter. The water
was clear as a crystal, and the sides were raised about eighteen
inches above the ground by the continuous flow of the mineral
waters, which left sulphur concretions. The inside of the 'Arctic
bathtub' was shaped like an inverted cone. We enjoyed the only*

warm bath we had had on the trip and judged the temperature of the water to be only ninety degrees. Some of the others were so hot they were almost boiling, and several good-sized areas of ground were warm and moist. "

After enjoying the hot springs and recording their observations, Mary Gibson Henry and her crew left the valley and returned to Fort St. John by a different route.

Convinced that the tropical valley of legend still lay hidden somewhere in the eastern Cassiars, Henry launched similar expeditions in northern British Columbia in the summers of 1932, 1933, and 1935. These adventures yielded some interesting experiences, such as an instance in which Henry and one of her daughters escaped from three armed men who harboured ignoble designs. They also gave the civilized world a better understanding of northern British Columbian geography; the Alcan Highway, for example, was constructed along the general route of Henry's final expedition. In spite of all this, Mary Gibson Henry never did find the fantastic tropical valley she sought.

Charles Camsell's Expedition

Another explorer who sought to find- or, perhaps more accurately, to disprove- the legend of a tropical valley in the Cassiars was Dr. Charles Camsell, founder the Canadian Geographic Society and Canada's contemporary Deputy Minister of Mines. In August 1935, Dr. Camsell boarded a rugged Fairchild 71 bush plane in the northern Pacific port town of Prince Rupert, British Columbia, and headed north.

His pilot was C.H. "Punch" Dickins, a WWI flying ace and a pioneer of subarctic aviation. Accompanying Camsell and Dickins were mechanic/photographer W. Sunderland and A.D. McLean, the Superintendent of the Civil Aviation Branch of Canada's Department of National Defence.

The official purpose of Dr. Camsell's expedition was to "investigate a number of matters on behalf of the Administrative Council of the North West Territories," and to aerially photograph and determine the nature of "a large area of unknown country in northern British Columbia and southeast Yukon." In addition to completing these official duties, Camsell was determined to squeeze in a side project of his own, namely an investigation into the tropical valley legend.

Camsell and company followed the Pacific coastline north from Prince Rupert to Wrangell, Alaska. From there, they took a route paralleling that of Dr. George Mercer Dawson, the Canadian geologist and surveyor after which Dawson City was named, who, along with peers William Ogilvie and Richard George McConnell, had conducted an exploratory expedition through northern British Columbia and Yukon in 1887 on behalf of the Geological Survey of Canada. First, Camsell and his team followed the Stikine River inland, flying northeast over the pristine wilderness of Stikine Country, past mighty glaciers, snow-capped mountains, volcanic plateaus, and the spectacular Grand Canyon of the Stikine to the remote frontier settlement of

Dease Lake, BC. That accomplished, they followed the Dease River northeast to its confluence with the Liard River just 8 kilometers (5 miles) south of the Yukon border, at the site of the tiny native settlement of Lower Post.

After taking a number of photographs there, Camsell and his companions flew east down the Liard River. In time, they arrived at the Liard River Hot Springs, a place with which Camsell was well acquainted.

The Liard River Hot Springs

Like the Toad River Hot Springs which Mary Gibson Henry and her crew came upon in 1931, the Liard River Hot Springs were another source of the tropical valley legend. Situated roughly 20 kilometres (12 miles) upriver of the rapids-riddled Grand Canyon of the Liard, these crystal clear, geothermally-heated waters constitute the second largest hot springs system in Canada. Instead of flowing directly into the Liard River, they spill along the muskeg-bottomed shore to form a steaming swamp and two picturesque pools which remain free of ice and snow all year long. With fourteen thermally-influenced plant species thriving in the area, it was easy to see how prospector yarns transformed the place into a tropical paradise.

History shows that the Liard River Hot Springs were no well-kept secret of the North Country. Of course, the local Kaska Indians had been aware of them for centuries. White men first learned of them in the 1830's, when explorers of the Hudson's Bay Company opened the upper Liard River as a fur trading route. In 1887, seventeen years after the HBC discontinued the route, the springs were recorded in the report of Richard George McConnell, who paddled down the Liard during his aforementioned expedition with Dawson and Ogilvie. A decade later, dozens of Stampeders passed by the hot springs on their way to the Klondike; the Liard River comprised one of the many branches of the all-Canadian overland trail from Edmonton. One of these Stampeders was 22-year-old Charles Camsell who, along with his brother Fred, big game hunters D.W. Wright and A.M. Pelly, and frontiersman Dan Carey and his son Willie, braved the Grand Canyon's frothing Hell Gate Rapids, deadly Rapids of the Drowned, and backbreaking Devil's Portage in a futile attempt to reach the Yukon goldfields. None of these men, in their journals and reports, ascribed the Liard River Hot Springs or the valley surrounding them with tropical characteristics. Some did not even deign to mention the hot springs at all, while others accredited them with attributes very much at odds with the tropical narrative. Camsell, for example, in a 1936 address to the Empire Club of Canada, stated, "I have never been able to appreciate why it has been described as 'tropical,' especially as during the two weeks I spent there the temperature ranged from 20 degrees to 40 degrees below zero." From whence, then, did the whispers of their tropical nature originate?

Further investigation revealed that tropical valley legend likely had its roots in a long-dead prospector named Tom Smith, whose broken down cabin Camsell and his crew discovered by the hot springs at the edge of "an open meadow with luxuriant vegetation." Nailed to the door of the cabin was an old, weather-beaten piece of paper bearing Smith's last message to the world:

"We are leaving for Fort Liard."

A sourdough from the Klondike, Tom Smith was one of the countless prospectors who roamed the subarctic wilderness in the wake of the last great gold rush. In the summer of 1921, he travelled down the South Nahanni River with an Indian guide, likely settling somewhere along the Liard River. In 1923, he travelled further down the Liard- this time accompanied by his daughter Jane, a fourteen-year-old halfbreed girl- to the hot springs. There, beside one of the springs' two pools, he built a cabin and established a trap line.

For two years, Tom and Jane trapped out of their cabin. The father and daughter supplemented their simple frontier diet of moose and caribou meat with onions, potatoes, and tobacco they grew in a nearby garden. In the spring of 1925, while he and his daughter were transporting their season's catch of furs upriver to Fort Liard, Smith's canoe capsized in the Rapids of the Drowned. The frontiersman was promptly sucked under the white water, joining the shadowy ranks of the voyageurs who went before him for whom the rapids were named. Sixteen-year-old Jane, however, survived the ordeal, somehow managing to clamber onto a sandbar. After being rescued by a party of Kaska Indians who happened to hear her screams, she was brought to Fort Liard.

Later that summer, she was sent to the Anglican Mission at Hay River, on the shores of Great Slave Lake, where she would remain until her untimely death in 1934.

When the traders at Fort Liard heard of the incident, they tasked Colonel J. Scott Williams of the Royal Canadian Air Force with searching for their friend during his mineral reconnaissance flights in the Liard River area- the first expedition of its kind in northern Canada. Colonel Williams obliged; accompanied by a mechanic named Caldwell and four other men, he landed his single-engine Vickers Viking at the site of Smith's cabin on the banks of the Liard River Hot Springs in 1925, where he stayed for some time. An exaggerated account of his visit to the area graced the pages of the September 24, 1925 issue of the *Wrangell Sentinel*, sparking that particular version of the tropical valley legend.

After the detour to the Liard River Hot Springs, Charles Camsell and his companions flew west back up the Liard River and over the northern Cassiars. Just before reaching the mouth of the Dease River, they veered north and flew over the taiga of northern British Columbia for 75 miles (120 kilometres). Near the Yukon border, they turned to the east and proceeded for 230 miles (370 kilometres) over previously uncharted territory, known thereafter as the Liard Plateau. There, they accomplished the primary goal of their expedition: to photographically prove, as Camsell put it in his 1954 autobiography *Son of the North*, "that the Rocky

Mountain system actually dies out about latitude 60° N in a broad, high plateau country, and that a great physiographic gap occurs in the eastern face of the Cordillera, separating the Rocky Mountains from the Mackenzie Mountains."

The party continued east to Fort Liard, Northwest Territories. They refueled there and continued on to explore much more of the Northland before finally flying to Edmonton, Alberta, by a circuitous route.

POSSIBLE EXPLANATIONS

Following Charles Camsell's 'debunking' of the tropical valley legend, it seemed as if most variations of the prospectors' yarn were accounted for.

Colonel J. Scott Williams' tale of a valley filled with "numerous hot springs, grass, and verdure of amazing growth" was almost certainly a reference to the Liard River Hot Springs, where the Royal Canadian Air Force officer searched for precious minerals and any sign of the missing prospector Tom Smith in 1925.

Frank Perry's account of "a vast paradise in the midst of the snow-covered mountains," replete with sixty-foot vines and rosebushes with "stems as thick as a man's forearm," was likely an exaggerated description of the Toad River Hot Springs, rediscovered by Mary Gibson Henry's party in 1931.

Somewhat more mysterious was the nature of Captain Samuel C. Scotte's tropical valley, warmed by strange hot springs in the nearby foothills. Although both of the *Alaska Weekly's* tropical valley articles- which described Scotte and Perry's stories, respectively- made it clear that the valley so vividly illustrated by Perry (likely the Toad River Hot Springs) was supposed to be the same valley in which Captain Scotte spent two winters, several aspects of Perry and Scotte's descriptions are inconsistent. Perry described his valley as being an incredible 200 miles long and 40 miles wide- dimensions perfectly congruent with, yet ten times the magnitude of, those of Captain Scotte's valley. Furthermore, while Perry's valley was located in the *eastern* Cassiars, Scotte's valley was said to be accessible by Telegraph Creek and the Stikine River- waterways which run through the *western* side of the Cassiar Range more than 300 kilometres to the west. If Scotte's tropical valley is indeed located on the western slopes of the Cassiar Mountains, it is possible that it is actually the valley at the mouth of the Stikine River, located on the Pacific Coast just 56 kilometres (35 miles) northeast of Wrangell, Alaska. There, the Choquette Hot Springs seep from the granite rocks at base of the Stikine Valley wall to form a warm water swamp reminiscent of the steaming marsh from Scotte's account.

The Choquette Hot Springs

The Choquette Hot Springs, also known as the Stikine Hot Springs, were well-known to both the white man and the Indian long before the tropical valley legend began to circulate throughout the North. These thermal waters were named after Alexander "Buck" Choquette, a French-

Canadian prospector, adventurer, and son-in-law of a powerful Tlingit chief named Shakes who discovered the gold that launched the Stikine Gold Rush in 1861.

For centuries before Choquette arrived in Stikine Country in the stern of a cedar canoe, the hot springs that would later bear his name were utilized by the local Tlingit natives. Russian fur traders who founded a trading post called Redoubt Saint Dionysius on the tip of a nearby island in 1833 made good use of the springs, as did the Hudson's Bay Company traders who renamed the post 'Fort Stikine' in 1839. By the time American troops occupied and renamed the post 'Fort Wrangel' in 1867, 'Choquette Hot Springs' was a household phrase on the Alaskan Panhandle. With unique vegetation growing in its vicinity all year round, however, it is not inconceivable that travelling prospectors, with no one to contradict them, might have augmented the springs into a wonderful tropical valley in whisky-fueled tales they brought with them into the interior.

The last of the published narratives of a tropical valley to be accounted for is the tale of Hank Russell and Jack Lee, the prospectors who discovered a primeval land of geysers, fumaroles, and the tracks of some huge, mysterious animal somewhere in the subarctic wilderness. Protective of their find, Russell and Lee did not disclose any significant hints regarding the location of their tropical valley. However, their story bears close resemblance to that of Perry's, which was likely an exaggerated description of the Toad River Hot Springs; perhaps Russell and Lee's tropical valley was also an embellishment of these waters.

As tempting as it might be to adopt, this explanation does not account for the volcanic aspects of Russell and Lee's valley. If their hypothesis regarding the valley's volcanic nature was correct, however, one wonders whether this subarctic Shangri-La might be located somewhere in one of the Northland's volcanic hotspots, such as the Wrangell Volcanic Field (which, in spite of its name, is situated more than 700 kilometres (435 miles) northwest of Wrangell, Alaska, on the southern border of Alaska and the Yukon); the Alligator Lake Volcanic Complex of south central Yukon; or the Fort Selkirk Volcanic Field in the upper Yukon Basin, where geological evidence and Dene tradition indicate an enormous volcanic eruption occurred in ancient times.

The Hot Springs of Mount Edziza

One northern volcanic hotspot which doubles as a likely candidate for both Russell and Lee's *and* Captain Scotte's tropical valley is the Mount Edziza volcanic complex, located in Stikine Country in the vicinity of Mount Edziza, one of Canada's highest volcanoes. Complete with steamy fumaroles, this area bears all the volcanic characteristics of Russell and Lee's oasis in the Arctic, and situated just southwest of the Stikine River and Telegraph Creek, it is in perfect geographic conformity with Scotte's subarctic paradise.

On the northwestern slopes of Mount Edziza are two sets of hot springs. The northernmost of the two, the **Elwyn Creek Hot Springs,** are composed of six separate springs, two of them warm, and four of them cold. These disparate temperatures strongly evoke the strange hot springs from Captain Scotte's account, which the military man claimed were ice cold in the summer and warm in the winter.

Just south of the Elwyn Creek Hot Springs are the **Tahweh Creek Hot Springs,** which lie in a steep-sided valley at the head of Tahweh Creek. Their waters are clear and taste distinctly of soda. With an average temperature of 44° Celsius (117° Fahrenheit), they are perhaps British Columbia's only hot soda springs.

The Mount Edziza 'tropical valley' terminates about 50 kilometres (31 miles) to the south, beyond the **Mess Lake Hot Springs,** to the point at which the **Mess Creek Hot Springs** empty into the waterway for which they were named. Just beyond lie the breathtaking Spectrum Mountains, brilliantly stained by mineral salts.

All things considered, this area coincides quite well with the tropical valleys described in the accounts of Russell, Lee, and Scotte, save for one important detail: the young igneous rock that characterizes the Mount Edziza volcanic complex, a far cry from Scotte's "rich, black loam," supports sparse vegetation.

THE LEGEND MOVES NORTH

In the first half of the 1930's, a rumour spread that the tropical valley of early 20th Century prospector lore- a misty land filled with lush and exotic greenery, well-nourished animals, and fertile, frost-free soil- was located not in the Cassiars, nor in the wilds of Alaska or the Yukon, but rather in the watershed of the mysterious South Nahanni River. Some versions of this legend were vastly more dramatic their precursors, alleging that this steaming valley was home to palm trees, banana trees, and colourful birds of the kind one might more likely expect to find in the jungles of the Amazon. Others were slightly more prosaic, claiming that the place abounded with exotic butterflies that fluttered among rampant fruit and flowers. All of these tales, however, maintained that the valley was heated by sulfurous hot springs, and that it was perpetually enshrouded by a heavy mantle of fog.

On September 26, 1933, after an Albertan prospector named Angus Hall disappeared in the Nahanni, the *Toronto Star* published an article under the headline "Prospector Vanishes in Dead Man's Valley." Amid paragraphs describing lost gold mines and Indian curses, the author squeezed in a section on the Nahanni's alleged tropical valley:

"Despite its position in northern latitudes, Death Valley is said to be almost tropical in nature. This is due to hot sulphur springs in the region, and rivers and streams of hot water that are semi-tropical in origin.

"*Fenley Hunter* [a gentleman explorer who led several expeditions up the South Nahanni River]... *describes the water of these streams as 'clear and quite warm' and says 'these sulphur hot springs appear to throw light on the stories of semi-tropical oases in this northern country.'*"

Two years later, in the summer of 1935, Dr. Alan E. Cameron, a geologist, mining engineer, and professor of metallurgy at the University of Alberta, ventured into Nahanni Country with his teenage son in order to see if there was any merit to the legends. The professor and his son travelled a total of 80 miles up the South Nahanni River from Nahanni Butte, taking rock and mineral samples as they went. Some years later, in a report of his expedition which graced the pages of the Canadian Geographic Journal, Dr. Cameron stated matter-of-factly that there was, indeed, a warm valley in the Nahanni which supported robust and prolific plant life. He suspected that the valley's pleasant climate was attributable to its hot springs, and to the chinooks (warm, east-bound winds from the Pacific Northwest) which frequently blew through it.

Before Cameron and Hunter's claims could be verified, war broke out in Europe. In no time, young Canadians all over the country were signing up for service overseas. The collective energy of the nation was directed towards the war effort, and the world forgot about the tropical valley for a time.

In 1945, when the dust of WWII finally began to settle, newspapermen all over the West were desperate for a good story; aside from the Nuremberg Trials, there seemed to be little of interest to report. As if on cue, in the fall of 1946, a bedraggled prospector named Frank M.W. Henderson (said to be the nephew of Robert Henderson, one of the three men who first discovered gold in the Klondike in the summer of 1896) staggered into civilization with a poke of coarse gold and a hair-raising tale.

Earlier that fall, Henderson claimed, he and John Patterson, his prospecting partner, had planned to search for gold around Watson Lake, Yukon, situated near the Liard River a short distance northwest of Lower Post, BC. Henderson, accompanied by two Dene guides, approached the place from his camp in the north, while Patterson trekked in from the east. The prospectors planned to meet up at a huge waterfall on the South Nahanni River, the junction of their respective routes, and travel together to their destination.

When Patterson failed to arrive at the rendezvous site, Henderson set out to look for him. Immediately, his Indian guides abandoned him, certain that Patterson had been taken by one of the sinister agents said to haunt the valley- spirits, monsters, and bad medicine which might take them, too, if they lingered. Henderson continued on alone, searching the tributaries of the Nahanni for any sign of his lost friend, and collecting 30 ounces of gold from the creek beds in the process. Of his partner, however, he found no sign; it seemed as if Patterson had vanished into the Nahanni Valley without a trace. When he finally returned to civilization in early fall, Henderson said of his experience, "all summer I moved with the utmost caution, mostly at night. There is absolutely no denying the sinister atmosphere of the whole valley. The weird, continual wailing of the wind is something I won't soon forget."

Henderson's chilling tale was a godsend to Canadian and American newspapers. With fresh wind in their sails, journalists picked up their telephones and started digging for stories on the Nahanni Valley. In no time, the old tropical valley legend resurfaced.

That October, one newspaper based out of Yakima, Washington, published a series of articles relating the adventures of James A. Watts, a short, husky geology teacher in his late twenties or early thirties who conducted a geological survey of the Nahanni Valley that summer. Watts had gone into the country with his brother-in-law, Edward Koss, and his wife on July 22. When the trio failed to return to civilization by mid-September, a party of Mounties went into Nahanni Country to search for them. Fortunately, the search and rescue team was unnecessary; the three geologists returned from the wilderness unscathed shortly after the Mounties' departure. Upon his return, Watts told journalists that "in a country where the thermometer drops to 72 below, there also is a sheltered semi-tropical valley, warmed by hot springs and geysers... It may sound fantastic, but there it is."

Other articles detailed the exploits of 29-year-old Walter J. Tully, another man who claimed to have visited the Nahanni's tropical valley that summer with partners Walter Budd and Jack Thorstein. According to one article, Tully claimed to have found "hot sulphurous springs that sent clouds of steam into the air, a low-lying mist that hides the valley from air view, lush vegetation, and a waterfall of breathtaking height." In another article, Tully described the valley's vegetation as "heavy" and "immense," and maintained that the trees there were unusually thick. "I'd say it was 30 or 40 degrees above the temperature of the outside country," he stated. "At least as warm as Vancouver." According to journalist Pierre Berton, who interviewed the explorer in a hotel on Hastings Street, Vancouver, Tully also claimed to have seen strange ice carvings atop the rocky bluffs of Nahanni River which "stood out like guardian angels."

The articles that generated the most public interest in the alleged tropical valley were those which supplemented recent exploratory reports with lurid tales of the Nahanni's past. One such article was "Nahanni... Valley of Mystery," by R.A. and Margaret Francis, a piece which opened thus: "The tumultuous Nahanni tells no secrets, but the winds above the river are heavy with the breath of mystery, of terror, of nameless, fearsome death dealt swiftly by unseen hands." After regaling the reader with stories of head hunters and prehistoric monsters, the authors went on to introduce the tropical valley. "In this valley," they wrote, "like a cloud-wrapped Himalayan Shangri-La, hidden among the frozen tundras, soft, fragrant breezes blow and tropical trees and flowers spring lushly from the fertile soil watered by hot springs."

Some journalists were openly skeptical of the newly-resurrected legend. Jack Scott of the *Vancouver Sun*, for example, caricaturized the Nahanni as "a bodyless valley where ripe bananas hang from the boughs of pine trees [and] dusky native girls swim about in the deep, warm pools." Others, like the *Vancouver Sun's* Pierre Berton, decided to treat the tale more seriously.

Pierre Berton's Expedition

By the winter of 1946, articles about the Nahanni Valley and its tropical paradise filled magazines and newspapers across the continent, engendering in adventurous souls a desire to be the 'first' to explore it. This desire quickly fomented a friendly competition which veritably exploded when a platoon of United States Marines formally announced their intention to launch an exploratory expedition in the Nahanni. Not to be outdone, Canadian Major-General F.F. Worthington, father of the Royal Canadian Armoured Corps, immediately declared that he would head a Canadian expedition into the region, and that he and his men would get there first. In no time, hundreds of adventurers from all over Canada and the United States were banding together, making preparations to explore the mysterious region which newspapers termed the 'Headless Valley.'

One man who hoped to capitalize on this furor was Hal Straight, editor of the *Vancouver Sun*. Straight realized that if he managed to land a reporter in the Nahanni before any of the competition, he could thrust the *Sun* into the international spotlight. In order to pull this off, however, he would have to ask his reporter to do the impossible- to fly out immediately, while the snow was still falling, braving the bitter cold of the subarctic winter while rival explorers sat around indoors, drawing up their springtime plans. For this formidable task, he appointed two champions- a grizzled bush pilot named Russ Baker, and a young, obscure journalist named Pierre Berton.

Like "Punch" Dickens, the pilot who flew Charles Camsell to the Liard River Hot Springs in 1935, Russ Baker was a pioneer of subarctic aviation. The Manitoba native had been freighting supplies all over the North since 1936, using Fort St. James, BC, as his headquarters. Said Pierre Berton of the man in his 1956 book *The Mysterious North*, Baker "was more than a pilot: he was a cartographer, trapper, doctor, prospector, ambulance-driver, listener to the troubles of lonely men in log cabins... Baker had done just about everything that can be done with a plane in mountain country."

Pierre Berton, on the other hand, was a bright young journalist who held a History degree from the University of British Columbia and, the year prior, a Captain's commission in the Canadian Intelligence Corps. Born in Whitehorse, Yukon, and raised in Dawson City, he seemed a perfect candidate for this northern beat. Little did he know that his upcoming Nahanni adventure would launch him into national stardom, inaugurating an illustrious, 58-year career in radio, television, and historical literature.

Accompanied by Art Jones, the *Sun's* photographer, Berton and Baker left Vancouver for Prince George, BC, on Wednesday, January 22, 1947. In that so-called "Northern Capital of BC", they were to meet up with one of Baker's crewmen, who would have the bush pilot's trusty old Junkers monoplane fueled and prepped for takeoff. The trio's departure was hasty and discreet; even Don Cromie, publisher of the *Vancouver Sun*, was unaware of Straight's audacious endeavour as Berton, Baker, and Jones boarded a Canadian Pacific Airlines plane bound for Prince George. The explorers' flight was delayed on account of a particularly ferocious blizzard; the reporter, pilot, and photographer finally arrived in Prince George the following Saturday.

In Prince George, Berton wired a short article to Hal Straight via telegraph. This piece was the first of what would become known as "The Headless Valley Expedition Series," a succession of newspaper articles detailing Berton, Baker, and Jones' northern escapades, which Berton's biographer Dr. A.B. McKillop described as "a mixture of mythic quest and modern adventure." Throughout their journey, Berton periodically submitted these articles to Straight by radio, outpost phone, telegraph, and air shuttle service. Straight, in turn, would publish them several days after receiving them.

Berton's first 'Headless Valley' article was published in the *Vancouver Sun* two days after Berton sent the telegram. The kicker read:

"An expedition is en route by ski plane to 'Headless Valley' in the Canadian northwest east of Yukon- a valley where men have met strange deaths and where bizarre legends abound regarding head-hunting cave-dwellers, prehistoric monsters, etc. The expedition, organized by the Vancouver B.C. Sun, is sending daily dispatches. "

The piece went on to describe the expedition's agenda, briefing the audience on some of the legends the party hoped to investigate. "Despite the tropical legends," Berton wrote, "we are fully equipped for any temperature and any occurrence."

Fort St. James

After a short trip to the telegraph office, Berton and Jones piled into Baker's tiny bush plane and struck out for the equally tiny village of Fort St. James, situated in the very centre of British Columbia. They reached their destination without incident and spent the night at Baker's home, an old saloon and dance hall rebuilt atop a 50-foot cliff.

Finlay Forks

The following morning, the three men, now joined by Ed Hanratty, Baker's mechanic, flew north over a vast tract of boreal forest. They made a brief visit to Pinchi Lake- a desolate, recently-abandoned mining town which supplied the Allies with mercury during WWII- before heading to Finlay Forks, a tiny old HBC trading post situated at the confluence of the Finlay and Parsnip Rivers, where the two joined to form the Peace River. There, they were received by Paul Vatcher, a young civil servant at whose cabin they spent the night, feasting on "great slabs of moose meat" and hot tea while a blizzard howled outside.

The four men attempted to leave the following morning, using axes, shovels, and crowbars to liberate the plane's skis from the drifts of hard-packed snow that entombed them, defrosting its frozen engine with a blowtorch, and thawing its battery in a cast iron oven belonging to trapper Roy McDougall, Finlay Forks' only other adult male resident. By the time they were ready to depart, it was too dark and too cold to fly. Defeated the four men settled down for another night at Finlay Forks.

The party met with similar difficulties the following three days, on each occasion spending countless hours in vain attempts to overcome them before finally retiring to Vatcher's cabin, frozen and exhausted. Roy McDougall tried to console the frustrated travellers, remarking, "We got lots of grub and lots of beds. When a Peace River blow comes up, all you can do is eat and sleep and let 'er blow."

Unbeknownst to the expedition crew at the time, the raging gale that kept them grounded may have saved their lives; on the day they reached Finlay Forks, the coldest temperature ever recorded in continental North America beset Snag, Yukon, a village situated at the exact same latitude as the Nahanni Valley. On that day, Yukon thermometers dropped to a mind-numbing -63° Celsius (-81° Fahrenheit).

During his stay at Finlay Forks, Berton submitted several articles to Straight, one of them describing the party's predicament. He concluded that piece with a remark on a unique aspect of Northern Canadian culture. "This is an odd country in many ways," he wrote. "They spread butter on home-made bread in inch-thick slabs and the eggs are the color of the setting sun. We have left the boundaries of Canadian rationing and are now in the land where they buy butter by the hundred-weight, bacon by the stone, and sugar by the sack."

Hal Straight responded to Berton's submissions with a telegram bearing good news. The editor had sold the 'Headless Valley' series to the International News Service, which meant that Berton's articles would reach a much wider audience. Berton had no way of knowing that one of his new audience members, Arthur Irwin of *Maclean's Magazine*, would give him a new job in Toronto once his Nahanni expedition was complete.

Fort St. John

Finally, on their fourth day at Finlay Forks, the four men managed to get Baker's plane off the ground. Shivering violently, the passengers perched themselves atop their gear while Baker flew east up the Peace River and over the eastern slopes of the Rocky Mountains to Fort St. John, BC. There, after checking into a hotel, Berton and Jones paid a visit to the Murray family, the four owners of the *Alaska Highway News* who, according to Berton, "started the recent wave of Headless Valley stories." Berton elaborates on the Murray family's influence on the Nahanni legends in his 1987 book *Starting Out*, stating that articles written by George Murray, the family's patriarch, "were made to order for the *Chicago Tribune* and the *Toronto Star*. The *Sun* in Vancouver picked them up and ran with them; within a few days, Headless Valley tales from other sources began springing up in print."

Fort Nelson

The following day, Baker learned that local air traffic control temporarily forbade planes from taking off on account of the cold. Defiant, Baker decided to fly anyway, and he and his three passengers were soon airborne and northbound. The party would later learn that theirs was the only plane in the air that day in all of Northern Canada. Two hours later, the four men landed at the little community of Fort Nelson, where they were forced to spend four days on account of the temperature.

During their stay at Fort Nelson, Hanratty discovered that the plane's cylinder was cracked from the cold; it was a miracle that it hadn't burst while the crew was flying over the godforsaken stretch of forest north of Fort St. John. Berton included this incident in his latest article, along with an ominous warning he and Art Jones received from a local postmistress:

"'The Nahanni?' she said. 'This is the worst time of the year you could choose to tackle it. Even in summer it is dangerous country. There are all sorts of stories about it. We don't know what to believe... I hope you come back with your heads."

Deer River

On their fifth day at Fort Nelson, the mercury rose a little, and the crew was in the air again. Before heading north, the men made a hundred-mile detour to a little cabin on the Deer River, where an Indian trapper's heavily-pregnant wife was stranded, expecting to give birth any day. There, Baker, Berton, Jones, and Hanratty helped the trapper's wife, mother, and infant son into the plane; the Indian's 10-year-old son was to stay behind with the huskies and hold the fort.

Although he had little trouble landing beside the cabin, situated as it was in a clearing in the middle of the woods, Baker had a difficult time getting out on account of the temperature and the snow. For a while, he feared that he and his charges might be stuck "playing stork" in the Northern bush. Fortunately, after Berton and Jones, struggling through waist-deep snow, helped push start the engine, he finally managed to get the plane back into the air. The expedition party delivered the expectant mother and her family to the Fort Nelson hospital before continuing north to Fort Liard.

The Tropical Valley

In that old fur trading town on the banks of the Liard River, Berton and Jones visited with Bill King, an old sourdough who regaled them with tales of his recent prospecting venture in the Nahanni Valley. They also interviewed Willie McLeod, nephew of the McLeod brothers who had lost their heads in the region in the early 1900's. Baker, in the meantime, was asked to ferry an Indian woman with a broken collarbone and her young son to the hospital at Fort Simpson- a task he completed with Berton, Jones, and Hanratty aboard. On the flights to and from Fort Simpson, the *Sun* correspondents got their first glimpses of the South Nahanni River, snaking as it did out of the Mackenzie Mountains. "The mountains through which it twists are breathtaking," wrote Berton. "They are like huge teeth jutting from bicuspids filed razor-sharp, others like monstrous molars ground to flattened tops. But our view of the mysterious Nahanni, now the most talked of river on the continent, was fleeting."

Nahanni Butte

After dropping the Indian woman and her son off at Fort Simpson, the four men flew to Nahanni Butte. There, they met with Jack LaFlair, a trapper and trader who had managed his own trading post there at the mouth of the Nahanni since 1914. When Berton asked him about the Nahanni's tropical valley, the old trader told him nonchalantly that it was located a short distance up the South

Nahanni, at the head of the Splits. It was not really a tropical valley, he maintained, but rather a pleasant stretch of riverbank warmed by hot springs, beside which a trapper named Gus Kraus lived with Mary, his Dene wife. Beside their cabin, in the valley's warm, fertile soil, the couple grew potatoes, cabbages, lettuce, carrots, radishes, and other vegetables.

Berton, Baker, Jones, and Hanratty spoke with LaFlair long into the night about the Nahanni and its various legends. At long last, they crawled into their sleeping bags and settled down for a restless sleep, flushed with the knowledge that the morrow would see them in the Headless Valley.

The Tropical Valley

The four men set out up the South Nahanni early the next morning, following the river as it wound into the mountains. Baker maintained a low altitude as he flew upriver, and in no time the men came to a deep section of the valley which, to Berton, "seemed to bury itself in the mountains." This, in accordance with LaFlair's directions, was the tropical valley.

Baker flew lower, almost to ground level, so that Berton and Jones could get a better view of the area. Below, the crew could see "the tiny square of Gus Kraus' cabin" standing out from the surrounding snow. There was no smoke rising from its chimney, nor were there any signs of life in its vicinity- Gus and Mary were likely out inspecting their trap line. Nearby, however, were clues as to how this stretch of the South Nahanni earned its 'tropical' designation. According to Berton in a later reminiscence, "Close by the cabin was a little creek, its ice rotten and yellow, and not far away steam rose from the hot springs, which looked like greenish spots on the snow. This was the sole hint of tropical conditions."

In the finale of his *Headless Valley Expedition Series*, in which he summarized the expedition's findings, Berton said of the valley's alleged tropical nature, "Tropical Valley? If you call a handful of hot springs a tropical valley, okay, but personally I kept my Arctic parka on." In that day's article, headlined "No Tropic Isle in Headless Valley," he put his assessment more bluntly: "It is not tropical."

Deadmen Valley

Convinced that the ice in the area was too thin to permit a landing, the four men flew upriver. Immediately, they plunged into a dark, gloomy limestone corridor known as the 'First Canyon' - a striking formation at which the party marvelled as they sailed past. A number of creeks drained into this gorge on both sides, forming deep, narrow, fissure-like ravines which snaked away into the rock. "It was a fantastic sight," wrote Berton. "Canyon upon canyon running off in every direction." In addition to these winding gaps, the First Canyon's sheer, 1500-foot (457-metre) walls were pockmarked with black, sinister-looking caves. Ancient Dene tradition told that these caverns were home to giant,

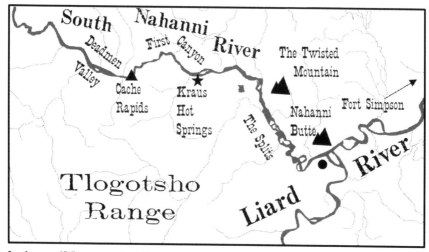

hairy wildmen who descended into the river valley at night to behead anyone foolish enough to camp in the area.

After fifteen miles, the party flew out of the First Canyon and into the saucer-like Deadmen Valley, where the headless remains of Willie and Frank McLeod were discovered in the early 20th Century. Berton described the place as "a great bowl, set in a circle of sharp-toothed mountains... Below us, the river wound lazily along its floor to vanish again into the mountain wall at the far end."

"I felt a sense of growing elation," the journalist wrote. "There, at last, was the valley that I had written so much about and read so much about. The setting was exquisite- the sawtooth pinnacles of the Mackenzie Mountains stood out, stark white against the sunless wash of the sky." Berton planned to explore some of Deadmen Valley on foot, and Jones hoped to take a few photos of it for the *Sun*.

Baker descended into the area and prepared to put the plane down on a stretch of river ice. According to Berton, "All of us were a little nervous because no one had ever landed a plane in the Nahanni in the winter and a good many people said it couldn't be done." Sure enough, as the bush plane's skis approached the snow-covered surface, the pilot realized that something was terribly amiss- the sun was obscured by fog that day, yet the shadow of the plane was clearly visible below. Baker started with the realization that the 'shadow' was, in fact, dark river water flowing beneath a thin layer of ice. He pulled up just in time, narrowly avoiding catastrophe, before circling around and making a successful, if bumpy, landing a short distance away. Baker later claimed that he would not attempt another winter landing in Deadmen Valley for $10,000, and would personally award $100 to any pilot who managed to pull off a similar stunt in February. To Berton, he said, "You can put this in your diary. It's the roughest ride you'll ever see and still stay in one piece."

Relieved to still be alive, the four men clambered out of the bush plane and surveyed Deadmen Valley. The place was as silent as the grave, due in part to the dampening effect of the thick blanket of snow that covered it, which wind had long since "whipped into frozen hillocks, some of them seven feet high." Scattered haphazardly among these snowdrifts were huge trees, mysteriously "strewn about as if uprooted by a giant paw."

The four men trudged through the thick snow of Deadmen Valley and headed out across the frozen South Nahanni River, on the opposite bank of which they had spied two dilapidated cabins from the air. In order to avoid falling through the ice- a potentially lethal scenario- Baker probed the path before them with a hatchet.

The party reached the opposite shore without serious mishap and soon located the two cabins. "The damp hand of decay lay heavy upon them," wrote Berton, "and it was impossible to enter their dank and gloomy confines without experiencing a shiver of depression." It appeared that the cabins had been abandoned long ago, their few remaining furnishings rusted and rotten. The identities of their former occupants were, and would forever remain, a mystery.

One of the items left behind by the cabins' former owners was a yellow, crumbing photograph of movie star Rita Hayworth, taken sometime in the previous decade, back when the "Love Goddess" was the top pin-up girl for American GIs of the Pacific Theatre and the Western Front. Berton included this discovery in the article he sent off to Hal Straight. Straight, in turn, supplemented the article with a few paragraphs of his own, which read:

"In the heart of this weird valley, deep in the grim sawtooth Nahanni Mountains where men have died for their gold, we found, of all things, a pin-up girl. Are you listening, Rita Hayworth? More important, is your press agent listening?

"Miss Hayworth, let us be the first to tell you that you are the official queen of Headless Valley. For it was your pretty head and scantily-clad torso that we found staring right at us out of a tattered and crumbling cabin in the forbidden valley.

"Who placed you here in this empty, forgotten log shack in this dead and silent banshee wind we have no way of knowing, but very nice you looked smiling at us from a sun-soaked California beach as you adjusted the zipper on your white-necked bathing suit. Believe us, Miss Hayworth, you brought the only breath of the tropics that has ever kissed the snow-locked wastelands that stretch across the 10 miles of this valley of dead men."

The article was accompanied by an Art Jones photograph depicting a bearded, wild-eyed Pierre Berton ogling the pinup poster, adhered as it was to a window frame in the old, ramshackle cabin.

Much to everyone's delight, Hal Straight's paragraphs were answered in a telegram, dated February 13. The message read:

"Am thrilled at being named Queen of the Headless Valley, but won't let it go to my head. Seriously believe Mr. Berton and his expedition have demonstrated extraordinary courage in their exploration of this unknown area of the Canadian Northwest. Would come to Vancouver to congratulate them myself, except that Orson Welles and I are busily trying to finish new film, "Lady from Shanghai," which we are making together, and

realize it is impossible to get away. Would like to take a look at bathing suit photograph, though, if only to see how I made out with that zipper. My very best to you all, Rita Hayworth."

———————◆—●—◆———————

After exploring the cabins, Art Jones cheekily snapped photos of Berton, knee deep in snow, holding street signs in his mittens. "As the first air-borne expedition," explained Berton in an article, "we have left mementoes for the half dozen other expeditions planning to invade the area next summer. We have planted street signs in the valley and have laid out streets and roads, avenues and boulevards... On Main Street, we nailed up this banner: 'To other expeditions, the Vancouver Sun, first into the Headless Valley.'"

That accomplished, the crew trekked back across the river to the Junkers and flew upriver. They explored more of the Nahanni Valley by air before returning back to Vancouver by a circuitous route. "We were glad enough to go," admitted Berton in a later interview, "for exploring that valley had been rather like spending a night in a haunted house."

THE NAHANNI'S TROPICAL VALLEYS

Before he set out on his 'Headless Valley' expedition, Pierre Berton read everything he could dig up on the Nahanni Valley. He quickly learned that the region was not quite as unexplored as contemporary newspaper articles made it out to be. For the past half century, a handful of trappers, big game hunters, and prospectors wandered into the Nahanni Valley in search of furs, hunting trophies, and gold. A few of those who returned documented their adventures in personal diaries, some of which found their way into print. Their anecdotes paint a picture of a wilderness as spectacular as it is unforgiving- a land of exquisite beauty and terrible danger. The names they gave to the region's landmarks- Cathedral Range, Headless Creek, Pulpit Rock, and Broken Skull River, to name a few- reflect a similar juxtaposition, suggesting a marriage between the sacred and the macabre.

Although none of these Nahanni explorers claimed to have discovered a truly tropical valley replete with parrots and palm trees, as some newspapers and magazines suggested, some of them came across a number of Nahanni hot springs eerily evocative of the oldest versions of the tropical valley legend. The most famous of these are the Kraus Hot Springs, also known as the Clausen Creek Hot Springs, which Pierre Berton and his party observed in February 1947.

The Kraus Hot Springs

Situated at the maw of the First Canyon just beyond the Splits, along a tributary of the South Nahanni called Clausen Creek, the Kraus Hot Springs were, for many years, the most accessible, and therefore the most well-known, of the Nahanni's hot springs. The handful of frontiersmen who ventured up the South Nahanni from the Liard River throughout the first half of the 20th Century were familiar with them, and it is likely that their descriptions of them formed the foundation upon which many variations of the tropical valley legend were based.

Despite Berton's dismissive description of them, the Kraus Hot Springs, particularly in summer, bear many of the characteristics ascribed to the legendary tropical valley of early 20th Century prospector lore, including exotic butterflies, rampant fruit and flowers, seven-foot-high vegetation, and cottonwood trees up to five feet in diameter. The area surrounding them is thick with wild timothy, chokecherries, golden rod, and aster. According to one explorer, whose statements sometimes require a grain or two of salt to swallow, the springs are even home to calliope hummingbirds, which migrate there from Brazil every summer.

One of the first men to write about these sulphur springs was Raymond M. Patterson (no relation to John Patterson), an Oxford-educated adventurer who explored the South Nahanni River in 1927, and again the following year with his friend Gordon Matthews, a fellow Englishman. Patterson documented his Nahanni adventures in his diary, relevant excerpts from which were edited and published posthumously in 2008 under the title *Nahanni Journals*. In 1954, Patterson himself published *Dangerous River*, a well-written adventure book in which he related his exploits on the

South Nahanni. Patterson's book has since become a cult favourite among canoeing enthusiasts.

In *Dangerous River*, Patterson included a colourful description of the Kraus Hot Springs area, and speculated as to its relation to the tropical valley legend:

"There were cleared spaces of old Indian camps... Many of the old campsites had become overgrown with an exuberance of wild roses and wild fruits- gooseberries, raspberries, and red and black currants. The springs themselves were of a clear, blue water; hot, but not too hot to lie in if you picked your spring, for the temperatures varied: they welled up close to the foot of the cliff, and the cliff was the end of the western precipice of the [First] Canyon as it swept away from the river. The meadow and the alleyways through the bush had been trampled by moose and bears, but everywhere one could see evidences of a riotous, almost tropical growth of grass, flowers, and bushes. There were gorgeous butterflies there, pale orange and blue, and in the red and yellow columbine that grew in the rocks at the foot of the cliff, humming birds were busy- tiny, flashing, bright-red jewels with their wives in bronze and iridescent green. One could well understand how the story of the Tropical Valley got around: the eager young reporter, the type ever prominent on the sucker list, and the old trapper, reminiscent in some tavern, and with the memory of all this beauty to spur the tongue...

"Hidden away in the mountains of the North-West, and preferably somewhere in the canyons of the upper Liard, there was a valley like the pleasant vale of Avalon from which the

storms and the cold winds turned aside, where the snow never lay and winter never came. The valley was a sun trap and a Chinook trap- the only wind that blew was the warm south-west Chinook and it blew all the time, softly through the mountain passes, bringing nothing but the gentle rain. And, better even than this, the grinding glaciers of ice ages had passed this valley by, and there were relics there of a pre-glacial flora: palm trees, even, could be relied upon to appear as the old trapper warmed to his story.

"A pleasant tale, though difficult to swallow, and we all liked to think that somewhere there might be an eternal garden cached away amongst the hills. These hot springs of the Nahanni added to the legend, and some writers made use of them in fanciful stories of the North... It was the dying kick, in Canada, of the Age of Marvels, in which, if a cartographer found himself with an embarrassingly blank space on the map, he felt free to write there whatever had pleased him most out of a tangle of travellers' tales."

Later on in his book, Patterson relates a conversation he had with Gordon Matthews in their Nahanni cabin in which the two of them "came to the conclusion that Deadmen's Valley [upriver from the Kraus Hot Springs] must be a 'Chinook trap' into which the Chinook is concentrated and funnelled from the southwest by the lay of the mountains and the passes. This, we decided, together with the hot springs and a little quite natural drawing of the long bow for the benefit of the always hopefully credulous townsman, could easily have given rise to the legend of the 'tropical valley' that was supposed to be cached away in these boreal solitudes." Seven years later, Patterson and Matthew's assessment was echoed by Dr. Alan E. Cameron, who concluded in his report on his 1935 Nahanni expedition that chinooks kept the air in Deadmen Valley "balmy and moist."

In addition to Dr. Cameron and his teenage son, other men who visited the hot springs that year were Charles Camsell and his crew, who flew over the place during their aforementioned aerial expedition of the Canadian North. The Nahanni hot springs were one of the many places the party visited following their stay at Fort Liard, although, curiously, they were perhaps the least publicized.

In 1941, a Chicago-born trapper and prospector named Gus Kraus built a cabin by the hot springs. For decades, he and his Dene wife Mary ran a trap line from this cabin, bathing in the springs in winter, growing vegetables in the fertile soil that surrounded them in the summer, and becoming such fixtures of the area that the place soon earned the name 'Kraus Hot Springs.' Native hunters who sometimes came up from the Liard River area had long referred to the place as *Todekthtsee*, or 'Stinking Water,' on account of the evil-smelling sulfur that permeated it. After the Kraus couple took up residence there, these Indians gave them names after the springs, instead of the other way around, referring to Gus as 'Stinking Water Man.'

"You could grow anything," said Kraus of his garden in a 1974 interview for Parks Canada, "for we growed even muskmelon there. One year we had watermelon, pumpkin, stuff like that. There was... real corn, that sweet corn... sacks full. Corn on the cob, great big vegetable marrows, tomatoes, name it. Everything you could raise in there... Parsnips six, seven feet high... Cabbages. Oh my God, yeah, I got cabbages galore, about twenty inches in diameter."

In addition to his garden truck, the hot springs had an interesting influence on Kraus' cabin. Due to the deleterious effects of the local sulphur on spruce and birch wood, Gus spent many summers repairing the base of his cabin. For the same reason, he eventually did away with wood flooring, laying linoleum over a cement foundation, which the heat of the springs kept warm all year round. "The cement would keep that thing so darn warm," said Kraus, "you'd have to have a ventilator... We wouldn't need no fire. Oh, it was surprising... only a little pile of wood done all winter. Oh yeah, you sure depend on it. You get up in the morning and you walk on the floor and just like what you never got out of bed. Feet are barefoot, just as warm as can be."

The Old Pot Hot Springs

As magnificent as it is, the area surrounding the Kraus Hot Springs is not the only valley in the Nahanni worthy of a 'tropical' designation, nor is it necessarily the most deserving of that appellative.

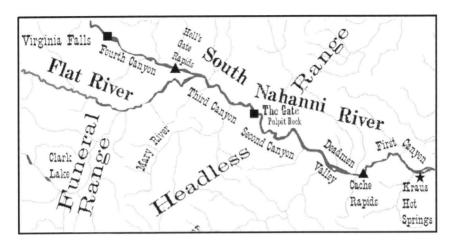

If you travel upriver from the Kraus Hot Springs, you'll come to the First Canyon, with its many caves and tributary gorges. The First Canyon is preceded upriver by the Cache Rapids, a frothing 800-metre (half-mile) stretch of white water sometimes called George's Riffle, immediately after which lies Lafferty's Riffle, where Metis brothers Jonas and Jim (or perhaps Frank) Lafferty once capsized their canoe. Further upriver, just beyond the rapids, is bowl-like Deadmen Valley, where Willie and Frank McLeod lost their heads.

Upriver from Deadmen Valley is the Nahanni's Second Canyon, another cave-pocked ravine very similar in appearance to the First Canyon, its walls rising a sheer 4,000 feet (1,220 metres) above the river's surface. From there, the South Nahanni winds its way through the Mackenzie's Headless Range towards a landmark known as the Gate, a narrow, watery passageway flanked by dizzying cliffs and a striking limestone pinnacle known as Pulpit Rock. The Gate serves as an entrance to the Nahanni's narrowest canyon, the Third Canyon, which cuts through the Funeral Range.

Beyond a lazy meander preceding the Third Canyon is the mouth of the Flat River, the South Nahanni's primary tributary and the setting of some of the region's most compelling legends. The Flat River is arguably as perilous to paddle as the watercourse into which it flows, containing thirteen rapids of varying severity. Beyond the first of these rapids, situated as it is near the river's mouth, the Flat plunges through what is known as the Low Canyon. Upriver, it is joined by the Caribou River, its own tributary, on the opposite bank of which lies an unearthly formation of hoodoos.

About 26 kilometres (16 miles) further up the Flat are the mysterious Old Pot Hot Springs, about which very little is known. These springs form a thermal pool on the east bank of the river. For many years, Albert Faille- an explorer who spent more time in Nahanni Country than any other in recorded history- maintained a log cabin near these hot springs.

The Wild Mint Hot Springs

Beyond the Old Pot Hot Springs, the Flat River crashes through a tumultuous succession of rapids. The most merciless of these is the Cascade-of-the-Thirteen-Drops (also known as the Cascade-of-the-Thirteen-Steps), a 1.2 kilometre-long stretch of white water riddled with rocks, high ledges, and standing waves, navigable by only the most skilled canoeists.

Just east of the Cascade-of-the-Thirteen-Drops, about a mile upriver from the Flat's confluence with the South Nahanni, are the Wild Mint Hot Springs, also known as the McLeod Creek

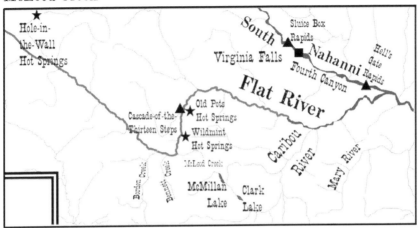

Hot Springs. These waters bubble from the side of a shallow hill to form long walls of tufa which help to contain three large pools, the largest being 75 metres in length, 30 metres in width, and 3 metres deep. Aquatic plants thrive in their bed, and a wide variety of luxuriant vegetation flourishes in their vicinity. One especially prolific plant in the area is wild mint, for which the hot springs were named.

According to Gus Kraus, the area surrounding the Wild Mint Hot Springs is perpetually free of snow and ice, much like the tropical valley in the prospector tales of old. "Green grass all winter there," said Kraus, "right on a big shore there on the river. You used to come along there and your feet were cold, just stand on the rocks. The rocks were nice and dry, big boulders just standing there. Heck, in no time your feet were nice. You feel the heat coming right up."

Billy Clark, a Highland Scot who spent time in the Nahanni, felt that the Wild Mint Hot Springs were the most superior thermal waters the region. In an interview with a representative of Parks Canada, he recounted bathing in their warm, bubbling pools, feasting on inch-round raspberries and gooseberries that grew in their vicinity "until [he] was just about bursting," and marvelling at a proximate series of inverse-conical sweet water wells, their banks thick with violets. "It would be a wonderful place, by Jove, to go in and relax if a person wanted to get away from it all," said Clark. "It would, by gosh!"

The West, East, and North Cantung Hot Springs

Far up the Flat River are the West and East Cantung Hot Springs, which empty into the same part of the river from their respective banks. About 17 kilometres (11 miles) further upriver is the mildly sulfurous North Cantung Hot Spring, thick with green algae.

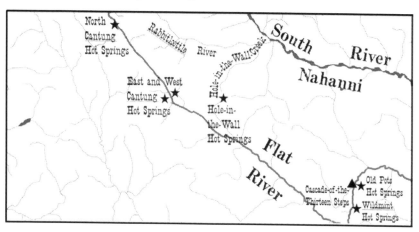

Rabbitkettle Hot Springs

Back on the South Nahanni, upriver from the mouth of the Flat River, lies what canoeist Peter Jowett, in his book *Nahanni: The River Guide*, described as "a very nasty, canoe-sucking whirlpool, a rotating river hole which has sent many paddlers into the drink." Immediately beyond this obstacle, referred to today as the Wrigley Whirlpool, is the equally deadly Figure Eight Rapid, a notorious strip of white water with a double hairpin turn, known in bygone days as the Hell's Gate Rapid and the Rapid-That-Runs-Both-Ways.

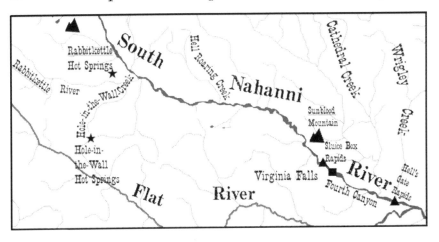

Beyond the Figure Eight Rapid and past a stretch of huge standing waves is the Nahanni's Fourth (and final) Canyon, also known as the Painted Canyon. On the other side of this ravine lies what is perhaps the Nahanni's most spectacular feature: a stunning 96-metre (315-foot) waterfall, bisected at the top by a limestone pillar called Mason Rock. Christened 'Virginia Falls' in the summer of 1928 by British gentleman explorer Fenley Hunter, who named the landmark in honour of his daughter, this roaring cascade is nearly twice the height of Niagara Falls.

Above Virginia Falls, preceded as they are by the Sluice Box Rapids, the South Nahanni twists through the Sunblood and Ragged Ranges of the Mackenzie Mountains. Far upriver, past Hell Roaring Creek, it is joined by Rabbitkettle River.

If you travel 1.6 kilometres up this tributary, past the mouth of Hole-in-the-Wall Creek, you'll come to a coulee known as Hot Springs Valley. In the midst of this place are the Nahanni's most visually spectacular thermal waters, the Rabbitkettle Hot Springs.

These mineral-rich waters seep from the tops of two towering 10,000-year-old tufa mounds, their many moss-fringed terraces flush with steaming water, before spilling down their slopes and into the river. During this process, the waters deposit the minerals with which they are saturated, building the tufa mounds layer by infinitesimal layer. With a height of 90 feet (27 metres) and a diameter of 225 feet (69 metres), the greater of these tufa mounds is the largest of its kind in Canada.

One of the first men to write about the Rabbitkettle Hot Springs was frontiersman Poole Field, a Mountie who cut his teeth in the Klondike during its heyday, and who travelled extensively with the Indians of the Mackenzie Mountains following his honourable discharge from the Force in 1900. In a letter to a friend, Field stated that the springs earned their name from a Dene legend which held that, in ancient times when the springs were boiling hot, Indians used them as 'kettles' to boil rabbits. He also revealed that the natives believed the place to be home to spirits. Passing Indians would leave gifts for these spirits, such as tobacco or knives, in order to ensure good luck or good health. In the 2013 film *Nahanni*, a Dene man named George E. Tetso elaborated on this belief, recounting a Dene myth which holds that the Rabbitkettle Hot Springs are the residence of Jambaleja (alternatively spelled "Zhamba Deja" and "Ndambadezha"), a spirit whom the Creator sent to earth to put the chaotic laws of man and nature back into order.

The Hole-in-the-Wall Hot Springs

If you travel about 21 kilometres (13 miles) up Hole-in-the-Wall Creek, Rabbitkettle River's primary tributary, you'll come to Hole-in-the-Wall Lake. Immediately west of the lake are the Hole-in-the-Wall Hot Springs- two vents of clear, warm water separated by a distance of about 300 metres (980 feet), each of them ornamented with green and pale algae.

The Broken Skull Hot Springs

Back on the South Nahanni, upriver from its confluence with the Rabbitkettle River, the river flows past Brintnell Creek, Glacier Lake, and a cluster of magnificent, towering cliffs known as the Cirque of the Unclimbables. As it begins to wind its way into the Backbone Mountains, the South Nahanni is met by Broken Skull River.

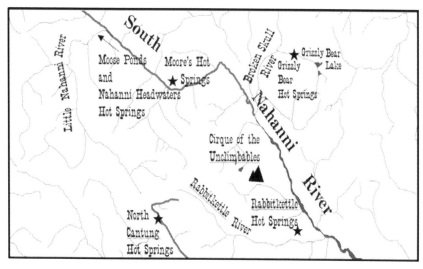

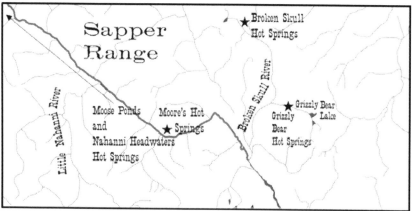

If you travel far up Broken Skull River, past the mouth of *Shuhzhie kajlj*, or The-Creek-that-is-Flowing-Out-of-the-Mountain, you'll come to the Broken Skull Hot Springs. These grey, murky waters bubble up from two vents, the cooler of them forming a tufa-walled pool, and the other flowing alongside it.

The Grizzly Bear Springs

About six kilometres (four miles) up Broken Skull River's only major tributary, *Shuhzhie kajlj,* are the Grizzly Bear Hot Springs. Situated only 3.5 kilometres (2.1 miles) west of Grizzly Bear Lake, these waters form a series of four steaming pools on the creek's southern bank, all of them surrounded by small tufa formations and thousands of tiny, delicate wildflowers.

Moore's Hot Springs

Back on the South Nahanni, beyond the soaring Vampire Peaks and their jutting Vampire Spires, and beyond the Elbow Rapids, lie Moore's Hot Springs. These thermal waters were named after John and Joanne Moore, a couple from Kingston, Ontario, who spent a year-long honeymoon in a cabin they built nearby them in the autumn of 1978. Joanne Moore, in her book *Nahanni Trailhead,* described her and her husband's impression of them thus:

"John and I were enchanted with the vegetation surrounding the springs. Oversized clovers and large waxy-leafed plants gave the forest a tropical appearance. The large ferns climbed to our waists and juicy red raspberries were ours for the taking.

"The greatest surprise was the meadow, where the springs bubbled up. Tall grasses and fireweed covered an area larger than a football field. The yellow poplar leaves quivered

in the wind on the hillsides banking the area, and off to the north we could see that crest of a snow-capped range. Moose had rested in the tall grass, as the ground covering was well flattened in spots, and hoof marks covered the dark soil."

According to Peter Jowett, "This is the warmest of the hotsprings you'll encounter [in the Nahanni Valley] *except* during flood conditions when the Nahanni backs up into the spring and makes it too cold for a pleasurable soak. The soils in the area benefit from the heated earth which in turn supports a very lush growth of cow parsnip and other species. By the way, mosquitos love it here, too!"

Nahanni North Hot Springs

Further upriver, the South Nahanni is joined by the Little Nahanni River. Up this tributary and further still up Lened Creek are the Nahanni North Hot Springs, also known as the Lened Hot Springs. These sulfurous waters issue from two separate vents, around which wild mint, ferns, and flowers grow in abundance. Rust-coloured algae thrive the springs' outwash.

It is possible that these thermal waters were what Poole Field referred to as the "Upper Hot Springs," which he claimed boiled up "through a sort of reddish sand". In a letter to a friend, Field recounted an incident in which an old Dene chief named Jim Pellesea, with whom he was travelling, asked him if he knew what made the springs red. Field pleaded ignorance and asked the chief his opinion on the matter. Pellesea told him that that he believed the springs belched forth "the blood of all the Indians and animals that have died on this earth. That is their blood coming up again."

Beyond the mouth of the Little Nahanni River are the two branches of the South Nahanni's headwaters. One branch extends 72 kilometres (45 miles) upriver, beyond a raging, boulder-strewn torrent known as the Rock Gardens, to a cluster of tiny lakes known as the Moose Ponds. In the distance are the towering, jagged Snyder Mountains, named after their discoverer Colonel Harry M. Snyder of Montreal, Quebec, who flew over them with northern pilot Leigh Brintnell and eight others in the autumn of 1937. The other branch of the Nahanni's headwaters follows Sapper River, one of the Nahanni's northernmost tributaries, northeast and then west into the mountains. At the terminus of these second headwaters, three clear, sulfurous hot springs, known as the Nahanni Headwater Hot Springs, flow down steep granite slopes into Sapper River. Green, orange, and cream algae grow in their outwash.

THE DEATH OF A LEGEND

From his research and his own experience in the North Country, Pierre Berton was fairly certain that there was no tropical valley in the Nahanni long before he first set foot in Russ Baker's Junkers monoplane. In the journalistic fashion of the day, however, he refused to allow facts to get in the way of a good story, entertaining the notion of the possibility of tropical valley in his articles until the end.

Years after the conclusion of his expedition with Baker, Art Jones, and Ed Hanratty, Berton described his bittersweet debunking of this great Canadian legend in a radio broadcast:

"The Myth of the Tropical Valley has been with us since the days of the Northwest Passage. It is our one genuine piece of folklore, as indigenous to our chill land as the leprechaun is to Eire. Indeed, it could only exist in a country like Canada where, for at least six months of the year, the entire population sits indoors longing for the sun. It is pleasant to contemplate a vision of a warm, green valley just over the horizon's rim, encircled by ice covered mountains, shrouded in mists, where- unlike Toronto or Winnipeg or even Vancouver- there lies perpetual summer."

Due to the efforts of Berton and other explorers, the mystery of a tropical valley in the Nahanni has been solved beyond a reasonable doubt. There is almost certainly no truly tropical valley in the region where "palm trees sprout from the permafrost," as Berton put it. There are, however, thirteen hot springs in the area, upon which a variety of 'tropical valley' legends were probably based.

———————

The myth of the tropical valley is a bit of an anomaly in terms of Nahanni legends, as it is one of just two to be resolved, and the only one to be truly debunked. Not every legend of the Nahanni Valley is so open-and-shut. The most mysterious of them all, upon which many of the others revolve, is the tale of Willie and Frank McLeod, whose headless corpses were discovered on the South Nahanni's shores in the early 1900's, and whose lost mine is said to lie somewhere on one of the river's many tributaries, promising untold riches to any prospector lucky enough to find it.

The Lost McLeod Mine

----------◆----------

"Of all the stories linked with this grim, austere land, that of Dead Man's Valley and the search for the Lost McLeod Mine is by far the most intriguing, and has mystified the North for forty years."

- Philip H. Godsell, *Romance of the Alaska Highway*, 1944.

THE TALE OF THE MCLEOD BROTHERS and their lost gold mine is perhaps the most mysterious of the Nahanni's legends. Like all good frontier legends, it has a number of different and often conflicting versions. No two articles on it tell the exactly the same story, and many credible, contemporary frontiersmen espoused versions of it which were completely incompatible with one another.

As disparate as many of them are, all versions of this great northern legend share a number of consistencies, the most important being their revolution around two main characters: brothers Willie and Frank McLeod.

THE MCLEOD CLAN

The McLeod brothers and their family are nearly as mysterious as the legends they have inspired. Records indicate that their father, Murdock (or perhaps Murdoch) McLeod was a Scotsman from the Western Isles who came to Canada as a young man to work for the Hudson's Bay Company. He spent his early twenties working at Fort Anderson, a remote, short-lived, severely undermanned HBC outpost servicing local Inuvialuit (Western Canadian Inuit) on the Anderson River about eighty miles upriver from the Arctic Ocean, before accompanying a Smithsonian Institute expedition on an enormous trek spanning a huge swath of Arctic coastline.

In 1865, Murdock transferred to Fort Liard, where he climbed the ranks to Chief Factor. There, he had a number of children with a local Metis[1] (or perhaps full-blood Dene) woman whom one record suggests might have been related to the Lafferty family, an old northern Metis clan. Two of these children were Willie and Frank. Sometime in the 1870's, after his first wife died, Murdock married a widow named Mary Emiline Kelberry (nee Collins), who bore him more children. Records show that Murdock had a total of ten children between his two wives, including Willie, Frank, Mary, Annie, John, Fred, Rose, Charlie, George, and Danny. Oral lore

---

[1] The Metis are an aboriginal people born of marriages between French and French Canadian , Scottish, and Orcadian fur traders and First Nations women.

Willie McLeod
Photo courtesy of the Glenbow Archives

Frank McLeod
Photo courtesy of the Glenbow Archives

indicates that he also had a son named Jake, while one ancient newspaper article suggests he had a son named Albert.

Willie and Frank McLeod grew up in and around Fort Liard, spending half their time at the fort, immersed in the world of the Hudson's Bay Company, and the other half on the trail, in the company of frontiersmen, Metis, and Indians. By all accounts, they grew up to be extremely competent outdoorsmen who could handle themselves in the wilderness as well as anyone in the Mackenzie region, "[reaching] manhood," as one writer put it, "with civilization as remote to them as their Indian friends." Willie, whom one contemporary maintained "showed most of the Indian in him and... liked their ways," was a particularly restless soul who felt more at home in the bush than at the fort. Although nearly all versions of the legend describe Willie as being the eldest of the McLeod brothers, one record suggests that Frank might have held that distinction.

In 1899, Murdock's failing eyesight prompted him to move south to Edmonton, Alberta, with his wife and most of his children.[2] Young Fred McLeod stayed behind and took up his father's mantle, becoming the new Chief Factor at Fort Liard, while Frank went to work as manager at Fort Nelson, in northeast British Columbia. It is on this stage that our legend is set.

---

[2] According to several sources, the McLeod family moved to Fort Norman, NWT, situated at the junction of the Great Bear and Mackenzie Rivers known today as Tulita; as opposed to Edmonton, Alberta .

THE TALE OF WILLIE AND FRANK MCLEOD

One day in the year 1900, a strange Indian sauntered into the trading room at Fort Liard. Unlike the trouser-wearing, mackinaw-clad Slavey Dene who typically visited the post, this dark-eyed, wild-looking brave wore a greasy, smoke-stained caribou skin robe in the old style. He was a Nahanni Indian- one of the mysterious, nomadic people who hunted deep in the Mackenzie Mountains, living the old way, as their ancestors had for a thousand years.

Young Fred McLeod, the fort's new Factor, was surprised at the lightness of the Indian's outfit. The Nahanni had no companions, nor did he carry any furs with which to trade. Aside from his primitive garb, his only possessions included an old rifle, a pair of snowshoes, and a medicine bag, which he wore around his neck. Fred stared in disbelief as the Indian reached into the latter item and withdrew a handful of solid gold nuggets[3], which he promptly spent with the abandon of a man who seemed to have no true appreciation of their worth.

At first, the Indian was reluctant to tell Fred where his treasure came from. After the curious trader plied him with tea and tobacco, however, the brave hinted that he had found his prize somewhere in the Nahanni Valley, south of

---

[3] Some say that the Indian produced gold dust, while others claim he produced chunks of quartz heavily-veined with gold.

the confluence of the Flat and South Nahanni Rivers.[4] With that, he collected his newly-purchased goods and disappeared into the wilderness, never to return.[5]

Fred McLeod was torn. On one hand, he desperately wanted to ditch the trading room for the trail, head into the Nahanni with a pick and pan, and find the source of the Indian's gold. On the other hand, he knew that duty dictated that he remain at his post. His father had bequeathed him the position of Chief Factor at Fort Liard the previous year, and he was duty-bound to fulfill the family's HBC contract obligation. He was the family's primary breadwinner now, and could not afford the luxury of a prospecting venture. Reluctantly, he consigned himself to reality and forgot about the incident.

Three years later, another Nahanni brave, this one a tall hunter named Little Nahanni,[6] arrived at Fort Liard. Like his predecessor, he paid for his goods with raw gold, which he kept in a moose skin poke. With some prompting,

[4] In many versions, the Indian was much less specific in his disclosure of the location of his find, stating that he had found his gold somewhere in the Nahanni Valley or in the Flat River area.

[5] In many versions of the legend, the trader who first learned of an Indian gold strike in the Nahanni was Fred's father, Murdock. Some say that Murdock acquired this information from a Nahanni Indian whom he had helped and befriended. In other versions, the McLeod family first learned of Nahanni gold from an Indian named Stewart, who hailed from somewhere in the Yukon either Lower Post or Dawson City), or from a Nahanni Indian named Big Charlie, who plays a more prominent role later in the chapter.

[6] In some versions, Little Nahanni was the Indian who appeared at Fort Liard in 1900; the man who appeared in 1903 was a stranger to the trader.

Little Nahanni revealed that he had panned his gold on Bennett Creek, a waterway which empties into the Flat River about five miles (nine kilometres) upriver of the Cascade-of-Thirteen-Steps.[7,8]

Fred could remain idle no longer. He sent word to his elder brother Willie in Edmonton[9] that a wealth of gold lay hidden somewhere in the Nahanni Valley. Willie immediately travelled north to Fort Nelson in northeast British Columbia, where his brother Frank now worked as manager, and convinced him to accompany him on a prospecting expedition. Frank quit his post late that fall, and the two brothers headed up the Liard River and into the Nahanni Valley.

The McLeod brothers met with some success that year, liberating an agreeable quantity of alluvial gold from the Nahanni's creek beds. When spring came, they returned to civilization and promptly squandered their hard-won earnings, losing much of it in poker games. They worked the best of their gold nuggets, however- a handful of gold chunks the size of beans- into a watch chain, which they gave to their

---

[7] In many versions, Little Nahanni did not disclose the specific location of his find.

[8] In some versions, Little Nahanni gave some of his gold to Bishop William Bompas sometimes incorrectly referred to as 'Bishop Brenner', an Anglican missionary from Fort Simpson. The bishop later had the gold worked into a watch chain and ring, both of which he wore until the day of his death. Frontiersman Albert Faille maintained that the Indian who gave the bishop this gold was actually Big Charlie, a character who appears later on in this chapter.

[9] According to one old frontiersman, Willie McLeod lived in Fort Nelson, along with his father, Murdock.

brother Fred, who had since transferred from Fort Liard to Fort Providence on the Mackenzie Delta just west of Great Slave Lake.

The following January, Willie and Frank McLeod decided to return to the Nahanni, certain that a golden bonanza awaited them somewhere in its misty recesses. This time, they were accompanied by their younger brother, Charlie.[10]

The three brothers began their journey in Edmonton, Alberta, where the majority of their family now resided. For some reason long lost to history, they reached their destination by an extremely circuitous route. First, they travelled by train to Vancouver, British Columbia, where they boarded a steamer that took them up the Pacific Coast to Wrangell, Alaska. From there, they travelled by dogsled up the frozen Stikine River to Telegraph Creek, two of the brothers breaking the trail on snowshoes while the third handled the sled and dog team. The trio continued further northeast to the remote frontier settlement of Dease Lake, and made a gruelling overland journey up the Cassiars and across the Liard Plateau. By the time they reached the upper Flat River, it was spring.[11]

---

[10] Few storytellers agree on the nature of the McLeods' 1904 expedition into the Nahanni. Although many maintain that the three brothers went in together that year, some say that Charlie was never present, while other say that Willie went in alone.

[11] According to some versions, the McLeod brothers began their journey in Fort Liard and travelled through the Mackenzie Mountains to the upper Flat River. Others claim that they began in Fort Simpson, where they purchased

There, on the shores of the upper Flat River, the McLeod brothers came upon a ragtag band of Slavey, Kaska, and Nahanni Indians. Among their number were Big Charlie, a stout, one-eyed sub-chief of a Nahanni band; Bobby Babiche, a Yukon Indian[12] who had married a Nahanni woman; Diamond C, a Cassiar prospector[13] who earned his unusual name in the Klondike Gold Rush; and two Nahanni Indians named Captain and Iron[14]- all men whom the McLeod boys knew well. These natives were also panning for gold, and had evidently met with some success. They showed the McLeod brothers samples of their findings: gold nuggets worth three dollars each, on average (a considerable sum in those days).[15]

Although the Indians neglected to disclose the site at which they had found their sizeable nuggets,[16] the McLeod

---

flour, tea, and ammunition before heading down the Liard and up the South Nahanni.

[12] According to one long-dead frontiersmen, Bobby Babiche was a Slavey from the Liard River area. "He was a very good hunter," the man said, "but he was no prospector, oh no. He was a hunter and a trapper."

[13] According to Gus Kraus, Diamond C was a Northern Tutchone Indian who hailed from Pelly Lakes, Yukon. Men who knew him agreed that Diamond C acquired his unusual name during the Klondike Gold Rush when a Stampeder asked him if he had seen any diamonds in the local creek beds. "Diamond, see?" the prospector said, gesturing towards a stone set into his ring. From then on, the Indian called himself 'Diamond C.'

[14] According to Gus Kraus, Captain and Iron were actually Beaver Indians from Northeast British Columbia and Northwestern Alberta.

[15] In some versions, the Indians showed the McLeod brothers samples of course gold dust. In others, they produced enormous gold nuggets the size of chicken eggs.

[16] In one version, the Indians simply "pointed northward" when the McLeod brothers inquired as to the source of their gold.

brothers suspected that they had done so somewhere in the immediate vicinity of their meeting place. They spent several weeks in the area searching for the source of the Indians' gold, panning the creeks there without success, before continuing down the Flat to the mouth of Bennett Creek-known thereafter as Gold Creek. There, they found quality placer gold (pronounced *PLASS-sir*; as creek bed gold is sometime called) in paying quantities[17], which they laboriously separated from the sediment and stuffed into various containers.

After a season of hard work, the McLeod brothers decided to head to Fort Liard, where they could restock their dwindling supplies before returning to the Nahanni the following spring; it was late fall, and Willie and Frank did not relish the prospect of spending a winter in that wild country without any tea or bannock.[18] Using sluice boxes that the Indians had abandoned upriver, they constructed a crude scow, packed it with supplies and the placer gold they had acquired, and set out down the Flat River. They successfully navigated a series of rapids before finally capsizing their craft on the treacherous Cascade-of-Thirteen-Steps. Although the

---

[17] In some versions, the McLeod brothers found a spectacular bonanza of gold-bearing quartz on Bennett Creek during their 1904 prospecting venture as opposed to placer gold in "paying quantities" . According to R.M. Patterson, however, the largest piece of gold they found on Bennett Creek was worth 50 cents.

[18] In this context, 'bannock' is unleavened wheat bread fried in animal fat, a staple of the Canadian frontier.

brothers survived the ordeal, most of their supplies, including nearly all of their gold, did not.

Undaunted, the brothers continued on down the river.[19] When they finally reached Fort Liard many days later, they were gaunt and emaciated, with nothing more to show for their trouble than an Eno's Fruit Salts[20] bottle stuffed with five to ten ounces of placer gold, which Willie had slipped beneath a sash tied around his waist in the hopes of protecting it.[21]

Nearly broke, yet determined to return to the site of their discovery, the McLeod brothers spent the rest of the year working for the Hudson's Bay Company at Fort Simpson in the hopes of earning a grubstake[22]; none of the northern traders would outfit them on credit on account of

[19] In some versions, the McLeod brothers completely destroyed their boat on the Cascade-of-Thirteen-Steps, recovering nothing but a rifle and 30 cartridges. Following the incident, some say that they hiked upriver back to the site of the Indian diggings, where the constructed another boat from sluice boxes or, in some versions, raw timber , shot and jerked a moose, prepared a moose-hide babiche rawhide cord trackline, and successfully tracked their boat down the rapids. Others say that they continued downriver on foot.

[20] Eno's Fruit Salts is a 19th Century pharmaceutical.

[21] According to Dick Turner, a frontiersman who spent much of his life trapping, trading, and prospecting in and around Nahanni Country, the McLeod brothers lost this gold bottle in the Liard River when they came upon a party of whites and Indians. The brothers told these men of their experience, and passed the bottle around from boat to boat. During this process, one of the men accidentally dropped the bottle into the river several frontiersmen mention that this man was a native named "Old Joe Hope"). Willie McLeod, the son of Fred McLeod and the nephew of Willie and Frank, told a similar story, substituting his father for the party of whites and Indians.

[22] In many versions, only Willie went to work for the HBC.

their gambling habits.[23] The Company pay was scant, and the brothers' accrual of prospecting supplies was painfully slow.

While the McLeod brothers toiled for their grubstake, a young, mysterious Scottish steamboat engineer named Robert Weir slipped into Fort Providence with a boatload of supplies for the HBC post.[24] Duty necessitated that he meet with Fred McLeod, Chief Factor at the time.

During their meeting, Weir noticed the golden chain on Fred's pocket watch and asked him where he had acquired it. Fred told him that his brothers had made it for him from Nahanni gold, and that they were preparing to embark on another prospecting expedition into the rugged country in which they had found it. They needed supplies, Fred informed him, and were unable to secure an outfit on credit from the local HBC traders.

The engineer thanked Fred for the information and promptly broke his HBC contract. Having come down with a bad case of gold fever, he travelled to Fort Simpson[25], met

[23] Some versions say that Fred McLeod, who served as manager at either Fort Providence or Fort Liard at the time, outfitted his brothers on credit.

[24] This character, usually referred to as Robert Weir, is one of the most enigmatic elements of the McLeod legend. He has been variously named W.J. Weir, Green, Wilderson, Ware, and George T. Wade, and described as being Scottish, English, American, and Australian. All accounts maintain that he worked as a steamboat engineer, however, and one frontiersman claimed he operated HBC steamers and gas boats on the Mackenzie River and Great Slave Lake. According to one account, this mysterious partner of the McLeod brothers is completely fictitious.

[25] In some versions, Willie and Frank were working for the HBC in Fort Liard instead of Fort Simpson.

with Willie and Frank, and agreed to stake them on the condition that he be allowed to accompany them on their expedition.[26] Willie and Frank took the mysterious engineer up on his offer, and the three men set out for the Nahanni that spring. For some reason, Charlie decided to stay behind this time.[27]

When the McLeod brothers failed to return to Fort Liard before winter, Fred McLeod at Fort Providence was not particularly concerned. Both Willie and Frank were seasoned outdoorsmen. Expert hunters and trappers, these two veterans of the subarctic could handle themselves in the wilderness as well as any Indian. Fred was sure that Willie and Frank would have little trouble living off the land if necessity required.[28]

Seasons came and went, and still there were no signs of Willie and Frank. Finally, in the spring of 1907, an abandoned canoe similar to the type the Metis brothers and their partner brought into Nahanni Country was found bobbing in a driftwood pile somewhere on the South

[26] Some say that the deciding factor that convinced Weir to accompany the McLeod brothers into the Nahanni was seeing Willie's small bottle of gold.

[27] Some versions have it that Charlie stayed behind because he had found work with the Hudson's Bay Company, perhaps in Fort Liard. Others maintain that he returned south to Edmonton.

[28] According to a number of reputable versions of the McLeod tale, Charlie McLeod attempted to look for his brothers in the fall of 1905, when they failed to return to Fort Liard on schedule. He was unable to complete this expedition on account of extreme cold and heavy snow. He attempted to search for them again in the spring of 1906, this time with a group of Mounties, but was similarly precluded by severe cold and snow.

Nahanni.[29] Word of the find spread quickly spread throughout the North Country via the 'moccasin telegraph'- the frontier equivalent of the grape vine- and Fred McLeod was soon notified. Fred informed the rest of his family in Edmonton of the disturbing news.

Charlie McLeod, determined to learn what had befallen his older brothers, travelled north the following year with his younger brother Danny.[30] At Fort Liard, the brothers put together a search party consisting of Poole Field, Sergeant Joy of the Royal Northwest Mounted Police, and two of the Lafferty boys.[31] Together, the six men headed up the South Nahanni in May, 1908, prepared for the worst.

After conquering the Splits, the notorious First Canyon, and the raging Cache Rapids, the party entered an open, bowl-like section of the valley. The men searched this area for some time, meticulously scanning the shoreline for any sign of human presence. Just as they were about to give up, one among them noticed a small clearing in the trees along the shore, its green foliage punctuated by the white flash of axe cuttings. The crew paddled over to investigate.

---

[29] According to one old frontiersman, Willie and Frank had gone into the Nahanni in a large, flat-bottomed scow as opposed to a birch bark canoe .

[30] In some versions of the legend, Charlie McLeod made this journey alone.

[31] According to one of the earliest printed versions of the legend, namely an article published in Winnipeg's *Manitoba Free Press* on January 13, 1909, Charlie McLeod's search party included Dawson miners J. Morrison and William Douglas, C. Young, O.B. Moore, and Albert McLeod. According to Gus Kraus, on the other hand, Charlie's party included Gus Morrison, Big Charlie, a Mountie named Nitchie Thorn, Poole Field, and a native named Alexi Lomond.

No sooner had the party stepped onto the riverbank than Charlie spied a dogsled runner lying in the grass.[32] On its side was an undated message pencilled in one of his brothers' scrawl:

"We have found a fine prospect."

When the party failed to find any additional clues in the area, they continued upriver. At the northern end of the saucer-like valley, just downriver from the entrance to the Second Canyon, they came upon another clearing, this one evidently the site of some long-abandoned camp. There, they made a grisly discovery.[33]

On either side of a long-dead campfire, beneath two rotting woolen blankets and atop beds of spruce boughs, lay a pair of human, adult, male skeletons. Both bodies, to the horror of their discoverers, were headless. One of them lay on its back, rolled neatly in its blanket, as if its former owner had died in his sleep.[34] The other was sprawled out on its chest, its blanket twisted about it haphazardly, one of its bony arms reaching out towards a rusted rifle which leaned against

---

[32] In some versions, the sled runner had been driven into the ground like a stake.

[33] According to some versions, this discovery was first made by Mary Adelle Lafferty, the Metis wife of a trader named Billy Atkinson, who had joined the search party along with her husband when Charlie McLeod and his crew passed by her camp on the South Nahanni River. She is alleged to have made her discovery near an old Nahanni Indian trail. In some of these versions, the headless skeletons of Willie and Frank McLeod lay beneath the same blanket, huddled together as if for warmth.

[34] According to some accounts, the blanket that covered this body was perforated by a bullet hole.

a nearby spruce tree.[35] The manner in which the bodies were displayed suggested a nocturnal ambush. The first man to be attacked- the one lying on his back- was evidently killed in his sleep before he had a chance to defend himself, while the second had leapt from his bedroll in a vain attempt to reach his rifle before being struck down. [36]

Charlie quickly identified the bodies as his brothers' from bits of tattered clothing[37], from Willie's gold ring, and from Frank's distinctive gold pocket watch, which dangled from a nearby tree branch. Shaken to the core, he and his companions proceeded to search the surrounding area for any evidence which might shed some light on the nature of his brothers' deaths. The company found neatly-stacked crates filled with supplies, although the picks and shovels the brothers had brought into the country appeared to be missing. They also discovered a box containing extraordinarily rich samples of gold-bearing quartz, indicating that the McLeod brothers had struck it rich somewhere in the Nahanni Valley before their untimely deaths- a "fine prospect," indeed. Of the engineer Weir, and of the McLeod brothers' missing heads, the company found neither hide nor hair.

---

[35] In some versions, this skeleton clutched the rifle in its hands.

[36] According to one version of the legend, which R.M. Patterson claimed originated in Fort Simpson, the headless skeletons were found tied to a tree. A nearby note indicated that they had found gold.

[37] In one version, the skeletons were only wearing long woolen underwear.

After burying their brothers' remains and marking the graves with a simple wooden cross, Charlie and Danny returned to Fort Liard, where they sent word to the Royal Northwest Mounted Police of their find, wholly convinced that Willie and Frank had been murdered. That accomplished, the two brothers likely returned to Edmonton together.

Suspecting foul play, the Mounties opened up an investigation into the McLeod brothers' deaths. The following year, a party of Royal North West Mounted Police (RNWMP)[38] officers from Fort Simpson accompanied Charlie McLeod up the South Nahanni to the scene of the crime, which had since acquired the ominous appellation 'Deadmen Valley'. The Mounties investigated the site and concluded that Willie and Frank had likely discovered a gold bonanza somewhere in the Nahanni, whereupon their partner Weir, crazed with gold lust, had murdered them in their sleep and made off with not only the fruit of their labour, but also, quite possibly, their heads.

---

[38] The 'Royal North West Mounted Police' RNWMP is one of the former titles of the iconic national Canadian police force whose members famous for their distinctive traditional uniform consisting scarlet serge and brown campaign hats are colloquially known as 'Mounties.' Initially entitled the 'North West Mounted Police' NWMP , this Force was established in 1873 in order to combat the illicit whisky trade the exchange of frontier whisky for Blackfoot buffalo robes which took place in what is now Southern Alberta and Southwest Saskatchewan. Its members played crucial roles in many of Western Canada's most turbulent events, including the surrender of Sioux Chief Sitting Bull, the North-West Rebellion, and the Klondike Gold Rush. The Force was renamed the 'Royal North West Mounted Police' RNWMP in 1904 following the participation of its members in the Second Boer War. In 1920, it merged with the older easterly Dominion Police to form the 'Royal Canadian Mounted Police' RCMP , the name it bears today.

The following year, a discovery was made which changed the Mounties' official opinion on the matter. In the woods about three miles south of Deadmen Valley, on some nameless tributary of the South Nahanni, a band of Slavey Indians came upon an unidentified skeleton[39] and reported their discovery to the RNWMP outpost at Fort Simpson. Corporal Arthur H.L. Mellor (or perhaps Mellow) of Fort Smith, NWT- the Mountie assigned to the McLeod case in 1909- assumed that the body was Weir's and, due to the fact that no gold was recovered along with it, made a controversial deduction. He concluded that Willie and Frank McLeod had lost their canoe, along with their supplies, through some freak accident and starved to death. While the brothers lay dying, Weir attempted to walk back to civilization, but perished from privation along the way. This theory was bolstered by a new revelation that the McLeod brothers had started out on their expedition ill-equipped and short of supplies, having headed into Nahanni Country with only 50 pounds of flour and 5 pounds of tea, which they purchased in Fort Simpson[40]. In light of the new evidence, the Mounties dismissed the deaths of the McLeod brothers as the result of an unfortunate accident- a position which they officially maintain to this day.

[39] According to one account, this skeleton was found with a revolver in its hand and a ragged hole in its skull, indicating its former owner had met his end through suicide.

[40] In some versions, the McLeod brothers purchased their 50 pounds of flour and 5 pounds of tea in Fort Liard instead of Fort Simpson .

Many frontiersmen who came into the Nahanni Country later on concurred with the Mounties' assessment. Woodsman Albert Faille, for example, believed that the McLeod brothers had lost their boat "when a weasel or wolverine had chewed through the babiche [rawhide] cord that was used at the time to tie [the] boat to shore." Their supplies gone, the brothers slowly succumbed to starvation and exposure. In an interview in later life, Gus Kraus speculated that the McLeods might have lost their canoe on the treacherous South Nahanni, relating a close call he had on the river involving an ice jam and a whirlpool. Others believed that the brothers contracted some sort of illness- perhaps scurvy or tuberculosis- in the bush and crawled into their bedrolls to die.

Other residents of the Mackenzie region held views contrary to the official narrative, seriously doubting the claim that the McLeod brothers were victims of natural forces. By all accounts, Willie and Frank McLeod were superior woodsmen who could handle themselves in the bush as well as, or better than, any of their contemporaries. Even if they did lose all of their supplies in a freak accident, many believed that they were quite capable of reaching civilization on foot, and would certainly not have succumbed to the elements at the same time, mere feet apart from each other. For many, it was obvious that Willie and Frank had been murdered.

Central to the debate regarding the nature of the McLeod brothers' deaths is the question of how Willie and

Frank lost their heads- a complicated query considering the conflicting information regarding the state of the brothers' corpses at the time of their discovery. According to some reports, it was clear from the ragged condition of the corpses' severed necks that the heads had been ripped, or perhaps twisted, from their bodies, as if by brute force. Others claimed that there were signs indicating that the heads had been chewed off by some large carnivorous animal. Conversely, Charlie McLeod maintained that his brothers' decapitations were almost surgically neat, as if done with a sharp implement, and believed that their murderer had dropped their heads into the South Nahanni River in order to conceal evidence of bullet wounds. And some claimed that the heads had evidently separated from their bodies through the natural process of decomposition. Whether Willie and Frank McLeod's heads were severed at the time of their deaths or sometime much later, and whether man, beast, time, or something else entirely was responsible for their removal, remains a mystery to this day.

Many frontiersmen believed that the McLeod brothers' heads were removed and carried off into the woods long after death by scavengers- bears, wolves, wolverines, and rats being the most frequently indicted suspects.[41] Willie McLeod, son of Fred McLeod, held this view, claiming that his uncles' bodies were actually identified by their hair, which had sloughed off

---

[41] In 1947, American journalist Phil Stong suggested that ants and mice were the culprits responsible for the McLeod brothers' headlessness, ending his article with a cynical directive: "Happy Dreams."

their respective scalps in the course of the decomposition process sometime before the skulls were taken.[42] Some proponents of this theory maintained that the scavengers only took an interest in the corpses' heads, neglecting to similarly make off with other body parts, due to a natural aversion to clothing and blankets, or due to the fact that the human brain takes an especially long time to decompose, thereby emitting a stench attractive to scavengers for a much longer period than other body parts.

Others were certain that the McLeod brothers' heads were amputated at the time of their deaths. Some Mackenzie Mountain trappers suspected that the brothers were slaughtered by a mad trapper or a fugitive from justice, perhaps an outlaw from the Yukon, who took their heads as trophies.[43] Others grumbled that the mysterious Nahanni Indians, fiercely protective of their hunting grounds, likely

[42] Willie McLeod son of Fred McLeod of Fort Liard told Pierre Berton, during the latter's 1947 expedition to the Nahanni, that the bodies of his uncles were actually discovered with their heads intact. In a much later interview with a Parks Canada representative, he claimed that the McLeod brothers' heads were, in fact, missing at the time of the discovery, but that their hair lay in tangled mats in their place, evidently haven "slipped off" as a result of decomposition. In an interview, Gus Kraus echoed Charlie's second testimony.

[43] Willie McLeod, son of Fred McLeod, heard a rumour, passed around by Slavey Indians, that a lawless Yukon native named Stewart had murdered his uncles. Willie told Pierre Berton, during the latter's 1947 expedition to the Nahanni, that this native "had a trapline in the country and killed [Willie and Frank] for their food." Years later, in a Parks Canada interview, he claimed that Stewart had murdered his uncles for their gold. Upon committing the deed, he allegedly traded the stolen gold in Dawson City, and never returned to the Nahanni Valley again. "Some of the rest of the Indians... they used to tell me about Stewart being quite an Indian," said Charlie. "I mean one of those tough Indians. Didn't care what he did."

had a hand in the McLeod brothers' untimely deaths[44], removing their heads in order to intimidate any whites who might come across their corpses. And some of the Slavey Indians who visited Fort Liard, when asked their opinion on the matter, whispered that the gruesome deed was the work of the Nakani, the giant, hairy, headhunting wildmen whom their people had long claimed haunted the Nahanni Valley.

Charlie McLeod, to his dying day, maintained that his brothers were murdered for their gold, which he was sure they discovered, by their mysterious partner, Robert Weir. He also hotly contested the official verdict that the skeleton discovered in 1909 constituted Weir's remains, and, according to a story he told to anyone who would listen, he did so with good reason.

THE HUNT FOR ROBERT WEIR

Following the discovery of Willie and Frank McLeod's headless remains, rumour spread that Robert Weir, the brothers' partner, was still alive and at large. Some claimed to have spotted the mysterious steamboat engineer in Telegraph Creek, British Columbia, with an enormous quantity of raw

---

[44] Some believed that the McLeod brothers did not find their bonanza themselves, but rather stumbled upon a small band of Nahanni Indians working a particularly rich creek bed. The Indians swore the brothers to secrecy, but allowed them to work alongside them. Later, one of their number murdered them, fearing that they would usher a gold rush into their hunting grounds upon their return to civilization.

gold in his possession.[45] Others reported that he was living like a king in Vancouver, BC, or that he was working as a tie gang labourer for the Canadian National Railway (in other versions, the Canadian Pacific Railway) under an assumed name, or that he was trapping in Northern Alberta, or that he had paid a visit to Fort Providence, NWT, his old stomping grounds. The Royal Northwest Mounted Police investigated some of these rumours, making inquiries in Telegraph Creek, Fort Providence, and Vancouver, and concluded that they were groundless.

Philip H. Godsell's Account

Chief among those perpetuating rumours of Weir's continued existence was Charlie McLeod. In the 1930's, '40's, and early '50's, Philip H. Godsell, a Hudson's Bay Company inspector-turned-historian who travelled about the Canadian North from 1906 until 1929, published a series of articles detailing the extraordinary story behind Charlie's allegation- a narrative which was corroborated by two pieces in the *Edmonton Journal* and the *Calgary Albertan*, respectively, both of them based on interviews with Charlie's sons and his nephew, Ike McLeod. Godsell claimed to have cobbled this story together from informal interviews with Frank Beatton, "a grizzled, irascible Orkney man... a hard-bitten old trader who hadn't an ounce of imagination in his whole makup," who served as Chief Factor at Fort St. John, the two of them

---

[45] Weir's raw gold has been variously described as dust, flakes, nuggets, and gold-veined quartz, and ascribed values of $4,000, $5,000, $8,000, $17,000, and $20,000.

"seated in a couple of babiche-netted chairs with a bottle of Old Buck rum between [them]"; from tales issuing "from the lips of tawny dog runners, bronzed canoemen, and white collared clerks" of the Hudson's Bay Company "in the snow-bound forests of Liard Country"; from Fred McLeod, then-Factor of Fort Liard, "a raw-boned... granite-faced... man in fringed buckskin, moccasins, and fur cap" with whom he conversed "in the sibilant patois of the Mackenzie Country," lounging in Fort Liard's "little den, redolent of smoked buckskin and adorned with colourful porcupine quillwork... while swirling flakes beat a muffled tattoo against the window panes and the box-stove cracked merrily"; and with Charlie McLeod himself, who told him his tale at Fort Resolution, "seated on a boulder overlooking the vast expanse of Great Slave Lake." Godsell, in his dramatic retellings of Charlie McLeod's story, paints a fascinating picture of a gruelling manhunt with a startling culmination.

According to this tale, sometime after the McLeod brothers' disappearance, "a band of mahogany-faced [Nahanni Indians][46] pitched their smoke-stained teepees" outside Fort Liard. These natives informed the Factor[47] that Weir (whom Godsell consistently referred to as either 'Ware' or 'George T. Wade') had been seen travelling west through the mountains,

---

[46] In some of Godsell's articles, these natives who informed the Factor at Fort Liard of Weir's westward journey were Slavey Indians as opposed to Nahanni.

[47] Although Godsell implies that Murdock McLeod was the Factor of Fort Liard at the time, other evidence indicates that the acting Factor at the time was likely someone else perhaps his son, Fred.

alone.[48] The Factor promptly relayed this information to Charlie McLeod in Edmonton, who decided to investigate the allegation.

With a strong hunch that Weir had murdered his brothers, Charlie set out west himself, quickly picking up Weir's trail. "Compact and wiry," wrote Godsell, "there was enough Indian blood in [him] to make him doggedly persistent." Charlie followed the trail southwest to Telegraph Creek, BC, where, he learned, Weir had been spotted with a large quantity of raw gold.

Charlie followed Weir's trail further west to the port town of Prince Rupert, BC, on the Pacific coast. After mingling with local fishermen, he learned that Reverend John Ellis, a missionary from the Yukon who had mushed into town a few days earlier, claimed to have met a stranger matching Weir's description. Back in a trading post at Telegraph Creek, Ellis noticed "a weird-looking man standing alone," reeking of putrefaction. Ellis spoke with the stranger, who told him, in hushed tones, that his partners had been slain in the wilderness by Indians. The rancid odour he exuded was attributable to the carcass of a caribou he had shot and skinned on his way to Telegraph Creek; by day, he dragged the animal's meat behind him, and at night he slept in its rotting hide.

---

[48] In Godsell's earliest article on the McLeod story, published in the 1936 issue of the RCMP's quarterly magazine *Scarlet & Gold*, Weir headed south instead of west. Charlie subsequently trailed him to Edmonton, Alberta, and then west via the Canadian Pacific Railroad to Vancouver, BC.

The man must have been wealthy, Ellis told Charlie, as he purchased a fine team of Alaskan malamutes, along with an outfit, before promptly heading west as if the Devil were at his heels.

For some reason, Charlie proceeded north up the Pacific coast to Ketchikan, Alaska, where, in a strange episode of clairvoyance, he learned that Weir was living in Vancouver. He travelled south by steamer to the city where, in a saloon on Water Street, in the heart of the old Gastown district, he "espied a broad-shouldered, flannel-shirted, hawk-faced man in a trail-battered Stetson, well-liquored and buying up drinks for the crowd. Then, as he turned on unsteady heels, Charlie found himself gazing into the sunken blue eyes of the man he'd trailed across the Rockies."

Charlie sat down with Weir at an empty table and, over a bottle of whisky, invited him to describe his misadventure with Willie and Frank. Weir, his voice thick with drink, recounted how he and the McLeod brothers, upon entering the Nahanni Valley, had been harried by hostile Indians at every step. "Food caches had been broken into and rifled. Twice, they had been fired on from ambush." At long last, on "some nameless creek in the shadow of three red buttes," they struck a spectacularly rich vein of gold. After another attempt on their lives, they decided to abandon their mine and return to it later with a larger party. The company quickly headed downriver. At Nahanni Butte, they divided the gold they had taken with them and went their separate ways; Willie and Frank headed east for Fort Simpson, while Weir struck out west across the mountains.

Charlie did not believe a word of the engineer's story; under no circumstances would his brothers, hardened rivermen that they were, have been defeated by the relatively tame water trail from Nahanni Butte to Fort Simpson, vanishing without a trace somewhere along the way. In spite of his misgivings, Charlie schooled his features into stoic compliance, careful to conceal his true sentiments from his brothers' partner. Over the next two weeks, he met frequently with the ex-engineer in order to glean what information he could from him. When Weir, under the influence, hinted as to the general location of his brothers' strike, the Metis assembled an outfit and headed north. He took a train to Edmonton, secured a ride on fur traders' carts to Athabasca Landing (the site of present-day Athabasca, Alberta), travelled to Fort Chipewyan, Alberta, via scow brigade, and made his way to Fort Liard by steamer and canoe. There, he stocked up on provisions and headed north into the Nahanni Valley.

Guided by a supernatural hunch, which Godsell suggested was a legacy of his Indian ancestry, Charlie McLeod "came to a willow-grown creek shadowed by three red buttes and choked with beaver dams." There, he found the headless skeletons of his brothers. Having proved to his satisfaction that Weir had indeed slain Willie and Frank in cold blood, Charlie vowed to take revenge. When he returned to Vancouver in the hopes of bringing his brothers' killer to justice, however, Weir was nowhere to be found.

Without any leads to follow, Charlie abandoned his manhunt and travelled to Fort Resolution, where he secured a position as interpreter for the Hudson's Bay Company (Charlie was reputedly fluent in eleven native dialects). Eventually, he headed Outside (as northerners sometimes refer to southerly civilization) to Edmonton, Alberta, where he started a small business.

Many years later, when Charlie was living on a farm he had purchased near Wetaskiwin, Alberta, just south of Edmonton, he learned, through some twist of fate, that Weir was working on a nearby stretch of railroad under an assumed name. Charlie confronted the man, who fled to a farm in "some obscure corner of Saskatchewan" near the Alberta-Saskatchewan border.

Charlie tracked his quarry and discovered Weir's hiding place without difficulty. As he approached the farmhouse, Charlie saw his brothers' old partner dash from the barn and climb atop a haystack, which he promptly set on fire. Before Charlie could reach him, Weir produced a revolver and shot himself in the head. Charlie barely managed to save Weir's smouldering corpse from the makeshift pyre. "A pair of field glasses and a pile of cigarette stubs near the window inside the [farmhouse] told their own story only too clearly," wrote Godsell. "[Weir] had spent nearly every waking hour watching the road way in an agony of suspense."

The Lost McLeod Mine

Charlie McLeod's Version

In the 1940's, the *Edmonton Journal* and the *Calgary Albertan* published several articles on the McLeod story, each of them ending with a description of Charlie McLeod's manhunt for Robert Weir according to Charlie's sons. Although these accounts, which were later echoed in a number of magazine articles, shared some similarities with the tales put forth by Philip Godsell, they had some fundamental differences.

According to these versions, sometime around 1926, Charlie McLeod entered a trading post outside Edmonton which specialized in the acquisition and sale of fox pelts. While browsing, he sparked up a conversation with a stranger who was similarly examining the store's wares- a man who looked vaguely familiar. Before long, the conversation gravitated towards the North Country, then to the Nahanni Valley, and finally to the deaths of Willie and Frank McLeod. "As a matter of fact," said the stranger in a conspiratorial whisper, "it was me who buried those fellows."

Charlie, his face grim, gripped the man by his arm. "I hope you're joking, mister," he growled. "I'm their brother, Charlie."

Ashen faced, the stranger broke from Charlie's grasp, fled the store, and retreated across the prairie. Charlie followed him. Acting on a tip, he trailed the man to a small farm outside Viking, Alberta- a relatively remote town east of Edmonton, not far from the Saskatchewan border. As Charlie made his way down the dirt road to the farmhouse, the fugitive he was tracking locked himself in the barn and shot himself through the head. The sparks which issued from his revolver ignited the surrounding hay, ultimately resulting in the barn's immolation. By the time the fire died out, smouldering ashes and a scattering of charred bones were all that remained of Robert Weir.

THE FATE OF MARTIN JORGENSEN

Back in 1908, following the discovery of Willie and Frank McLeod's headless skeletons, word spread that the Metis brothers had stumbled upon a fabulous golden bonanza sometime prior to their deaths- a rumour supported by the fact that samples of rich, gold-veined quarts were found along with their corpses. Before long, a handful of hardened, fearless prospectors decided to search for this lost gold, taking their chances in the mist-shrouded vale to which their resultant misfortunes would soon bequeath a ghastly epithet: 'Headless Valley.'

In 1909- the same year in which the Royal North West Mounted Police officially closed their case on the McLeod brothers- the first of these prospectors, a Norwegian[49] named Martin Jorgensen (or perhaps 'Jorgenson'), went into the Nahanni Valley in search of the McLeod brothers' lost gold.

---

[49] Many say that Martin Jorgensen was Norwegian. Some say that he was Swedish, others claim he was Danish, while others still maintain that he was Swiss.

By all accounts, Jorgensen was a healthy, robust, and extremely competent woodsman endowed with sterling character, liked and respected by Indian and white man alike. Frontiersman Billy Clark described him as "a strapping fellow, well-versed in woodcraft and prospecting," while Philip Godsell characterized him as "hard-boiled sourdough... a genial giant of a man [who] laughed to scorn the thought that any curse could hover over" the Nahanni Valley.

Like that of the McLeod brothers, the tale of Martin Jorgensen has a number of different and often conflicting versions. In the words of W.D. Addison, a Parks Canada historian who attempted to document these variations in the 1970's, "the discrepancies in the different versions of this event and mystery of circumstances are greater than that for any other [Nahanni] disappearance except the McLeods." Minor details notwithstanding, however, most of these variations can be roughly distilled into two main narratives, distinguished most prominently by their appointment of two different partners to the unfortunate protagonist: Poole Field and Osias Meilleur, respectively.

The Field-Atkinson Version

According this this version of the tale, Martin Jorgensen made his way into the Nahanni Valley sometime in 1909 or 1910. The details regarding the route he took into the country and the state of his business relationships at the time are obscured in a haze of inconsistencies. According to some versions of the legend, Jorgensen was partnered with Poole

Field, who ran a trading post for the Northern Trading Company at the time. Others claimed that he was allied with Billy Atkinson, a grizzled prospector and trapper who happened to be a close friend and former partner of Poole Field.

Whatever the case, Jorgensen secured an outfit from Poole Field and headed into the Nahanni Valley in search of the McLeod brothers' lost gold. Most versions agree that Field's trading post was located at the confluence of the Pelly and Ross Rivers- two waterways situated in the Yukon west of the Mackenzie Mountains, their headwaters located a short distance from those of the South Nahanni- and that Jorgensen travelled alone up the Ross River from Field's store, hiked overland to the headwaters of the South Nahanni, built a canoe, and headed

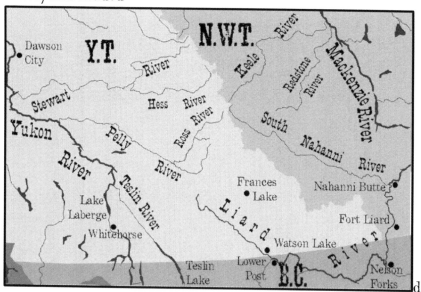

ownriver. Other storytellers, however, claim that Jorgensen

started out from Fort Simpson and travelled up the South Nahanni River. In many of his articles, for example, Philip Godsell describes seeing Jorgensen off at Fort Simpson, shooting the breeze with him as he loaded his canoe and cautioning him to beware of the legendary Nakani- a jest which Jorgensen dignified "with a throaty laugh [as] he dipped his paddle and swung out into the current."

While Martin Jorgensen was prospecting in the Nahanni Valley, Billy Atkinson was convicted of manslaughter; during a heated altercation with a rival trapper in a Dawson City saloon, the sourdough clubbed his adversary to death with a glass bottle. While Atkinson was serving his five year sentence in a RNWNP jail, his Metis wife, Mary (nee Lafferty), went to live with his good friend Poole Field, for whom she had agreed to work as a housekeeper. Ultimately, this arrangement resulted in Field taking Mary as his wife, apparently with Atkinson's blessing[50] (Field's first wife, a Dene woman named Tanny (or perhaps Kitty Tom), lost her life during an early 20th Century flu pandemic which swept through the Northwest Territories).

In 1913, a travel-weary, pockmarked Slavey trapper named Jules stumbled into a trading post at Pelly Lakes, Yukon,[51] bearing a letter for Billy Atkinson.[52] He had just

[50] According to some versions of the legend, Poole Field married Mary Atkinson after Billy Atkinson's death.

[51] In other versions, Jules brought his letter to Dawson City.

completed an arduous journey up the South Nahanni River and over the Mackenzie Mountains, he told the traders at Pelly Lakes- a journey for which he had been paid handsomely in raw gold by the strange, broad-shouldered white man who had entrusted him with the task.

The traders advised the courier to deliver his letter to Atkinson's former wife, Mary, who happened to be visiting the post with her new husband, Poole Field, as Billy was still locked up in a Mountie jail. Mary accepted the letter on Atkinson's behalf and immediately showed it to Poole Field. The letter consisted of a crude, grease-stained map indicating a cabin located about a mile upriver from the mouth of the Flat, along with short message from Martin Jorgensen instructing Atkinson to come quickly- the burly Scandinavian had struck it rich.

As Billy Atkinson had authorized him to stake claims on his behalf while he was in prison, Poole Field felt justified in following up on the lead. In 1914, he assembled an outfit and set out for the Nahanni Valley, hoping to hook up with Jorgensen and stake a gold claim for himself and his incarcerated friend. According to a letter, which Field wrote many years later to a man named Jack[53], he was accompanied on this expedition by a Dene adventurer named Oskar, a

---

[52] In many versions of the legend, this letter was addressed to Poole Field.

[53] Poole Field's friend Jack was likely either trader Jack LaFlair or John "Jack" Moran, former Inspector of the Northwest Territories & Yukon Branch.

spectacular guide with whom he had travelled extensively in the past.

That year, Poole and Oskar travelled over the mountains and down the South Nahanni to Virginia Falls, where they decided to spend the winter. There, they spent the next few months trapping out of their tents, accumulating a sizeable quantity of marten pelts in the process, before returning the way they had come with their season's take of furs.

Poole Field returned to the Nahanni Valley the following year, once again determined to find Jorgensen. Some say that he went into the country alone that year. Others contend that he was accompanied by his friend Oskar, or by his wife, Mary. Others still maintain that he went in with a trapper named Olaf Bredvic, and with Billy Atkinson, freshly released from prison.

The route that Field and his party took to get to the Nahanni that year is another subject of contention. Some say that they travelled down the South Nahanni River, while others claim that they trekked over the Mackenzie Mountains to the headwaters of the Flat River. Others still claim that they portaged from Virginia Falls to the head of Irvine Creek, a tributary of the Flat, where they found a temporary a-frame cabin which Jorgensen had constructed, on the central column of which was inscribed a crude map and a message directing the reader to look for Jorgensen at either of his two main cabins, one of them situated at the Flat's confluence with the South Nahanni and the other located on a creek nearby it.

Whatever the case, Poole Field and his party travelled deep into the heart of the Nahanni Valley, prospecting as they went. Field, in one of his letters, stated that he and his companions were finding fine colours in the creek beds, and suspected that they might have "made a strike" were it not for a lurid turn of events.

In time, Field and his companions came upon a trail blazed through the forest which, they discovered, led to one of Jorgensen's main cabins. Most storytellers agree that this cabin was located on a creek situated a short distance from the mouth of the Flat River. Whether this waterway was the stream known today as Jorgensen Creek, a tributary of the Flat situated just above the mouth Caribou River, or Clearwater Creek, a tributary of the South Nahanni located across from the Flat's mouth just upriver from the Figure Eight Rapids, which Albert Faille, for reasons which will soon become obvious, dubbed 'Murder Creek,' is another detail on which storytellers disagree. What storytellers *do* agree on is that Poole Field and his companions, upon approaching Jorgensen's main cabin, knew immediately that something was very wrong.

The scene which confronted Poole Field and company on September 28, 1914 is one of the most controversial elements of the Nahanni legends. There are more versions of this scene than almost any other in the Nahanni story. When stripped to their core, however, every version agrees on two things: that Martin Jorgensen's cabin was little more than a pile of cold ashes, and that Martin Jorgensen's headless skeleton lay somewhere in its vicinity.

According to one version, Jorgensen's corpse lay on its chest between the ashes of his cabin and the creek beside which it was built. An empty bucket, which lay on its side closer to the creek, suggested that Jorgensen had been in the process of retrieving water with which to douse a fire in his cabin when he saw something that scared him. He dropped the bucket and ran towards his cabin to get his rifle, but was struck down in the process.

Another version has it that Jorgensen's skeleton was found about 65 yards from his cabin at the bend of a narrow game trail, clutching or lying next to a loaded rifle, the barrel of which, in some variations, was twisted. Two spent shells lay in the grass nearby, indicating that the sturdy Norseman had put up a fight for his life.

Most variations of the legend include some remark on the condition of Jorgensen's firearms. Some say that his rifle and revolver were nowhere to be found, while others suggest that their roasted skeletons, fully loaded in some versions and completely empty in others, were discovered among the cabin's ashes. According to one story, Jorgensen's .38-55 Savage rifle, which he had acquired in Fort Simpson the previous summer, was later found for sale in the same store in which he had purchased it. On the other hand, Billy Clark maintained that Jorgensen's .38-55 was found propped up against a tree near his body "with the hammer cocked and a shell in the barrel."

Another detail on which some storytellers disagree is the condition of Jorgensen's head. Although most versions of the legend maintain that Jorgensen's skull was nowhere to be found, some allege the contrary. Gus Kraus, for example, claimed that Jorgensen's skull was discovered near the cabin with a ragged hole in the crown. Others claimed that his skull was found in the bush. And Billy Clark maintained that, while the majority of his skull was missing, Jorgensen's jaw was found lying somewhere in the grass.

Perhaps the last word on the matter should be afforded to Poole Field, who described his gruesome discovery in a letter to a friend, dated July 14, 1939:

"After rooting around for a while there seemed to be a pretty well cut out trail leading up the river so I started following it out. About fifty yards from the cabin there was a bunch of large spruce and the trail made a short turn around it. Just here I found an axe in the trail. I picked it up and just around behind the tree I found Martin's bones or what was left of them. His gun lay close by, loaded and cocked. We never found his skull, all tho [sic] we stayed all next day to examine the place well."

Although some versions have it that Poole Field, being an ex-Mountie, left the scene undisturbed in an effort to preserve the crime scene for the Mounties who would examine it, Field admits in his letter that he and his companions buried Jorgensen's bones and marked his grave with a wooden cross before heading to Fort Simpson to inform the Mounties of their find. According to a Nahanni park ranger who heard the tale from an old northern frontiersman, Field left the scene with eerie sensation that he was being watched.

The Osias Meilleur Version

According this this version of the tale, Martin Jorgensen first entered the Nahanni Valley in 1909, lured by tales of lost gold. En route, he briefly encountered Corporal Arthur H.L. Mellor of the RNWMP, who was on his way back to Fort Smith following his investigation into the deaths of the Willie and Frank McLeod. He also ran into a prospector named Osias Meilleur, who was on his way out of the country at the time.

Jorgensen met with little success that year, and had similar luck in 1910. In 1911, while refreshing his outfit in Fort Simpson, he ran into Osias Meilleur again, with whom he decided to partner. The two prospectors returned to the Nahanni, building a cache and a cabin on a particular creek about a mile up the Flat River (or perhaps on Clearwater Creek, opposite its mouth). They spent the winter there before returning to Fort Simpson in the spring of 1912.

After restocking their supplies, Jorgensen and Meilleur returned to their Nahanni camp. Jorgensen planned to spend another winter at the cabin, while Meilleur decided to return to Fort Simpson in the fall. Before Meilleur's departure, the two men agreed to meet up in Fort Simpson the following summer.

When Jorgensen failed to show at the appointed time, Meilleur was not particularly perturbed. He later claimed that a party of Dene hunters had informed him that they had seen Jorgensen heading west up the Flat River only a few weeks earlier.

In the fall of 1914, Meilleur returned to the site of his and Jorgensen's Nahanni camp. There, he discovered that his partner's cabin had burned to the ground. Near the ashes, he found a loaded rifle, a revolver, and some clothes, including trousers which he recognized as Jorgensen's. Curiously, he failed to report his discovery to the Mounties, opting instead to spend the winter in the area.

———————————————

On August 14, 1916, Corporal David Churchill and Special Constable Joe Hope of the RNWMP departed from Fort Simpson, tasked with conducting an investigation into Martin Jorgensen's death.[54] The Mounties arrived at the site of Jorgensen's cabin on September 21. Their first order of duty was to exhume the big Scandinavian's remains. Unfortunately, they were unable to glean much from the potential crime scene due to the degree to which the evidence

---

[54] According to Philip Godsell, the Mountie assigned to Jorgensen's case was an officer named Constable Clark.

had been tampered with. Without any leads to follow, the Mounties decided to drop the case.

How Martin Jorgensen met his gruesome fate in the winter of 1913 remains a mystery to this day. Pierre Berton believed that Jorgensen had a run-in with "a mean old bear," which subsequently made off with his head. Gordon Matthews, Raymond Patterson's partner, suspected that Jorgensen starved to death. Some contemporary Slavey were convinced that he had been dispatched by a wild Nakani. And many frontiersmen, including Gus Kraus, Billy Clark, and Albert Faille, believed to their dying day that the stalwart Norwegian had been murdered for the gold which his letter to Billy Atkinson indicated he had discovered.

Poole Field, in one of his letters, made the startling claim that the Mounties did, in fact, determine who had murdered Martin Jorgensen, writing that he "and the police... just about had things all set to arrest the murderer when he died in California." This statement is in direct conflict with an inexplicable RCMP response to a query submitted by Raymond Patterson, dated October 27, 1952: "As to Jorgensen, we have no file or record of such a person being reported missing in the South Nahanni Country. In all probability, a man by that name could have made a trip into that country and, like many other prospectors and trappers, returned to the Outside safe and sound."[55]

---

[55] Patterson's letter from the RCMP is rendered even more bizarre in light of another letter sent from Constable R. C. Clark of Fort Liard to 18-year-old

In the 1970's, a tough Ukrainian bush pilot named Nazar Zinchuk, who spent many years trapping and prospecting in the South Nahanni in the first half of the 20th Century, related a new and interesting, if unlikely, rumour he heard regarding the mysterious death of Martin Jorgensen. This rumour, which Zinchuk first heard in Fort Liard, allegedly originated with a Dene woman, who is said to have heard the story from her mother, who, in turn, heard it from her husband, Diamond C, while he lay on his deathbed. According to this story, a certain Nahanni Indian had wandered into Jorgensen's cabin sometime in 1913, while the Scandinavian was out prospecting. The native helped himself to some of Jorgensen's moose meat, cooking it over a fire and seasoning it with what he thought was salt. Unfortunately for the Indian, the 'salt' that he sprinkled over his roast was actually crystalline strychnine, a deadly toxin which Jorgensen had brought into the country for trapping purposes. The Indian, oblivious, gorged himself on the poisoned meat and promptly passed away.

The story goes that two of the Indian's friends, Diamond C and a well-known Nahanni hunter named Charlie Yohin, held Jorgensen responsible for their friend's death.

Loren E. Coleman, a man who would become one of America's foremost cryptozoologists, on January 28, 1964. In response to Coleman's request for information on the various legends surrounding the Nahanni Valley, Clark all but dismissed the legends as fantasy before closing with this cryptic line: "The above information has not come from Police files, as it is not the policy of the RCMP to divulge such information from their records."

One cold winter night, they took their revenge, murdering the prospector and setting his cabin on fire.

Although it does not bring us any closer to solving the mystery of Martin Jorgensen's death, it is interesting to note that Philip H. Godsell received a letter from Jorgensen's 50-year-old brother, a Vancouverite named John A. Vatne, dated October 30, 1940.

"Only last Saturday," Vatne wrote, "I accidentally came across a copy of the North West Mounted Police Annual, *Scarlet and Gold*. With keen interest, I read the story entitled 'Dead Men's Gold.'[56] Suddenly I became literally transfixed at the words 'Jorgensen Strikes It Rich.' It was with mingled suspense and horror that I finally came across the facts relating to the disappearance of my long lost brother...

"We knew that Martin had partly outfitted in Winnipeg and set out in the wilderness in search of the yellow metal," Vatne went on. "Knowing the peculiar nature of my brother it was not surprising that he maintained a long silence. Years passed with no news. Rumours, as brought out by sourdoughs and travellers, reached us; one rumour contradicting another, leaving us in a painful state of uncertainly."

---

[56] 'Dead Men's Gold' is Godsell's earliest article on the tale of the lost McLeod mine.

Vatne finished his letter by thanking Godsell for bringing his family some closure, asking a number of questions regarding Jorgensen's fate, and explaining that he had a different surname than his brother due to his adoption into another household following their mother's death.

THE NAHANNI GOLD RUSHES

Inevitably, the tales of the lost McLeod mine and of Martin Jorgensen, the prospector who had lost his head in an attempt to find it, began to spread throughout the North Country. For the first few years following Jorgensen's death, fear of the Nahanni's mysterious dangers evidently eclipsed the lure of its lost gold; aside from Poole Field, the Lafferty boys, and a handful of trappers, few men dared to try their luck in the remote watershed which had come to be known as 'Headless Valley.'

The Rush of 1922

Out of the blue, in March 1922, a short, somewhat inconspicuous article appeared in the *Edmonton Journal* informing readers of a gold strike which had been made in the Nahanni Valley. "At present time," the article went, "it is impossible to state the exact extent of the find, but it is thought by men who know the country that it will be of considerable importance."

This 'strike' had been made by Poole Field, who presented several chunks of what he erroneously believed to be

Rare photos of the Nahanni Valley's 1922 gold rush, courtesy of archivist Gina Payzant and the Athabasca Town and County Archives.

gold-bearing quartz at Fort Simpson. Field claimed to have found his samples some sixty miles upriver from Nahanni Butte. Hard on the heels of his modestly publicized discovery, a handful of prospectors from Fort Smith, NWT, made their way down the Slave River, across Great Slave Lake, up the Mackenzie and Liard Rivers and into the Nahanni Valley.

Inspector Fletcher, an RCMP officer stationed at Fort Fitzgerald, Alberta, on the Slave River, reported to his commanding officer, "There has been quite a little local excitement about this strike and all the local people have either been up to stake or are going up to stake in the near future. There will probably be a small local rush in the spring," he predicted, "and of course there is the possibility of this news getting Outside and causing a large rush, but you will be in a better position to estimate the possible size of a rush from the Outside than I am. Sgt. Thorne informs me that Field is confident he has made a big discovery."

Fletcher's commanding officer dutifully related the information to his superiors in Ottawa, cognisant of the humanitarian disaster which could potentially result if a full-blown gold rush in the Nahanni Valley got underway. "I have not allowed this information to become public," he wrote, "as I do not wish to create a rush into that country upon such meagre evidence."

The *Edmonton Journal*, however, felt no such constraints, and proceeded to cover the small gold rush that ensued. Years later, Gus Kraus claimed to have discovered relics of this event on Bennett (a.k.a. Gold) Creek, which he believed were left by Nahanni hunters Captain and Iron. Unfortunately, when it was all said and done, this tiny rush yielded neither the fabled lost McLeod mine nor the legendary strike of Martin Jorgensen.

The NAME Expedition

Following the rush of 1922, the South Nahanni once again became, as Raymond Patterson put it, "a river that men avoided, except for the odd summer prospecting party- and the Indians and Poole Field. Faille and I broke the spell in 1927."

Indeed, both Raymond Patterson and Albert Faille entered the Nahanni Valley in 1927, ostensibly in search of the lost McLeod mine. Patterson chronicled his 1927 adventure in his journals, and later in his famous book *Dangerous River*. At that time, Poole Field and Jack LaFlair were perhaps the region's only permanent white residents; the two men ended up operating rival trading posts at Nahanni Butte.[57] Patterson and Faille both made their way up the South Nahanni as far as Virginia Falls before travelling a short distance downstream, up the Flat River, and up its primary tributary, the Caribou, prospecting as they went. Patterson returned to civilization that August, while Faille decided to remain in the country, alone. For Albert Faille,

---

[57] Frontiersman Billy Clark purportedly teased the two men for their rivalry, calling LaFlair "Baron Butte" and Field "Lord Goldfield."

this quest for the lost McLeod mine would evolve into a lifelong obsession.

The following year, Patterson returned to the Nahanni Valley with a friend and fellow Englishman, Gordon Matthews. The two men built a cabin in Deadmen Valley, out of which they spent the whole of 1928 prospecting and hunting. On their way into the country, they encountered two prospectors named J. Starke and R.J. Stevens, who planned to search for the lost McLeod mine at the mouth of the Caribou River. The two parties travelled upriver together as far as Deadmen Valley before going their separate ways.

Later that summer, a wealthy American adventurer named Fenley Hunter made a prospecting expedition up the South Nahanni River at the behest of Charles Camsell, with whom he was acquainted. His companions on this journey included a prospector from Dease Lake named George Ball and an Indian named Albert Dease. Although the three men initially planned to ascend the South Nahanni, portage overland to the Keele (a.k.a. Gravel) River, paddle downriver to the Mackenzie, and return to civilization via that great northern river, they ended up turning back prematurely on account of what historian Kerry Abel termed a "complete lack of exciting prospecting." Before leaving the country, Hunter reached the spectacular Virginia Falls, which he named after his daughter.

That year, Charlie McLeod decided to return to the Nahanni Valley after an absence of thirty years in order to search for his brothers' lost mine, doing so under the auspices of a Toronto-based prospecting company called Northern Aerial Mineral Exploration Ltd. (NAME). He was accompanied on this expedition by prospectors C.M. "Grizzly" Simmonds, Jake A. Davidson, "Professor" W.H. Wrigley, and perhaps Gus Morrison.

Philip Godsell, in most of his articles on the lost McLeod mine, described meeting with Charlie and his companions at Fort Resolution immediately prior to their departure. While he was chatting with Pierre Mercredi, the fort's French Canadian Factor, a bush plane flew in and landed nearby, frightening many of the Yellowknife and Dogrib Indians who had come to trade their furs (the bush plane, at that time, was a recent innovation in the Canadian North, and most of the Indians, as well as the Fort Resolution traders, had never seen one before). While the plane's pilot, Captain Harry "Doc" Oakes, set about refueling his craft, the passengers- namely the men of the NAME expedition- mingled with the fort's staff. On this occasion, Godsell heard the story of the lost McLeod mine from Charlie McLeod himself. After "Doc" Oakes had finished refuelling, the prospectors piled into his tiny plane and, to the accompaniment of the well wishes of the Fort Resolution traders, took off for the Nahanni Valley.

Godsell learned the sequel to this story late that fall, while "seated beside the crackling box-stove in the Mess Room at Fort Simpson," shoulder to shoulder with "Mounted

Police, trappers, traders, and black-robed priests who, like
[himself], were awaiting the return of the stern-wheeled
Distributor from the Arctic to carry [them] south to Fort
Smith."

"Suddenly," Godsell wrote, "the door swung open. Into
the room reeled four animated skeletons in the last stages of
exhaustion. Bearded and begrimed, their clothes patched with
greasy strips of buckskin, I recognized the human caricatures
as the prospectors who had flown in search of Dead Man's
Valley."

Godsell promptly supplied the emaciated prospectors
with shots of rum and slabs of fried moose meat before sitting
down with them to hear their story. Charlie McLeod
explained that "Doc" Oakes had dropped them off at a tiny
lake deep in the Flat River watershed, which was known
thereafter as Landing Lake. When he failed to pick up him
and his companions at the scheduled time, Charlie and the
NAME crew made the decision to shoot and jerk a couple
mountain sheep, bolt together the flimsy, three-part
collapsible canoe with which they were equipped, and commit
themselves "to the turbulent waters of some unnamed
stream."

"At race-horse speed," wrote Godsell, "they were
swirled along in their cockle-shell craft. Rock walls closed in
until the serpentine channel, twisting in hairpin turns, was
crushed between rock ramparts that reared thousands of feet
above them. Onward they swept over black chutes roaring

through narrow chasms so deep that the sky seemed but a silver thread in the blackness that engulfed them, while the air vibrated from the roar of the angry waters that spattered in their faces and half-blinded them. Warned by the menacing roar of still another cascade, the men scrambled ashore, barely in time, and perched precariously on the foam-bespattered ledge as the river leaped a precipice and roared in a boiling torrent to the rocks... below."

The prospectors spent all of autumn searching in vain for the lost McLeod mine before finally making their way out of the rugged valley that had nearly claimed their lives, dejected and miserable.

In his journal, and in *Dangerous River*, Patterson described encountering Charlie McLeod- "a little, dark, clean-shaven man with black hair and Indian features"- and his wet and weary companions in Deadmen Valley while the NAME crew was on its way out of the country. The Oxford-educated adventurer recounted how "Grizzly" Simmonds had grumbled about the decided unflatness of the Flat River, arguing that the waterway should have instead been named the 'White Water.'[58]

Patterson described how Charlie McLeod, upon learning that Patterson had recently made a trip up the Flat River, began acting very strangely, refusing to stay the night at his and Matthews' cabin or to discuss any more details

[58] Incidentally, the old Dene name for the Flat River translates to "White Boiling River."

regarding NAME's recent prospecting venture. Patterson privately suspected that Charlie's bizarre behavior was an indication that he and his crew had discovered gold somewhere in the Flat River watershed.

The 1929 Rush

Raymond Patterson and Gorden Matthews spent the winter of 1928/29 in the Nahanni Valley before returning Outside. Following their departure, some northerners suspected that the Englishmen had discovered gold. Before long, the Nahanni Valley was invaded by another handful of prospectors, including Billy Clark; an old Metis named George Sibbeston; Harry Camsell (Charles Camsell's nephew); and Norwegians Carl Aarhuis and Ole Loe. As before, none of these prospectors found the lost Macleod mine or the source of Jorgensen's strike. As soon as it had started, the tiny gold rush abated, and the Nahanni Valley was quiet once again.

THE TREASURE MAP

In the winter of 1932, Scottish frontiersman and ex-HBC man Billy Clark snowshoed into Fort Liard with his elderly British partner, "Sourdough" Jack Stanier- a man who had, at that time, made a total of nine trips into the Nahanni Valley in search of the lost McLeod mine.

By the time of his and Clark's visit to Fort Liard in 1932, Jack Stanier was a thoroughly seasoned prospector and a veteran of many a northern trail. In fact, the old Sourdough and his former partner, Joe Bird, were two of the brave few who ventured into the Nahanni Valley during the Stampede of 1897/98, hoping that the legendary valley long shunned by the natives might serve as a shortcut to the Klondike. According to some, they were the only Stampeders who hazarded this rugged branch of the all-Canadian route and lived to tell the tale.

Legend has it that Stanier and Bird, sometime in 1898, entered the Nahanni Valley with a reluctant native guide who was doubtless well aware of the Nahanni's sinister reputation. They conquered the Splits, the Nahanni's four rapids-riddled canyons, and the gruelling portage at Virginia Falls. When they had reached a point near the Rabbitkettle Hot Springs, the Stampeders' Indian guide abandoned them, frightened by a horrifying dream. According to some versions of the legend, the two Stampeders continued on alone, reaching the Moose Ponds at the South Nahanni's headwaters and following an Indian trail across the Mackenzie Mountains to the Ross River, which led them to the Pelly, and to the Yukon goldfields beyond. According to another version, the men spent the winter in the Nahanni Valley before returning the way they had come and travelling to the Klondike by way of the Liard.

Father Le Guen's Map

On that cold winter day in 1932, Jack Stanier and Billy Clark paid a visit to the Oblate Mission at Fort Liard, where they were received by the Mission's Superior, Father Joseph Turcotte. There, in the rectory, the three men, along with a visiting fur trader named Patty Crickmore, filled their pipes with pungent kinnikinnick[59] and their mugs with steaming tea and settled down for a game of bridge.

As the four northerners played cards, talk gradually turned to the lost McLeod mine. Sometime during the conversation, Father Turcotte mentioned, rather nonchalantly, the existence of a treasure map said to lead to the McLeod brothers' lost diggings. Clark and Stanier were intrigued, and pressed the missionary to elaborate. Father Turcotte scratched his head, his eyes absently scanning the rectory ceiling, and told the frontiersmen that, if memory served, he had heard once that the McLeod brothers had entrusted the map to old, grey-bearded Father Le Guen, who had served at the Fort Liard Mission back in Willie and Frank McLeod's day, and who now headed the Mission at Fort Providence. He agreed to ask the old missionary about the map if the opportunity arose.

In Lent, 1933, Father Turcotte's superiors dispatched him to Fort Providence, where he was to temporarily relieve Father Le Guen of his duties; the elderly Oblate was heading Outside for medical attention. While filling in for Father Le Guen, Turcotte, with the old priest's permission, began rummaging through the missionary's old papers. Sure

---

[59] Kinnikinnick is an Indian smoking blend often consisting of tobacco, bark, leaves, and bearberry, which was once a staple of the northern frontier.

enough, he unearthed a crude, age-yellowed map depicting a creek with a wide fork at its head. Alongside the main body of the creek sat two small lakes, and north of the creek's fork was another creek which evidently flowed northward. At the bottom edge of the map was the signature of Willie McLeod, and on a particular section of the northerly creek was the tantalizing inscription: "GOLD".

Father Turcotte sealed the ancient document in an envelope and had it delivered to Clark and Stanier via Mountie patrol. The two frontiersmen, upon receiving it, could barely contain their excitement. Their enthusiasm turned to pure elation when they saw what Willie McLeod had drawn; both prospectors knew exactly which area the map depicted.

It just so happened that, shortly after Clark and Stanier received Father Le Guen's old map, a bush pilot named Stan McMillan stopped at the fort on a business errand. At that time, McMillan worked for bush pilot Leigh Brintnell, who owned the Fort Simpson-based airline company Mackenzie Air Service. Clark and Stanier spoke with McMillan and arranged for the pilot to drop them off in the Nahanni Valley sometime that spring.

In June, 1933, Stan McMillan made good on that arrangement, flying Clark and Stanier deep into the Nahanni and dropping them off at the edge of what is known today as Clark Lake. Clark and Stanier laboriously packed their gear down a stream now known as Leigh Creek to another small body of water, known today as McMillan Lake. There, they came across a game trail leading north. They decided to follow it.

The game trail led to another stream known as Sheep Creek, which, they knew, flowed into the Flat River at a location just upriver from the Cascade-of-the-Thirteen-Steps.

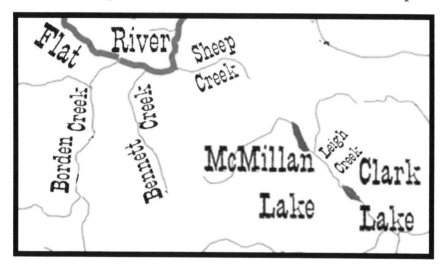

By the time Clark and Stanier had hauled their gear over to Sheep Creek, it was beginning to get dark. Stanier decided to make camp, while Clark opted to take a hike up the creek.

After following the creek for some time, Clark spied, in the dim light of the early evening, something peculiar lying in the grass. His heart hammered in his chest as he approached the object, and veritably leapt into his throat when he parted the veil of greenery that concealed it. Clark had stumbled upon a pair of ancient, age-silvered sluice boxes.

Could these be a relics of Willie and Charlie McLeod's lost diggings?

Clark raced back upriver to inform his elderly partner of his discovery. Upon hearing the news, Stanier stopped what he was doing and accompanied Clark to the scene of his find. Although the prospectors' subsequent search that evening failed to turn up any additional items of interest, Clark and Stanier crawled into their bedrolls that night certain that they had uncovered remnants of the legendary lost McLeod mine.

The next day, the two prospectors moved their camp down to the site of Clark's discovery and began to look around. Stanier described their subsequent discoveries in a newspaper interview later that year thus:

"We found Willie McLeod's old workings, just as he left them. There were his sluices boxes, two of them carefully piled on two dry logs, so Willie evidently intended coming back. There were his riffles- one pole riffle and one filled with auger holes- where he had used quicksilver.[60] There were his stakes and the old saw pits where he whipsawed his lumber for his boxes, and two old camps. His tools he evidently had cached. However, some of them turned up later in a rather peculiar way.

"I am not romancing. This is a true story, and those who believe in dreams will understand. My partner, Bill Clark, is Highland Scotch, and at times has remarkable dreams. One

---

[60] 20th Century prospectors sometimes used quicksilver, or mercury, to separate fine gold dust from sluice box sediment.

morning, he told me that he had dreamed where some of McLeod's tools were. That day, we went up the creek, and coming to a bend. Bill exclaimed, 'there is the place!' Sure enough, there was the business end of a shovel sticking out of a rockslide."

Stanier and Clark discovered additional mining equipment, including rusted picks and gold pans, piece by piece. They also found good showings of flake gold in adjacent Sheep Creek, which was soon renamed McLeod Creek in honour of Willie and Frank- a label which it bears to this day.

Initially, Stanier and Clark were certain that they had stumbled upon the lost McLeod mine, or at least one of Willie and Frank's outlying mining camps. However, the absence of gold-veined quartz, samples of which were allegedly discovered along with the McLeod brothers' headless bodies, along with evidence that whipsawing had likely taken place in the area,[61] hinted that the ancient sluice boxes, pans, picks, and shovels might have belonged to someone other than the McLeod brothers.

The Rush of 1933 34

That summer, Clark and Stanier staked two claims on McLeod Creek and began sinking shafts to bedrock. Later that September, Stan McMillan flew in to Clark Lake, picked up Clark and Stanier's trail, and landed a short distance from

---

[61] Most versions of the McLeod legend maintain that Willie and Frank were lightly equipped when they entered the Nahanni Valley, and were probably without a whipsaw.

their camp. Along with him was Poole Field, who had heard about the McLeod map and was curious as to how Clark and Stanier had made out. Field did some subsequent panning in McLeod Creek and, according to Clark in his diary, "said surface indications were better than some of the best creeks" that he had ever panned in Nahanni Country.

That fall, the four men flew to Fort Simpson, where they formed a mining syndicate with a number of locals. Company members included Father Turcotte, Patti Crickmore, bush pilot and WWI flying ace Wilfrid "Wop" May[62], mechanic Gerald Hansen, trappers Bill Epler and Jack Mulholland, Willie McLeod (son of Fred), and several others. In 1914, after partnering with Great Bear Lake Mines, a Toronto-based mining company, members of the syndicate put together an 11-dog sled team and set out for McLeod Creek. Trapper Dick Turner, in his autobiography *Nahanni*, summarized the miniature, ultimately unsuccessful gold rush in this way:

> "*A dozen or so local people, trappers and others, flew in from Fort Simpson. Only one man, I believe, stayed in to work his claim; the others came right back out hoping to sell their*

---

[62] "Wop" May was the Canadian aviator tailed by German fighter ace-of-aces Manfred von Richthoven, the formidable "Red Baron" of WWI fame, when the latter was fatally shot down over the Somme on April 21, 1918. After the War, May became a northern bush pilot. On New Years' Day, 1929, he and fellow aviator Vic Horner made a mad aerial dash from Edmonton to Little Red River, a tiny frontier settlement in Northern Alberta on the Peace River, to deliver medicine needed to combat an epidemic of diphtheria. May and Horner's daring exploit was dubbed "The Race Against Death" by the Canadian media.

claims. About twenty trappers from the Liard area went in by dog team in January 1934. The Nahanni Indians guided them in, through the valleys, up over high passes and along creek beds... Like many others, their trials were for naught."

That same year, prospector Bill King made his own independent prospecting venture in the Nahanni Valley. He was led into the country by Big Charlie, who assured King that Clark and Stanier and their associates were looking for Nahanni gold in the wrong place, and that he knew where the gold really was. Like the Great Bear Lake Mines expedition, however, Bill King and Big Charlie ultimately returned to civilization with little to show for their efforts.

That winter, Jack Stanier departed for Edmonton, where he underwent an operation on either his bladder or his prostate. He would never return to the Nahanni again; two years later, the elderly prospector who had spent his life in search of northern gold passed away in an Edmonton hospital.

Father Angerand's Map

Frontiersmen Dick Turner and Gus Kraus, in their respective writings and interviews, maintained that the map which Jack Stanier and Billy Clark had in their possession was fraudulent. The McLeod brothers *had* produced a treasure map, they maintained, but the real one made its way into the hands of Gerald Hansen, a mechanic from Fort Liard.

According to Gus Kraus, Stanier and Clark had actually acquired their map from a Catholic missionary named Father Angerand, who served in the Mission at Fort Liard. Stanier frequently spoke about this map with Gerald Hansen, who began to harbour some jealously towards the old sourdough. Eventually, Hansen approached Father Angerand and demanded that he retrieve the map from Stanier and give it to him. Hansen argued that, since he was a Catholic and Stanier a man without any particular religious leanings, Angerand ought to give him the map instead.

Father Angerand informed him that he had another map in his possession and, after rummaging through his trunks, produced a mildewed treasure map which was signed by both Willie and Frank McLeod. The landmarks on this map, Kraus claimed, were assigned their old, late 19th / early 20th Century names. The Flat River was labelled "*Tu Negaa Dehe*"; Meilleur Creek, a waterway which enters the South Nahanni near Deadmen Valley, was marked "Little River;" Caribou River was designated "Deer River;" and, most importantly, Bennett Creek was called "Gold Creek." Gus Kraus believed that this map was legitimate, and that it proved that the lost McLeod mine was actually located on Bennett Creek.

CHARLIE MCLEOD'S FINAL EXPEDITION

Throughout the 1930's and '40's, the Nahanni Valley's reputation as a sort of subarctic El Dorado spread throughout Canada by way of newspapers and popular magazines. Every once in a while, intrepid adventurers would make the journey north to Fort Simpson or Fort Liard, enter the Nahanni Valley via canoe or bush plane, and join resident pioneers like Albert Faille in the ongoing search for the lost McLeod mine.

In 1950, an elderly Charlie McLeod decided to take one last crack at the Nahanni. He had met with moderate success nearly a decade earlier, during a 1942 expedition on which he found promising colours in McLeod Creek, and hoped that a more thorough search of the area might yield the legendary mother lode. Accompanied by his sons Cecil, Frank, and Ivan, as well as his sons-in-law Ben Smith and Jack Gourtey of Edmonton, Alberta, he made his way up the South Nahanni and Flat Rivers in a motor-powered scow towards the gloomy canyon of McLeod Creek.

Many of those who knew him well described Charlie McLeod as a highly superstitious man who put great stock in the efficacy of spiritualism. At night in his farmhouse outside Wetaskiwin, Alberta, the old Metis would sometimes douse the lamps, light up some candles, and conduct séances, during which he purported to communicate with his long-dead brothers, Willie and Frank. It was on the advice of his ghostly brothers that Charlie decided to search for their lost gold one last time.

As Charlie and his sons made their way up McLeod Creek,[63] the old northerner suddenly threw up his hands and yelled "Stop! No further! My brothers told me it's right here."

---

[63] In one version of this story, Charlie did this in the South Nahanni's Second Canyon as opposed to in the McLeod Creek canyon .

Charlie McLeod, in right foreground, with his companions during their 1950 Nahanni Valley expedition. Photo from August 1972 issue of the magazine *Treasure*. Magazine courtesy of Gary Mangiacopra

The party pulled over to the shore, whereupon Charlie led them up a dizzying section of the canyon wall. At one point during his ascent, Charlie lost his footing and slipped, nearly plummeting over a cliff to certain death. He was saved at the last second by a spruce tree, which broke his fall. Charlie's rifle, on the other hand, was not so fortunate.

While Charlie's sons scrambled to free him from the spruce tree, the old Metis noticed a faint shimmer in a nearby shelf of rock. His eyes glowing with emotion, he pointed the phenomenon out to his companions. Could it truly be the long-sought gold which Willie and Frank had discovered in 1905?

As it turned out, Charlie and his crew had stumbled upon a particularly rich vein of copper. Although it was not the golden bonanza that they had hoped for, the men were nonetheless pleased with their discovery. Using miner's picks, they spent the next few days liberating large chunks of ore from the shelf before returning home to Edmonton, satisfied.

ALBERT FAILLE'S QUEST

Men from all walks of life searched for the lost McLeod mine throughout the 20th Century. Foremost among them was Albert Faille, a tough frontiersmen who spent most of his adult life prospecting and trapping in the Mackenzie region in general, and the Nahanni Valley in particular. From 1927-1962, this hardy prospector- known to the local Slavey as "Red Pants" for the red, handmade woolen trousers he affected- made a total of eight expeditions up the South Nahanni and Flat Rivers in search of the fabled treasure.

In 1962, the National Film Board of Canada produced *Nahanni*, a documentary following Faille's eighth and final prospecting expedition into the haunted valley. In the film, the stooped, 74-year-old frontiersman, regarding his lifelong quest for Nahanni gold, was quoted as saying, "I'll be dead or drowned before I quit."

The search for the lost McLeod mine came to an abrupt halt in 1972, when Canadian Prime Minister Pierre Elliott Trudeau's regime designated the Nahanni Valley a Canadian National Park, forever outlawing serious prospecting in the region. Perhaps not unpredictably, Albert Faille gave up the ghost on New Years' Eve the following year. In the words of historian Norman Kagan: "As he had lived, Albert died humbly, leaving this world with the passing of 1973. He was found around Midday on January 1, 1974, fully clothed and seated in the outhouse behind his shack. The certifying physician declared death came the previous night."

THEORIES

Over the years, there have been many ideas put forth as to the location of the McLeod brother's lost diggings. Charlie McLeod, who passed away in Coquitlam, British Columbia, in 1969, long believed that his brothers had made their find on McLeod (a.k.a. Sheep) Creek- a belief he shared with Jack Stanier and Billy Clark. Gus Kraus, on the other hand, was sure that Willie and Frank had struck it rich on Bennett (a.k.a. Gold) Creek, an adjacent tributary of the Flat River, although he was quoted in a 1986 *New York Times* article as having said, "there's about fifteen creeks in [the Nahanni Valley] with gold, and it's good gold." As for Martin Jorgensen's strike, some believe it was made on Clearwater (a.k.a. Murder) Creek, others on Jorgensen Creek, and others still on Wrigley Creek, which flows into the South Nahanni just below the Figure Eight Rapid.

Interestingly, Albert Faille, in later life, came to believe wholeheartedly that the lost McLeod mine would be found on one of the tributaries of the South Nahanni River, not on one of the Flat's. Although he once hinted in an interview that he thought the McLeod diggings might be located on the north fork of a waterway called Johnny Creek, the route which Faille took on some of his last expeditions indicated a keen interest in Marengo Creek, a tributary of the South Nahanni located upriver from Virginia Falls.

This theory is doubly interesting when considered in conjunction with a fascinating discovery made by Mel and Ethel Ross, an adventurous Canadian couple who documented their recreational 1957 expedition up the South Nahanni River in a charming, quaintly witty film entitled "Headless Valley."

The Discovery of Mel and Ethel Ross

During their expedition, Mel and Ethel made a trip above Virginia Falls. There, on one of the South Nahanni's tributaries, they discovered a hidden valley, its creek bed littered with chunks of some soft, malleable substance which appear to be large gold nuggets. In the film, an elderly Mel, his voice quavering with age, reminisced on the discovery, saying:

"When at last we reached the base of that odd-shaped mountain that we had been heading towards, the last creek which we had been following seemed to disappear right into the cliff. At first, we thought there must be a spring flowing out from under the cliff, but as we came closer, we could see that the stream was flowing out of a narrow cleft in the cliff, which was practically invisible except from one angle. There was a very faint trail heading into that defile- a trail which looked as if it

hadn't been used for years and years. We couldn't have gone home happy without knowing where that trail led, so we followed on in just hoping that we wouldn't meet some grizzly bear coming down.

"In this narrow gap between the cliffs, with that ice-cold stream running, there was a damp chill in the air. No sound except rolling water. It really had been a great place to get up close to grizzlies, but I can assure you that was one time I just wasn't interested in game pictures.

"Ethel got in a hurry to catch up there. Sometimes it would be steep rock shoulders to climb over, and the trail kept leading on and up. It looked like we were getting a long ways back into the mountain, but it probably wasn't as far as it seemed, for a lot of the going was pretty steep. The trail kept rising, and all the time it seemed to be bearing a little more and more to the left.

"After an hour or so of steady climbing, the cliffs above us got lower, and we could look out through a gap down into a mountain ring valley where a half dozen little spring-fed creeks joined together and formed another small river which was going out through another gap in the cliffs.

"Well, we were satisfied that this hidden valley was going to be the end of our trip, and, as the main stream seemed to be heading in the direction of the Nahanni, we decided to follow it as long as it continued in the right direction. I was just getting myself a drink in one of the smaller creeks before leaving when I

spotted something glittering in the water, and called Ethel over to see it. It was a long-shaped lump of yellowish metal, and it seemed to be rather heavy for its size.

"Now, at that time, I had never seen any gold, but this looked suspiciously like what I had always imagined gold should look like. When Ethel came over to examine it, she spotted something else in the water. We found that, glittering there in the stream, were several more of those same kind of nuggets. Whatever they were, we were certain that they were a mineral of some kind. Here's the large nugget that I picked up first."

Here, the camera shows a much younger Mel, crouched beside a creek, with a small chunk of some sort of raw metal in his hand which strongly resembles a gold nugget.

"I was quite sure that I had never seen something quite like it before.

"So, we got out our frying pan and tried panning in that patch of gravel, just rolling the pan around and picking up the largest rocks. Whatever they were, those nuggets seemed to be in quantity. When I finished washing out the sand and dirt and picking up the gravel, every pan had a layer of that gold, or fool's gold, or whatever it was. And it all appeared to be extremely heavy."

Here, we see a younger Mel panning in a creek with a cast iron frying pan. Inside the pan, along with water and sediment, are a significant quantity of gold-like nuggets.

"At that time, I had never seen either gold or fool's gold, but I remembered reading somewhere that fool's gold was hard and brittle and couldn't be shaped or flattened, while real gold should be quite soft and workable. Whatever it was, those nuggets turned out to be very soft. When I tested one, I found that I could whittle off fragments with just a pocket knife, and when I laid one of the little round nuggets on a rock and pounded it with the back of the build axe, it spread and flattened out until it turned out almost real like a coin."

Here, the camera shows Mel doing both of these things. Sure enough, the substance gives way under Mel's knife, and flattens out upon being pounded.

"Well, along with the weight, to me, it added up to a pretty good indication to gold. In fact, I was convinced enough that I set to work panning all that I thought I could carry out of there.

"We debated on whether to show these sequences or not, but felt that you would enjoy seeing them, and that it wouldn't be fair not to show our entire trip. However, just one word of warning: when I finally decided to show these scenes, I camouflaged the location of this little hidden valley so that I'm quite sure that nobody is going to locate it from my directions."

Mel and Ethel proceeded to stuff a large wool sock full of these nuggets before making their way back to the South Nahanni. While crossing a stream on their way out of the valley, Mel was hit on the ankle by a rolling rock, which caused him to drop the pack containing the sock and his and Ethel's provisions. After a long search for the pack, which had disappeared under the water, the couple conceded that it was lost for good.

Despite the setback, both Mel and Ethel Ross made it out of the Nahanni Valley in one piece. In this respect, they followed in the tradition of Albert Faille, Raymond Patterson, Jack Stanier, and Gus Kraus- frontiersmen who explored the Nahanni Valley and lived to tell the tale. Like Martin Jorgensen and Willie and Frank McLeod, however, many more were not so lucky.

———————◆—◆———————

Legend has it that the lost McLeod mine is still out there, hidden away in some corner of the Nahanni Valley, just waiting to be found. Instead of wealth beyond his or her wildest dreams, however, some say that the fate that awaits its discoverer is the stuff of nightmares.

Poole Field hinted at this belief in one of his letters, dated July 17, 1939. In it, he related the following piece of advice, given to him by the elderly Chief Jim Pellesea, the leader of a band of Mackenzie Mountain Indians with whom he was travelling at the time:

"As the old chief said to me, 'My friend, why do you want gold? Haven't we everything we need- lots of game, meat and fish, lots of fruit in season, and enough fur . . . to buy anything we need- to lead a happy life? Maybe if you found gold, it would

change all.' Yes, I suppose it would, and maybe not for the better."

Out of context, the chief's suggestion appears to be a friendly impartation of philosophical wisdom. The statement that precedes it, however, reveals it as an ominous warning. Before referring to the words of the chief, Field informed his letter's recipient of the following observation he made regarding the fate of Martin Jorgensen, the McLeod brothers, and other prospectors believed to have struck it rich in the Nahanni Valley prior to their untimely deaths:

"There seems to be a hoodoo or jinx that follows you around when you reach the Nahanni Country."

The Curse of the Nahanni Valley

"During recent research I have discovered something strange about the Valley of the South Nahanni River which may be of some importance to the expedition. Under no circumstances must they prospect nor remove minerals from the soil whilst in this valley. Men who leave the soil of the Valley alone go unharmed; prospectors are found dead."

- Mr. Harridge of Ancoats as cited by Sir Ranulph Fiennes, *The Headless Valley*, 1973.

O NE OF THE OLDEST AND DARKEST legends surrounding the watershed of the South Nahanni river has it that a curse hangs over the valley, or, sometimes more specifically, over its gold. Whether attributing the Nahanni's accursed nature to the ancient spell of an Indian medicine man, the presence of a malevolent supernatural entity, or some sort of mysterious quality inherent to the land itself, all versions of this legend are bolstered by the disturbing fact that, throughout the first half of the 20th Century, the Nahanni Valley was a place where men (and at least one woman) died mysterious deaths and disappeared with uncanny frequency.

THE KLONDIKERS

Martin Jorgensen and the McLeod brothers were not the first men to lose their lives in the Nahanni. Oral lore indicates that many a Dene hunter disappeared in the valley long before the first white man dipped his paddle into the 'Dangerous River'. For centuries, the Slavey Dene of the Liard River area avoided the Nahanni whenever possible, claiming that it was a land filled with *michili*, or "bad medicine"- a sinister, nebulous aura conducive to misfortune.

In 1897, a handful of enterprising Stampeders wandered into the Nahanni Valley, hoping that it might serve as a shortcut to the Klondike. Little is known about the fate of these gold-seekers, although it is believed that very few survived the forbidding stretch of the all-Canadian route to which they committed themselves. For many years, the only evidence of their journey were a scattering of strange-looking cabins built from vertical logs.

Three decades after the Klondike stampede, Raymond M. Patterson and Gordon Matthews stumbled upon the ruins of some of these Klondikers' cabins in Deadmen Valley. Patterson described these gold rush relics and weird sensation they evoked thus:

"There was an eerie, uncanny feel to them that could not be wholly accounted for by the silence of the place, hidden away up this snye and removed from all the rush and turmoil of fast water; or by the dark, old trees with their long grey-green streamers of moss that swayed in ghostly fashion at the faintest whisper of a breeze. There was something wrong about those old cabins; something happened there to the men who built them."

A Klondike-era story attributed to Jack Stanier, who entered the Nahanni Valley during the last great gold rush and lived to tell the tale, may shed some light on the fate of the cabin's former occupants. According to trapper Dick Turner in his book *Nahanni*:

"Jack [Stanier] said that on the winter trip from Fort Liard through the mountains he and his group were following a trail with many other gold rushers ahead of them. There were also others coming behind. Around dusk one night, his party came upon a cabin and were delighted to find a place to camp. Inside the cabin he was feeling around for the bunks, stove and table when he discovered that the three bunks contained men who had been dead for some time and were now frozen stiff. Jack said he and his companions went on a ways farther and camped in the open that night."

Half a century later, during Pierre Berton's expedition to the Nahanni, Jack LaFlair described another grisly relic of the Stampede left behind in the Nahanni Valley. On the night that Berton, Baker, and Hanratty spent in his cabin at

Nahanni Butte, the trader told his guests of a Stampeder corpse buried on the banks of one of the Nahanni's tributaries. "The bank's been washing out near the grave," LaFlair told the explorers with a ghoulish grin. "You can see his feet sticking out."

THE DEATH OF JOHN O'BRIEN

Two decades after the Klondike Stampede, following the death of Martin Jorgensen and the proliferation of the legend of the lost McLeod mine, some Mackenzie Mountain sourdoughs began to speculate that the curse that the natives had long maintained hung over the valley was real, and that it was particularly relevant to those who sought Nahanni gold, or to those who came close to finding it. Martin Jorgensen and Willie and Frank McLeod, they observed, had all stumbled upon a fortune of Nahanni gold, and had all lost their heads shortly thereafter.

The resurrection of this old Indian legend led to wild speculation regarding the source of the Nahanni's accursed nature, and that of its gold. Perhaps, some sourdoughs surmised, a Nahanni shaman had put a spell over the valley in order to prevent white prospectors from invading his people's hunting grounds, or maybe the Nahanni's gold was guarded by some sort of otherworldly entity whose nature was beyond Man's comprehension. Whatever the case, the so-called 'curse of the Nahanni' sufficiently discouraged prospectors from trying their luck in the valley for a number of years.

Although the legend of the curse initially succeeded in keeping gold seekers at bay, the Nahanni Valley was soon invaded by a handful of trappers who hoped to capitalize on the North Country's other famous resource, fur. One trapper who entered the Nahanni Valley in the early 1920's was John O'Brien, a World War I veteran whom Billy Clark believed hailed from the Peace River area. He built a cabin on Jackfish River, a waterway which flows into the South Nahanni a short distance upriver from Nahanni Butte, and established a trapline with his partner, whose name has long been lost to history.

On January 27, 1922, O'Brien left his cabin to inspect some traps. He told his partner that he expected to return in eight to ten days. Some versions of the legend say that, when O'Brien failed to return after two weeks, his partner went to look for him, but was unable to find him. Others suggest that his partner abandoned him to die. Whatever the case, Jack LaFlair and Metis woodsman Jonas Lafferty, who shared a cabin with several others across the South Nahanni from the Clausen Creek Hot Springs at that time, learned that O'Brien was missing about a month after his departure and set out to find him.

LaFlair and Lafferty trudged across the frozen, snow-covered South Nahanni on snowshoe and travelled north up the rugged slopes of what Raymond Patterson later named the 'Twisted Mountain.' There, on a rocky shelf near the mountain's peak, at the end of his trapline, the two frontiersmen discovered John O'Brien's frozen corpse.

The body was crouched over a pile of tinder with a box of matches in his icy hand. They were "those big matches," said Billy Clark. "You know, those big boxes, [those] travelling . . . type." It appeared as though O'Brien had frozen to death in the process of lighting a fire.

LaFlair and Lafferty buried the trapper on the shelf on which they found him. From then on, until Raymond Patterson arrived in the Nahanni Valley, the site of the tragedy was known as 'O'Brien's Mountain.'

THE VANISHING OF MAY LAFFERTY

Several years after O'Brien's death, a Metis girl named May Lafferty vanished in the Nahanni Valley. Her disappearance remains one of the strangest episodes in valley's history to date.

May "Annie" (or perhaps "Tanny") Lafferty[1] was a younger cousin of Poole Field's wife, Mary. She was, by all accounts, a strange little girl whom one frontiersman described as neurotic. She was from Fort Simpson, and often pined for her home and family while on the trail.

---

[1] According to one frontiersman, May was the daughter of a trapper named Mattson, who lived in a cabin at Nahanni Butte.

In the summer of 1921, May accompanied Poole and Mary Field and a party of Nahanni Indians on a journey through Nahanni Country. The band had just spent the winter trapping deep in the Mackenzie Mountains, and were on their way to one of the trading posts on the Liard or Mackenzie Rivers, where they planned to exchange their season's take of furs for ammunition, flour, tea, and other such goods.

It is said that May had been unwell and acting more strangely than usual for some time prior to this trip. "Very often she appeared to be quite depressed and wanted to be back with her folks at Fort Simpson," wrote woodsman Al C. Lewis in his book, *Nahanni Remembered*, paraphrasing the words of his trapping partner, Harry Vandale, who told him the story in January, 1937.

One day, while the party was following an old Indian trail along a southern branch of what would one day be called Mary River (this waterway, which was named in honour of Poole Field's wife, enters the South Nahanni in the Third Canyon), May Lafferty disappeared. Initially, it was presumed that the girl had wandered into the bush to answer the call of nature, and little was thought of her absence. As the day drew on, however, Mary Field became increasingly concerned that something had befallen her younger cousin. Eventually, when too much time had elapsed, she called a halt to the expedition and tasked her husband with finding and retrieving the girl.

Immediately, Poole Field set out into the wilderness with five native hunters- Diamond C, Boston Jack, Charlie Yohin, George Tesou, and Big Charlie, all of them veterans of a thousand hunts. In no time, the men picked up May's trail and followed it into the woods; it appeared that the girl had lost her way and wandered away from the trail.

Although Poole Field was strong, fit, and a perfectly competent frontiersman in his own right, he quickly found himself outstripped by his Indian companions; all of them were natural-born woodsmen who had spent their entire lives in the wild, as their ancestors had for untold generations, and knew how to move through the bush. Incredibly, these expert native trackers soon found themselves similarly outclassed by little May Lafferty, whose slender moccasin prints indicated that she had plunged through the wilderness as if on the wings of the wind.

Field and his companions followed May's trail for a total of nine days. Along the way, they found articles of her shredded clothing hanging from tree branches at irregular intervals; it appeared that the Metis girl had divested herself of her attire as she ran until she was completely naked. The mosquitoes at that time of year were innumerable, and would have made short work of even the hardiest hunter had he been similarly exposed. Yet May's trail went on and on, windings its way up into the mountains.

The next development in the search for May Lafferty was perhaps best described by Dick Turner in his book *Nahanni*:

"By now she had got into rugged country where she had to do some very steep climbing. She must have been without fear for she climbed some cliffs where the men were afraid to go and had to go away around and pick up her track on top.

"About the fifth day the hunters came to the bottom of a very rugged high cliff, which was actually the side of a five thousand foot mountain. Her tracks were visible at the bottom, but they could find no sign that she had turned to the left or the right. Poole said there was just no way that any sane person could possibly have gone up that wall of rock. There was an indication that she might have tried, for there was a narrow shelf-like ledge up for a hundred feet or so. Some of them went part way up but turned back. Poole thought for sure they had come to the end of the trail, but they worked their way round to the top and sure enough, there was her track again heading south and east. Sane or not, she was heading in the direction of her home, which was Simpson."

Field and his five companions followed May's trail for four more days before finally giving her up for dead. After the incident, the creek on which she disappeared was named 'May Creek' in her memory.[2]

---

[2] According to river guide Neil Hartling in his book *Nahanni: River of Gold, River of Dreams* 1993 , the Slavey name for May's Creek is *Ts'eli Ets'odehtlah Dehe*, meaning "A Little Girl Lost Creek."

May Lafferty's body was never found, and to this day, her fate remains a mystery.

THE FATE OF YUKON FISHER

One of the most fascinating and enigmatic characters known to frequent the Nahanni Valley was a veritable giant of a man known only as 'Yukon Fisher'.[3] Fisher was a Stampeder who had made his way to the Klondike via the Ashcroft Trail, a miserable, gruelling route through British Columbia. In some Yukon saloon, the enormous sourdough got into an argument with the bartender and opened his head with a glass bottle. "There was blood all over," said Billy Clark of the incident. "[Fisher] thought he'd killed this fellow, so he took off into the bush."

For years, Yukon Fisher lived as an outlaw in the wilderness of the Northwest Territories. He survived in total isolation, avoiding Indians and white men alike. On rare occasions, the bearded, fur-clad fugitive would hazard a visit to some remote northern trading post, like Poole Field's store on Ross River or the trading post at Frances Lake (located on the Frances River, a tributary of the Liard), where he would stock up on tea, salt, matches, and ammunition before disappearing into the wilderness once again. Poole Field, who had more contact with the huge bushman than any of his

---

[3] According to a number of sources, Yukon Fisher's real name was Charles Taylor.

contemporaries, said that Fisher had developed the senses of a wild animal as a result of his primitive lifestyle, and could easily tell a moose, caribou, bear, and man apart from the sounds they made walking through the brush. Field also claimed that Fisher only ever paid for his staples in coarse alluvial gold.

Every once in a while, a couple of trappers or a band of Indians would come across the abandoned remains of one of Fisher's camps. These typically consisted of a small, conical hut made from tree branches. "He'd pack them with moss all around," said Clark, "leave a place in the top for the smoke to [escape], and he'd have his fire inside. When the snow came in the winter time, he'd have a nice, warm place."

One day, Jules- the Indian who had delivered Martin Jorgensen's letter to Poole Field- tracked Fisher down and informed him that he was a free man; the bartender whom he believed he had murdered was alive and well, and all charges against him had been dropped. Fisher refused to believe the Indian and remained a subarctic recluse for the rest of his life.

According to Philip Godsell, Charlie McLeod and the men of the NAME expedition, during their arduous 1928 odyssey down the Flat River, stumbled upon "a headless skeleton of a giant white man" somewhere on Bennett (a.k.a. Gold) Creek, the waterway along which many believe Willie and Frank McLeod made their legendary strike. Beside the body was a .44-40 carbine rifle, its barrel badly bent, and a short distance away were the tumbledown[4] remains of a primitive cabin. "Nearby weathered axe cuttings," wrote Godsell, "indicated that the nameless pioneer had perished some fifteen years before [i.e. 1913]." Although there was little evidence to prove it, most Mackenzie frontiersmen who heard the tale believed that Charlie McLeod and his crew had stumbled upon the headless remains of Yukon Fisher, another victim of the curse of the Nahanni Valley.

THE DISAPPEARANCE OF ANGUS HALL

In 1929, a year after Charlie McLeod's NAME expedition and Raymond Patterson and Gordon Matthew's return from Deadmen Valley, the Nahanni Valley was the site of a minor gold rush; the curse, it seemed, no longer exercised a deterrent power. Among the prospectors who headed into the valley during this stampede were three partners named J.M. Gilroy, Andy Hay, and Angus Hall.

Raymond Patterson described Gilroy, the leader of this party of three, as "strong as a bull, square-built with tremendous shoulders on him and designed by Nature for carrying a pack." He and Hay, both natives of Edmonton, Alberta, set out for the Nahanni in April, 1929.

When they reached Fort St. John, BC, on April 18, Gilroy and Hay teamed up with another north-bound

---

[4] In some versions of the Yukon Fisher tale, the cabin discovered by the crew of the NAME expedition was found burnt.

prospector named Angus Hall. Hall hailed from Mayerthorpe, Alberta, a small farming village located about 120 kilometres northwest of Gilroy and Hay's hometown. He was a seasoned prospector whom Godsell described as a "brawny veteran of a hundred gold camps."

Hall's backcountry experiences had made him a staunch proponent of light travelling, and he had packed himself accordingly. So strongly did the Albertan believe in the principal of a light load that he had brought along a black and white dog onto which he had packed some of his gear.

Gilroy, Hay, and Hall decided to approach Bennett Creek- the epicentre of the rush- by an unorthodox route, boating and portaging their way to the Liard River, and the South Nahanni beyond, via Fort Nelson. They reached the South Nahanni River by May, whereupon they were beset by a series of flash floods. The three prospectors tackled the South Nahanni's high waters head on and managed to make it beyond the Second Canyon to the mouth of Scow Creek before their motor gave out.

Following this setback, the three prospectors paddled to shore and headed up Scow Creek on foot. "The going was difficult in the steep, narrow valley," wrote Raymond Patterson, "but evening found them camped in a little clump of firs well up into the timberline country, tired, tempers short, and Hall grumbling about the slowness of the other two and the pile of junk they insisted on carrying."

The following morning, after a heated argument with his two companions, Angus Hall decided to travel on alone. Gilroy and Hay, with their heavy packs, were progressing far too slowly for his liking, and Hall, a veteran of many a gold rush, knew that the degree to which a Stampeder met with success was largely dependent upon the order in which he arrived at the diggings relative to his competition. Anxious to reach the goldfields of Bennett Creek before rival prospecting parties, Hall grabbed his rifle, shouldered his meagre pack, and trudged ahead of his partners, his motley mutt ranging before him.

Later that day, Gilroy and Hay, according to Patterson, "caught a glimpse of [Hall] climbing, away up a long valley against a background of grey boulders, green grass, and alpine flowers. And then they saw him again, once, silhouetted for a moment against the blue, summer sky- and that was the last time that any man ever set eyes on Angus Hall."

After losing sight of their partner, Gilroy and Hay made their way northwest along the timberline, past May Creek and Mary River. Eventually, they descended into the valley of the Caribou River, which they followed to the Flat. There, the came upon a prospecting party of four, consisting of Fred Hasler, Billy Hill, W. "Curly" Cochrane, and George Spangler. The six men shared a meal together.

Patterson claimed that the two parties joined forces then and there and travelled upriver together. Historian

W.D. Addison, on the other hand, maintained that "the two parties didn't unite until they reached the diggings." Whatever the case, both parties continued upriver towards Bennett Creek.

The six prospectors arrived at their destination sometime in late May. Alarmingly, they found neither Angus Hall nor any sign of his presence. Up until that time, Gilroy and Hay had not been particularly concerned that Hall had failed to rejoin them; their fellow Albertan was an experienced woodsman who seemed perfectly capable of handling himself in the wilderness. Now, they suspected that some misfortune had befallen their partner. They travelled further up Bennett Creek where, on the creek's shore, they discovered a solitary footprint made by a hobnailed boot, the type of footwear that their missing companion wore.[5,6]

The body of Angus Hall was never discovered, and, according to many versions of the tale, his hobnailed boot print was the only trace of him that ever turned up in the Nahanni Valley. In the words of Philip Godsell, the prospector had disappeared "as utterly as though the earth had swallowed him."

Years later, Billy Clark introduced an entirely new piece to the puzzle of Angus Hall in an interview for Parks

---

[5] In some versions of this story, the hobnailed boot print was found on the shore of the Flat River.

[6] According to Raymond Patterson in *Dangerous River*, the hobnailed boot print found on the bank of Bennett Creek might have been his own.

Canada. He claimed that Andy Hay later discovered a note from Hall in a communal emergency cache near Landing Lake. The note was a small list of items that Hall had taken from the cache, including some rice, a little flour, and a pound of rendered fat. "It was very little he took," said Clark. "There were just a few necessary items and some tea. It was a short list that he'd set forth. That was the last clue outside of his imprint."

"There was a sequel to that that I'd rather not discuss," Clark revealed cryptically, later on in the interview. He went on to briefly describe how, sometime after Hall's disappearance, he came upon a party of men alongside whom trotted the same black and white dog that Hall had brought with him into the country. Clark refused to disclose the identities of these men, maintaining that he had no proof that any one of them had a hand in Angus Hall's disappearance.

THE DEATH OF PHIL POWERS

One year after the disappearance of Angus Hall, a trapper named Phil Powers arrived in the Nahanni Valley. Those who knew him described him as a tough, honest, and extremely competent frontiersman. Philip Godsell (who consistently referred to him in his articles as 'Bill' instead of 'Phil'), maintained that Powers hailed from Fort Nelson, and that he had slept in his cabin on the banks of the Sikanni Chief River for a few months while blazing a Hudson's Bay

Company fur road from Fort St. John- a precursor to the Alaska Highway, which runs from Dawson Creek in east-central BC, through the Yukon, to Delta Junction in the heart of Alaska. After arriving in the Nahanni Valley, Powers built himself a cabin at the mouth of Irvine Creek, across the Flat River from the Old Pot Hot Springs, and established a trap line.

At that time, Phil Powers was engaged to a woman named Ms. Swensen, a writer from Peace River. He had planned to meet his sweetheart at Nahanni Butte in the spring of 1932, whereupon the couple were to travel to Fort Simpson to get married. When Powers failed to arrive at the appointed time, a distraught Ms. Swensen accosted Jack Stanier and Billy Clark, who were visiting Jack LaFlair at his Nahanni Butte trading post, and demanded that they take her upriver to find her fiancé. The two prospectors acquiesced, but managed to ferry her only as far as Mattson's cabin (a trapper's shack located below the Splits) before being forced to turn back on account of high waters.

Exasperated, a frantic Ms. Swensen proceeded down the South Nahanni and up the Liard to Fort Simpson, where she asked the local RCMP to send out a patrol to find her missing fiancé. Only after badgering them persistently did she convince Constable Duncan C. Martin and Special Constable Billy Edwards to make a trip into the Nahanni Valley to see what had befallen Phil Powers.

By the time that Martin and Edwards reached Nahanni Butte, the river had lowered considerably, and the Mounties were able to make their way up the South Nahanni and further up the Flat River without much difficulty. On the way, they were joined by Poole Field and Albert Faille.

"Some distance beyond the spot where Jorgensen had met his sudden and mysterious death," wrote Godsell, "they came upon the first evidence of disaster; skeletons of lynx and foxes caught in traps that had been set and never tended." Further on, they founded a sawed-off 30-30 carbine rifle lying on the riverbank. Further still, at the confluence of the Caribou and Flat Rivers, they came upon the remains of Powers' 22-foot freighter canoe, which had long since snagged in a large pile of driftwood.

Finally, the party of four came to the mouth of Irvine Creek and proceeded upstream on foot. There, a short distance from the Flat River, they came to the site of Phil Powers' cabin, or what was left of it.

The scene was eerily evocative of that which Corporal David Churchill and Special Constable Hope had stumbled upon sixteen years prior, only a short distance away. Similar to Martin Jorgensen's, Powers' cabin had burned to the ground, evidently having done so sometime in the winter of 1931/32. "She was a hot fire!" declared Gus Kraus. "All that was left was a piece of a log about two feet, maybe a little bigger... And he had some porcelain kettles. They were just melted together."

Among the ashes were the fire-blackened bones of Phil Powers. There are a number of conflicting accounts regarding the condition of his corpse. Some say that Powers- like Yukon Fisher, Martin Jorgensen, and Willie and Frank McLeod- was found headless, and that his skeleton clutched a six-shooter revolver in its bony fingers, each of its chambers containing an empty brass casing. Others maintain that the charred remains of the trapper's skull were found lying at his feet, and that the remnants of a rifle with a length of wire fastened to the trigger- perhaps a 'set gun' used for trapping- lay nearby. Others still say that the conflagration that destroyed the cabin had consumed most of Powers' bones, and that all that remained of him was a charred femur, a few blackened finger joints, and eight tiny globules of gold which were once tooth fillings.

Powers' 20-foot-tall cache, which had somehow escaped the inferno, stood a short distance away. "There was only one odd thing about that find," wrote Patterson, "but it was decidedly odd" considering the evidence that the fire had occurred in the winter of 1931. Nailed to one of the cache's poles was a piece of wood bearing the following message, written in pencil:

"Phil Powers— his finis Aug. 1932"

Most frontiersmen, when asked their opinion on the matter, believed strongly that Phil Powers' death was not the result of some sort of unfortunate accident. "And he was certainly not the type to commit suicide," said Billy Clark.

Dick Turner likely echoed the sentiments of many of his fellow frontiersmen when he wrote, "I have since thought that if a man of that calibre could make serious mistake in the bush, then God help the rest of us."

THE DISAPPEARANCE OF
JOE MULHOLLAND AND BILL EPLER

Sometime in the early 1920's, two trapping partners arrived in Nahanni Country. Their names were Jack Mulholland and Bill Epler.

Epler was a plainsman from Winnipeg, Manitoba. Those who knew him described him as man of good character, who was honest, intelligent, loyal, truthful, and courageous. For about fifteen years, he and his American partner, Jack Mulholland, were inseparable; the two frontiersmen trapped all throughout the Nahanni Valley, becoming fixtures of the region as much as Poole Field and Albert Faille.

In the fall of 1935, Bill Epler and Jack Mulholland opened an independent trading post at Nahanni Butte alongside Jack LaFlair. They were soon joined by Jack's Mulholland's brother Joe, who flew in to the country from Minnesota for the season. That winter, the two Mulholland brothers managed the trading post while Epler tended the trapline.

When it became clear that the trapline would produce little in the way of fur that winter, Epler decided to move it far up the South Nahanni, above Virginia Falls to remote Rabbitkettle Lake, located a short distance northwest of the Rabbitkettle Hot Springs. For some reason, it was decided that Joe Mulholland, Jack's brother, would accompany Epler on this trapping excursion. This decision was not entirely unreasonable; although Joe was a newcomer to the subarctic, he was certainly no stranger to the backcountry.

Sometime after Christmas, 1935, a tough bush pilot named George C.F. Dalziel, sometimes referred to as the 'Flying Trapper,' flew Joe Mulholland and Bill Epler to their destination (according to many versions of this story, this was not Rabbitkettle Lake but rather Brintnell (a.k.a. Glacier) Lake, a body of water nestled in the shadow of the Cirque of the Unclimbables a relatively short distance northwest of Rabbitkettle Lake). The two trappers had brought several yards of canvas along with them. They planned on using this material to construct a watercraft in the style of an Indian skin boat, which would carry them and their furs down the South Nahanni River to Nahanni Butte after spring breakup. According to Al Lewis, Albert Faille, who had once paddled down the South Nahanni in a skin canoe, thought that this plan was tantamount to suicide. "And when Faille talks about this river," he wrote, "you listen."

Spring breakup came and went that April, but the rushing water brought with it no sign of Epler of Mulholland. At first, Jack Mulholland was not particularly alarmed. He thought that his brother and partner might be taking their time, hunting beaver along the river as they went. When the missing trappers failed to returned after three weeks, however, he and Bill Epler's friends became concerned and decided that a search upriver was in order. For this task, they nominated the Flying Trapper, George Dalziel.

At that time, Dalziel was grounded in Edmonton on account of an alleged game infraction or a smuggling violation. In order to get the Flying Trapper airborne so that he could search for Epler and Mulholland, trappers Harry Vandale and Dick Turner's brother, Stan, created a petition, which they asked all the residents of Fort Simpson to sign. "If I recall correctly," wrote Dick Turner, "Stan said everyone was more than willing to sign. For example, Stan told me of the two Catholic priests. He presented the petition for them to sign and they grabbed a pen immediately. Stan said, 'Just a minute, this says that the undersigned will take all responsibility if there is a question of legality of Dalziel breaking the seizure of his aircraft for the purpose of the search.' 'Yes, yes,' they said, 'we understand,' and signed right away."

The petition convinced the RCMP to lift Dalziel's flying ban prematurely, and the Flying Trapper headed north immediately, accompanied by Harry Vandale. Dalziel flew deep into the Nahanni Valley and landed at the site at which he had dropped off Epler and Mulholland earlier that winter. There, he made an ominous discovery. A short distance from the site at which they had been dropped off,

Epler and Mulholland had evidently built a cabin. Just like Jorgensen's and Powers', however, all that remained of it was a pile of ashes.

Dalziel and Vandale searched the vicinity of the burned cabin, but found no other signs of Epler and Mulholland. "They returned to Simpson without seeing a sign of the lost men," wrote Turner. "Dal [was] an excellent bush pilot and we all thought it extremely unlikely he would have missed the boys if they were anywhere to be seen." It seemed as if Epler and Mulholland had vanished into thin air.

After refuelling his craft, Dalziel, accompanied by Constable Winston C. Graham and Regis "Dick" Newton of the RCMP, proceeded to comb the Rabbitkettle and Glacier Lakes areas, as well as the length of the South Nahanni River, for any trace of the missing trappers, but to no avail. Nazar Zinchuk also claimed that Darryl Searle, a hard, petulant bush pilot, similarly searched for Epler and Mulholland throughout the Nahanni Valley in 1936 and met without success. Although a rigorous investigation that lasted several months followed Dalziel and Searle's preliminary flyovers, only a handful of potential clues as to the missing trappers' fate were ever found.

The Clues

Back in May 8, 1936, Albert Faille, Gus Kraus, and Billy Clark arrived at the mouth of the Flat River, where they were joined by Nazar Zinchuk. They had spent the previous few weeks camping at Irvine Creek, waiting for the ice to go out. There, at the confluence of the Flat and Nahanni Rivers, at the base of what is known as Direction Mountain, the four frontiersmen came upon the remains of campfire which Zinchuk claimed was only a few days old. They proceeded down the South Nahanni, along the banks of which they found several recent axe cuttings. The only other men known to be in the Nahanni Valley at that time were Epler and Mulholland, and so, naturally, after the two trappers were confirmed missing, many presumed that the campfire ashes and axe cuttings constituted their last traces.

The following winter, Al Lewis and Harry Vandale, who were trapping together at Rabbitkettle Lake, stumbled upon what Lewis described as "a neatly folded green tarpaulin... an empty Turret tobacco tin... one front leg of a wolf," and the ashes of a long-dead campfire buried in the snow at the mouth of the Rabbitkettle River. "Trappers and prospectors are not in the habit of leaving tarps wherever they happen to stop along the way," wrote Lewis, speculating that the item was placed there by Epler and Mulholland sometime immediately prior to their disappearance.

The vanishing of Bill Epler and Joe Mulholland sparked all sorts of rumours and conjecture. Some speculated that the two had attempted to travel down the South Nahanni in their canvas canoe following spring breakup and had capsized and drowned. Others were sure that they had attempted to travel down the South Nahanni while it was still frozen and had disappeared through a hole in the ice. Others still were certain that the trappers had been murdered by the same sinister forces that had taken the lives of their predecessors. Ultimately, as one writer put it, Epler and Mulholland were "two more to add to the tally of missing souls in Nahanni Country."

Dick Turner's Theory

In his book *Nahanni*, trapper Dick Turner related a fascinating side note to the mysterious disappearance of Bill Epler and Joe Mulholland. "I believe that I am the only one alive who knows about it," he began.

Turner went on to explain how, one day in January, 1938, while he was in Fort Simpson, he paid a visit to a local hotel owned by his friend Andy Whittington. Late that evening, while sitting in the quiet kitchen of Whittington's establishment, he and the hotelier chatted about trapping, prospecting, and the Nahanni Valley. "The talk got around to Bill and Joe," wrote Turner, "as it did so often among friends."

Sometime during the conversation, the hotel manager dropped his voice to a whisper and looked Turner dead in the eye. "Dick," Whittington began, "I will tell you something I have never told anyone before."

Andy Whittington proceeded to relate a strange experience he had the previous winter during a visit to Vancouver. One day, while waiting to cross the street, a taxi stopped beside him, waiting at a red light. "There was a passenger in the front seat beside the driver," the hotelier said. When the passenger turned his head to look out the window, a bewildered Andy Whittington found himself face to face with none other than Bill Epler. "I knew Bill Epler as well as anyone," Whittington declared. "With that one eye and pug nose of his, I could never mistake him."

Dick Turner followed up on this tale by describing a story which Bill Epler had told him many years before. When Epler was eighteen years old, he got into an argument with a Greek restaurant owner in Winnipeg, Manitoba, his hometown. After exchanging heated words with the man, Epler stormed out of his establishment.

To let off some steam, he decided to go for a walk. After a few blocks, he came to a vacant grassy lot where a group of younger boys were playing baseball. He decided to stop for a while and watch the game.

At one point, one of the batters made a tremendous hit, sending the ball sailing towards the end of the lot where Epler stood. The boys searched for their baseball in the grass for some time before accusing Epler of stealing it. "Honest, I didn't!" Epler laughed. "You can search me." The boys took him up on his offer, patting him up and down before they were satisfied that he was telling the truth. The ball was found shortly thereafter, and the boys resumed their game.

The following day, Epler was arrested by the police. The Greek restaurant owner whom he had confronted the previous day had been shot to death, and he was the prime suspect on account of the heated words he exchanged with him shortly before the shooting. At that time, Epler was a poor, unemployed orphan and could not afford to hire a good lawyer. While he awaited his trial in the local jail, his cellmate was hanged for murder, and Epler despaired that he was next for the noose.

Fortunately, during his trial, the baseball-playing boys whom Epler had encountered on the day of the murder were called to the stand. They assured the jurors that they had searched Epler thoroughly when looking for their baseball, and that he most certainly did not have a gun on his person at the time. On the strength of the boys' testimony, Epler was declared 'not guilty' and was subsequently released from prison. When he later told Turner of this traumatic experience, he assured the trapper that he would never, under any circumstance, allow himself to face another trial.

After hearing Whittington's story and reflecting on Epler's words, Turner envisioned a hypothetical scenario. Perhaps, sometime during the winter of 1936, Joe Mulholland had met with some terrible accident while on the trail. Rather than return to civilization without his partner and potentially face another murder trial, Bill Epler might have decided to fake his disappearance and flee the country. "It was not likely," admitted Turner, "but it was possible, if he had returned without Joe, he might have thought, 'Australia for me, boy, here I come.'"

THE DISAPPEARNCE OF OLLIE HOLMBERG

In 1940, the *Edmonton Journal* published an article stating that an aeronautical engineer named William Gilbertson was found dead in his cabin somewhere in the Nahanni Valley. Little is known of Gilbertson or the nature of his demise, although, according to Nazar Zinchuk, there was a vague, unsubstantiated rumour that George Dalziel, on whose planes the man worked, somehow had a hand in his death.

That same year, a frontiersman named Ollie Holmberg was rumoured to have disappeared in the Nahanni Valley. Godsell described the Scandinavian as "a brawny prospector from the gold camps of Great Bear Lake and Yellowknife... Big and strapping, his bronze face radiated good nature."

In his various articles, Godsell related how Holmberg had departed Fort Simpson for the Nahanni sometime that winter. When he failed to return in the spring as scheduled, an RCMP patrol set out to find him. Neither they nor any subsequent patrols discovered the slightest trace of the lost prospector. Similar to Gilbertson, some suspected that Holmberg had been murdered by the Flying Trapper.

When Pierre Berton made his Headless Valley expedition seven years later, he wrote that Holmberg was not, in fact, swallowed up by the Nahanni Valley as was popularly believed, but had actually disappeared in the Smith River area of British Columbia, located more than 150 miles to the southwest. Over the years, his claim has been both affirmed and denied by a number of frontiersmen.

Like so many of others who sought gold in the Nahanni Valley, Holmberg's fate remains a mystery to this day.

THE CASE OF ERNEST SAVARD

In 1945, Walter J. Tully, whom Pierre Berton interviewed prior to his Headless Valley expedition, made a prospecting expedition to the Nahanni Valley along with two partners, Walter Budd and Jack Thorstein. Near Virginia Falls, the three men discovered a badly decomposed body of a man lying in a sleeping bag on the banks of the river, his head nearly severed from his shoulders.

When Tully returned to civilization and told journalists of his discovery, many suspected that the body was that of Ernest Savard, a 40-year-old French Canadian prospector well known in the mining camps of British Columbia and Ontario. Savard had previously brought rich samples of gold ore out of the Nahanni Valley to Fort Nelson, and had disappeared into the forbidding country again in the spring of 1945, never to return.

When asked his opinion on the cause of Savard's death, Tully speculated that the man had succumbed to a combination of scurvy and starvation. "Hunger made him tired," he suggested, "so he crawled into his sleeping bag and died. The coyotes couldn't get at his body, but they gnawed away at his head."

For others, Tully's description of Savard's remains conjured up images of Willy and Frank McLeod, Martin Jorgensen, Yukon Fisher, and Phil Powers, whom legend says were all found in the Nahanni Valley without their heads. Naturally, some wondered if Savard and his headless predecessors were all dispatched by the same sort of culprit.

During his 1947 expedition, Pierre Berton wrote that Savard could not have died in the Nahanni Valley in 1945, as he was reportedly alive and well in 1946, toiling away in the newly discovered goldfields of Yellowknife, at the northern end of Great Slave Lake. Billy Clark and Gus Kraus echoed Berton's claim, saying that Savard actually died some years later at the mouth of Hay River, on the southern shores of Great Slave Lake. "Tully may or may not have found a body in the Nahanni," Berton concluded in one of his articles. "It certainly wasn't Savard's."

THE DISAPPEARANCE OF JOHN PATTERSON

In the autumn of 1946, a bedraggled prospector named Frank Henderson returned to civilization from the wilderness of the Nahanni Valley with a poke containing 30 ounces of coarse alluvial gold and a chilling tale.

Henderson was a nephew of Robert Henderson, one of the three co-discovers of the gold that launched the Klondike Gold Rush, and had spent most of his life in the wilderness of the Canadian North moiling for gold. He was no greenhorn, and was intimately familiar with the dangers inherent in northern prospecting. For example, only two years prior, he and a party of geologists and Indian guides had found what appeared to be the body of prospector John Jacobson near the junction of the South Nahanni and Flat Rivers. As it turned out, Jacobson was comatose, having been left for dead by his party nearly two weeks earlier. Miraculously, he recovered consciousness while Henderson and his party were in the process of digging his grave.

In spite of Henderson's extensive wilderness experience, the hardened frontiersman was visibly shaken when he recounted his experience in the Nahanni Valley in the fall of 1945 to journalist George Murray of Fort St. John. That fall, Henderson explained, he had planned to prospect with his partner, John Patterson[7], at Watson Lake, Yukon, situated near the Liard River a short distance northwest of Lower Post, BC.

Patterson was another man with considerable backcountry experience. The 55-year-old prospector,

---

[7] No relation to Raymond Patterson.

reportedly well known in Vancouver and Calgary, had served as an advisor on the Alaska Highway alongside seasoned frontiersmen like Philip Godsell. He was a veteran of the South African Gold Corp. and, according to Henderson, had "done any amount of field work, and the toughest, roughest country would not bother him."

Henderson and Patterson planned to meet at Virginia Falls that summer, whereupon they would travel down the South Nahanni and up the Liard to Watson Lake. Henderson approached the meeting place from the north, travelling down the Pelly River and the Canol Road from his camp on Pelly Lake. Patterson, on the other hand, accompanied by three Indian guides and a dogsled packed with six months-worth of provisions, trekked in from the east, travelling from Russell Lake, NWT, down Great Slave Lake, up the Mackenzie River, and apparently up the Trout River to Trout Lake, NWT. In June, he travelled overland from Trout Lake to the Liard and up the South Nahanni River and was never heard from again.

When Patterson failed to arrive at Virginia Falls at the appointed time, Henderson's Indian guides abandoned him, convinced that the prospector had been taken by the sinister agents whose head-hunting, cabin-burning activities fulfilled the curse of the Nahanni Valley. Patterson spent the rest of the season alone, searching the haunted vale for his lost partner. "All summer," he said, "I moved with utmost caution, mostly at night. There is absolutely no denying the sinister atmosphere of that whole valley. The weird continual wailing of the wind is something I won't soon forget."

When asked if he believed in the curse of the Nahanni Valley, Henderson replied, "of course, there's something to this legend. I don't think the murderers are native headhunters so much as possibly fugitives from justice in Northern law courts who are hiding out in that valley."

Later that fall, Henderson left Fort St. John for Watson Lake and Whitehorse, where he chartered a plane to fly over the Nahanni Country and searched for any sign of his missing partner. Despite his efforts, no trace of Patterson was ever found.

THE DEATH OF JOHN SHEBBACH

In the fall of 1946, Nazar Zinchuk's partner, a novice trapper and fellow Ukrainian named John Shebbach, was flown deep into the country south of the Flat River. He entered the country alone with very little supplies and next to no food. Before departing for the Nahanni, Zinchuk assured him that, if he found himself in dire straits, he could find relief in a cabin situated at the confluence of the Flat and Caribou Rivers, built many years earlier by prospectors J. Starke and R.S. Stevens. He himself would be in the Nahanni by that time, he told his partner, and would meet him there.

In spite of his promise, Zinchuk did not go to into the Nahanni Valley that year, nor did Shebbach return from it. A year went by without any word from the Ukrainian greenhorn. Then, in June 1948, an old Metis frontiersman named George Sibbeston travelled into Fort Simpson with a disturbing report.

Sibbeston told the Mounties at Fort Simpson that, in Starke and Stevens' old cabin, located just a mile up the Flat River from his own cabin, he had discovered the mutilated remains of an unidentified man. Immediately, a couple of officers hired Gus Kraus as a guide and travelled into the Nahanni Valley to investigate.

Kraus and his charges arrived at the cabin without incident. Inside, they found the body of John Shebbach, or what was left of it. "It was just a mess," said Kraus. "Scraps of clothing and bones had been gnawed and dragged around by bears, wolves, and every other damned thing that could chew."

Alongside Shebbach's mutilated remains, Kraus and the Mounties discovered the Ukrainian's diary. Its entries told a harrowing tale of privation and starvation. Upon arriving in Nahanni Country, Shebbach had built himself a cabin at what are known as the Skinboat Lakes and proceeded to establish a track line. Unfortunately, neither fur bearing animals nor big game were plentiful in that corner of the region at that time, and Shebbach soon found himself in real danger of starvation. Remembering Zinchuk's assurance, he packed all the gear that he could carry and made his way towards the Flat River on foot.

Finally, after an arduous trek, Shebbach arrived at Starke and Stevens' old cabin at the confluence of the Flat and Caribou Rivers, hungry and trail-weary. Of course, Zinchuk was nowhere to be found. Shebbach decided to wait for his partner, and settled in for the winter. Due to either a lack of game in the area or his incompetence as a hunter, or perhaps some combination thereof, Shebbach failed to procure any meat for himself and soon began to starve. After several weeks of fasting, malnutrition began to take its toll. As his energy steadily dwindled, Shebbach spent less time chopping firewood and searching for food each day and more of it lying in the cabin's bunk until he became completely bedridden. His final journal entry, dated February 3, 1946, indicated that he had survived for at least 43 days without food.

Kraus and the Mounties shook their heads ruefully as they gathered up Shebbach's remains, lamenting the grotesque irony inherent in the fact that, all throughout the Ukrainian's ordeal, George Sibbeston's well-stocked cabin lay only a mile down the Flat River.

OTHER DEATHS AND DISAPPEARANCES

Although John Shebbach was typically the last victim of the curse of the Nahanni Valley to be mentioned in classic Headless Valley literature, he was certainly not the last man to lose his life in that menacing tract of the Mackenzie Mountains.

The Curse of the Nahanni Valley

Leonard Brunchnik

In 1957, an eighteen-year-old adventurer named Leonard Brunchnik set up the South Nahanni with a prospector's pick, a gold pan, and a mining book in search of the lost McLeod mine. Several months later, his body was found on the shelf of a cutbank of the South Nahanni, lying face-down in a mat of dried vomit. The remains of a crude raft tangled in a drift pile downriver told his tragic tale all too clearly.

Angus Blake Mackenzie

In the fall of 1961, two strong, healthy bush pilots named Angus Blake Mackenzie and John Langdon decided to produce a motion picture on the legend of the curse of the Nahanni Valley, and succeeded in convincing Jack Mulholland and trapper Tom Haggerty with assisting them in their endeavour. Langdon was an experienced bush pilot who dabbled in photography, while Mackenzie was an aerial veteran of WWII, having served as a navigator in the Royal Canadian Air Force (RCAF). In October, 1961, the filmmakers leased a Cessna 180 light utility aircraft, replaced its floats with skis, and began scouting for a location. Eventually, they decided to film the majority of their picture on Bennett Creek.

That December, Mackenzie and Langdon began ferrying supplies from Smith River, British Columbia, to their base camp on Bennett Creek. At one point, around the middle of December, the snow was so heavy and the weather so inclement that the two men were forced to spend two weeks at the home of Dick Turner and his wife, Vera, who traded and trapped out of their cabin at Nahanni Butte.

On January 5, 1962, Angus Blake Mackenzie took off solo from Smith River on another 50-minute supply run to Bennett Creek. When he failed to return on schedule, Langdon suspected that he had been forced to land on a lake somewhere in the Nahanni Valley and was simply waiting for the weather to clear. When Mackenzie failed to appear after the storm abated, however, an RCAF Search and Rescue team set out to look for him.

In spite of their efforts, the Search and Rescue team was unable to find any trace of Mackenzie or his aircraft and, after forty days, the missing pilot was given up for dead. "We heard many... explanations for Blake's disappearance," wrote Dick Turner in his 1980 book *Wings of the North*. "Some said it was all done on purpose, he had wanted to escape something or other and had flown to Alaska or South America. Or that John Langdon and he had found a gold mine and Blake had escaped with the money, and that putting the plane down in the bush was the only ploy to further his ends. Others said, 'Find the woman and you will find Blake.'"

Since the majority of their film equipment had already been flown in, Langdon decided to commence filming without his partner. Six months after Mackenzie's disappearance, he, Jack Mulholland, and Tom Haggerty, while shooting footage for the movie's finale, spotted an object glinting in a distant valley between McMillan Lake and the headwaters of McLeod Creek. They hiked over to investigate.

Upon closer inspection, the object revealed itself to be part of the remains of Mackenzie's aircraft. In and around the wreck, Langdon, Mulholland, and Haggerty found a neatly-arranged assortment of supplies, including a chainsaw, jerry cans filled with gasoline, motor oil, a stove-heated canvas tent, and about 100 days-worth of provisions; Mackenzie, it appeared, had survived the crash, and subsisted in its vicinity for some time. They also found two of Mackenzie's diaries, one of them written with a pen, and the other evidently inscribed with the sharpened head of a .303 bullet. Of the pilot himself, however, there was no trace.

The stories contained in the diaries discovered at the site of the wreck indicated that Mackenzie had survived the crash with only minor injuries, and had lived well for some time afterwards, surviving off of an ample supply of food he had brought along with him as a precaution against such a predicament as the one he found himself in. He wrote of making huge signal fires, tramping out large 'SOS's in the snow, and crafting a flag from a pole and his red sleeping bag in an effort to attract the attention of the crews of the RCAF Search and Rescue planes that flew overhead. Curiously, the area in which Mackenzie's plane was discovered was covered thoroughly by the Search and Rescue team, and although the sky was often clear enough for steam and smoke from drilling rigs to be visible from over 50 miles away, none of the RCAF pilots involved in the search saw any sign of the signal fires, SOS messages, or red flags indicated in the bush pilot's journal.

Angus Blake Mackenzie's journal entries suddenly ceased after 46 days with no indication as to the reason for their termination. Inexplicably, Mackenzie's body was never found.

Stockwall, Hudon, Goertz, and Busse

That same year, on September 29, a bush pilot named Kenneth Stockwall, whom Dick Turner maintained "was considered to be one of the best bush pilots operating out of Yellowknife," flew men named Victor Hudon, Gunther Goertz, and Henry Busse into the Nahanni Valley in his Cessna 185. That day, Stockwall flew directly into the heart of what Gus Kraus described as "one of the worst storms, I think, that ever hit the Nahanni."

Sometime later, Stockwall's shattered aircraft was discovered near Virginia Falls, along with Hudon's corpse. The bodies of Stockwall, Goertz, and Busse were never found.[8]

Wuethrich, Wiesmann, and Mihncke

On June 22, 1963, three Swiss canoeists named Martin Wuethrich, Fritz Willy Wiesmann, and Wolfgang Mihncke

---

[8] According to Dick Turner, the ruins of Stockwall's craft were discovered in Sundog Creek, a waterway situated in the northeastern corner of the Nahanni Valley, a short distance from a body of water called Little Doctor Lake.

flew in to Glacier Lake, far above Virginia Falls, and set out down the South Nahanni River in a canoe. Wiesmann, Mihncke, and the canoe were never seen again.

In either late July or early August, a Mountie patrol found the body of Martin Wuethrich trapped beneath a wall of the Figure Eight Rapids with a poncho around his neck. The corpse was in a state of almost complete preservation due to the conservational effects of the cold rushing water in which it was immersed.

The three Swiss men, the Mounties surmised, had likely capsized their canoe on this particularly mean stretch of river and drowned.

***

Many more men in addition to those mentioned in this book have died or disappeared in the Nahanni Valley. The fates of these others, while tragic, can largely be attributed to the natural forces that characterize similar stretches of rugged, remote, uninhabited wilderness. Most of them died in canoeing accidents, some perished in plane crashes, others were killed by wild animals, and other still succumbed to privation after losing their way in the woods. Father Mary of Fort Liard, a northern Oblate Missionary, perhaps summarized the fates of these men most aptly thus:

"Those men who disappeared up the Nahanni, they were no fools, you know. They were all men who knew the bush well,

but in that country, one mistake is too many. One mistake, and-whoosh- it is too late."

TALES OF MADNESS

In addition to being a place where men were known to die mysterious deaths and vanish without a trace, the Nahanni Valley is a region in which an alarming portion of its inhabitants have slipped into insanity. May Lafferty included, it could be argued that, over the course of the 20th Century, at least eight people have lost their minds somewhere in the Nahanni Valley.

In his book *Nahanni*, Dick Turner described four men whom he know personally who he claimed were driven mad by loneliness and isolation in the Nahanni bush. One of these unfortunates, Turner wrote, "died of 'Shanty Rot.' He lay on the bed in his cabin for the best part of two years and gradually rotted away." The other three suffered from paranoia, certain that something or someone was out to get them. "One man would lie on his bunk with his face to the wall when his neighbour came to see him. Another one would accuse his friends and neighbours (behind their backs) of stealing from him... The third man was really gone far. Talking with him on commonplace subjects, I found him as normal as anyone... But suddenly, in the middle of a conversation, he would lower his voice, and in a somewhat obscure manner, make reference to 'them'... The strange thing about all this is that one spring he did fail to return... and was never seen again..."

Another frontiersman who included tales of insanity in his memoirs of the Nahanni was Poole Field. In one of his letters, he wrote of the adventures had by him and his Yukon Indian friend, Oskar, while travelling through the Nahanni Valley with Chief Jim Pellesea and his band of Mountain Indians in 1905. One of the more tragic anecdotes he related in this letter revolved around one of the band's most prominent members- a strapping young Mountain Indian brave named Afah.

The Tragedy of Afah

Afah was an excellent hunter and a sort of leader amongst the band's youth. Poole Field estimated that the young man weighed about 200 pounds- a considerable weight in those days, especially for a Dene, many of whom, at that time, were chronically undernourished.

Like most young men of the band, Afah had openly taken a romantic interest in Nahkah, the 16-year-old daughter of Big Foot, the brother of the chief. "She was a tall, slim girl," wrote Field, "and when she was dressed up in her dancing costume of fine deerskins decorated with fringed beads and porcupine quills and joined the dancing in the evening, she made quite a striking figure." Although Big Foot had given Afah his blessing to marry his daughter, Nahkah was undecided as to whether or not she wanted to take the burly brave as her husband. Her father respected her indecision and did not pressure her to marry until she was ready.

At that time, if a Dene man wanted to marry a particular bachelorette, custom dictated that he present her father with a gift, which served as a sort of bride token. Traditionally, if the father was pleased with the suitor, he accepted the gift, thereby giving the man consent to marry his daughter. Conversely, if he was displeased with the supplicant and wanted to deny him his blessing, he returned the gift.

At that time, Afah was the most dominant of all the young men in that particular band of Mackenzie Mountain Indians in both strength and temperament, and was therefore thought to have the best chance with Nahkah. In spite of this, many of his peers showered Big Foot with choice cuts of meat and other such gifts in the hope that they might win the maiden's hand instead. As Big Foot had decided to allow his daughter to choose her husband herself, however, he gratefully accepted all the gifts that came his way. "Old Big Foot was living high," wrote Field, "and, of course, as I was camped close to Big Foot... I came in for a good share of the goodly things handed around."

As the band made their way up the Ross River and over the Mackenzie Mountains towards the headwaters of the South Nahanni, Field's Indian companion, Oskar, similarly took a fancy to Big Foot's beautiful daughter. This lean and wiry newcomer from the Yukon had become quite popular among the band's youth, and some thought that he had as good a chance of wooing Nahkah as did the indomitable Afah. Eventually, Oskar decided to take his chances and offer Big Foot a bride token of his own. The chief's brother accepted the gift without hesitation, telling Oskar, as he had the other young hopefuls, that he could have his daughter's hand if he managed to win her heart.

One evening, after a long day of travelling, the young men of the band decided to amuse themselves with a friendly wrestling competition. Afah, by far the strongest of the bunch, quickly came out on top. When he ran out of opponents to best, he challenged Oskar, who had been watching from the sidelines, to a bout. The youthful Yukoner readily accepted.

Although Oskar was about 40 pounds lighter than the stocky Afah, he was several inches taller than him, and had a longer reach. Perhaps more importantly, he was also an experienced fighter, having honed his combat skills in the gold camps of the Yukon, where recreation among the hardy white prospectors often consisted of wrestling and bare-knuckle boxing. When Afah rushed him, Oskar lowered his shoulders, wrapped his arms around his opponent, and tossed him over his head. The big hunter landed heavily on his back, the wind knocked from his lungs.

It was apparent from the reaction of the onlookers that this was the first time that Afah had been thrown. Infuriated, the defeated brave picked himself up, drew his hunting knife, and lunged at Oskar, who was still grinning triumphantly, hoping that his victory had impressed Nahkah. The Yukon Indian became aware of the attack just in time. With lightning speed, he sidestepped his powerful adversary and knocked him out cold with a haymaker to the chin.

Unbeknownst to Oskar, who had come of age in the rough-and-tumble world of the Klondike, the superstitious Mountain Indians held fist fighting as taboo. "Of course, there was the devil to pay," wrote Field. "In vain I tried to explain to Afah and his relations that Afah had no business drawing a knife, but they couldn't see it." Big Foot and Chief Pellesea were on Oskar's side, however, and after a long and heated argument between the two camps, things began to settle down.

A few days later, Field, Oskar, Afah, and a handful of hunters hiked up to a place in the mountains where four bull moose had been killed. The band was moving camp soon, and Field and his companions were tasked with dressing and packing the meat. As they approached the site, the Indian dogs that had been ranging ahead of them suddenly raced back towards them, yelping fearfully. Hot on their heels was an enormous mother grizzly bear, snorting with rage as she crashed through the brush.

Poole Field narrowly avoided the furious animal by leaping to the side. Afah, on the other hand, was not so fortunate. The charging bear converged on the Indian and raked viciously at his head, sending him sprawling head over heels with a single swipe of her mighty paw. She proceeded to rear up on her hind legs and roar, whereupon Oskar, who had hitherto managed to evade the monster, darted in and plunged his skinning knife hilt-deep into her abdomen. The bear fell with a tremendous crash, apparently breaking her spine in the process. As she bellowed and swiped at her assailant from her prone position, a hunter named Big Moose put a bullet through her ear, killing her instantly.

Immediately, the party turned its attention towards Afah, who lay prostrate on the forest floor. The fallen brave was unconscious and bleeding profusely from a gaping gash that opened his head from crown to throat, narrowly missing his left eye. Field and the Indians bandaged the injured hunter as best they could and transported him on a makeshift stretcher back to the camp.

It took Afah a full three weeks to physically recover from his wound. Mentally, however, the young brave was never the same again. "I think the skull had been cracked or something," surmised Field, "as he seemed to have crazy spells at times afterwards, and the scar, after it had healed, sure spoiled his beauty."

When Afah was fit to travel, the band headed down the South Nahanni River, down the portage trail at Virginia Falls, and overland through the mountains to the Flat River. Further to the west, at the headwaters of a tributary of the Liard called the Hyland River, Field and the Indians began panning for gold. "I had been pretty well through Alaska and Dawson Country," wrote Field, "and, to my mind, we were in the ideal spot to find something."

"However," he continued, "Man proposes and God disposes, and my friend Oskar, in a way, again threw a monkeywrench into the machinery." During Afah's recovery, the Yukon Indian had finally won Nahkah's affection, and was welcomed by her family. All that remained was to name the day of their wedding.

Afah was bitterly jealous of his rival's conquest, and began to blame Oskar for all of his recent misfortunes. A few of the band's medicine men fed his suspicions by suggesting that Oskar was secretly a medicine man himself, and had sent the bear to kill him. It seemed that a violent confrontation between the two rivals and their respective supporters was inevitable.

In order to prevent bloodshed, Big Foot decided that Oskar and Nahkah ought to be married as soon as possible, thereby settling the matter once and for all. There, on the shores of the Hyland River, the Mountain Indians held a massive wedding feast. "[We] danced our heads off and gambled," wrote Field, "and everybody had a good time." Everyone except Afah, that is. In the morning, the young brave was nowhere to be found. "He had just taken a light outfit with him" wrote Field, "-a 45-70 black powder rifle and an old double barrel muzzle loader shot gun- and disappeared without saying a word to anyone."

About a week later, Field and the Indians found themselves camped in a stand of heavy timber. One dark and moonless night, at around 2 o'clock in the morning, the whole band was awakened by a deep, unearthly howl that seemed to erupt from the middle of the camp. Terrified, the hunters sprang from their beds, seized their rifles, and stood by the entrance of their teepees, listening intently.

"Every dog in the camp started howling..." wrote Field, "and made such a noise [that] you could hear nothing, but when it quieted down, Afah spoke out of the darkness."

The resentful brave told Oskar to pack his outfit, leave his new bride, and make his way back to the Yukon. If he refused, Afah promised to kill him. All night long, Afah repeated his threat. Whenever Field or another hunter attempted to reason with him, he responded with another hair-raising howl which all the dogs in the camp took up with him. He finally departed into the woods sometime before dawn, leaving the Indians fearful and exhausted.

The deranged brave repeated his performance the following five nights. "He pretty near had us bugs," wrote Field, "what with want of sleep and scared that he might do as he said." Soon, Field and some of the Indians began searching for the disgruntled brave during the day. Try as they might, however, they were unable to find him anywhere. "He was too smart for us," wrote Field. Eventually, they attempted to ambush Afah at night, but were similarly evaded by the wily hunter.

After several days, Field decided to head alone to a small creek located about 10 miles from the camp, where an Indian boy had found coarse gold. Field found the colours there so promising that he spent the entire day prospecting in the area. When it became too dark to return to the main camp, he made a siwash camp[9] beside the creek, building a large fire and laying a blanket over a bed of spruce boughs. There, he enjoyed the first fitful sleep he'd had in a week.

The following morning, Field returned to the Indian camp and found the whole place in an uproar. He quickly learned that, the previous night, a bloodthirsty Afah had returned to the camp with his rifle in one hand and his shotgun in the other, both of them loaded, primed, and cocked. There, he found Oskar waiting for him, crouched beside a campfire.

As he had the previous five nights, Afah ordered the Yukon Indian to pack his belongings and hit the trail. Oskar calmly told the Mountain Indian that he had no quarrel with him, and began to stand up, whereupon Afah bashed him in the head with the butt of his rifle, skinning him from forehead to crown. Before Afah could land another blow, Oskar grabbed him by the legs and upset him, causing him to drop his weapons, and in no time, the two Indians were

---

[9] A 'siwash camp' is a crude outdoor camp constructed by subarctic frontiersmen. It typically consists of a rectangular bed of spruce boughs arranged on a patch of snowless ground, bordered by three, roughly 2-foot-high windbreaks which are typically composed of green saplings)- and one large fire situated at the opening.

rolling together on the forest floor, engaged in ferocious hand-to-hand combat.

By this time, all the Indians in the camp had emerged from their teepees to watch the duel. None of them dared interfere. At one point, when both braves were severely battered and bloodied, Afah broke free and ran for his weapons. Oskar followed in hot pursuit. In moments, the two braves were locked in a deadly struggle for the possession of Afah's black powder shotgun. During this scuffle, Oskar managed to get the muzzle of the firearm against Afah's stomach. He pulled both triggers, and as quickly as it had started, the battle was over; Afah lay stone dead on the forest floor.

Joe the Mad Prospector

Another tale of insanity that Poole Field related in one of his letters revolved around a mad prospector whom Field referred to only as 'Joe'. While Affah's lunacy likely stemmed from a traumatic brain injury resultant of his brush with the mother bear, it is likely that Joe's mental malady was attributable to the debilitative psychological effects of long periods divorced from civilization. To use the vernacular of the sourdoughs of the day, Joe probably got 'bushed'.

Joe was a prospector whom Field knew from his post-Klondike days in Yukon and Alaska, when he worked as a dog team courier running mail between Dawson City and Nome. Joe and his partner Red, the latter being another of

Field's Yukon-Alaskan acquaintances, travelled to a location near the headwaters of the South Nahanni sometime around 1912, hoping to strike it rich. In 1914, when Field entered the Nahanni with Oskar in order to look for Martin Jorgensen, he decided to make a side trip to search for his old friends.

Field and Oskar travelled up the Ross River and into the mountains where, not too far from the headwaters of the South Nahanni, they found a log cabin, smoke billowing from its stove pipe chimney. As they approached the cabin, they both let out a loud "Halloo!" Their salutations were met with silence.

Field and Oskar worked their way around to the front of the cabin and found that its door was wide open. In the middle of the room stood Field's old friend, Joe, clad in nothing but a suit of woolen underwear and staring at the wall with a vacant expression on his face. "Halloo, Joe, how are you?" Field asked cautiously, to which Joe replied, "shoot, shoot, shoot..." over and over again, never once taking his eyes off of the wall.

Disconcerted, Field approached the man and saw that his face was badly scratched and one of his eyes swollen shut. "For God's sake, Joe!" he exclaimed. "Have you and Red been fighting?"

"Oh," said the prospector, still staring at the wall, "Red got scared of me and ran away. Say, you know, there are a lot of blue devils around here, but I'll fix them. I have them shut up in a box." With that, he ran over to a corner of the cabin, seized a small wooden box, and ran outside, yelling, "Follow me!" A bewildered Field and Oskar obliged.

As he trailed after the deranged prospector, Field began to suspect that Joe's box was packed full of gunpowder. He said as much to Oskar and, in order to prevent a potentially deadly accident, the two of them tackled Joe to the ground. The prospector put up a fierce fight, and Field and Oskar managed to subdue him only with considerable effort. The box, as it turned out, was filled with matches, and contained a few tins of baking powder.

"Oh! Hello, Poole!" said Joe, when he had finally cooled down, evidently having recognized his old acquaintance. "How are you? Where did you come from?"

Field told the prospector that he and Oskar had come from his trading post on the Ross River before inquiring, once again, as to the whereabouts of Red. Again, Joe told him that Red was frightened of him and had ran away. When Field asked him how he had acquired his injuries, the demented prospector pointed to the peak of a nearby mountain and claimed that he had rolled down its slopes.

Baffled, Field and Oskar took Joe into the cabin and sat him down on the bunk. In a Dene dialect which Joe did not understand, Field instructed Oskar to collect any knives or guns that might be lying outside the cabin and cache them in a safe place, and to search the area for any sign of Red.

While Oskar went about his errand, Field continued to interrogate Joe in an effort to come to a better understanding of the situation. At one point, Joe made a move to stand up. Afraid that he might catch Oskar handling his weapons, he grabbed a handful of Joe's undershirt and roughly forced him to sit down again. The prospector howled in agony, whereupon Field, looking down the neck of his shirt, noticed that Joe's back appeared to be caked with dried blood.

"How on earth did you get in this shape?" asked Field as he examined the man's extensive injuries.

"Oh, just rolling down the mountain."

At that point, Oskar returned to the cabin with news that he had found Red's tracks going up a nearby creek. Whatever his reason for leaving, Red had evidently departed with haste, judging from his tracks. After talking it over, Field and Oskar concluded that Red had probably gone looking for someone to help him deal with Joe, and decided that their best course of action would be to remain at the cabin and look after the deranged prospector until Red's return.

Later that evening, Joe informed his guests that he was going to make another trip up the mountain. When Field and Oskar attempted to stop him, he put up a ferocious struggle. The two adventurers eventually subdued the belligerent prospector and, panting and sweating, convinced him to allow them to dress his wounds. "So I stripped him and gave him a wash up," wrote Field, "bandaged the worst of the cuts and fixed him up as comfortable as I could to avoid another wrestling match."

That accomplished, Field and Oskar tied Joe's knees together to prevent him from running, and bound his arms at the elbows, "but not too tight that he couldn't rest fairly comfortably." The two partners spent the rest of the night watching the crazed prospector in shifts.

"About eleven the next day," wrote Field, "I was standing in front of the cabin looking down the creek in the direction Red had gone when I saw his old red head poking out from behind a stump, and the muzzle of his rife pointing straight at me. I don't know who was more surprised, him or I."

"Red, it's me!" Field exclaimed, throwing his hands up in the air in surrender. The redheaded prospector lowered his weapon and went over to greet his old acquaintance.

When he learned that Joe was tied up inside the cabin, Red let out a sigh of relief and fired a shot into the air. Soon, the men were joined by Ole Loe, another frontiersman known to frequent Nahanni Country.

"There are lots of us now," said Red. "We might as well turn Joe loose." As soon as they did so, however, the crazy prospector launched himself at his old partner. Before the other men could intervene, Red threw Joe on his back, knocking the wind from his lungs, and sat on his chest. "Now, young fellow," he said, "you were boss long enough. I am the boss again, and don't forget it. Any time you get fresh, I will just do this over again, only a little harder. You understand?"

"Yes, Red," said Joe, as though he were completely sane.

Later that afternoon, Red sat down with Field and told him his story. Joe, as Field knew well, was a devout Catholic who spent long hours praying and reading the Bible. Several months earlier, his religious fervour began to devolve into a sort of zealous mania. He started practicing extreme and unorthodox forms of worship, and would often enlist Red in his strange sectarian schemes.

Years earlier, Red had developed a general aversion to religion when his wife deserted him for a preacher. In spite of this, he decided to appease his partner and take part in the various pseudo-religious ceremonies that he organized in order to keep the peace. As time drew on, Joe's rituals became increasingly bizarre, and Red soon began to fear for the future.

One day, Joe decided to build a sacrificial altar on the top of a mountain similar to that which Abraham had built atop Mount Moriah in the Book of Genesis. Like the Hebrews of the Old Testament, he and Red would atone for their sins by making burnt offerings on the altar. Red's offering, Joe declared, would be his gold pocket watch, while his own sacrifice would consist of all the gold dust he and Red had panned from the creek, as well as a batch of bread and doughnuts that he had baked specially for the occasion.

This was too much for Red. As Joe climbed up into the cache to retrieve the gold dust, Red grabbed his rifle, hitched his dogs to a sled, and took off upriver, where he eventually found Ole Loe.

"We decided the best thing to do was to take Joe to Dawson for medical treatment," wrote Field. Before setting out on the journey, however, he and Red decided to hike to the top of the mountain in order to see what had become of the gold dust.

Field and Red found Joe's altar without much difficulty. The pious prospector had built what looked like a small fort, on top of which lay a heap of burnt bread and doughnuts surrounded by about twenty beeswax candles. "Someday, someone will find it and think he has found the ruins of a lost civilization," wrote Field.

As the two frontiersmen searched the vicinity of the altar for any sign of the missing gold dust, they found Joe's clothes scattered about haphazardly. Traces of dried blood on some nearby rocks indicated that Joe had stripped naked before rolling down the mountainside, just as he claimed.

When they finally conceded that the gold dust was lost for good, the two frontiersmen descended the mountain and returned to the cabin. Red and Loe took Joe with them to Dawson City, where the mad prospector underwent medical treatment and eventually made a full recovery. Field and Oskar, on the other hand, set out to find Martin Jorgensen.

The Starvation Cabin

In the fall of 1959, five prospectors from Yellowknife, Northwest Territories, flew into McMillan Lake, near McLeod Creek, to prospect for gold. Their names were Alex Mieskonen, Orville Webb, Thomas Pappas, Dean Rossworn, and John Richardson. In addition to a sled and a dog team, they had brought 100 pounds of flour and several months' worth of rice, beans, sugar, and tobacco along with them into the Nahanni Valley, all of which was to last them until January, when the pilot who had dropped them off was scheduled to return to McMillan Lake with supplies.

In late December, Gus Kraus and Frank Bailey, the Game Warden of Fort Simpson, decided to pay a visit to the five prospectors. While inspecting their tiny cabin and surrounding camp, the two men found evidence that the prospectors had shot a number of moose and caribou- an illegality in light of the fact that they were not in possession of a big game hunting licence. Bailey informed the prospectors of their infraction and forbade them from killing any more caribou or moose unless they were in danger of starvation. He proceeded to seize all the meat they had stored in their cache before flying out of the country with Kraus and pilot James Roy Franklin.

Frank Bailey immediately reported the prospectors' game infraction to Constable Vic Werbiki of Fort Liard. "Vic Werbiki was cool headed, tactful, and was well liked and respected by all who knew him..." wrote Dick Turner. "I thought he was of the best tradition of the RCMP, a man who might overlook some minor items but with whom no one would care to tangle if he were investigating something serious."

The following day, pilot James Franklin flew Bailey, Kraus, and Constable Werbiki to the five prospectors' camp. The easygoing Mountie did not levy any charges against the gold seekers, but instead asked them if they wanted a free lift back to civilization. When the prospectors refused his offer, Werbiki inspected their provisions, ensured that they had enough to last until their scheduled January shipment, and left them to their own devices, flying out of the country with Bailey and Kraus.

Nothing more was heard of the prospectors for the rest of the winter. Months later, in May, brothers Chuck and Jim McAvoy, bush pilots who operated a small airline service out of Yellowknife and had heard tell of the prospectors' scheme, decided to fly in to McMillan lake to see how the gold hunters had fared.

As they flew over the lake, the McAvoy brothers noticed the letters 'SOS' tramped out on the soft ice. They landed nearby, located a trail, and followed it to the prospectors' tiny cabin. Inside, they found Dean Rossworn and John Richardson, both of them severely emaciated. As they helped the starving prospectors to their craft, the McAvoy brothers heard Rossworn and Richardson's harrowing tale.

Back in January, the shipment of provisions that the prospectors had counted on failed to arrive. Their flour stores all but exhausted, the five prospectors slowly began to go hungry. More than just their physical health, however, this lack of food seemed to have an extraordinarily deleterious effect on their mental states.

At first, when they realized that they were on their own, the five prospectors attempted to fill their larder with moose and caribou meat. Although they managed to kill a number of animals without much difficulty, they were inexplicably unwilling to do the work necessary to avail themselves of the carcasses they procured. Instead of dressing the meat and packing it a mere two miles back to their cabin, they decided to butcher and eat their dogs. One prospector shot a dog and interred it in a hole he had chopped in the ice of McLeod Creek. When the carcass was so rotten that its hair slipped off at the slightest touch, he took it out, cooked it, and ate it. Another did the exact same thing with the guts of a caribou he slaughtered, leaving the rest of the good, red meat for the wolves.

The strangest segment of this bizarre tale involved Alex Mieskonen, the bespectacled sponsor of the prospecting expedition. One day, after a failed ice fishing expedition on

McMillan Lake, Mieskonen grabbed his camera, his field glasses, and his packsack and set out from the prospectors' tiny cabin, claiming that he would return with some wire with which they could build snares. After he had been gone for some time, the prospectors heard a loud boom in the distance. Curiously, none of them deigned to investigate the unusual noise.

When Mieskonen failed to return after several hours, one of the prospectors followed his trail through the snow to see what had befallen him. About a mile from the cabin, he found Mieskonen's red and ragged remains scattered about the snow. It appeared that prospector, whose fear of explosives was well known, had committed suicide with the last of their dynamite.

Following Mieskonen's demise, Orville Webb and Thomas Pappas set out into the wilderness to find help. None of them were ever seen again.

When the McAvoy brothers discovered the skeletal Dean Rossworn and John Richardson in May, 1962, both prospectors were in the final stages of starvation. Miraculously, the two of them survived the ordeal and were eventually nursed back to health.

Although it may not have any connection with this particular legend of the Nahanni Valley, it is interesting to note that George McAvoy, one of the two brothers who rescued Rossworn and Richardson from almost certain death, disappeared two years later while flying geologists Doug Thorpe and A. Kunes over the arctic barrens south of Bathurst Inlet, Nunavut. Until the discovery of his plane in the summer of 2003, the fate of George McAvoy remained one of Canada's most famous aviation mysteries.

THEORIES

In 1971, Sir Ranulph Fiennes- a British Army officer, explorer, and adventurer- led an expedition into the Nahanni Valley. Most of his companions on this journey were fellow members of the Royal Scots Greys, a 293-year-old cavalry-turned-armoured regiment of the British Army which was destined to amalgamate with the Prince of Wales' Dragoon Guards later that year to form the Royal Scots Dragoon Guards. Two years later, Fiennes published a book about this expedition entitled *The Headless Valley*. On the subject of the curse of the Nahanni and the men it is alleged to have claimed, he remarked:

"The fact remains... that most of these missing men were hardened prospectors who had spent much of their lives in the far north. And it is curious that, though there are a thousand equally remote and hostile valleys in the north where far greater numbers of prospectors live from year to year, there are no other regions half as rich in tales of death and burnt-out cabins."

Unlike Fiennes, some of those who have commented on the alleged curse over the years dismissed the alarming preponderance of mysterious deaths and conflagrated cabins in the Nahanni as coincidence, chalking the incidents up to animal attacks, accidents, and other hazards endemic to the subarctic wilderness. Others levied accusations against some of those already suspected in the deaths of Martin Jorgensen and the McLeod brothers, namely the mysterious Nahanni Indians, the dreaded Nakani of Indian legend, or crazed frontiersmen. One particular frontiersman supposed by some to have a connection with the curse of the Nahanni Valley was a mysterious white man known only as the Mad Trapper of Rat River.

The Mad Trapper of Rat River

The so-called 'Mad Trapper of Rat River' first appeared in the vicinity of Rat River, a tributary of the Mackenzie Delta located a short distance from the Arctic Ocean, in the summer of 1931. The few who met him described him as a dour, taciturn woodsman with the faintest hint of a Scandinavian accent who went to great lengths to avoid human contact. He went by the name of 'Albert Johnson,' although he almost certainly borrowed this name from the brother of another trapper who lived in the region at the time.

In December, 1931, a native trapper named William Nerysoo arrived in the tiny settlement of Arctic Red River Post, situated at the confluence of the Arctic Red and Mackenzie Rivers just south of what is now Inuvik, NWT, and informed the local RCMP that someone was springing his traps and hanging them up on tree branches. He suspected that Johnson was behind the mischief and asked the Mounties to investigate him.

On December 26, Mountie Constable Alfred "Buns" King and a Gwich'in Indian Special Constable named Joe Bernard trekked to Johnson's cabin on snowshoes in order to question the mysterious trapper about Nerysoo's allegation. Although Johnson was inside his cabin at the time of the Mounties' arrival, as evidenced by the smoke that issued from the chimney, he refused to speak with them, let alone open the door to them, and put a burlap sack over the window when they attempted to look inside. Knowing they could not force their way inside Johnson's cabin without authorization, the two Mounties made their way 80 miles (129 kilometres) down the Husky River to the settlement of Aklavik, NWT, where another RCMP outpost was located.

Five days later, on New Years' Eve, King and Bernard returned to Johnson's cabin with a search warrant and two additional RCMP officers from Aklavik, Constable R.G. McDowell and Special Constable Lazarus Sittichinli. As before, wood smoke issued from the cabin's chimney, indicating that Johnson was inside.

As the Mounties approached the cabin, King called out to Johnson from a distance, asking him to come outside and informing him that he was authorized to break in his door if he did not comply with his request. As before, there was no reply. The Mountie approached the cabin cautiously and rapped on the door. His knocks were answered by a rifle blast which hurled him backwards into the snow; Johnson had shot King through the door.

The wounded Mountie scrambled back towards the sled, one gloved hand clamped tightly over his injury, as his companions returned fire. Alarmingly proximate bullets zipped by as the Mounties lashed their fallen comrade to the sleigh and took off at breakneck speed, bound for Aklavik. Due to atrocious weather conditions, the patrol arrived at their destination after 24 hours of hard travelling. King was rushed to the local hospital, where he eventually made a full recovery.

Upon hearing the Mounties' report, Inspector Alexander Eames, commander of the Western Arctic Sub-District of the RCMP and head of the garrison at Aklavik, decided to lead a ten-man patrol to Johnson's cabin and arrest the trapper for his offence. This patrol consisted of himself, McDowell, Bernard, and Sittichinli; three of Eames' own men, Ernest Sutherland, Karl Gardlund, and Knut Lang; Constable Edgar "Spike" Millen of Arctic Red River Post, who had actually met and briefly spoken with Albert Johnson earlier that summer; and Charley Rat, an Indian guide. The nine men, along with 42 sled dogs, arrived at Johnson's cabin on January 9, 1932 by an obscure Indian trail and, after a brief reconnaissance mission during which they determined that he was still inside, approached it cautiously.

At first, the Mounties beseeched Johnson to surrender himself peacefully; he would not be hanged for murder, they informed him, as he had not managed to kill Alfred King. Their entreaties were met with a fusillade of gunfire, which the lawmen quickly returned. As they circled about his cabin, firing as they went, the Mounties learned that the trapper had bored loopholes on all sides of his cabin, turning his log shack into a veritable fortress, and was able to harry his assailants from every angle.

All day long and well into the night, the nine Mounties exchanged gunfire with the lone desperado. Try as they might, the RCMP officers, special constables, and Indian scout, all of them experienced hunters, were unable to get the upper hand on the mysterious Scandinavian trapper. Finally, sometime after midnight, the besiegers managed to breach Johnson's cabin by lobbing several lit sticks of dynamite onto the roof. A tremendous explosion ensued, obliterating the cabin's roof and partially caving in its walls. Before the smoke had cleared, Eames and Garland stormed the breach, whereupon Johnson, who had sheltered himself from the blast in a pit he had dug in the cabin floor, shot Garland's flashlight out of his hand. The Mounties retreated back into the darkness and, at about 4:00 in the morning, decided to return to Aklavik in defeat.

One week after the shootout, a second posse, composed of seven men, left Aklavik for Albert Johnson's cabin. On the way, they were joined by eleven Gwich'in Indians. The eighteen-man party arrived at the remains of Johnson's cabin without incident. Despite their best efforts, however, they were unable to find any sign of the trapper or his tracks. Eventually, it was decided that, for logistical purposes, a four-man team would continue to search for Johnson further up the Rat River. This team consisted of Karl Gardlund, Noel Verville, Quartermaster Sergeant R.F. Riddell, and Constable Edgar Millen.

The four men spent several day combing the Rat River for any sign of Albert Johnson. They had nearly reached the limits of their endurance and were dangerously low on provisions when Riddell spied a faint pair of snowshoe tracks which Gardlund and Millen recognized as Johnson's. With fresh wind in their sails, the Mounties took up the chase.

Gardlund, Verville, Riddell, and Millen followed Johnson's tracks for days. The wily trapper travelled on hard-packed snow wherever possible in an effort to leave a less visible trail, and took an erratic, circuitous, and often circular route over all manner of obstacles in the hope of throwing off his pursuers. To the Mounties' dismay, he seemed to have almost superhuman stamina; Johnson, with a heavy pack on his back and a pair of snowshoes on his feet, appeared to be travelling twice as fast as they were in spite of the sled dogs that aided their efforts. Even more disturbing was the fact that the outlaw trapper, as evidenced by his leavings, only built small fires beneath snowbanks in an effort to avoid detection, and subsisted entirely on squirrels and rabbits that he snared, apparently cognizant of the likelihood that firing his rifle at bigger game would give away his position.

With the help of an Indian hunter, the four Mounties finally managed to locate Johnson's camp and approach it by way of a shortcut. The lawmen attempted to ambush the fugitive and soon found themselves engaged in a bitter firefight with him. During this confrontation, Constable Edgar "Spike" Millen was killed instantly by a bullet through the heart. According to some accounts, Johnson let out a gruff laugh when he shot the Mountie- the only utterance any of his pursuers would ever hear from him.

Riddell headed back to Aklavik to report the tragic news to Eames, and Gardlund and Verville interred Millen's body in cache to preserve it from scavengers. The Mounties did not feel the need to press the attack, as Johnson was trapped between them and a sheer cliff, near the base of which he had built his camp, and had nowhere to run. Incredibly, Johnson made his escape by climbing the cliff that bounded him with the aid of a woodcutter's axe.

Upon hearing of Millen's death, Inspector Eames requested that his superiors give him leave to commission a bush pilot to aid in the search. His Edmonton superiors forwarded the request to General J.H. MacBrien, Commissioner of the RCMP, who approved the use of a plane in the manhunt, and in no time, WWI flying ace, celebrated bush pilot, and Nahanni prospector "Wop" May was given the order to ready his plane.

While May made his preparations, Inspector Eames set out towards Rat River with a compliment of seven

Mounties, three special constables, and a number of trappers. Among the party was Arthur Blake, a former Mountie and the owner of a trading post on the Peel River who, along with the recently deceased Millen, was one of the few northerners who had actually spoken with Albert Johnson.

By this time, the 'Mad Trapper' had crossed over into the Yukon Territory and was heading west for the Richardson Mountains. Determined to get their man, increasingly disconcerted RCMP headmen in Edmonton dispatched patrols from Whitehorse, Dawson City, Fort Norman, Aklavik, Fort Simpson, and Mayo, Yukon. Soon, "Wop" May was in the air, delivering much-needed supplies to Inspector Eames' human bloodhounds.

In early February, May began flying over the Aklavik, Barrier, and Rat River Countries in an effort to pick up Johnson's trail. On February 8, he noticed a pair of lone snowshoe tracks- almost certainly Johnson's- near the headwaters of the Barrier River and reported his discovery to the Mounties.

The following day, a raging blizzard precluded May from investigating the tracks further and the Mounties from continuing their pursuit. For the lawmen, this setback was not particularly perturbing on account of the fact that Johnson was now trapped at the foot of the Richardson Mountains. His only way over the divide was through the Wright or McDougall Passes, which the RCMP were now guarding.

Incredibly, Johnson used this opportunity to pull off an extraordinary stunt that has bewildered mountain guides ever since- during the blizzard, Albert Johnson scaled the Richardson Mountains. Instead of crossing the divide by way of the Wright or McDougall Passes, the 'Mad Trapper' opted to climb up and over the mountains' high ridges- an enterprise which local trappers and Indians assured the Mounties was impossible at that time of year for all but the most skilled mountaineers. Yet, incredibly, Albert Johnson achieved this spectacular feat of endurance without any technical equipment in the middle of a howling blizzard. To this day, mountaineers are baffled as to how Johnson managed this prodigious achievement.

Several days later, an astounded "Wop" May discovered Johnson's tracks on the other side of the Divide, heading southwest towards Yukon's Eagle River. Hoping to head him off, Eames ordered the pilot to fly William Carter (May's spotter), Gardlund, Riddell, and himself to La Pierre House, an HBC post situated north of Johnson's location. After taking on supplies at the outpost, the four men travelled south on foot, eventually falling in with another eight-man Mountie patrol similarly tasked with bringing Johnson to justice. This other party consisted of Constable Sid May (no relation to "Wop"), Special Constables John Moses and Lazarus Sittichinli, Staff Sergeant Earl F. Hersey, Frank Jackson, and Peter Alexie.

After dropping off his passengers, May headed south to the Eagle River, quickly picking up Johnson's trail. As soon as he found it, however, he lost it again; Johnson had found the trail of a migrating caribou herd and had taken the opportunity to conceal his tracks within it. On February 14, May picked up his quarry's trail again, finding it twenty miles up the Eagle River.

On February 17, Staff Sergeant Earl F. Hersey, who had been ranging ahead of the Mountie posse, ran head-on into Johnson, who was in the process of stepping back through his own tracks. Hersey quickly overcame his surprise, raised his rifle, and started shooting at the outlaw. Johnson, in turn, ran a few paces towards the frozen Eagle River before suddenly whirling around and firing a single shot at his pursuer. Johnson's bullet hit Hersey in the left elbow, passed through his left knee, and buried itself into his chest, lifting Hersey clean off the ground in the process.

By this time, the rest of the 12-man posse had caught up with Hersey. Believing their fallen comrade to be dead, they broke into three groups and closed in on the 'Mad Trapper'. With no time to run, Albert Johnson planted his heavy pack in the snow in the middle of the Eagle River, took cover behind it, and prepared to make his last stand.

Johnson was subjected to a withering barrage as the Mounties took up positions around him, firing as they went. Gardlund, Jackson, Moses, and Ethier worked themselves into a particularly advantageous position, flanking Johnson by climbing up to a high bank behind him, before shooting him three times. One bullet passed through his shoulder, another buried itself into his side, and a third detonated a cluster of ammunition in his pocket, blowing a chunk of flesh out of his thigh. Incredibly, the 'Mad Trapper' seemed impervious to his wounds, firing round after round at his assailants with unnerving accuracy.

As the shootout raged on, "Wop" May circled over the battlefield in his bush plane. After a particularly long spell between shots, he flew in for a better look. He described this moment in a later reminiscence, saying:

"As I flew over the fugitive's lair it seemed as though he was lying in an unnatural position. Swinging back, I nosed the Bellanca down till our skis were tickling the snow. Johnson, I could plainly see as I flashed past, was lying face down in the snow, his right arm out-flung grasping his rifle. I knew as I looked that he was dead."

May landed his plane nearby as the Mounties cautiously approached Johnson's lifeless body. "As I stooped over and saw him" said the pilot, "I got the worst shock I've ever had. For Johnson's lips were curled back from his teeth in the most terrible sneer I've ever seen on a man's face ... It was the most awful grimace of hate I'd ever seen -the hard-boiled, bitter hate of a man who knows he's trapped at last and has determined to take as many enemies as he can with him down the trail he knows he's going to hit."

Both Johnson and the wounded Hersey were flown back to Aklavik, where the latter eventually made a full recovery. A crude autopsy revealed that the Mad Trapper had sustained seven bullet wounds during the firefight, the mortal wound being a devastating shot through the pelvis which wreaked havoc upon his internal organs. On his person, the Mounties found $2,410 in Canadian bills; five American banknotes; a glass jar containing five pearls and five pieces of golden dental fillings; a jar of alluvial gold; a Model 99 Savage 30-30 rifle and thirty-nine 30-30 cartridges; a 16-gauge Iver Johnson shotgun and four shotgun shells; a Winchester .22 rifle; a compass; thirty-two Beecham's Pills (a 19th Century "cure-all" patent medicine); a woodcutter's axe; a packsack; a can of lard; a dead squirrel; and a dead whisky jack.

In the wake of Johnson's death, many ideas were put forth as to the identity of the mysterious 'Mad Trapper of Rat River,' who had evaded the indomitable RCMP for 48 days in one of the most rugged regions in the world. Some thought that he was simply a trapper who lost his mind after years of isolation in the bush. Others were certain that he was ex-military, perhaps a shell-shocked veteran of WWI. Many suspected that he was an illegal immigrant looking to lie low, or perhaps an intelligence operative for a foreign nation. Others still suspected that he was a criminal, perhaps a bank robber, who fled north in the hope of evading justice.

Dick North- a Yukon-based author who wrote a number of excellent non-fiction books on the history of the Canadian and Alaskan North- made a compelling case in his 1972 book *The Mad Trapper of Rat River: A True Story of Canada's Biggest Manhunt* that 'Albert Johnson' was really Arthur Nelson, a strange, silent, extremely antisocial woodsman who roamed the North Country from 1926 until his disappearance in the early 1930's. He went on to suggest that Nelson might have made occasional forays into the Nahanni Valley during the 1920's, where he murdered Yukon Fisher, Angus Hall, Phil Powers, and perhaps a number of other prospectors for their gold teeth. After killing his victims, Nelson pried out their gold dental work before cutting off and disposing of their heads in order to disguise his crime. This, North suggested, might account for the eight mysterious gold fillings the Mounties found in a glass jar among Mad Trapper's personal effects.

North's theory that Johnson killed Fisher, Hall, and Powers for their dental work was called into question in 2009, when a forensic team exhumed the Mad Trapper's remains and conducted a series of tests on them. The team's efforts were showcased in *Hunt for the Mad Trapper*, a documentary produced and directed by Canadian filmmaker Michael Jorgensen in partnership with Discovery Channel Canada. In this documentary, forensic odontologist (an expert in the study of teeth) David Sweet, upon examining Johnson's teeth, voiced his opinion that the eight gold fillings that Johnson carried in a glass jar at the time of his death were, in fact, his own.

———————◆———————

Although many of the Nahanni's mysterious deaths and disappearances could potentially be blamed on rogue frontiersmen like the Mad Trapper of Rat River, the same cannot be said for the disproportionate number of adventurers who have lost their lives (or their minds) in the region under supposedly natural circumstances, nor the strange, haunting atmosphere which many feel hangs over the valley like a spell. For some, the only explanation for these and other chilling phenomena lies in the realm of the supernatural.

The Evil Spirit

———————+———————

"For many years, the Indians had told of evil spirits roaming through a valley on the South Nahanni River... Here, among fog-bound caves, evil spirits lurked, ready and able to do away with any interloper."

- Al Masters, *Lost Gold Mine of Shangri-La Valley*, 1972.

ANCIENT DENE LEGEND has it that the Nahanni Valley is a haunted place home to ghosts and spirits. These include the restless souls of those who have died there, as well as timeless supernatural entities endemic to the area. At least one of the vale's supposed spectral residents, the spirit called Ndambadezha, for whom travelling natives left gifts at the Rabbitkettle Hot Springs in order to ensure safe passage through the region, was believed to be benevolent. Many more, however, were reputedly malicious, and were said to beleaguer those who trespassed on their haunts.

The spirit that the Dene of the Mackenzie Mountains feared most of all was a malevolent entity most commonly associated with the caves that overlook the South Nahanni River. It was said that this demon could make men vanish "like smoke in the wind", and that, on windy nights, hunters brave enough to camp in the valley could sometimes hear it wailing in the canyons.

In the early 20th Century, when white frontiersmen began trickling into the Nahanni in search of gold and furs, few paid any heed to the legends. When their counterparts began dying and disappearing under mysterious circumstances, however, some began to wonder whether the old Indian tales might have some truth to them. Others flatly refused to give the stories any credence, dismissing these traditional native beliefs as fantastic myths based on unusual yet completely natural phenomena.

THE DENE PANTHEON

In order to contextualize the various supernatural entities Dene legend says haunt the Nahanni Valley, we must first come to a general understanding of traditional Dene beliefs regarding ghosts and spirits. One of the most comprehensive summaries of these beliefs can be found in the article *On the Superstitions of the Ten'a [Dene] Indians* by Canadian Jesuit missionary Father Julius Jette, first published in the 1911 issue of the anthropological and linguistic journal *Anthropos*. Jette, who lived among the Indians of the Yukon Valley from 1898 to 1929, divided the supernatural beings of Dene mythology into five broad categories: 1) The Greater Spirits; 2) The Souls; 3) The Shadow-Souls; 4) The Familiar Demons of the Shamans; and 5) The *Nekedzaltara*. We will take a look at the first four types of supernatural beings here in this chapter; the fifth category, the *Nekedzaltara*, will feature more prominently later on in this book.

The Greater Spirits

"Among the spirits with which the writer has become acquainted," wrote Jette, "there are four that stand in conspicuous prominence, and considerably outrank all the others." These include: a) The Spirit of Cold; b) The Spirit of Heat; c) The Spirit of Wind; and d) The *Tso-neteye*. The first three of these mythical beings are inextricably linked with natural elements, and might be classified by modern-day students of the occult as 'Elementals' – terrifying, ethereal, often hostile phantasms which embody particular forces of nature. The fourth of the Dene's Greater Spirits, the *Tso-neteye*, is an even more sinister entity than its malicious elemental counterparts.

The Spirit of Cold

Dzada-Kaka, the Spirit of Cold, reigns supreme during the winter. It delights in freezing people to death, yet subsequently covers the bodies of its victims in a blanket of snow in a perverse display of respect. Jette remarked in his article that an unusual number of Dene natives seemed to die at the approach of snowstorms, eerily corroborating the legend of the *Dzada-Kaka*, before suggesting that their deaths were actually attributable to atmospheric disturbances associated with the abrupt change in weather which usually preceded such storms.

Whether or not the Dene of the Mackenzie Mountains supposed this Greater Spirit to be responsible for the death of John O'Brien, who was found frozen solid near the peak of the Twisted Mountain in February 1922, crouched over a pile of kindling with a box of matches in his hand, is unknown.

The Spirit of Heat

Rolet-Kaka, the Spirit of Heat, holds sway over the earth in the summer months. This generally-benevolent entity battles with *Dzada-Kaka*, the Spirit of Cold, during the spring and autumn, and is perpetually at war with his frigid counterpart inside every human being, fighting to keep him or her from freezing to death. Legend has it that the crackling of the campfire is the *Rolet-Kaka's* way of asking for food, which one can provide by throwing small bits of meat into the flames.

The Spirit of Wind

The *Altsih-Kaka*, the Spirit of Wind, is the ruler of the aerial elements. According to Jette, Dene natives often invoked this spirit with songs and sacrificial offerings before embarking in their canoes in an effort to secure a safe journey.

Tso-Neteye

"The most dreaded of the Greater Spirits," wrote Jette, "is undoubtedly... *Tso-neteye* [literally 'The Bad Thing'] ... [Its] occupation is to kill men, and for this purpose, [it] sends over the earth sickness or disease, which the [Dene] conceive as a phantom-like spectre, prowling about, especially at night, when it is always dangerous to walk outside." *Tso-neteye* is assisted in its heinous endeavours by a shadowy legion of lesser demons, the aforementioned *nekedzaltara*.

The Souls

Long before missionaries brought Christianity to the subarctic, the Dene believed in reincarnation and the immortality of the *nokobedza*, the human soul. They also believed that the soul leaves the body after physical death, lingering for some time in the vicinity of the corpse. On the condition that the body in which it once resided is properly interred and the grave sufficiently tended to, the *nokobedza* eventually embarks upon a journey towards one specific location on earth called *Na-radenilna-ta*. Interestingly, to the Dene of the Yukon River, this spiritual destination was the site at which Dawson City was eventually established. The spirits dwell in this "transitional paradise" for some time before transmigrating into the zygotic body of a human or animal, thus repeating the cycle.

While waiting to be reincarnated, disembodied *nokobedza* "often wander about, at night, under the cover of darkness, or in the bright winter moonlight. In this respect, they resemble the ghosts of the white man's lore. People generally do not see them, but dogs and shamans sometimes enjoy this privilege. If a dog barks or howls at night... the conclusion is invariably that the animal has seen a ghost or devil."

According to Dene tradition, many a native hunter disappeared in the Nahanni Valley long before the arrival of the white man, never to return. As a *nokobedza's* ability to make the journey to *Na-radenilna-ta* is contingent upon the proper treatment of his or her earthly remains, it holds that the spirits of these victims still linger in the Nahanni where their bones lie, trapped between reality and the beyond, waiting in vain for a proper burial.

The Shadow-Souls

Ancient Dene tradition has it that *yega*, or shadow-souls, are protective spirits which inhabit all people, animals, plants, and most inanimate objects. While each human being has his or her own *yega*, there is only one *yega* for each individual "species" of lesser animal, plant, and object. "The *yega*," wrote Jette, "is a protecting spirit, jealous and revengeful, whose mission is not to avert harm from the person or thing which it protects but to punish the ones who harm or misuse it."

The Familiar Demons of the Shamans

Altaa, the ancient Dene maintained, are a special kind of *yega* far more powerful than the ordinary variety, yet subservient to shamans who command them to do their bidding. In many ways, these entities resemble the helpful *daemon* of Ancient Greek mythology- semi-divine spirit guides which constitute the souls of dead heroes- and the 'familiar spirits' of medieval European folklore- ethereal, animalic beings believed to aid witches and folk healers in their arcane enterprises. In both Dene and Inuit tradition, *yega* (called *tornat* in Inuktitut) serve as guardians and servants to medicine men who manage to secure their allegiance. With the help of an *altaa*, a shaman can perform all manner of extraordinary feats, such as casting curses, conferring luck, curing diseases, conversing with spirits, and learning hidden secrets.

In his letter on the subject, Poole Field mentions that the madness of Atah the Mountain Indian was nurtured by the medicine men of his band, who told the young brave that the grizzly bear with which he had a nearly-fatal encounter was sent after him by Field's friend Oskar, his romantic rival and a shaman in his own right. It is likely that these Mountain Indian medicine men believed that Oskar was able to control the bear through an *altaa*, or that the bear was, in fact, the physical manifestation of an *altaa* whose powers Oskar had harnessed.

THE WIND

One theme that recurs in nearly every version of the legend of the evil spirit of the Nahanni Valley is the entity's haunting vocalizations. Variously described as a wail, a moan, a howl, and a shriek, this chilling lamentation is almost always associated with wind, evoking images of the *Altsih-Kaka*, the Spirit of Wind.

Over the years, a number of frontiersmen have commented on the uncanny human quality of the sound the wind makes rushing through the Nahanni's canyons. Frank Henderson, for example, upon returning from a fruitless search for his missing partner, inflamed the imaginations of Canadians by declaring: "There is absolutely no denying the sinister atmosphere of the whole valley. The weird, continual wailing of the wind is something I won't soon forget."

The following year, Pierre Berton made his famous expedition to the Nahanni with Russ Baker, Art Jones, and Ed Hanratty. In a later reminiscence, the journalist eloquently illustrated the chilling effect that the sound of the Nahanni's wind had on him and his companions during their time in Deadmen Valley, writing:

"And as we stood there in the silence... we heard in the distance an eerie and spine-chilling sound. A low, howling whine swept out of the mountain down into the valley, died, and rose again in greater intensity. Was this the great evil spirit which the Indians claimed lurked in the mountains? ...Standing there in Deadman's Valley, not far from the spot where the McLeod bodies were found, on that cold day in 1947, I felt it as strongly as anyone could. The wind was beginning to rise in the canyons, and bursting into the great bowl of the valley it began to whine

almost like a living thing. The banshee wail made our hackles rise, for this was, without a doubt, the spirit sound so many men talked and whispered about."

Berton went on to describe how this same wind, sometime prior to their arrival, had evidently whipped the snow of Deadmen Valley into massive hillocks, among which were strewn trees that had been uprooted as if by "a giant hand."

Raymond Patterson also made note of the strange sounds of the Nahanni's winds in an interview, characterizing the Nahanni's canyons as "wind funnels". In his personal journal, he recounted a spooky wind-related experience in Deadmen Valley which he neglected to include in *Dangerous River*: "In the afternoon, a curious wailing came on the wind from us downstream, like the voice of a man in danger- probably the call of a lynx."

Mel Ross, during his 1958 expedition with his wife, Ethel, also made a few remarks on the sound in his documentary *Headless Valley*, saying:

"With… one of the famous winds of the Nahanni whistling and moaning through the crags above, we could easily understand how the natives had allowed their taboos about those canyons. When one of those winds funnels down through the canyon, there's howling and laughing and shrieking like millions of devils. Every crack and crevice of the canyon walls gives off some sort of weird sound."

SPOOKY FORMATIONS

Many of those who disregarded the legends of the Nahanni's phantoms believed that these stories stemmed not only from the eerie, human-like quality of the Nahanni's winds, but also from some of the region's strange-looking natural formations, such as the foreboding caves of the First Canyon or the spectacular Rabbitkettle Hot Springs. Dene hunters who came upon these unearthly landmarks centuries ago, they argued, regarded them with fear and awe, and concluded that their strangeness was an indication that they attracted, engendered, or were created by ghosts and spirits.

Caribou River Hoodoos

One of the Nahanni's many bizarre-looking natural structures is a cluster of sandstone hoodoos situated across the Flat River from the mouth of the Caribou. The Flat River being the site of so many mysterious incidents, it is not inconceivable that superstitious Dene natives took these concretions as evidence of a supernatural presence in the area.

Devil's Kitchen

Although it is not certain whether local Dene natives ascribed the Caribou River hoodoos with supernatural qualities, one section of the Nahanni Valley which definitively aroused superstitious terror is a strange place known today as Devil's Kitchen, or the Sand Blowouts. This area, situated on the southeast slopes of Mattson Mountain near the Splits, is littered with otherworldly, wind-sculpted sandstone pillars which Peter Jowett likened to the sculptures of English artist

Henry Moore.[1] According to Jowett, "many of these features have a layered appearance caused by ribbons of different coloured sand, and range in colour from gleaming white to purple."

As weird as they are, these aeolian formations are not the Devil's Kitchen's eeriest attributes, especially when considered in conjunction with the legend of the Nahanni's evil spirit. As one writer put it, "A banshee wild wails [there], and men are said to have plunged through a brittle crust of soil- and disappeared..."

In an interview, Gus Kraus described Devil's Kitchen in detail, supplementing his depiction with a chilling tale which may shed some light the origin of its sinister reputation. "Nobody went to that thing, you know," he began.

Many years ago, while visiting Nahanni Butte, Kraus asked Poole Field and Jack LaFlair what they thought of the strange place near the summit of Mattson Mountain, which appeared as a white blemish on the mountainside when viewed from the river. The two traders suspected that its irregular colour was attributable to some sort of salt or soda, but admitted that they had never seen the place up close.

Later on, Kraus asked the same question to an elderly Indian named Matou. "Never go there," the old man warned him. "We call that 'The Wind'... Long time ago, somebody

---

[1] Most of Henry Moore's sculptures are smooth abstractions of the human figure characterized by hollow spaces and lack of detail.

tracked a moose in that place, and pretty soon the moose didn't come out. So he made a complete circle, and finally hit his track again. He followed him, and that was it... no more track. The Wind took him. Dangerous place."

For Kraus, Matou's tale evoked the old Indian legend of the evil spirit who could make men vanish into thin air. Instead of frightening him, however, the elder's story imbued in him a burning desire to see what really lay at the top of Mattson Mountain. Kraus told the tale to Mary, his Dene wife, and in no time the fearless couple were bushwhacking their way towards the mysterious location.

"Heck, it was no goldarn patch on the mountain," said Kraus. "It's just darn near flat up there, just as flat as can be. All sand... as fine as talcum powder, like flour, to any grade of sand you want... and every colour you can think of. There's brown, there's red, there's blue, purple..." As Parks Canada puts it on their website, "the entire setting seems more evocative of a beach or desert environment rather than its actual location in a pine forest high on a mountain."

Kraus went on to describe the strange sandstone formations there, including spheres of all sizes, some of them stacked upon one another in seemingly unnatural arrangements; weird structures eerily akin to flying saucers; and a hollow, thirty foot pillar shaped like a harp. "You'd swear it was made [by humans]," he said.

Some of the concretions looked "like bones," Kraus continued. "Like old, cooked-out bones... So Mary says, 'It's the Devil's Kitchen. He [threw all the bones out] here on the sand.' So we named it 'Devil's Kitchen.'"

"So anyhow, you walk on this sand and you'd swear you're walking on a drum... boom, boom... every step. So, we fooled around there for a while and then we left.

"So the next time we came up, we told this to the game warden, Vic Shattuck, and him and his brother comes in. They wanted to see it and take some pictures. So, we went up again, and of course, Vic, he started walking all around and... bang! He went through. Up to his goldarn... hip! We would pull his leg out and the sand [would] just go and pour and fill up again. So, I see now where that guy's moose went in the wind. That thing is hollow underneath. That moose went through."

Kraus went on to describe a nearby seam of coal which burned day and night for decades on end, as well as a number of smooth, shiny trees which stood a short distance away, their trunks and limbs polished to a sheen by wind-blown sand.

The Cemetery

Later on, in the same interview in which he described Devil's Kitchen, Gus Kraus alluded to another strange area in the Nahanni Valley near the head of Mattson Creek.

"In the wintertime, when you come in there," he said, "you'll see these big frost forms, some five feet, six feet high, and all sizes- some almost two feet in diameter, some a foot. It looks just like a cemetery- a graveyard with the tombstones. When you go over there and just give it a tap, the whole thing falls in, and up- poof! – comes a warm, real warmed-up air... It really would be a dangerous place to walk if it wasn't frosted, because, should that be covered with snow, and you come without snowshoes... you'll fall in... That's it. You can't see the bottom of it." Kraus suspected these frost formations were formed by seams of burning subterranean coal similar to the one near Devil's Kitchen.

THE STAPHYLOCOCCUS MENINGITIS THEORY

In September, 1946, a novel theory was advanced purporting to explain a number of Nahanni legends, including the fate of the fabled Naha tribe, the reason for the disproportionate number of mysterious deaths and disappearances, the origin of the valley's 'curse', and the phenomena behind Dene legends of ghosts and evil spirits. This theory strongly evokes the *Tso-Neteye*, "the most dreaded of the Greater Spirits," said to kill men with sickness and disease, aided in its task by demonic minions, the *nekedzaltara*.

While on a business trip in Ottawa, Donald Carroll, a member of the United States Geological Survey, proposed that, many years ago, the original inhabitants of the Nahanni

Valley- members of the legendary Naha tribe- were wiped out "by an epidemic of a very virulent staphylococcus type of meningitis, which is extremely infectious." Carroll suggested that this flesh-eating, brain-addling bacteria may have been introduced to the region "by Russian trappers from Alaska." Dene warriors who stumbled upon the remains of the Naha villages deduced that their ancient enemies had been stricken by an evil spirit that lived in the area, and decided to give the Nahanni Valley a wide berth in order to avoid its wrath.

"The half-ruined stone huts [of the Naha tribe] are still standing," Carroll reported, "and whoever takes shelter in them contracts the extremely infectious disease. The bacteria is of the type which can remain dormant for considerable time. It appears that when trappers, hunters, and prospectors were in the region, they naturally sought the shelter of the huts which were still standing. The warmth of the camp-fires would quickly rouse the bacteria from its dormant state." The prospectors and trappers were subsequently devoured by the disease, their mysterious fates giving rise to the legend of the curse.

A number of contemporary newspaper and magazine articles reported that, subsequent to Carroll's proposition, a doctor made a special journey to the Nahanni Valley with the aim of collecting samples of the bacteria, hoping to either affirm or refute Carroll's claim. Whether or not this physician was successful in his endeavours remains a mystery.

STRANGE EXPERIENCES

Although it might be tempting to dismiss the old Indian legends of ghosts and spirits in the Nahanni as superstitions derived from a healthy respect for the forces of nature, spooky natural formations, the unearthly acoustics of the valley's canyons, or an epidemic of deadly bacteria, these explanations cannot account for a variety of odd happenings which have plagued the region's explorers since the days of Willie and Frank McLeod. One frontiersman who related his own unexplainable experiences in the Nahanni to the author of this book is Anthony Roche, a Northern Canadian of aboriginal descent who has spent much of his life in the subarctic bush.

In July 2010, while in the employ of Parks Canada, Roche was flown in to Rabbitkettle Lake, where he was tasked with clearing trails and stocking the warden cabin with firewood in preparation for winter. It was a lonely job, especially since canoeists were precluded from the river above Virginia Falls at that time on account of forest fires. Roche, however, had no other plans that summer, and was happy for the work.

After two weeks of solitude at Rabbitkettle Lake, Anthony Roche was joined by two colleagues whom we will refer to as Mike and Jen. The three coworkers spent their days labouring in the bush, and shared the warden cabin at night.

"One day," said Roche, "after a morning of splitting and hauling wood, we all jumped in the lake to cool off. Mike and I cooked lunch, and it was Jen's turn to do the dishes. While Jen did the dishes, Mike went for a nap, and I dozed off, too.

"I could hear Jen fiddling with the dishes and walking through the cabin, and at some point, it was quiet." After a few minutes of silence, Roche heard someone, who he assumed was Jen, walk through the kitchen and into the room where he and Mike were snoozing. Mike was dozing on the upper level of a bunk bed, while Roche lay face-down on the bottom level.

"I felt a light tap on my heel," said Roche, "and presumed Jen wanted me to dry the dishes. So I mumbled, 'yeah, yeah,' and fell asleep again.

"A short time later, the footsteps returned to the room, but from the living area this time, and I felt a light shake on my right shoulder. Again, thinking it was Jen trying to wake me up, I just shrugged it off and tried to get more sleep.

"The footsteps came back, a little more stern-sounding, like she was angry. I then felt an almost violent shake on my right shoulder. The footsteps left the room, and I woke up."

Upon rising, Roche made a trip to the outhouse just outside the cabin. When he returned, he found Jen asleep on the couch. Thinking it odd that she had fallen asleep so quickly, he roused her and inquired as to her reason for waking him up. Puzzled, Jen told him that she had been asleep for some time, and had not so much as entered the bunkroom after finishing the dishes.

Roche felt a chill run down his spine. "I looked at the clock, and it was 5:34 in the evening. Mike was on the top bunk, and I would have known if he had gotten off the bed, but I woke him and asked him anyway." Mike claimed to have heard the footsteps, too. Like Roche, however, he assumed that it was Jen who had been walking around the cabin.

"I didn't think too much of it," Roche concluded. "I've lived in the bush and tundra all my life. Weird stuff does happen, whether people want to believe it or not."

Who or what strove to attract Anthony Roche's attention that summer day in 2010? Is it possible that he had a brush with one of the spirits whose inhabitation of the Nahanni Valley the Dene of the Mackenzie Mountains have long affirmed? Perhaps Roche was visited by the forlorn ghost of one of the region's many victims, doomed to wander the accursed valley that had claimed its earthly body. These unsettling suppositions gain credence when considered alongside another strange event which took place in the same area shortly afterwards.

"About a month later," Roche told the author, "I was back at Rabbitkettle with two more coworkers and a student who was making promotional videos for the Parks in the southern Northwest Territories." One evening, after a long day of filming, the four companions settled down for a meal beside an open fire. The sky was overcast, and thunder rolled ominously in the distance, heralding an oncoming storm. Once they had finished eating, Roche and his fellow guides took out their field glasses began to casually scan the hills for bears and other wildlife. Nearby, the film student went about editing his day's footage.

While they looked through their binoculars, Roche and his coworkers heard a peculiar sound emanating from somewhere in the woods. To Roche, the noise was unmistakable: it was a man attempting to imitate a raven. "Growing up," he explained, "my brothers and I would often imitate ravens. We did it for years, and we weren't close to the real thing. Neither was what I heard."

Roche was bewildered, as he had been under the impression that he and his companions were the only people on the river at that time; canoeists were still forbidden from the valley upriver from Virginia Falls due to the forest fires. He looked to one of his older colleagues, who casually said, without offering any further explanation, "He's just letting us know he's there."

"Almost immediately after," said Roche, "the wind picked up, and we could clearly hear a woman singing. Again, I asked if either man had an idea of who or what it was. Both shook their heads and looked as puzzled as I did.

We all grew up on the land, and knew the wind doesn't sing like a woman."

What did Anthony Roche and his companions hear that day at Rabbitkettle Lake? Were they the calls of the Nahanni's timeless spirits come to declare their presence? Were they the anguished wailings of tormented souls returned to haunt the living? Or was it all just a trick of the wind?

———◆———

In addition to ghosts and spirits, the Dene of the Liard River and the Mackenzie Mountains believed that another type of being, more corporeal yet no less menacing, haunted the caves, canyons, and forests of the Nahanni Valley. This somewhat indefinable entity is perhaps best separated into three often-conflated sub-categories: the Naha tribe, the Nahanni Indians, and the Nakani.

The Nahanni Indians

———◆———

"The Nahanni, they said, was straight suicide. The river was fast and bad, and if a man ever did get through those canyons what would he find in that little-known country of the Yukon divide? Gold–gold without end, guarded quite likely by horned devils for all anybody knew to the contrary, but certainly by the wild Mountain Men–Indians who never came in to any trading post either in the Yukon or in the Northwest Territories. They lorded it over the wild uplands of the Yukon-Mackenzie divide and made short work of any man, white or Indian, who ventured into their country. Just ask the Indians here, or better still, the Indians at Fort Wrigley. Why, you couldn't bribe them with all the marten in the North to go back west more than thirty miles from the Mackenzie! No–we'd better all have another drink and be sensible and forget about the South Nahanni."

- Raymond M. Patterson, *Dangerous River*, 1954.

IN THE SPRING OF 1908, when word spread of the discovery of Willie and Frank's headless skeletons on the banks of Deadmen Valley, many regional mountain men were convinced that the brothers had met their ends at the hands of Nahanni Indians. Very little was known about these mysterious mountain-dwelling natives, seldom seen but for their infrequent visits to trading posts on the Liard or Ross Rivers, although the Slavey of the Liard River, the Kaska of southeastern Yukon, and the Mountain Indians of the Mackenzie Mountains seemed to be deathly afraid of them. Many frontiersmen agreed that the Nahanni were fiercely protective of their territory, the watershed of the South Nahanni River, and that they were notoriously hostile to trespassers.

When the Nahanni Indians learned that they were suspected in the murders of the McLeod boys, they retreated deeper into the wilderness and refused to speak with any inquiring Mounties on the subject of Willie and Frank McLeod. Without any evidence to incriminate them, the Mounties decided to leave them in peace.

RAYMOND PATTERSON'S ENCOUNTER

Twenty years later, following the mysterious deaths of Martin Jorgensen, John O'Brien, and Yukon Fisher, Raymond Patterson found himself alone in Deadmen Valley; Gordon Matthews, his partner, had just departed for Nahanni Butte. The two Englishmen, cognisant of the sinister reputation of the Nahanni Indians, had brought Chinese firecrackers and rockets into the country in order to frighten off the natives if necessity demanded, but had used them all to celebrate New Years' Eve, by which time it had become clear to them that "the dreaded Nahannis were down to a small, miserable remnant, gathered round the posts on the Liard."

Apparently, in the two decades that followed the discovery of the McLeod brothers, tuberculosis and other ailments had reduced the Nahanni Indians to a relatively harmless scattering of hunters and trappers reliant upon HBC trade goods.

One cold day in January, 1929, while alone in his cabin in Deadmen Valley, Patterson was suddenly and unexpectedly visited by a party of Nahanni Indians. The natives had approached the cabin in complete silence, and Patterson only became aware of their presence when their leader stepped into his doorway, casting a shadow across the floor. "Not being addicted to jumps and sudden starts," wrote Patterson, "I contrived to show no surprise, which was the reverse of what I felt."

Patterson invited the Indian inside for tea and set about preparing a fire. The Nahanni obliged, silently entering the cabin and sitting on Matthews' bunk "without the faintest flicker of expression on his face." He was soon joined by seven equally-taciturn companions. "There they sat watching me intently; no murmur came from them nor any sign, and the place looked like some primitive woodcut that might well have been entitled 'The Council House.'"

When he got a fire going in the cast iron oven, Patterson placed a large aluminum pot on the stove top and filled it with water. The prospect of such a large quantity of tea elicited some nudging and grinning amongst the Indians.

While the water heated, Patterson asked his Nahanni visitors a number of questions, which they attempted to answer using signs and gestures, and ascertained that they had come from the west through the valley of the Meilleur River, a tributary of the South Nahanni. "They seemed quiet enough and peaceful," he wrote, "and I thought of the sinister reputation that rumour had assigned to them. Here was I alone with them, and, by all the rules, I ought very shortly to be headless. Yet there was no sign of immediate action, and they were intensely interested in the preparations for tea. The water was boiling now in the bucket: I threw in a huge handful of Orange Pekoe, followed it up with about half a pound of sugar and stirred the bubbling concoction vigorously with a stick. A murmur of satisfaction went round and from a shadowy corner came, in a deep voice, 'Lots of tea!' followed by a quiet chuckle. So they were not mute, after all."

Soon, the nine men were joined by a mustachioed, mackinaw-clad, Stetson-wearing Yukon Indian named Barney who was travelling with the Nahanni Indians at that time. Barney spoke both English and the language of the Nahanni Indians in addition to the Yukon Dene dialect of his own people, and served as an interpreter for both Patterson and his unexpected guests. Through Barney, Patterson learned that this band of Nahanni had returned from a hunting excursion on the Beaver River- a tributary of the Liard River which runs parallel to the South Nahanni in the southwest- and had travelled to Deadmen Valley by way of the westerly Meilleur River. After exchanging some pelts for tea and sugar at Jack LaFlair's trading post at Nahanni Butte, the Indians planned to make another trip to the Beaver River for the spring beaver hunt before returning to the South Nahanni in moose skin boats by way of the Liard.

"They must have been well tanked up on my tea now," wrote Patterson, "but they stayed with it manfully and drained that bucket to the last dregs. Then they rose up and departed, without a word or a smile, and I sat there and scratched my head and thought, well, it was probably their way of doing things..." No sooner had he set to washing out the tea pot, however, than Patterson heard a thud on the roof of his cabin. When he went outside to investigate, he found the Nahanni Indians retreating down the frozen South Nahanni on dogsled. Turning around, he discovered a large quantity of moose meat sitting on a corner of his cabin's roof- a gratuity for his hospitality, courtesy of the Nahanni Indians.[1]

It is possible that Raymond Patterson was one of the last white men to lay eyes on true Nahanni Indians. According to Mary Kraus in an interview with Northern Canadian writer Lyn Hancock, the mysterious tribe was all

---

[1] It is interesting to note that, while Patterson described the story of his surprise encounter with the Nahanni Indians in *Dangerous River* and elaborated upon it in an interview conducted by a representative of Parks Canada, he curiously failed to mention it in his personal journal.

but wiped out in an epidemic of influenza that ravaged the North Country in 1929, a year after Patterson's encounter.[2]

FLYNN HARRIS' STATEMENT

Although the theory that the Nahanni Indians were behind many of the Nahanni Valley's unexplained deaths and disappearances was a popular one in the Mackenzie region throughout the first half of the 1900's, not every northerner believed the reclusive natives to be habitual murderers. Quick to leap to their defence was Thomas William "Flynn" Harris, the Indian Agent at Fort Simpson- a truly remarkable individual who deserves a brief profile here, if only for the purpose of entertainment.

Even in a land characterized by colourful characters, "Flynn" Harris was positively kaleidoscopic. "A thick-set man, with low brow, close cropped hair, and a terrible squint," wrote Philip Godsell of the man, "Flynn went to school with Sir Robert Borden[3] and was well on his way to becoming an

---

[2] Although Mary Kraus believed that the last of the Nahanni Indians succumbed to disease in 1929, Pierre Berton, in the aftermath of his 1946 expedition to the Nahanni, wrote: "There are few Nahanni Indians left now, but those that are still around are highly primitive and superstitious people who believe in medicine men and won't shoot a wolf because they think it might be their own grandmother." Similarly, Canadian writer James Harley Marsh, in his 1996 book *The Canadian Encyclopedia*, reported that, as of 1996, there were 2,407 registered 'Nahani' Indians in Canada.

[3] Sir Robert Laird Borden served as the 8th Prime Minister of Canada from 1911-1920.

outstanding criminal lawyer when the Call of the Wild and an excessive thirst drove him into the arms of the Mounted Police, whom he assisted in the capture of Chief Big Bear[4]."

Following a ten-year career with the NWMP, Harris found employment with the Hudson's Bay Company. He worked his way up the company's ranks to become Factor of Fond-du-Lac, a tiny HBC trading post on the shores of Lake Athabasca, located in what is now Northern Saskatchewan. Much to the astonishment of his superiors, Harris, while stationed at this godforsaken outpost, requisitioned two pencils, a daybook and ledger, and a whopping five gallons of red ink. When the RCMP Commissioner inquired as to what Harris intended to do with such a prodigious quantity of ink, the Factor replied, "What I don't use, I abuse!" Apparently, Harris had an enormous appetite for alcohol, and would often resort to red ink, shoe polish, and antiseptics when more conventional beverages were unavailable. According to Jean Godsell, Philip's wife, Harris, "when in his cups... would conduct the business of the agency or the post office in his birthday suit, calling between splurges of work and copious draughts for Caroline, his [Chipewyan] wife, to slap him vigorously on the back and *'bust me gall!'*"

---

[4] Chief Big Bear was a 19th Century Plains Cree chief and an ally of Metis revolutionary Louis Riel in the 1885 North-West Rebellion, a military conflict fought between Metis rebels and their Cree and Assiniboine allies and Canadian government forces in what is now Central Saskatchewan and East-Central Alberta.

By all accounts, Harris was an extraordinarily learned man in both the academic sense and the practical. By the time he was appointed Magistrate and Indian Agent at Fort Simpson in 1911, he was fluent in French, German, Spanish, Esperanto[5], Cree, Chipewyan, and six native dialects in addition to his native English, all of which he spoke with a lisp. He was also purported to have a remarkable grasp of Dene culture and perspective, and was often criticized for the leniency he extended towards the Indians and Metis with whom he was tasked with dealing.

In 1929, "Flynn" Harris attempted to combat the sinister reputation of the dwindling Nahanni Indians under his charge, reportedly asking Raymond Patterson and Gordon Matthews, as they prepared to leave Nahanni Country for the Outside, to "go to the *Edmonton Journal* office and try to put an end to 'all [those] damn fool stories about the headhunting Nahanni Indians.'" Later that year, when interviewed by a journalist during the 1929 Nahanni gold rush, Harris said, "There's no denying there have been some sudden deaths on the Nahanni, but no Indians were responsible for them. The Nahanni native is merely a slave, taking his name from the region in which he lives, and he has neither the inclination nor the ambition to go on the war path against the whites. I personally am convinced that [the dead and missing whom the

---

[5] Esperanto is an artificially constructed language designed specifically for international communication.

Nahanni Indians were accused of murdering] starved to death
and that the clues held up as proofs of crime were the work of
wolves or other animals that discovered the bodies."

EARLY ACCOUNTS

Although frontier legend and popular opinion held
that the Nahanni Indians were a violent and reclusive people,
both Flynn Harris' statement and Raymond Patterson's
experience suggest that members of this mysterious tribe may
have been unfairly maligned. Unfortunately, there are no
Nahanni Indians alive today whose oral lore might affirm or
refute these notions. In light of this uncertainty, the following
questions arise: Who really were these people and what role, if
any, did they have in the deaths and disappearances which
have given the Nahanni Valley such a sinister reputation? In
order to answer these questions, we must turn to history.

Nor' Wester Accounts

The first written reference to the Nahanni Indians
appears in the journal of Alexander Mackenzie, the Scottish
explorer who first navigated the mighty northward-flowing
Mackenzie River in 1789 on behalf of North West Company[6]
(NWC), hoping that it might constitute the legendary

---

[6] The North West Company, established in 1779, was a fur trading company
headquartered in Montreal, Quebec. In 1821, the enterprise, under pressure
from the British Crown, merged with its historic rival, the Hudson's Bay
Company.

Northwest Passage[7]. At the time of Mackenzie's expedition, the Canadian North was a sprawling, largely unexplored expanse of wilderness peopled almost exclusively by various Dene and Inuit tribes; in 1789, the only other non-aboriginals in the region were a handful of rugged Russian and Siberian *promyshlenniki* (sailors and fur trappers) who manned the trading posts of the Russian-American Company on the coast of Alaska, more than 550 miles to the west.

Throughout their expedition, Mackenzie and his crew made contact with the Slavey Indians of the Mackenzie River area and probed them for information on the flora, fauna, geology, and ethnology of the surrounding country. During one such interrogation, the Slavey told the explorers of a mysterious tribe of "Mountain Indians" who inhabited the westerly Mackenzie Mountains.

Although Alexander Mackenzie and his crew discovered a vast wilderness rife with fur-trading potential (eventually dubbed the 'Mackenzie District') during their 1789 expedition, the North West Company waited for seven years before attempting to avail themselves of its resources. In 1796, the company tasked a clerk named Duncan Livingston with founding a fur trading post on the Mackenzie River a short distance from its head at Great Slave Lake. Three years

---

[7] The Northwest Passage is a legendary waterway through North America which was said to connect the Atlantic Ocean with the Pacific. Alexander Mackenzie hoped that the Mackenzie River might prove to be this waterway, and allegedly named it 'Disappointment River' when he discovered that it emptied into the Arctic Ocean.

later, he and his crew attempted to retrace Alexander Mackenzie's route to the Arctic, but were massacred by Inuit warriors about 200 miles from their destination.

Undaunted, the Nor'-Westers, as the men of the North West Company were known, proceeded to establish a string of fur trading posts along the Mackenzie River and its tributaries throughout the early 1800's, at which they began trading with the local Slavey, Dogrib, Sahtu, and Hare Dene. One of these posts, built at the mouth of the Liard River in 1803 and christened 'Fort of the Forks', would later become Fort Simpson. Another post, built about 150 miles (240 km) down the Liard River from its confluence with the Mackenzie, was Fort Riviere-du-Liard, or Fort Liard.

During these early years of the Mackenzie Region fur trade, the watershed of the Liard River, and by extension the Nahanni Valley, was largely a mystery to the men of the North West Company. As historian Theodore J. Karamanski put it, "the traders had traveled the first 250 miles or so regularly, but nothing broke the obscurity of the Liard's upper stretches but the flickering lights of legends and Indian reports."

In 1807, the factor of Fort of the Forks, a Norwegian-born fur trader named Willard Ferdinand Wentzel, learned that the residents of this mysterious land to the west- the "Mountain Indians" alluded to in Alexander Mackenzie's journal- in fact consisted of three tribes: the Dahoteena, the Nombahoteenais, and the Nahanni. "The only information I can get concerning these Natives," Wentzel wrote in a letter to fellow NWC clerk Roderick McKenzie (a cousin of Alexander Mackenzie), "is that they inhabit these rocks, live upon caribou and goat flesh, and make war upon each other."

Hudson's Bay Company Accounts

In 1822, the North West Company, under pressure from the British Crown, merged with its main fur trading rival, the British-backed Hudson's Bay Company. That same year, the reclusive Dahoteena Indians of the Mackenzie Mountains, much to the delight of the fur traders, began appearing at Fort Norman and Fort Good Hope (two NWC-turned-HBC trading posts situated on the Mackenzie River) bearing furs for trade. Not long after that, westerly Indians who called themselves the "Umbahotinne" similarly came down from the mountains to trade at Fort of the Forks, which had been renamed 'Fort Simpson' that year in honour of Sir George Simpson, the Governor of the Hudson's Bay Company. The Umbahotinne, the traders discovered, were almost certainly the "Nombahoteenais" whom Wentzel learned inhabited the Mackenzie Mountains back in 1807. In this way, the HBC came into contact with two of the three Indian tribes said to inhabit the Mackenzie Mountains. The only mountain-dwelling Dene the fur traders had yet to meet were the mysterious Nahanni.

The Hudson Bay Company traders in the Mackenzie Valley quickly established rapport with their new clients and began to learn their language. Edward Smith, the Chief

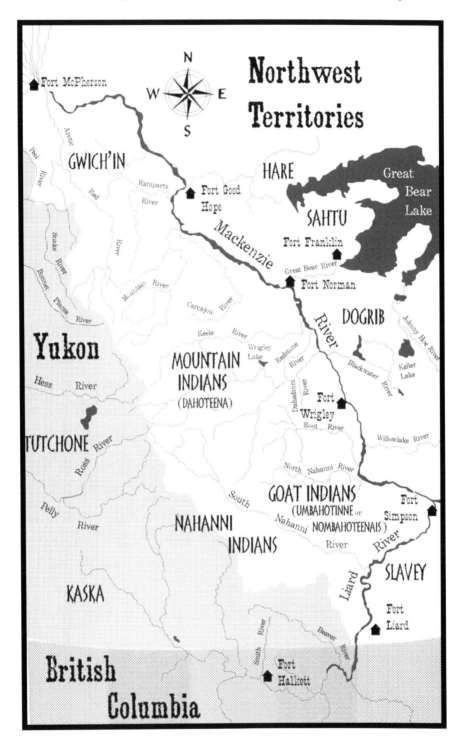

Factor of Fort Simpson, soon learned that the Dahoteena and the Umbahotinne were, in fact, members of the same tribe, and had different names only because the Nombahoteenais, who inhabited the southern Mackenzie Mountains, lived in mountain goat territory, while the more northerly Dahoteena did not.[8]

Edward Smith also learned from his Umbahotinne customers that a remote waterway called the *Naha Dehe*- the river we know today as the South Nahanni - was the dividing line which separated the Umbahotinne from the territory of their westerly neighbours, the Nahanni Indians. Smith and his companions were peripherally familiar with this watercourse, as its mouth entered the Liard River roughly halfway between Fort Liard and Fort Simpson, but had not yet explored it.

On the subject of the Nahanni Indians themselves, the Umbahotinne were curiously tight-lipped, almost as if they feared that mere mention of the mysterious tribe might somehow invite misfortune. This sentiment was shared by the Slavey of the Mackenzie River, who whispered that the Nahanni were a tribe of fearsome giants cursed by the gods for their evil and unnatural practices.

---

[8] According to ethnographer Beryl C. Gillespie, the Dahoteena were probably the people known today as the 'Mountain Indians' the natives with whom Poole Field travelled in the early 1900's , while the Umbahotinne were likely the people known today as the 'Goat Indians.'

In spite of their reticence to discuss their westerly neighbours in any detail, the Umbahotinne disclosed that Nahanni territory was rich in beaver. Smith relayed this exciting information to his superior, George Simpson, and in no time, the Governor made plans for an expedition up the *Naha Dehe* with the objective of contacting the Nahanni Indians.

Alexander McLeod's Expedition

That winter, Alexander Roderick McLeod (no relation to Willie and Frank), the HBC's Chief Trader of the Mackenzie District, hired a handful of Slavey trappers and headed up the frozen Liard River from Fort Simpson, bound for Nahanni territory. Little is known about this first HBC expedition into Nahanni Country, although historians surmise that Alexander McLeod and his party reached the mouth of the South Nahanni River without incident and began travelling upriver. To McLeod's dismay, the party did not encounter any of the legendary Nahanni Indians, and were eventually forced to retreat to Fort Simpson.

John McLeod's 1823 Expedition

Upon returning to the trading post, Alexander McLeod wrote a letter to George Simpson informing him of his failure to contact the reclusive Nahanni Indians while at the same time assuring him of his intention to promptly appoint a promising young Scotsman named John M. McLeod (no relation to Alexander, Willie, or Frank) "to command a party... on a voyage of discovery to the Westward."

John McLeod, the man whom Alexander McLeod nominated to lead this second HBC expedition up the South Nahanni, was a tough, no-nonsense frontiersman respected by Indians and white men alike for his skill as a woodsman and his effective leadership style, which one historian described as "firm yet flexible." On June 5, 1823, he set out from Fort Simpson, bound for the South Nahanni. His team consisted of two French-Canadian voyageurs, a Metis translator, and seven Slavey guides.

After their first day struggling through the current of the Liard, McLeod rewarded his voyageurs with a glass of rum, and granted "a small quantity of very weak stuff to the Indians."

After four days of toiling up the Liard, the company made it to the mouth of the South Nahanni and began tracking their large, gift-laden canoe up the Splits. "The Courses of this river is very various," wrote McLeod in his journal, "and the Channels much obstructed by shoals and drift wood." When the party reached the mouth of what is now Mattson Creek, McLeod decided that they would make better time on foot and had his men cache the canoe on the shore. Instead of following along the banks of the South Nahanni, McLeod and his men shouldered their gear and struck inland, to the west.

As they hiked up and over the sharp, rocky ridges of the Tlogotsho Mountain Range, John McLeod and his crew supplemented their trail diet of pemmican and hardtack with fresh venison and mountain lamb. At regular intervals, they built huge bonfires near mountaintops, feeding them pine boughs and green branches so that they belched forth huge clouds of smoke. In those days, it was customary for the Dene to build such signal fires when entering the territory of a foreign tribe. If the tribe on whose territory the visitors encroached wished to meet the newcomers, they built smoky signal fires of their own. An absence of such fires meant that the natives wanted the newcomers to leave their territory. Ominously, the first few signal fires that McLeod and his men built went unanswered.

John McLeod and his men continued northwest, crossing five mountain ridges and what is now the Meilleur River. At the base of the sixth mountain ridge were a cluster of teepee rings, a scattering of age-weathered meat-drying racks, and the ashes of old campfires- evidence of an abandoned Nahanni spring camp. Beyond the seventh range, the explorers came upon a similar site, this one evidently an old Nahanni winter camp.

The HBC men proceeded to explore the area surrounding these camps before continuing west over two more ridges. After camping west of the ninth ridge for several days, John McLeod and his crew headed southeast. Four days later, while hiking above the treeline on a high mountain, bound for the South Nahanni, they came upon fresh moccasin tracks heading down a game trail in Indian file- signs that

Nahanni Indians were close at hand. The company men decided to follow them.

The Indian trail led down into the valley of what is now Jackfish River, which enters the South Nahanni near the head of the Splits, before twisting back up the mountainside towards the summit. The explorers managed to follow it, albeit with some difficulty. "The Nahany Indians make no scruple in climbing up precipices with their Women and Children," John McLeod noted in his journal, "where none of my men, and very few of the Indians would venture."

Upon reaching the summit, the explorers saw a plume of smoke in the distance- the unmistakable product of a Nahanni signal fire. They hastily built a signal fire of their own, indicating their willingness to meet with the mysterious Indians. They continued down the ridge towards the distant smoke, and soon the two groups came within sight of one another.

"Both parties approached each other very slowly," wrote McLeod. "Yelling, Singing and Dancing as they advanced, at 7 P.M. both partys joined unarmed, each holding a small piece of meat in their hand- shortly after a Dance was formed, which amusement continued for the remainder of the day."

The Nahanni Indians were fourteen in number and appeared to be in excellent physical condition. McLeod observed that their language "was fluent and harmonious, but they vociferate it out with such incredible force, that it is on the whole disagreeable." He summarized his first impressions of the Indians themselves thus:

> "The Nahanys appear to be a manly race of men and good hunters, they are smart, active and quick in their motions, and are not haughty, but seem to be peaceably inclined without the appearance of fears or meanness. They are Cleanly, Hospitable and Sociable."

The two parties camped beside each other that night and exchanged gifts in the morning. To the leader of the Nahanni band- a grizzled old hunter named White Eyes whom McLeod described as "a tall strong and robust built man" with a beard which gave him the "looks of an old Roman Sage"- the HBC men gave a "Chief's Coat" and a "Half Ax, Hand Dag. Knife [i.e. Dagger], Looking Glass [i.e. Mirror], Small Kittle [i.e. Kettle] and a small piece of Red Oriell feathers- which articles he seemed to be highly satisfied." To the rest of the band, they distributed fire strikers[9] and vermillion[10].

From the Nahanni Indians, John McLeod received a gift of seventeen martin pelts. McLeod allowed the Slavey under his command to trade some of their personal effects for

---

[9] Fire strikers are pieces of carbon steel used to start fires. When struck against sharp flint, they produce sparks.

[10] Vermillion is a rich red pigment made from powdered cinnabar mercury sulfide , historically used to produce red paint.

the Nahanni's remaining furs, which included, "a few Martins, some Beavers, Cats and a Bear Skin or two."

Later that day, John McLeod conversed with White Eyes through his Metis interpreter and learned much about the surrounding country. He also discovered that most of the Nahanni Indians lived in the so-called 'West Branch' of the Liard River (i.e. the upper Liard River; as opposed to the 'East Branch,' the watercourse we know today as the Fort Nelson River). Later that evening, he and his men joined the Nahanni around the campfire and spent much of the night singing and dancing to the throb of a moose-skin drum.

The following day, John McLeod and his crew made arrangements to meet with White Eyes and his Nahanni band the following year before bidding them *adieu* and starting for Fort Simpson. They arrived at the trading post on July 10, 1823, having sustained themselves on caribou, mountain sheep, moose, and a black bear on their homeward journey.

John McLeod's 1824 Expedition

One year later, on June 18, 1824, John McLeod set out from Fort Simpson with three voyageurs- two of them Metis, and the third a French-Canadian- and five Slavey Indians, determined to make good on his arrangement and rendezvous with White Eyes and his band. At that time, the Liard River was much higher and the current much stronger than it had been the previous year. To make matters worse, a sheet of ice skirted the riverbank, adding an element of danger to the gruelling process of tracking. In spite of the obstacles,

McLeod and his crew made it to the mouth of the South Nahanni on June 12 without serious mishap.

After lighting a huge signal fire, the explorers spent the night camped at the foot of Nahanni Butte. "Weather very Warm and Musquitoes worse and worse," wrote McLeod. The following morning, the party learned that some of their paddles had washed away down the Liard, the South Nahanni having risen three feet in the night to lap at their canoe and gear. Undaunted, they proceeded up the Splits.

After conquering a mere forty miles of the South Nahanni, John McLeod and his crew cached their canoe, shouldered their gear, and marched west up Jackfish River and into the Tlogotsho Mountains. As they had done in 1823, they lit signal fires at regular intervals atop the ridges they crossed, but received no reply.

On June 18, when they had reached a point at the very heart of the Tlogotsho Range, the Slavey under McLeod's command refused to proceed any further into Nahanni territory, afraid that the dreaded men of the mountains would slaughter their tiny party. As moose and mountain sheep were plentiful in the area at the time, McLeod agreed to camp there until the Indians worked up the nerve to continue.

On June 22, one of McLeod's crew spotted the smoke of a distant campfire. The following day, the party broke camp and set out in the direction from which it came in spite of the Slaveys' misgivings. McLeod wrote that his Indian employees "remonstrated for some time, but seeing that I was determined on going, they began to arrange their little bundels to follow."

The following day, the company encountered a lone Nahanni hunter to whom they gifted a steel knife. Later on, they came upon four more Nahanni, who they treated similarly.

On the afternoon of June 25, McLeod and his crew met up with White Eyes' band. They quickly learned, to their disappointment, that the Nahanni had endured a very hungry winter and, as such, had managed to accumulate very few furs. Determined to wrest some benefit from the expedition, McLeod then asked White Eyes if he would accompany him to Fort Liard. The chief vehemently refused when he learned that Fort Liard was situated in the territory of the Kaska Indians, with whom his people were at war. Alternatively, McLeod invited the Nahanni chief to accompany him and his men Fort Simpson- a proposal to which White Eyes reluctantly agreed. After an evening of singing, dancing, and gift-giving, the two parties retired for the night.

The following day, the Nahanni band escorted McLeod and his men on the first leg of their homeward journey. On the way, the party happened upon a herd of mountain caribou and managed to bring down nine animals in the ensuing hunt. After giving the grateful Nahanni most of the meat, the fur traders said their goodbyes and carried on alone, accompanied by White Eyes and his son and nephew.

The following morning, White Eyes awoke with a start, troubled by a terrifying dream, and expressed his desire to return to his people. John McLeod, however, "assured him that his dreams would turn out quite the reverse of what he then anticipated, after some time had elapsed in Interpreting the Old Leaders dreams, with some fine words and few promisses, he with some reluctance agreed to follow, and was under way at 5.0 a.m."

And so the company continued on through Nahanni Country, braving thunder and lightning, a swirling blizzard, and a spell of torrential rain. When they finally arrived at their cached canoe, hungry and frozen, they found that their pemmican had been eaten by martens. Inured to the privations of the trail, the hardy frontiersmen swallowed their disappointment in lieu of their rations, disembarked, and began paddling down the South Nahanni. The three Nahanni Indians were initially terrified when they found themselves afloat atop the rushing water, having never travelled by canoe before, but were eventually put at ease by McLeod.

The party made it safely down the South Nahanni and headed down the Liard without stopping, the voyageurs paddling throughout the night in shifts. The company men reached Fort Simpson at 5:00 p.m. on July 2, 1824 and showed the Nahanni Indians around the fort. The natives "seemed lost in astonishment and surprise" as they savoured their first taste of the white man's world.

After allowing the Indians a day to adjust to their new environment, Edward Smith, the Chief Factor of Fort Simpson, sat down with them and asked them a number of questions about their territory through an interpreter. After learning what he could, the company man instructed the Nahanni on how to dress skins so that the valuable fur was preserved.

That night, the fur traders treated their wide-eyed Nahanni guests to song and dance, regaling them with various Scottish, French Canadian, and Metis fiddle tunes. "Music seems to delight them," wrote John McLeod, "and in short they were lost in wonder and admiration." White Eyes thanked his hosts for their hospitality, saying:

"I am like a Child now in my own estimation, you treat us so well. That I have nothing to give makes me ashamed to speak, which is the reason I appear silent... all my Party and Children will be curious to come here and see what I have seen, it is the Whites who have made the Earth, we see that now."

The next day, John McLeod ferried the three Nahanni Indians over to the western shore of the Liard River. They provided them with 44 pounds of provisions and several gifts, leaving the White Eyes and his relatives "pleased and elated beyond description."

White Eyes' 1824 visit to Fort Simpson was the first serious step in a long, if tenuous, relationship between the Nahanni Indians and the Hudson's Bay Company. In no time, the Nahanni were making sporadic pilgrimages from their mountain homes to Fort Simpson, where they traded pelts for knives, hatchets, kettles, muskets, shot, and powder. By the late 1820's, some intrepid Nahanni even began to appear at Fort Liard.

The first written hint that the Nahanni Indians may not have been as "peaceably inclined" as John McLeod initially deduced came in November 1829, when Edward Smith, Chief Factor of Fort Simpson, wrote of these natives:

"In return for good usage, they are obedient and willing to please— in their general character there is something secret and treacherous— and once irritated very sanguinary— numerous and in a rich country might be very independent if it were not for their habits of indolence."

In spite of their perceived faults, however, the Nahanni Indians enjoyed a business relationship with the Hudson's Bay Company throughout the 19th Century and well into the 20th. Wrote Edward Smith to George Simpson on the subject of these occasional customers: "Altho' they inhabit a rich country, their wants few once completed they will not exert themselves." In the 1910's, the Nahanni also began taking their furs to independent trader Jack LaFlair and

Poole Field, who represented the Northern Traders Company, at Nahanni Butte.

Although the acquisition of firearms and metal tools greatly improved the quality of life of the Nahanni Indians, the Hudson's Bay Company's influence on these primitive mountain people was not entirely positive. In additional to European goods, the fur trade also inadvertently brought the Nahanni into contact with various 'white man diseases' to which they had no natural immunity. Epidemics of tuberculosis, smallpox, and influenza devastated their population throughout the latter half of the 19th Century, and tragically, sometime in the early-mid 1900's, the Nahanni Indians were completely wiped out.

IDENTITY

Early accounts indicate that the Nahanni Indians were a relatively friendly people whose territory stretched from the South Nahanni River west to the watershed of the western headwater of the Liard. As is the case with most Nahanni legends, however, there is more to the story than meets the eye.

Territory

White Eyes' 1823 claim that most of the Nahanni lived in the vicinity of the West Branch of the Liard was first called into question in the summer of 1825, when twenty-eight-year-old Murdock McPherson of the Hudson's Bay

Company led an exploratory party up the river from Fort Liard. Although McPherson and the handful of Kaska Indians under his employ tracked and portaged one hundred miles up the Liard's West Branch, passing through what White Eyes claimed was the heart of Nahanni Indian territory, they failed to see a single Nahanni Indian. This is perhaps not entirely surprising considering the information Raymond Patterson gleaned during his surprise visit in January, 1929, namely that the Nahanni Indians were a nomadic people who regularly travelled in pursuit of game. More mysterious, however, was the fact that the only abandoned campsites McPherson and his crew stumbled upon were so old that the drying racks they contained were cracked and silvered with age, indicating that the Nahanni had left the country long ago.

John McLeod led a similar expedition up the 'West Branch' of the Liard in the summer of 1831 along with six voyageurs, two Indians, and his "faithful dog" named Spring. McLeod and his men managed to reach one of the distant headwaters of the Liard River, conquering the Hell Gate Rapids, the Rapids of the Drowned, and the Devil's Portage. Throughout the course of their long and arduous journey, they encountered only two groups of people, one of them a band of Kaska, and the other a mysterious stranger who hurled stones at their camp at night, concealed by shadows and brush.[11]

Instead of shedding light upon the question of Nahanni territory, anthropological findings only sowed further confusion. In the 1940's, a Professor of Anthropology at the University of Carolina named John J. Honigmann conducted an investigation into the ethnology of the Nahanni Indians and learned from different sources that these natives were believed to have hunted all over the Canadian North, from the Kechika River area in Northern British Columbia, located not too far from the Toad and Liard River Hot Springs, to the Pelly River area in Southern Yukon, the historic home of the **Tutchone** Indians.

Many of Honigmann's native informants placed the Nahanni Indians in territory believed to have been controlled by the **Kaska**. In addition to the aforementioned source who claimed that the Nahanni frequented the Kechika River area, a popular Kaska haunt, another of Honigmann's informants placed Nahanni Indian territory in the vicinity of McDame Creek, a tributary of the Dease River situated in the middle of Cassiar Country, telling him that the Dease River was actually once called the 'Nahani River'. Yet another informant assured Honigmann that "'Nahani' merely constituted another name for the Kaska Indians". Similarly,

---

[11] Incidentally, two of John McLeod's voyageurs perished on the return journey from the headwaters of the Liard, disappearing beneath a boiling stretch of whitewater known as the Portage Brule Rapids.

Oblate missionary Emile Petitot, who tended to the spiritual needs of the Dene along the Mackenzie River in the 1860's and '70's, claimed that the Nahanni lived along the southwestern slopes of the Mackenzie Mountains- the eastern border of Kaska territory. Likewise, Canadian geologist and surveyor Dr. George Mercer Dawson, in his report regarding his aforementioned 1887 expedition through northern British Columbia and Yukon, wrote: "The Kaska form a portion of the group of tribes often referred to by the Hudson Bay Company's people as Nahaunie or Nahaunie..."

Another of Honigmann's sources claimed that the Nahanni were actually the more westerly **Tahltan** Indians, whose traditional homeland was the Stikine River Country. This assertion was corroborated by German-American anthropologist James Alexander Teit, whose learned that some of the Tahltan even considered themselves Nahanni, but only because the they were "so called by the Indians living east of them."

American ethnographer George T. Emmons, who learned much of Tlingit and Tahltan culture while serving as a U.S. Navy Lieutenant on the Alaskan coast in the late 1800's and early 1900's, added two subdivisions of the **Tlingit** of the Pacific Northwest to the list of tribes bearing the appellation 'Nahanni'.

To top it off, the writings of cultural anthropologist Catherine "Kitty" McClellan suggest that the **Tagish** of southwestern Yukon might also have been lumped into this category- a notion corroborated by Teit.

Tribe

Various frontiersman further muddied the waters by labelling the Nahanni as, or assigning them characteristics consistent with, other Dene tribes. For example, in an interview for Parks Canada, Raymond Patterson indicated that he was under the impression that the Nahanni were simply a subgroup of the **Slavey**, whose territory stretched from the Mackenzie River to the shores of Great Slave Lake and farther south into BC and Alberta.

Conversely, Billy Clark described how the Nahanni Indians would often camp along Wrigley Creek, a tributary which flows into the South Nahanni opposite the mouth of the Flat River, before travelling north through the mountains, building huge 25-foot-long moose skin canoes, and paddling down the Gravel (a.k.a. Keele) River to Fort Norman, where they traded their furs- a practice which Charles Camsell, in his book *Son of the North*, attributed to the **Mountain Indians** (a.k.a. Dahoteena), "the most intelligent and resourceful of all the Indians trading at Fort Norman." This notion that the 'Nahanni' were actually Mountain Indians is echoed in the journals of Alexander Hunter Murray, a 19th Century Hudson's Bay Company fur trader who founded Fort Yukon, Alaska, at the confluence of the Yukon and Porcupine Rivers (in the heart of Gwich'in territory) in 1847.

To make things even more confusing, Dick Turner, in his book *Nahanni*, wrote that, "the famous and war-like Nahanni Mountain Indians who wore Dall sheepskins as clothing were called 'Sheep Men' by the other northern Indian tribes"- an appellative suspiciously similar to that applied to the Umbahotinne: the **'Goat Indians'**.

Language

Another spin on the nature of the Nahanni Indians can be found in the journal of HBC fur trader Willard Ferdinand Wentzel. Having sat in on White Eyes' interrogation at Fort Simpson on July 3, 1824, Wentzel likened the language spoken by the Nahanni chief to that of the Kaska of Fort Liard. He also suggested that the Nahanni language had "a strong affinity to the [the tongue of the] **Beaver Indians** of Peace River." This last statement is doubly intriguing when considered alongside a letter written by George Keith- an HBC clerk who would go on to become the Chief Trader of the Athabasca, Mackenzie, and Great Bear Lakes Districts- to fellow clerk Roderick Mackenzie on January 7, 1807. In his letter, Keith related a story about an ancient tribe called the "Na ha ne", whose members inhabited the upper Liard River area for many years. Sometime in the late 18th Century, Keith claimed, this Stone Age tribe was driven out of Nahanni Country by a band of Beaver Indians, who migrated north into the region from their home in what is now northern British Columbia and Alberta, having been similarly displaced by Cree Indians.

The first Northern frontiersman to seriously analyse the language of the 'Nahanni' was an Oblate missionary named A.G. Morice. While working among the natives of Northern British Columbia in the 1880's, he attempted to classify the various dialects of the Dene. According to ethnographer Beryl C. Gillespie, who wrote an excellent article on the Nahanni Indians for Volume 6 of the Smithsonian Institution's 1981 tome *Handbook of North American Indians* (which focuses on the First Nations of the subarctic), Morice "described the Nahani as a dialect grouping of peoples known at present as Tahltan, Kaska, Taku [a subdivision of the Tlingit], Mountain, and perhaps the **Tsetsaut** [a Dene tribe which traditionally inhabited the land surrounding the Alaska-British Columbian border between the Stikine River and present-day Prince Rupert, BC]."

The Word 'Nahanni'

A final subject of contention regarding the nature of this mysterious tribe is the meaning of the word 'Nahanni'. English travel writer Michael H. Mason, who mushed about the North Country in 1920, claimed in his 1924 book *The Arctic Forests* that "Nahani" means "People of the West". Somewhat similarly, Gus Kraus, in an interview, said that, according to Oblate Missionary Father Le Guen (whose map of the McLeod diggings Jack Stanier and Billy Clark obtained through Father Turcotte), the word 'Nahani' means "setting sun", and the Nahanni Indians were called the "setting sun people". This interpretation was corroborated by Gus' Dene wife, Mary, who told an interviewer that 'Nahanni' means "the sun is tired and just... setting down."

Renowned Canadian anthropologist Diamond Jenness espoused a different interpretation of the word, which he included in his 1932 book *The Indians of Canada*. Jenness maintained that the term "Nahani" translates to "people over there, far away." John Honigmann, on the other hand, contended that the sub-word "Na" signifies "Enemy" or "Hostile". Conversely, Raymond Patterson, in *Dangerous River*, wrote that, according to Archie Gardiner, a frontiersman from Fort Nelson, the word "Nahanni" is "a sort of corruption, a white-man word. The proper Indian pronunciation for the Nahanni tribe is Na'anike, and it means, 'The people who speak like ducks'- their language being very different from the Slavey.'" According to an online Dogrib dictionary, the word "Nah'aa g t'ii," which bears some resemblance to 'Nahanni', means "Mountain People." And Dene language expert Allan Adam told the author of this book that "Na'aa" means "giant(s)," and that "Na'aahdee" – a word for the Nahanni River- means "River of Giants," evoking the old Slavey legend that the Nahanni were really a race of enormous, wicked Indians.

Theories

When one considers all of this conflicting information as a whole, two possibilities seem to present themselves. The first is that the Nahanni Indians were a nomadic people who travelled frequently and widely throughout the North Country, from the Yukon to Stikine Country to the Cassiar region to the Nahanni. The second- a theory put forth by John Honigmann- is that the Nahanni were not a distinct people at all, and that the word "Nahanni" was simply a term applied by various Dene people to distant and mysterious tribes whom they considered evil, untrustworthy, or hostile. "European visitors borrowed the appellation without fully understanding the context of use," Honigmann suggested. "By applying it to specific groups of Indians, they have complicated the tribal distribution pattern."

If Honigmann's hypothesis is correct, then who were the Indians who inhabited the watershed of the South Nahanni River? Despite the notion, espoused by several frontiersmen, that the Nahanni Valley was a sort of no-mans-land which served as a buffer between various native tribes, the Nahanni Valley clearly supported at least a semi-permanent Indian population throughout the 19th and much of the 20th Centuries. So-called 'Nahanni Indians' like Big Charlie, Charlie Yohin, Captain, and Iron undoubtedly lived in the Nahanni area in the days of Willie and Frank McLeod, and many frontiersmen have alluded to their dealings with Nahanni Indians in their writings and interviews. Perhaps most compellingly, Indian Agent "Flynn" Harris, who took great pride in his familiarity with the natives under his charge, went so far as to publicly defend the honour of the Nahanni Indians, whom he felt the Canadian press unfairly maligned in the 1920's. Evidently, there were natives who lived in the Nahanni Valley. The question is, who were they?

According to historian W.D. Addison, "what little evidence there is suggests that the South Nahanni watershed may never have contained a year-round resident Indian population because of the low productivity of the land. Indians, living a nomadic life, apparently travelled into the area periodically from different sides of the Northern Cordillera." Addison's assertion, coupled with Honigmann's hypothesis, suggests that the 'Nahanni Indians' were actually Mountain Indians, Goat Indian, Kaska, and Slavey who periodically wandered throughout the Nahanni area, "[taking their] name," as Harris put it, "from the region in which [they lived]." Is it possible that the mythical, mountain-dwelling tribe, so feared by the Slavey and Kaska, was actually an illusory phantom- a product of over-active imaginations, rich oral tradition, and a systemic fear of strangers?

Hostility

What of the supposed sinister nature of the Indians who inhabited the watershed of the South Nahanni River? Local Dene certainly feared the valley's reclusive residents, and, according to at least one sourdough, with good reason. In a letter to Poole Field, an elderly woman named Ida Mary Goulter, who hailed from Carmacks, Yukon, wrote that the "Nahanni or the mountain men... were hostile to the [Indians of the] Yukon", and that "it was not until Poole Field came to this side that these Indians got over some of their bloodthirsty doings." Goulter's testimony seems to support White Eyes' claim that the Nahanni warred with the westerly Kaska. Mrs. Goulter concluded her commentary on the Nahanni with the cryptic words: "I knew of such terrible things they done..."

Many frontiersmen who lived in and around the Mackenzie Region were also afraid of the Nahanni Indians. Jack LaFlair, for example, during his days as an independent fur trader at Nahanni Butte, purportedly kept a revolver in his trade room at full cock as a precaution against them.

Were the 'Nahanni Indians' truly guilty of the gruesome crimes they were charged with? Did they really decapitate prospectors and burn down their cabins in the 'Headless Valley'? Although old Canadian newspapers and magazines are riddled with vague references to the brutality of the Nahanni Indians, no member of that mysterious tribe, to the best of this author's knowledge, was proven beyond a reasonable doubt to have committed murder. The same cannot be said for the members of other subarctic tribes, however.

According to English explorer Warburton Pike in his 1898 book *Through the Sub-Arctic Forest*, the Kaska Indians had "the greatest objection to white men trapping on their own account in their country; gold dust they can take as much as they like, but the fur is the Indian's equivalent for gold and must be left for the Indian. They are very firm on this point- so much so that a couple of white men who were trapping on the Liard some years ago were killed by the

Indians because they refused to let the furs alone." If any of the First Nations of the Mackenzie Region had the motive to murder frontiersmen, it would have been, in Pike's opinion, the Kaska.

Another Dene denomination with a history of violence is the aforementioned Beaver Tribe, whose members lived along the Peace River of British Columbia and Alberta. As George Keith mentioned in his 1807 letter to Roderick Mackenzie, the Beaver Indians clashed with the northern Plains Cree in the late 1700's when the latter ranged northward into their territory in search of furs.[12] According to Keith, some of the Beaver Indians subsequently fled north into the Liard River area, where they fought with and ultimately displaced the indigenous "Na ha ne". Not long afterwards, in the winter of 1812-13, a band of Beaver Indians butchered the residents of Fort Nelson- a North West Company fur trading post situated at the junction of the Liard and Fort Nelson Rivers (located about 106 km (56 miles) northwest of present-day Fort Nelson, BC). The Beaver warriors slaughtered the fort's occupants with impunity, sparing neither the Factor's wife nor his children.

---

[12] The Peace River received its name when the Cree and Beaver Indians smoked the pipe of peace on its shores sometime in the late 1700's, ending their feud. Thereafter, the river served as the boundary separating the territories of the two rival tribes; the Beaver lived north of the river, while the Cree inhabited the land to the south.

Headhunting

While the First Nations of the Mackenzie Region were not as warlike as many of their Canadian counterparts (ex. Haida, Blackfoot, Iroquois, Inuit, etc.), history shows that they were not completely averse to bloodshed. Whether or not the 'Nahanni' had a propensity for headhunting is another question. According to John Honigmann, the Kaska practiced scalping, but not decapitation. As for the warlike Tlingit, however, who resided on the coast of Alaska and Northwest British Columbia far to the west, "heads were taken... and scalped as the expedition neared home 'unless they had time to do so on the spot.' Scalping is specifically stated to have been done in such a way as to exclude the ears."

Incendiarism

Finally, we must address the question of the Nahanni's proclivity for arson. A number of men who lost their lives in the Nahanni- namely Bill Epler, Jack Mulholland, Martin Jorgensen, Phil Powers, and perhaps Yukon Fisher- had their cabins burned down around the time of their deaths. Was this the work of Nahanni Indians?

The Tlingit of the Pacific Northwest certainly seemed to have a penchant for pyromania. In 1802, they massacred the Russian garrison at Redoubt St. Michael (a.k.a. Old Sitka; a Russian outpost located at what is now Sitka, Alaska; not to be confused with the fort of the same name established in 1833 at the mouth of the Yukon River at the site of what is now St. Michael, Alaska) and burned the fort to the ground. In 1804, they razed another Russian colony on Alaska's Yakutat Bay, and in 1852, they the burned down HBC's Fort Selkirk, situated at the confluence of the Pelly and Yukon Rivers. The natives of the Mackenzie Region, on the other hand, were not famous fire starters. If they did set cabins in the Nahanni Valley ablaze, they were not acting in accordance with their people's historical habits.

———————•——————•———

The debate regarding the nature of the Nahanni Indians and the question of whether or not any of them had a hand in the deaths of the Nahanni Valley's many victims will likely never be truly resolved. Another legend of the Nahanni Valley, however- one inextricably linked with that of the Nahanni Indians- has a startling and undeniable truth at its core. This legend, believe it or not, is the tale of the White Queen.

The White Queen

"Nahani... They are a hardy, virile people, but have suffered much from white influence. They were hostile to strangers, and many white pioneers have been done to death by them. This tribe was for many years under the complete domination of one woman, supposed to be partly of European descent."

- Michael H. Mason, *The Artic Forests*, 1924.

THROUGHOUT THE FIRST HALF of the 20th Century, various books, magazines, and newspaper articles made cursory references to a beautiful woman of European ancestry- a so-called "White Queen"- said to have once ruled over the wild men of the Nahanni. Most writers refused to give this character, seemingly more at home on the pages of a C.S. Lewis fantasy novel than the wilds of the Canadian subarctic, any serious consideration. Pierre Berton, for example, in his writings and speeches, consistently dismissed her as a mythical figure; an inevitable inclusion in tales of lost worlds. Even Mary Kraus, who spent much of her life in the Nahanni Valley, described her as "a dream that somebody put... in the paper, just for stories." As strange as it may sound, however, the story of the White Queen is, along with the tale of the Tropical Valley, one of just two legends of the Nahanni Valley to be definitively resolved, and the only one proven beyond a reasonable doubt to be true.

BACKGROUND

Like the legend of the Nahanni Indians, the story of the White Queen has its roots in the early years of the Northwestern fur trade. In order to fully appreciate the events from which this legend derives, a little historical context is required.

Samuel Black's Expedition

In the summer of 1824, while John McLeod and his crew made their second trip up the South Nahanni River, another HBC expedition was underway further to the southwest. Led by Samuel Black- a notorious old Nor' Wester who served as George Simpson's nemesis during the days of the NWC-HBC rivalry- a party of ten headed up Northern British Columbia's hitherto uncharted Finlay River[1]. Black's motley crew consisted of six voyageurs (of English, Metis, and Iroquois extraction); a Metis interpreter and his wife; and a Scottish officer. Their objective was to discover a great northward-flowing waterway which paralleled the Mackenzie

---

[1] The Finlay River joins with the Parsnip River at Finlay Forks where Pierre Berton and his companions were stranded for four days during their Headless Valley Expedition to form the Peace River. It was first discovered and partially explored in 1797 by Nor' Wester John Finlay.

River to the west of the Mackenzie Mountains- a hypothetical river which, as it turned out, existed only in the mind of Governor George Simpson.

During their expedition, Black and his men encountered an impoverished band of Sekani Indians, several members of which they enticed into service. A handful of Sekani guides led the explorers northwest beyond the Finlay River into the territory of the Thloadenni, a friendly branch of the Tahltan tribe with whom the fur traders hoped to make contact.

On the eve of July 15, 1824, while Black and his crew relaxed around a campfire after a hard days' march, a band of Thloadenni materialized from the brush and approached the explorers' campsite. Evidently hoping to make a positive first impression on Black and his crew, the Indians were resplendent in what Black described as:

"...their newest apparel, consisting of white or new dressed skin coverings, Leggings Fringed, painted and garnished with Porcupine quill work, bunches of Feathers stuck wildly into the Hair of their Heads."

The explorers greeted the Thloadenni and invited them to join them by the fire. After giving them gifts of tobacco, the fur traders inquired as to their way of life, hoping that the natives were experienced trappers. In hushed tones, the Thloadenni proceeded to tell the HBC men that they lived a precarious existence, eking out a living in perpetual fear of another band of Tahltans to the west, with whom they were at war. These westerly Tahltans were hostile by nature, the Thloadenni informed the explorers, and were strong and numerous due to the muskets and ammunition they received from the powerful Tlingit of the Pacific Northwest. The Tlingit, in turn, acquired these weapons from white men on the Pacific Coast, whom Black correctly assumed were Russian *promyshlenniki* of the Russian-American Company. Because of their mercantile exploits, the Thloadenni called their powerful Tahltan enemies the "Trading Nahanni."

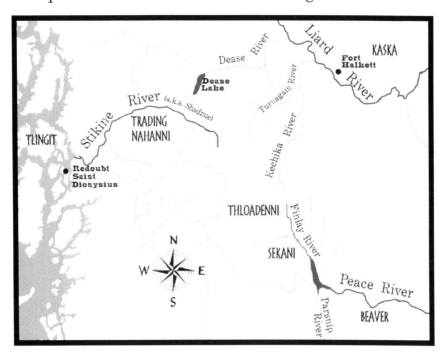

In spite of their remarkable strength and vigor (Black noted, in his journal, that the Thloadenni braves were much more physically imposing than their half-starved Sekani counterparts), the Thloadenni seemed deathly afraid of the

Trading Nahanni. So great was their fear of these belligerent, musket-wielding Tahltans that they refused to guide Black and his crew northwest, as that route would take them near the border of their territory.

Although he failed to secure their assistance, Black managed to elicit some information from the natives regarding the country to the west. The Thloadenni informed Black that the Trading Nahanni lived in the watershed of a great river which flowed southwest all the way to the Pacific Ocean. Today, we know this waterway as the Stikine River, which winds southwest through Stikine Country before emptying into the Pacific just north of Wrangell, Alaska. The Thloadenni, however (and, by extension, Samuel Black), knew this river as the *Schadzue*.

After spending several days in the company of the Indians, Black and his men bid their Thloadenni acquaintances farewell and continued north along what they called the "Thloadenni Road," a rugged, swampy trail that wound through the mountains. After several days of slogging through waterlogged moss and tangled tree branches, they reached what were almost certainly the headwaters of the Stikine River. Frustrated that his official objective precluded him from exploring this waterway, Black wrote in his journal, "I wish I had wings to go and see for in this country our progress is slow."

The explorers proceeded northeast, and, after hiking for some time, came to a river which Black correctly surmised led to the Liard. Satisfied that there was no great northward-flowing river that paralleled the Mackenzie to the west- at least, none which started south of the Liard- Black and his men followed this tributary, which Black dubbed 'Turnagain River', to the Kechika River. They followed the Kechika to the Liard and returned to civilization.

The *Dryad* Affair

As a result of Samuel Black's 1824 expedition up the Finlay River, HBC Governor George Simpson knew that *promyshlenniki* of the formidable Russian-American Fur Company- an Imperial Russian fur trading enterprise sponsored by the Tzar- acquired furs from the powerful Tlingit Indians of the Pacific Northwest who, in turn, acquired them from various Dene Indians who inhabited the interior. These Russians, along with independent American traders (both of whom conducted their business on the Russian-owned Pacific Coast of Alaska), constituted the Hudson's Bay Company's main competitors in the North Country since the HBC's absorption of the North West Company in 1821.

Nearly a decade after Black's expedition, Governor Simpson resolved to steal business away from his Russian and American rivals on the Northwest Coast. In the summer of 1833, he tasked veteran fur trader Peter Skene Ogden- a former Nor' Wester and one of Black's closest friends- with sailing up the Pacific Coast and up the Stikine River into British territory. There, on the banks of the river, Ogden was to build a fur trading post. Simpson reasoned that, if the Hudson's Bay Company managed to establish themselves along Tlingit trade routes- one of which, they surmised, was the Stikine River- they could intercept the flow of furs to the coast.

It must be mentioned that, at that time, the Stikine River was a bit of a mystery to George Simpson and the men of the Hudson's Bay Company, as no company men had yet navigated its length. In fact, the river's mouth had been discovered just two years prior, in the spring of 1831, when Lieutenant Aemilious Simpson of the British Royal Navy (Governor Simpson's distant relative and old schoolmate) sailed past it on an exploratory expedition up the Pacific Coast. Although Samuel Black had discovered the river's headwaters during his Finlay River expedition in 1824, George Simpson and the men of the Hudson's Bay Company were unaware that the stream which the Tahltan of the interior called the *'Schadzue'* was the same waterway which the coastal Tlingit called the *'Stikine'*.

On Simpson's orders, Peter Ogden set out from Port Simpson, an HBC trading post on the coast of British Columbia located a short distance north of present-day Prince Rupert, on June 15, 1833. On a brig called the *Dryad*, Ogden and his crew of thirty eight sailed up the Pacific Coast towards the mouth of the Stikine River. As they approached their destination, the sailors discovered, to their dismay, that the mouth of the Stikine was guarded by a Russian fort newly-constructed on the shores a nearby island, its palisaded parapets bristling with cannons. Ogden lowered the anchor and waited for the fort's commander to address him.

Soon, the *Dryad* was approached by a whaleboat bearing Russian emissaries. Ogden invited the occupants of this smaller craft onto his ship, only to receive a letter notifying him that British vessels were prohibited from entering the waters surrounding the fort. These waters, Ogden learned, included the Stikine River.

The Russians, it seemed, were one step ahead of the Hudson's Bay Company. Apparently having foreseen Simpson's plan to take control of the Stikine, they had built a bastion, called Redoubt Saint Dionysius, on the tip of an island fronting the river's mouth several months earlier. They believed that by building this fort, they were legally justified in blocking the British from the river. According to an article in the Treaty of Saint Petersburg of 1825, a formal agreement between the Russian and British Empires which defined the boundaries between Russian America and British possessions in the Pacific Northwest:

"Subjects of his Brittanic Majesty shall not land at any place where there may be a Russian establishment, without permission of the Governor or Commandant; and, on the other hand, that Russian subjects shall not land, without permission, at any British establishment, of the Northwest coast."

In other words, the HBC men were legally unable to enter the Stikine River so long as Redoubt Saint Dionysius stood at its mouth.

Ogden knew that the Russians were cherry-picking from the 1825 Treaty, and that the agreement decreed that British citizens had the right to navigate all rivers which flowed through Russian territory to the Pacific Coast, fort or not. He said as much to the Russian emissaries, who subsequently claimed that they would have to pass Ogden's grievance on to Baron Ferdinand von Wrangel- Chief Manager of the Russian-American Company and *de facto* Governor of Russian territory in what is now Alaska- before they could allow the British to pass. Ogden had no choice but to acquiesce. He anchored the *Dryad* off the coast of what would become Zarembo Island and awaited Baron von Wrangel's response.

Ultimately, the incident at Redoubt Saint Dionysius, which came to be known as the *Dryad* Affair, sparked a long, drawn-out bureaucratic battle between London and St. Petersburg. Until the disagreement was resolved, Ogden and the men of the Hudson's Bay Company were officially forbidden from entering the Stikine River from the Pacific Ocean.

ORIGINS

Until the British and Russian Empires could come to a formal agreement on navigational rights in the Pacific Northwest, the men of the Hudson's Bay Company had no choice but to seek an alternative route to the Stikine if they hoped to compete with their rivals on the West Coast. Their subsequent expeditions into the heart of northern British Columbia would bring them into contact with the Trading Nahanni, the warlike Tahltans who inhabited the watershed of the Stikine River. Their hair-raising encounters with these natives formed the foundation upon which the legend of the White Queen is based.

Discovery of the *Schadzue*

One year after the *Dryad* Affair, while the headmen of the Hudson's Bay and Russian-American Companies were still embroiled in a diplomatic war over British access to the Stikine River, John McLeod set out on yet another westward expedition from the Mackenzie Region. As mentioned briefly in the previous chapter, he successfully reached the headwaters of the 'West Branch' of the Liard River in 1831. Now, his HBC employers wanted him to explore the 'East Branch' of the Liard, the waterway we know today as the Fort Nelson River.

McLeod, however, had other plans. Ever since Samuel Black's Finlay River expedition in 1824, he harboured a desire to explore the upper reaches of the river which the Thloadenni called the *Schadzue.* He suspected that the best way to reach this river from the Mackenzie Region was by way of the waterway which would come to be known as the Dease River, a tributary of the upper Liard that he and his men discovered during their expedition three years earlier. McLeod decided to use his expeditionary commission to test his hypothesis.

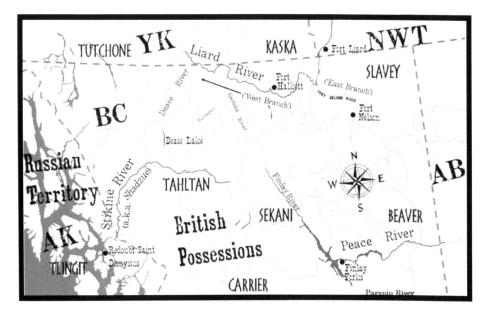

On June 25, 1834, John McLeod, accompanied by five
voyageurs and two Indians, set out from Fort Halkett- an
HBC post situated at the mouth of the Smith River (a
tributary of the Liard), established by a clerk named John
Hutchinson back in 1829. He and his men tracked, poled, and
portaged their way up the hazardous West Branch of the
Liard. They reached the mouth of Dease River on July 10.

McLeod and his crew proceeded south up the Dease,
conquering a succession of rapids. Two weeks later, they
arrived at the river's source: a long, narrow body of water
which McLeod named Dease Lake in honour of his friend and
fellow fur trader Peter Warren Dease. Upon paddling to the
western shore the lake, McLeod and his men built a cache and
secured their canoe before plunging west down an Indian trail
through the forest.

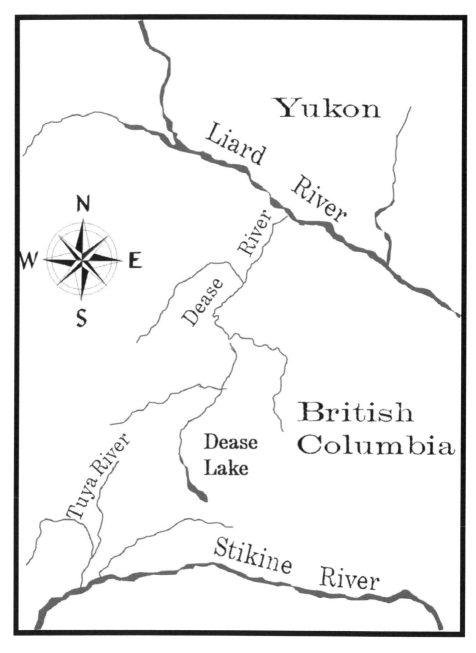

The following day, the explorers came to a swiftly-flowing river, which they managed to cross via a precarious Indian log bridge. Later that day, they came to yet another...

"River, but frightful to look at, a similar Bridge with the one of the morning was thrown across by the natives, but so very slender was its construction, that only one of the Men (John Norquoy) would venture across."

The next day, John McLeod, accompanied by Norquoy and another of his voyageurs, crossed this terrifying log bridge a second time; the remainder of the crew, too afraid to hazard the crossing, remained on the opposite bank. The three explorers followed the river- known today as the Tuya- south and discovered that it merged with another stream before flowing into a great river that flowed southwest. John McLeod, flushed with a sense of accomplishment, knew that this watercourse could only be the legendary *Schadzue*.

Having attained his personal goal, McLeod led his three intrepid companions back up the river and over the log bridge, where the reminder of the crew was waiting for them. McLeod and his men proceeded overland to Dease Lake, down the Dease River, and down the Liard to Fort Halkett.

Hutchinson's Misadventure

John McLeod's discovery that the Dease River served as a suitable route to the *Schadzue* was a boon to the Hudson's Bay Company, whose headmen endeavoured to expand their commercial empire further into the interior. George Simpson was especially impressed with McLeod's work, as he correctly suspected that the *Schadzue* and the Stikine were one and the same, and that McLeod's route to the river might constitute a backdoor to the tantalizing waterway so tenaciously guarded by the Russians. The HBC Governor rewarded McLeod for his contributions to the company by promoting him to a position which necessitated his transfer to Oregon Country (which was not yet officially a territory of the United States) far to the south.

Following McLeod's departure from the Mackenzie Region, George Simpson decided to establish a post on Dease Lake, from which an expedition deep into *Schadzue* Country could be launched in the future. Before he could set his plan into motion, however, a couple of Metis *engages* (as Hudson's Bay Company employees were sometimes called) murdered a number of Mountain Indians at Fort Norman, an HBC post situated on the Mackenzie River. This incident forced George Simpson to temporarily abandon his plans for expansion and focus on mending the HBC's relationship with the Fort Norman natives.

By 1836, the situation at Fort Norman was much improved, and George Simpson once again turned his attention towards Dease Lake. That summer, he tasked the *engages* stationed at Fort Halkett with building a trading post on the lake's shores. The man he nominated to lead the expedition was John Hutchinson, the HBC clerk who founded Fort Halkett back in 1829.

As a younger man, John Hutchinson had conducted several successful exploratory expeditions in the Mackenzie

Region on behalf of the Hudson's Bay Company. He had since grown weary of frontier life, however, and now much preferred the comforts and securities of the fort to the rigours and perils of the trail. When he received word of his new assignment, he tendered his resignation from the HBC. In accordance with company policy, however, his superiors refused to allow him to quit the business until his application for resignation had been properly reviewed- a process which typically took about a year. Reluctantly, Hutchinson, accompanied by a crew of voyageurs and Indian guides, set out up the Liard that summer, bound for Dease Lake.

Several weeks later, a bedraggled John Hutchinson and his wild-eyed crew stumbled into Fort Simpson. The fort's supervisor- a broad-shouldered young Highlander named Robert Campbell- was surprised by Hutchinson's unexpected visit, as he was under the impression that the clerk and his crew were at Dease Lake. Before he had a chance to voice his confusion, Hutchinson launched into a harrowing tale of near disaster.

Several days after leaving Fort Halkett, Hutchinson and his crew arrived at Portage Brule, a trail which circumvented one of the Liard's more dangerous rapids. They arrived at the trailhead at dusk, and were only able to transport their canoe and gear a short distance up the trail before they were forced to make camp.

The following morning, Hutchinson's voyageurs discovered, to their horror, that a mysterious Indian had visited their camp during the night; an unmistakable pair of moccasin tracks encircled the camp just beyond what would have been the reach of the firelight. Fearing that their nocturnal visitor might be the advance scout of an Indian war party, Hutchinson dispatched two of the Indians under his command on a reconnaissance mission up the trail. After they had been gone for some time, the natives raced back into camp, breathless, with the alarming news that a hundred Nahanni braves were creeping down the portage trail in their direction. The spears and flintlock muskets they brandished, coupled with the fierce black war paint that stained their faces, betrayed their malicious intentions beyond a doubt.

Despite Hutchinson's efforts to organize an orderly retreat, the *engages*, overcome by panic, fled pell-mell for the river, leaving behind everything but their muskets, paddles, and canoe. Hutchinson had no choice but to follow his fearful crew. The party leapt into their boat and paddled furiously down the Liard. They raced past Fort Halkett and Fort Liard, not daring to stop until they reached the safety of Fort Simpson.

Robert Campbell's Expedition

For many months following the incident at Portage Brule, Hutchinson's terrifying tale was the talk of the Mackenzie District. Although many voyageurs agreed that the men of Fort Halkett were lucky to have escaped with their lives, some, including George Simpson and the level-headed Robert Campbell, suspected that Hutchinson's

Nahanni war party was, as Simpson put it, "nothing more or less than the production of a timid mind."

In the spring of 1837, Robert Campbell decided to risk personally finishing what Hutchinson started. That March, he snowshoed from Fort Simpson to Fort Liard, where he bullied a number of voyageurs and Indians into accompanying him to Dease Lake.

Campbell and his crew set out on their journey in May, 1837. After only three days on the trail, however, the Indians deserted the party, afraid that they would be ambushed by Nahanni warriors if they continued any further up the Liard. That same afternoon, about half of the voyageurs defied Campbell's orders and refused to carry on, haunted by Hutchinson's tale. Campbell, disgusted with his crew's cowardice, returned with them to Fort Liard, where he promptly assembled another team.

Several weeks later, Robert Campbell embarked upon his second journey up the Liard with a brand new crew. The Scotsman, much to his irritation, soon learned that his new companions were no less fearful of the Nahanni Indians than their predecessors and, after refusing several of their requests to return to the fort, sternly chastised them for their lack of heart. Shamed by Campbell's diatribe, the voyageurs begrudgingly pushed on up the Liard to the abandoned Fort Halkett, which Hutchinson's Nahanni warriors apparently left undisturbed. Campbell led them further up the Liard to

Portage Brule, where Hutchinson and his men claimed to have had their encounter with the wild men of the mountains.

A short distance up the portage trail, the voyageurs met with a sobering sight that cast serious doubt on Hutchinson's story: at a clearing in the woods beside the trail were a scattering of rusted and rotten trade goods, evidently the commodities abandoned by Hutchinson and his crew. "Of course everything was spoilt," wrote Campbell in his journal, "except such articles as ball, shot, & the provisions eaten by wild animals." If Hutchinson's Nahanni war party had truly passed by the area the previous summer, they had neglected to avail themselves of the food, tools, and ammunition that Hutchinson and his men had hauled into the country.

By that time, it was too late in the summer to push on to Dease Lake. Accordingly, Campbell and his crew decided to spend the winter at Fort Halkett. The winter passed by relatively uneventfully, and by the spring of 1838, Campbell and his crew, along with a handful of reinforcements sent from Fort Simpson, were back on the trail to Dease Lake.

Powwow on the Stikine River

The journey to Dease Lake was relatively uneventful. Upon reaching the area, Robert Campbell tasked the leader of the reinforcements from Fort Simpson[2] with constructing a

---

[2] Incidentally, the officer who Campbell appointed to oversee the construction of the fort at Dease Lake was A.R. McLeod Jr., the Metis son of HBC Chief Trader Alexander Roderick McLeod (who first journeyed up the South Nahanni River in the early 1820's).

fort on the lake's shore. While his men went about their task, Campbell, along with an interpreter named Francis Hoole and two young Indian hunters named Lapie and Kitza, headed west through the woods, determined to explore the *Schadzue* River.

Campbell and his companions evidently headed down the same Indian trail that John McLeod had discovered four years earlier, as they crossed the first log bridge that McLeod had mentioned in his journal. When they came to the second bridge, they noticed the smoke of an Indian campfire rising above the treetops of the opposite bank. Campbell, eager to speak with the area's locals, crossed the bridge with Lapie and Kitza. Hoole, on the other hand, though "very handy, a splendid hunter & canoe maker, & most ingenious at all kinds of work, was exceedingly timid & afraid of strange Indians," and refused to cross to the other side.

While Hoole waited on the opposite bank, Campbell, Lapie, and Kitza made their way towards the Indian camp, which proved to be a lone tent. To their surprise, they found the place abandoned; apparently, its occupants had fled at the explorers' approach.

Within the dwelling, Campbell and his Indian companions found three metal pots of Russian manufacture. Inside one of them was a quantity of boiled salmon which the hungry frontiersmen happily devoured, leaving behind a knife and some tobacco as payment. When they finished their meal, they returned across the log bridge, rejoined Hoole, and retired for the night.

Early the following morning, Campbell was roused by the cry of, "Indians! Indians!" He crawled from his blanket to find a band of sixteen natives peering at him and his companions from across the river. Ignoring Hoole's frantic entreaties to flee, the Scotsman calmly hoisted the Hudson's Bay Company flag he carried with him and invited the Indians to join him and his crew on their side of the river. After deliberating amongst themselves, the Indians cautiously crossed the log bridge to the explorers' encampment and sat with them around their fire.

Once everyone was seated, the chief of the Indian band produced a pipe, packed it with some of the tobacco that the explorers had left in the tent the previous evening, and began to smoke. When he had finished, he passed the pipe to Campbell, who took a deep drag before passing the device on to his companions, who similarly took a puff each before passing it on to the mysterious Indians, who did likewise. As soon as the pipe made a full revolution around the fire, the chief began to speak.

The natives, Campbell and his companions learned, were the dreaded Trading Nahanni who lived in the vicinity of the *Schadzue* River. They had come to this particular part of the country in order to attend a massive Indian gathering hosted by the Tlingit, who came upriver twice every summer to trade with the natives of the interior. The chief confided that the Tlingit had always instructed him and his people to kill any white men that appeared from the east, as they were the enemies of the whites who provided the Tlingit with guns and steel. Fortunately for Campbell and his crew, this sub-chief of the Trading Nahanni was not particularly fond of his domineering Tlingit trading partners, and decided to let the explorers live.

When Campbell expressed his desire to attend the great Indian rendezvous, the chief was alarmed. He told the Scotsman that a powerful Tlingit chief named Shakes presided over the gathering, and would surely kill Campbell and his men if they fell into his hands. "Though I & my band would be willing to protect you," the chief warned, "we could not do so as Shakes' men are as the sands of the beach."

Undeterred, the Highlander implored the chief to take him to the assembly. When the leader, seeing Campbell's determination, reluctantly agreed to escort him to the camp, the fur trader loaded a brace of flintlock pistols, slipped a dagger into his belt, grabbed his double-barrelled percussion lock rifle, and followed the Indian down the Tuya River. Lapie, Kitza, and a terrified Francis Hoole fell in behind him.

Like John McLeod before them, Robert Campbell and his companions followed the Tuya River to its confluence with another stream and continued on to the *Schadzue* River. As they walked, they were accosted by several of the sixteen Trading Nahanni with whom they had smoked. These natives beseeched them to abandon their folly, apparently fearing for their safety. "If you persist," they told the explorers, "you will never return, Shakes will kill you." Heedless of the danger, Campbell and his men carried on.

After hiking fifteen miles down the *Schadzue*, the explorers crested a high hill. They were rewarded for their efforts with an incredible view of the Indians' mega-camp- a sprawling assortment of smoky campfires and moose skin tents that stretched down the valley. Wrote Campbell of the scene:

"Such a concourse of Indians I had never seen assembled. They were gathered from all parts of the Western slope of the Rockies & from along the Pacific Coast."

As Campbell descended the hill towards the camp, he was surrounded by a throng of inquisitive Indians who were astounded to see a white man from the east. One native who knew some English bombarded the fur trader with a litany of questions. Whenever Campbell made a reply, the Indian shouted his answer out loud in his own language. These words were "taken up & yelled by a hundred throats till the surrounding rocks & the valley re-echoed with the sound."

Near the heart of the encampment, Campbell was approached by a tall, muscular warrior who, judging from the deference and respect that his compatriots afforded him, could only be Shakes, the powerful head chief of the Tlingit- the man whom the Trading Nahanni had warned him to avoid.[3] The chief, stone-faced, solemnly shook Campbell's hand and directed him towards his tent. Realizing that he had no other choice, Campbell obliged.

Inside the tent, the Scotsman was surprised to find four ragged Russian *promyshlenniki-* evidently esteemed guests of the chief. The leader of the party, who was equally surprised to see Campbell, introduced himself as "Mr. Monrobe" before offering the Highlander a glass of whisky. According to a letter written by Murdock McPherson- the fur trader who led an expedition up the West Branch of the Liard River in 1825- the Russian officers treated Campbell with courtesy, but were unable to conceal their immense "jealousy of his appearance in that Quarter."

As Campbell acquainted himself with the ambassadors of the Russian-American Company, a great commotion erupted outside the tent. Suddenly, the tent's moose skin covering was ripped off by the sixteen Trading Nahanni who had accompanied Campbell to the rendezvous, each of them poised for battle. The Trading Nahanni, it seemed, suspected that Shakes intended to murder their new friend. "If the

---

[3] Since the 18th Century, 'Shakes' was an honorary title reserved for great Tlingit clan leaders. The 'Chief Shakes' who Robert Campbell met in 1838- a renowned warrior named Keishishk- was the fourth Tlingit chief to bear this title. His nephew and successor, Chief Shakes V, became the father-in-law of Alexander "Buck" Choquette, the French-Canadian prospector after whom the Choquette Hot Springs were named, whose 1861 discovery launched the Stikine Gold Rush.

White Chief is killed," they warned the Tlingit leader, "there will be plenty of blood spilled here!"

Once the Tahltan warriors were satisfied that their friend was safe, at least for the time being, Shakes asked Campbell to give him a demonstration of his double-barrelled percussion lock rifle- a true novelty to the natives, whose experience with firearms was limited to the smoothbore flintlock muskets they acquired from the Russians. Campbell did as requested, firing off one of his two rounds at a distant target to a chorus of whoops and cheers. Suspecting that the Tlingit chief planned to seize him once his weapon was empty, Campbell reloaded the empty barrel before taking another shot. He repeated this procedure for as long as Shakes required him to shoot, never giving the chief the opportunity to catch him unarmed.

At one point, Shakes became distracted long enough for Campbell to slip away from him and his Tlingit countrymen. For some reason, he was forced to leave his gun behind. He made his way back up the hill from which he had first descended, and found Kitza, Lapie, and Hoole waiting for him at the top. Alongside Campbell's masculine companions stood a fairer figure- the woman who would serve as the inspiration for the legend of the White Queen.

THE CHIEFTESS OF THE TRADING NAHANNI

Robert Campbell quickly learned that the lady who had joined his companions in his absence was the head chieftess of the Trading Nahanni. The Scotsman was instantly smitten with this enchanting Indian noblewoman, writing in his journal:

"She commanded the respect not only of her own people, but of the tribes they had intercourse with. She was a fine looking woman rather above the middle height & about 35 years old. In her actions & personal appearance she was more like the Whites than the pure Indian race. She had a pleasing face lit up with fine intelligent eyes, which when she was excited flashed like fire."

After introducing him to the chieftess, Kitza, Lapie, and Hoole inquired as to Campbell's experience in the camp. The company man told his fellows about the Russian traders, described his brush with Chief Shakes, and lamented the loss of his gun, fire bag[4], kettle, and axe, which the Indians had stolen from him. When the Tahltan chieftess learned the source of Campbell's displeasure, she immediately set off down the hill towards the encampment. Shortly thereafter, she returned with all of the Scotsman's belongings and presented them to their bewildered yet grateful owner. This chieftess, it

---

[4] A fire bag is a pouch containing flint, steel, kindling, and other materials used to make fire.

seemed, had a great deal of influence over the red men of the Northwest.

In addition to Campbell's effects, the chieftess brought with her words of warning for the Scotsman and his crew, cryptically informing them that their lives depended on their speedy departure. Campbell and his men thanked the lady for her kindness and, after hoisting the HBC flag and emblazoning the company's logo on a tree, allowed her to accompany them several miles up the *Schadzue*.

When the time came for the explorers to part with their new ally, Campbell gave the chieftess his handkerchief as a token of his friendship. In return, the queen of the Trading Nahanni slipped two silver bracelets from her wrists and placed them in the trader's hands. With that, Campbell and his crew bid the lady farewell and returned to Dease Lake.

Winter at Dease Lake

Upon their return to Dease Lake, Campbell, Kitza, Lapie, and Hoole regaled their fellow *engages* with tales of their adventures on the *Schadzue*. Campbell, to his pleasure, discovered that his men had done a magnificent job of constructing the fort. They were not nearly as successful in their quest to fill the fort's larder, however. Accordingly, Campbell decided to make the journey to Fort Simpson, where he hoped he might secure some winter provisions for his men.

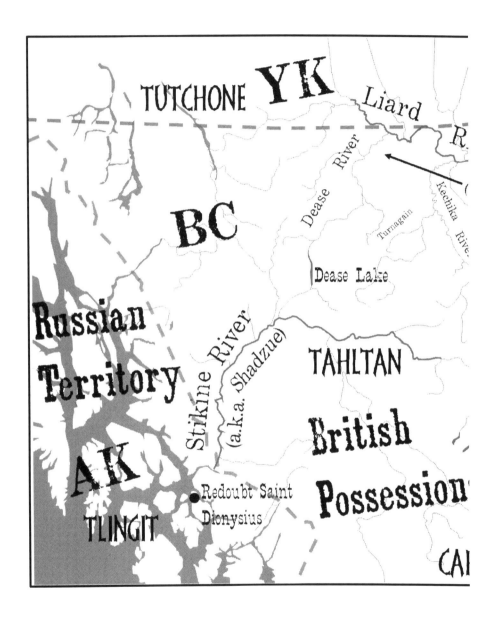

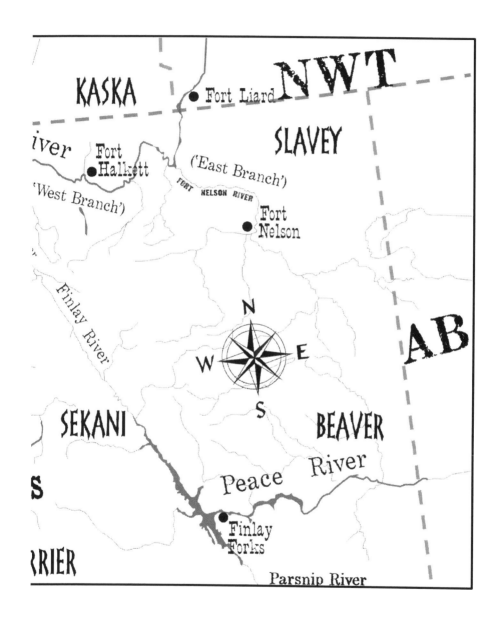

Campbell, accompanied by Lapie, immediately set off down the Dease River in a small birch bark canoe. The pair reached Fort Simpson on August 20, 1838, having narrowly avoided what might have been a fatal spill in the Hell Gate Rapids on account of a leak that sprang in their canoe. There, in that capital of the Mackenzie District, Campbell reported to Chief Trader Murdock McPherson, informing him of his experience on the *Schadzue*. McPherson was immensely pleased with Campbell's work, knowing that the presence of Russian traders at the Indian rendezvous almost certainly confirmed that the *Schadzue* was, in fact, the Stikine.[5]

Although he was delighted with Campbell's discoveries, Murdock McPherson refused to grant the voyageur's earnest request for provisions. Frustrated beyond measure, Campbell and Lapie returned to Dease Lake with nothing to show for their efforts.

Robert Campbell and his men would face a bitter winter at Dease Lake- a season characterized by extreme privation and suffering. As both fish and game were scarce in the region at that time, the *engages* endured many months of severe malnutrition. Three of their number succumbed to

---

[5] Unbeknownst to the Scotsmen, Campbell's expedition would prove to be in vain. In a years' time, Governor George Simpson and Baron Ferdinand von Wrangel would come to an agreement on navigational rights in the Pacific Northwest. Specifically, the Russians would lease the British their southern coastal territories for the annual price of two thousand beaver skins, inadvertently nullifying the value of Campbell's remote outpost at Dease Lake.

hunger, while the remainder were reduced to eating the leather netting on their showshoes and the parchment that covered the fort's windows in a desperate attempt to stave off starvation. To make matters worse, they were constantly harassed by the Trading Nahanni, who made it their mission to terrorize the traders at every opportunity. These aggressive Tahltans took casual potshots at the fort when they came to trade, manhandled a voyageur on at least one occasion while conducting business, and eventually raided the post's storeroom of its meagre contents.

As terrible as that winter proved to be for Campbell and his crew, it began on a much sweeter note than the one on which it ended. During their first visit to the post on Dease Lake, the Trading Nahanni were on their best behavior due to the presence of their leader, the beautiful, fair-skinned chieftess from the Stikine River. When she saw the fur traders' pitiable circumstances, this Dene Duchess had her people prepare a sumptuous feast of salmon steaks and caribou meat for her hosts.

Later that night, while the fort was asleep, a handful of brash Tahltan braves burst through the trade room door screaming war whoops. Before any of the voyageurs could react, the Indians snatched up the muskets that hung from the fort's walls and leveled them at the fur traders. As they prepared to murder the *engages*, the chieftess of the Trading Nahanni, who had been sleeping at the other end of the fort, rose from her furs to admonish her unruly warriors. Seething with rage, she strode into their line of fire and withered the young men with a ferocious glare. Immediately, the braves lowered their weapons, silent and shamefaced, unable to abide their queen's indignation. Having averted the massacre of Campbell and his crew, the chieftess "found out the instigator of the riot, walked up to him, and, stamping her foot on the ground, repeatedly spat in his face, her eyes blazing with anger."

Several days later, when the chieftess had concluded her business at Dease Lake, Robert Campbell and his crew saw her off, bidding her a hearty farewell. The voyageurs watched as the Tahltan princess disappeared into the trees with her retinue, their hearts filled with admiration for the extraordinary woman who had saved their lives. And that was the last they ever saw of the chieftess of the Trading Nahanni.

Barring the possibility that she was the Metis daughter of a Russian *promyshlenniki*, the woman who served as the basis for the legend of the White Queen was probably not of European extraction, nor is it likely that she ever set foot in the Nahanni Valley. Nevertheless, Robert Campbell's account of her, when considered alongside the vague legend his tale spawned, supports the notion that even the most bizarre folktales, when stripped of their mythological trappings, tend to reveal underpinnings of solid, substantive truth.

Another legend of the Nahanni Valley proven to have some basis in fact (and, like that of the White Queen, a connection with the legend of the Nahanni Indians) is the mystery of the Naha tribe, an ancient Stone Age people said to have inhabited the Mackenzie Mountains in bygone days... before inexplicably vanishing without a trace.

The Naha Tribe

"Near the end of the trail, I... look 60-metres down at the spire that splits the falls in two. Paddlers affectionately call this Mason's Rock... To the Dene of the Mackenzie River Valley, the spire represents one of the spirits of the Naha, a tribe of mountain warriors who wore sheepskin clothing and armoured vests made of tightly woven sticks. Legend has it that this fierce people would descend from the mountains from time to time to raid the Dene camps below. By the time the victims pulled themselves together to track down the marauders, they would only find a burning campfire."

- Ed Struzik, *Ten Rivers: Adventure Stories from the Arctic*, 2005

L EGEND HAS IT has it that the mountains of Nahanni Country were once populated by a violent Stone Age people known as the Naha. In ancient times, these wild tribesmen raided Dene settlements in the lowlands of Mackenzie Country. Renowned for their ferocity and barbaric practices, their menacing reputation struck fear into the hearts of their enemies.

This article of Dene folklore is closely related to that of the Nahanni Indians, and indeed, the two legends are identical in many respects. Both the Naha and the Nahanni were said to be a primitive, hostile, nomadic people of whom their Dene neighbours were deathly afraid. And, as one might suppose, the words "Naha" and "Nahanni" almost certainly share similar etymological roots; as Peter Jowett put it in his book *Nahanni: The River Guide*, both of these names essentially "meant the People Over There Far Away, the Enemy, the People of the Setting Sun, the People Who Speak Like Ducks, or the Giant Enemy, depending who was speaking of them." In accordance with this information, many of those who have written on the subject have considered the Naha and the Nahanni Indians to be one and the same.

While the legends of these two tribes certainly bear great resemblance to one another, there are two fundamental differences which set them apart. The first is the degree of primitiveness ascribed to the two tribes. Although the Nahanni Indians were purportedly less inclined to espouse modern technology (i.e. HBC muskets and other European trade goods) than their Kaska and Slavey counterparts, the Naha were typically portrayed as downright barbaric. Nearly every written reference to them remarks upon the crudeness of their tools and their brutal state of existence. Some versions even describe them as troglodytes, or cavemen, who made their homes in the caverns that pockmark the slopes of the Nahanni Valley.

The second major difference between the Naha and the Nahanni Indians pertains to their collective demises. The Nahanni Indians were generally believed to have survived in the Nahanni Valley well into the 20th Century, dwindling and possibly dying out in the late 1920's or early 1930's on account of Old World diseases. Legend has it that the Naha, on the other hand, disappeared quickly and quite mysteriously long ago, in the dim recesses of the Nahanni's dark history.

THE LEGEND

According to Dene tradition, the Naha tribe was the first nation to inhabit the Mackenzie Mountains. Most storytellers agree that the Naha were a nomadic people who travelled from place to place in search of game. They worshipped the spirit Ndambadezha, whom they considered their protector, and left gifts for him whenever their travels brought them to the Rabbitkettle Hot Springs. Some say that they dwelled within the caves of the Nahanni Valley, while others maintain that they kept a base camp at the mouth of Prairie Creek, a tributary of the South Nahanni which enters the river at Deadmen Valley.

Unlike the reclusive Nahanni Indians, who largely confined their activities to the remote domain over which they reigned, the Naha were said to be a warlike people who regularly raided their Kaska and Slavey neighbours along the Liard and Mackenzie Rivers for the purpose of stealing women. Before embarking upon such forays, Naha warriors donned thick sheepskin robes and rod-armour cuirasses, the latter made from wooden dowels bound closely together with sinew. Armed with birch wood shields and stone-tipped knives, spears, axes, and clubs, they left Deadmen Valley and proceeded down the warpath to Nahanni Butte, on the slopes of which they set up camp. From the mountain's heights, these Paleolithic savages scanned the valley of the Liard River for the smoke of distant campfires. When they located an enemy camp they deemed worth raiding, they descended the mountain and set off through the woods towards their quarry. If the ensuing skirmish was a success, the Naha tortured the surviving enemy warriors, mutilated the bodies of their fallen comrades, executed their children, and carried their wives and daughters off into the mountains.

According to Herb Norwegian, the current Grand Chief of the Dehcho (i.e. Slavey) First Nation, "It came to a point where the people in the flats and lowlands couldn't put up with the continuous raiding every year, so finally the elders got together and said 'we got to put a stop to this.'" It was decided that a massive Dene war party would head into the Nahanni Valley to eliminate the Naha threat once and for all.

The Dene warriors marched into Naha territory without meeting any resistance and soon espied the smoke of a distant campfire. Upon rushing into the camp with their weapons drawn, however, they found that the Naha were nowhere to be found. It was as if their enemies had vanished into thin air. Terrified that they would suffer a similar fate if they lingered, the Dene braves beat a hasty retreat back to the lowlands. They never saw the Naha again.

THEORIES
Nahanni Indians

As mentioned, many writers who have commented upon the legend of the Naha tribe have argued or assumed, with good reason, that this Dene folktale is simply another facet of the legend of the Nahanni Indians. For example, Richard C. Davis, the editor of *Nahanni Journals* (the 1927-1929 journals of Raymond Patterson, published posthumously in 2008), in his *Introduction* to the aforementioned book, describes the Naha (or, as he calls them, the "Nah'aa") as "the mysterious indigenous people referred to as Nahannies by early traders." Others have suggested that the Naha were simply the ancient ancestors of the Nahanni Indians.

In a similar vein, some writers, such as canoeist Neil Hartling, have argued that the Naha were probably the Kaska Indians, a tribe which some ethnologists have conflated with the Nahanni.

A Distinct Tribe

Some of those who have written on the subject have taken the Dene legend at face value and considered the Naha a unique and distinct tribe which inhabited Nahanni Country, and which died out sometime in the distant past. The latter half of this notion (although perhaps not the former) is corroborated by what is arguably the earliest written allusion to the Naha tribe- a letter written by NWC (and future HBC) clerk George Keith to fellow clerk Roderick Mackenzie on January 7, 1807 (mentioned briefly in the chapter on the Nahanni Indians). Keith spent a portion of his letter describing the country surrounding Biscaga Fort, a NWC outpost situated on the Liard River near the mouth of the Muskeg River, which would later be abandoned in 1811 or 1812 when Fort Nelson was built.

Not far from the fort," wrote Keith, "and so called from the flint stones very common in the place[1], and which the old inhabitants the Na ha ne tribe, made use of as knives and axes. This tribe of Indians has abandoned the country on account of the encroachments of its present possessors." Keith went on to explain that these "present possessors" called themselves "Beaver Indians, a name which they claim as descendants from the Beaver Indians at Peace River, from when they separated some ages ago, when attacked by enemies."[2]

Other writers have similarly claimed that the Naha were driven out of Nahanni Country in the 1880's (roughly a century after the alleged supplantation alluded to in Keith's

---

[1] "*Biskaga*", apparently, was a Dene word for flint.

[2] These "enemies" who drove the Beaver Indians north from their territory on the Peace River were almost certainly the northern Plains Cree.

letter) by the Slavey. This notion is not necessarily incompatible with Dene oral lore. According to Herb Norwegian, "In some versions of the story, the Naha were tracked down and killed, in others the warriors simply disappeared."

The Navajo Theory

One fascinating theory regarding the fate of the Naha tribe contends that these people, for one reason or another, decided to abandon the Nahanni Valley and migrate south; the deserted camps that the Dene war party stumbled upon in the Mackenzie Mountains contained artifacts which the Naha considered too burdensome to transport. After leaving their mountain homes, the Naha slogged through the boreal forests of Northern Canada and hiked 2,000 miles south down the Canadian prairies and Great Plains to the arid deserts of the American Southwest. There, they became the Navajo- today, the second largest federally-recognized Native American tribe in the United States.

Linguistic Evidence

This wild theory is supported by several tantalizing pieces of circumstantial evidence. First, the Navajo language is closely related to those spoken by the Dene of the Canadian-Alaskan subarctic, and to the Yeniseian languages of Northeastern Siberia, where the Dene people are believed to have originated.[3] For example, although the Navajo, being

---

[3] Today, most anthropologists believe that the first inhabitants of the Americas crossed the Bering Strait from Siberia to Alaska via an ancient land bridge thousands of years ago, in three separate waves. The Paleo-

desert dwellers, had no word for "boat", the word they used to describe the gliding of an owl in flight was the same word that the northern Dene used to describe the movement of a canoe over water. According to Herb Norwegian, "Slavey Dene visiting Arizona have found they can converse quite comfortably with the Navajo."

Today, the Navajo tongue, along with Western Apache and a handful of other languages spoken by the natives of Southwestern United States, is considered to belong to the Southern Athabascan language group, a subfamily of the Athabascan languages, which is, in turn, a subfamily of the Na-Dene language family. Clearly, the Navajo language, and the Southern Athabascan language subfamily in general, has its roots in the subarctic. Is it possible that it was brought to the American Southwest by the legendary Naha?

Another Native American people of Southwestern United States culturally related to the Navajo, and with similar linguistic ties to the subarctic Dene, are the Apache. Interestingly, according to American anthropologist Frederick W. Hodge, the Apache earned their name from the Zuni, an ancient Pueblo people endemic to western New Mexico. The Zuni called their warlike neighbours from the

---

Indians, the Pleistocene ancestors of most Amerindians south of the Canadian border, are believed to have crossed the Bering Strait land bridge somewhere around 11,500 B.C. A second migration- that of the ancestors of the Dene peoples- is believed to have occurred between 10,000 and 8,000 B.C. The third and final migration from Siberia to the Americas began around 3,000 B.C., and involved the Thule people, the ancestors of all modern Inuit, and the more ancient Dorset people, who we will learn more about later on in this book.

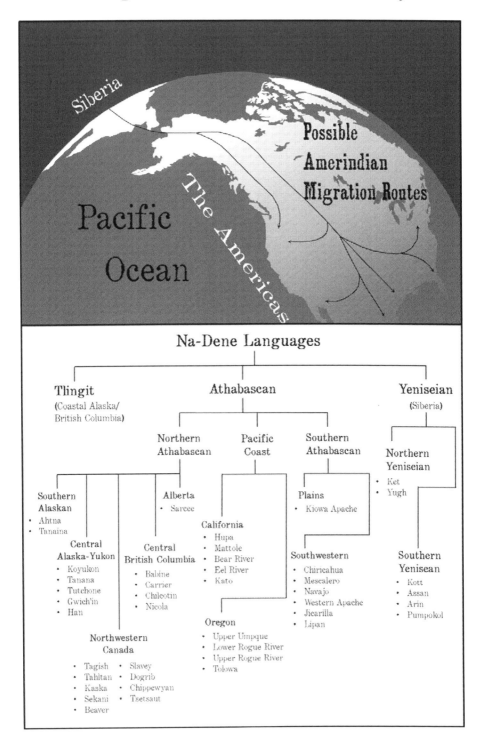

Siberia

Pacific
Ocean

The Americas

Possible
Amerindian
Migration Routes

Na-Dene Languages

Tlingit
(Coastal Alaska/
British Columbia)

Athabascan

Yeniseian
(Siberia)

Northern
Athabascan

Pacific
Coast

Southern
Athabascan

Northern
Yeniseian
• Ket
• Yugh

**Southern
Alaskan**
• Ahtna
• Tanaina

Alberta
• Sarcee

Plains
• Kiowa Apache

**Central
Alaska-Yukon**
• Koyukon
• Tanana
• Tutchone
• Gwich'in
• Han

**Central
British Columbia**
• Babine
• Carrier
• Chilcotin
• Nicola

California
• Hupa
• Mattole
• Bear River
• Eel River
• Kato

Southwestern
• Chiricahua
• Mescalero
• Navajo
• Western Apache
• Jicarilla
• Lipan

**Southern
Yenisean**
• Kott
• Assan
• Arin
• Pumpokol

**Northwestern
Canada**
• Tagish   • Slavey
• Tahltan • Dogrib
• Kaska   • Chippewyan
• Sekani   • Tsetsaut
• Beaver

Oregon
• Upper Umpque
• Lower Rogue River
• Upper Rogue River
• Tolowa

north *"Apachu,"* or "Enemy," a name strikingly evocative of one interpretation of the word "Naha." It must be mentioned that, although proponents of the Naha-Navajo theory might be tempted to draw a similar parallel between the phonetically-comparable names "Naha" and "Navajo", the word "Navajo" actually derives from the Pueblo word *"Navahu"*, meaning "large field," which Spanish conquistadors applied to the tribe in question; the name that the Navajo called themselves was *"Dine"*, or "People"- another clear connection between this desert tribe and the Dene of the subarctic.

———————

Many authorities on the subject contend that archaeological and historical evidence further supports the notion that the ancestors of the Navajo and Apache tribes entered the American Southwest from the north. However, most experts agree that these southerly migrations took place somewhere between 1100 and 1500 A.D., several centuries before the Naha were said to have disappeared from the Nahanni Valley (at least, according to two different versions of the legend).

Mythological Connections

A number of aboriginal folklorists, including Herb Norwegian, have vaguely suggested that similarities between the legend of the Naha tribe and the traditional Navajo origin myth further corroborate the connection between these two indigenous peoples. Unfortunately, few of these experts, in their interviews and articles, have deigned to specify which similarities they were referring to. Their omissions were not necessarily born from negligence, and may, in fact, have been deliberate; historically, many Native American and First Nations storytellers have shown an aversion to sharing the sacred stories of their ancestors with outsiders.

Fortunately for outsiders, the Navajo creation myth, also known as the *Dine Bahane*, or the "Story of the People," is now a well-documented piece of oral tradition. Like most tales passed down by word of mouth, it has a number of different versions. All versions, however, similar to those traditionally espoused by the Pueblo, the Aztec, and the Hopi, tell of four different worlds through which the first humans passed on their way to the Fifth World, in which we live today.

The **First World** of the Navajo creation story, also known as the Dark World, was a small island surrounded by four seas and inhabited by spiritual beings. From there, the First Man and First Woman travelled east and ascended into the **Second World,** or the Blue World, home to blue and gray-furred and feathered animals.

The First Man and Woman eventually left the Second World for the Third, travelling south on the advice of the Wind and exiting through an opening in the sky. The **Third World,** or the Yellow World, was dominated by two great perpendicular rivers and six Sacred Mountains. Here, the First Woman bore many children- the First People- who learned weaving and agriculture from their supernatural neighbours. Here also, some of the First Women gave birth to various half-human monsters.

After a mischievous Coyote stole two children from a river monster called the Big Water Creature (sometimes called the "Water Buffalo"), the First People were beset by a Great Flood, which approached from the North, East, and South. The People fled up the Sacred Mountains and, with the help of the Holy People who inhabited these heights, scrambled up into the **Fourth World.**

The Fourth World, or the White World, consisted of a small, barren island surrounded by water. At the behest of the People, a supernatural being called Water Sprinkler threw great stones in each of the four directions, creating holes in the ground through which the water drained. Gradually, a land to the east began to emerge. The island on which the People were stranded was connected to this mainland by a lane which was too muddy to cross. The People called upon the Wind to dry the mud, and soon were making their way across this bridge to the new world, the **Fifth World.**[4]

In this new land, the People, with the help of supernatural forces, created the Sun, the Moon, the Seasons, and, inadvertently, Death. That accomplished, they created the Stars and Constellations, and recreated the six Sacred

---

[4] In some versions of the story, the Fifth World was located above the Fourth World rather than to the east of it, and the People reached it with the help of either a Badger or a Locust.

Mountains that they had revered in the Third World. Shortly after furnishing their Fifth World with these things, the People were attacked by the half-human monsters that the First Women had spawned in the previous world. From then on, the people lived in fear of these creatures.

Around this time, two extraordinary Twins were born. Their mother was once a small turquoise figurine who the First Man and Women discovered atop a Sacred Mountain and raised as their daughter, at the behest of the Holy People. The Twins eventually learned that their father, a mysterious figure who had no hand in their upbringing, was the Sun, who lived far to the east. After a series of ill-fated hunting excursions, the Twins were chased east by monsters. Aided by the guidance of a supernatural being called Spider Woman, they continued east along the Holy Trail, conquered a succession of obstacles, and ultimately arrived at the home of their father. After subjecting them to a number of dangerous tests, the Sun accepted the Twins as his sons and gave them magic weapons with which to fight the monsters back west. The Twins returned home and, with the help of the Wind and other allies, slaughtered the half-human creatures that had caused their people such grief.

Some of those who have attempted to connect the Navajo origin legend with the tale of the Naha tribe have suggested that the Fourth World (the White World) represents subarctic Canada, and that the Fifth World represents *Dinetah*, the traditional homeland of the Navajo (a territory encompassing northwestern New Mexico, northeastern Arizona, southwestern Colorado, and southeastern Utah). However, in the version of the legend described above, the People travelled east from a small, barren island to the Fifth World via an isthmus surrounded by water- a scenario much more evocative of the migration across the Siberian land bridge than the long southerly trek the Naha are said to have made down the length of North America.

Although this potential connection between the Fourth World and Northern Canada is fairly weak, the Navajo creation story certainly has some similarities to various Dene origin tales. According to many ethnographers, some Dene creation stories involved a migration from the west, not unlike the Navajo emergence from the Fourth World to the Fifth. Others involved a Deluge, similar to the Great Flood which drove the Navajo from the Third World to the Fourth.[5] And some featured characters called the "Two Brothers", who killed off giants and other monsters that terrorized their people, much like the heroic Twins of Navajo lore.

It must be mentioned that these similarities are not necessarily proof that Navajo and Dene creation stories are related to one another. Through what is probably sheer

---

[5] According to some Dene legends, after the Deluge, the Beaver, the Otter, and the Muskrat all dove down in an effort to retrieve mud with which to build habitable land. In this way, it is nearly identical to a similar origin legend espoused by the Ojibwa, or Chippewa, of the Great Lakes area.

coincidence, these same themes also feature in stories embraced by civilizations from all over the world, most of them with no discernable connections to the Dene. For example, a west-to-east migration characterizes the Exodus of Hebrew scripture; a Great Flood features in the Ancient Mesopotamian poem *The Epic of Gilgamesh*; and warrior brothers called the Hero Twins are central figures of Maya mythology.

Although the Navajo and Dene creation myths certainly share some common themes, there are also several ways in which they differ. According to ethnographer Cornelius B. Osgood in his 1933 article *The Ethnography of the Great Bear Lake Indians,* a report on the ethnography of the Sahtu Dene: "Myths of origin, flood legends, and tales of monsters, vary from tribe to tribe, and from individual." Some Dene origin stories tell of "descent from a woman and a medicine man who assumed the form of a dog", while others revolve around a battle between two children over the possession of an owl- elements of which the Navajo story is devoid.

If anything, the Navajo origin myth, with its Five Worlds, bears a closer resemblance to those of the Pueblo, Aztec, and Hopi- three nations related by common cultural and religious aspects- than it does to the various creation myths of the subarctic Dene. If the Navajo people truly derive from the Dene, as linguistic, anthropological, and historical evidence seems to suggests, then the similarities between the

Navajo origin myth and those espoused by their southern U.S./Mexican counterparts indicate that the Navajo may have borrowed the story from their southerly neighbours rather than brought it with them from the North. Barring the possibility that the Navajo imbued this story with elements unique to their own native folklore, this notion suggests that the story in question may have no connection with the Naha legend.

Although the Navajo creation story (or "emergence myth," as it is sometimes called) may or may not have any connection with the subarctic, another tale might. According to historian Kerry Abel in her 1993 book *Drum Songs: Glimpses of Dene History*, Father Leopold Osternmann (presumably a missionary who worked with the Navajo) wrote in 1905 that the Navajo were well aware of their subarctic relatives, and referred to them as *"Dene nahodloni,"* or "they who are also Navajos". According to Osternmann, legend had it that "a party once set out to meet the Dene, but after living with them briefly, the Navajo returned home, unable to convince the Dene to come south with them."

Spooky American Parallels

THE STORY OF THE ANASAZI

It is interesting to note that, for centuries prior to the Navajo-Apache migrations, the Southwestern United States was dominated by members of an ancient, archaeologically-advanced Amerindian civilization- a tribe whose tale, in many ways, eerily parallels that of the Naha. These remarkable people lived in permanent villages called *pueblos*, some of them composed of multi-storied buildings built from brick and stone, and others consisting of intricate apartment complexes carved from the living rock of sandstone cliffs. Incidentally, around the time of the Dene migration to the American Southwest, these people quickly and inexplicably abandoned their ancestral homes, taking to the deserts of New Mexico and Arizona, where they gradually fractured into the tribes known today as the Pueblo nations. This tribe's troglodytism and sudden and mysterious diaspora are not the only aspects in which it resembles the lost tribe of the Nahanni Valley. The name that the Navajo gave these people was *"Anasazi,"* which translates to "Ancient Enemies". For centuries, these Dene migrants avoided the lonely stone ruins that the Anasazi left behind, certain that they were haunted by evil spirits.

LEGENDS OF THE SUPERSTITION MOUNTAINS

Although it likely has no real connection with our legends, it is interesting to note that, in addition to the similarities between the story of the Naha tribe and the tale of the Anasazi, there is another legend of the American Southwest which eerily evokes the folkloric essence of Nahanni Valley. In south-central Arizona, on the western frontier of what was once Apache territory, lies a range of mountains known as the Superstitions. The legends that surround this region- tales of supernatural forces, mysterious beheadings, Indian curses, and lost gold mines- bear remarkable resemblance to many of the legends of the Nahanni Valley.

For centuries, local Apache Indians considered the Superstition Mountains to be sacred, believing that they were inhabited by an angry Thunder God who dwelled in a deep hole which served as the mouth to Hell. Legend has it that the violent dust storms for which that part of Arizona is notorious are attributable to diabolical winds which emanate from this stygian chasm.

In about 1540 A.D., Spanish conquistador Francisco Vazquez de Coronado led an expedition through what is now Arizona. He hoped to discover Cibola, one of the legendary Seven Cities of Gold, and appropriate its riches for the Spanish Crown. Upon entering the Superstition Mountains, his men began to mysteriously disappear in the night, one by one, only to be found decapitated, their desiccated corpses withering under the steady glare of the desert sun. Convinced that the area was cursed, the Spaniards fled the mountains, dubbing them *"Las Montanas de Supersticion"*, the Iberian version of the name they bear today.

In 1748, the Superstitions came under the control of Don Miguel Peralta, a cattle baron from the Mexican state of Sonora. The businessman soon learned, to his delight, that the Arizonan mountains he owned were rich in gold and silver. For the next hundred years, the Peralta family made occasional mineral-hunting excursions into the region, ever wary of the hostile Apache Indians, who were said to slaughter any white men that they found desecrating their sacred grounds.

In 1846, four of Peralta's descendants made another prospecting foray into the Superstition Mountains. This time, they returned to Sonora with a wealth of gold ore, having evidently stumbled upon a spectacular bonanza. Although they initially planned to return to the site of their diggings the following year, three of the Peralta brothers ultimately decided to remain in Mexico on account of the Mexican-American War. The fourth brother returned to the Superstitions alone, determined to liberate as much of their auric contents as he could before the area officially became the territory of the United States.

While they worked, the miners under Peralta's employ learned that an Apache attack was imminent. Accordingly, they disguised the location of their mine and loaded their donkey carts with as much gold ore as they could carry. Unfortunately, on their way out of the mountains, Peralta and his men were ambushed by Apache warriors and massacred, almost to a man.

Several decades later, sometime in the 1860's, a German prospector named Jacob Waltz discovered a fabulously rich gold mine somewhere in the Superstition Mountains- perhaps the lost diggings of the Peralta family. Waltz purportedly murdered his partner in order to avoid sharing the treasure with him, and took the secret of the mine's location with him to the grave. Following the prospector's death, the legendary bonanza he discovered was dubbed the Lost Dutchman's Mine.

ARCHAEOLOGICAL EVIDENCE

Although the question of whether or not the Navajo and Apache nations are the progeny of the Naha tribe is a subject of debate, archaeological evidence indicates that the Nahanni Valley was indeed once inhabited by an ancient Dene tribe, and may have even served as migration route for the ancestors of more southerly Dene groups. According to Pierre Berton, "in the late thirties, a scientific expedition from the University of Texas visited the Nahanni Country with the object of tracing the path of the Indian migration from Siberia down through the Canadian North. They found evidence of this deep under the leaf mold of some of the natural caves in the limestone mountains- in the form of flint arrowheads."

According to Peter Jowett, preliminary archaeological surveys indicate that "a hunter-gatherer culture, using leaf-shaped spear points, may have been the first group of people in the Nahanni, arriving between ten and nine thousand years ago. The most significant example of prehistoric occupation was uncovered at Yohin Lake," a body of water situated beside the South Nahanni's First Canyon. Here, "lithic artifacts indicate an extensive use of the area between 6,000 and 2,500 year ago."

Another archaeological site known as Chimney Point, located near the village of Nahanni Butte and so named for the ancient stone chimneys discovered there, appears to have been the site of "a historically extensive occupation" extending from ancient times up until the 19th Century.

The 1986 discovery of a fluted arrowhead atop the Tlogotsho Plateau, a vast alpine prairie overlooking Deadmen Valley, prompted another archaeological excavation which yielded evidence of a primitive stone quarry, another fluted arrowhead, a *chi-tho* (a tool used to soften hides), stone scrapers, and archaic fishing implements. These ancient artifacts, coupled with a teepee ring containing nails and fragments of an old tin can, suggest that the Plateau was occupied by Dene natives from pre-contact times up until the days of the fur trade. "Although the discoveries made on Tlogotsho Plateau are inconclusive," concluded Jowett, "they add fuel to the suggestion that the plateau may have been used as a migration route between 10,000 and 9,000 years ago".

In an interview with writer Lyn Hancock, Mary Kraus claimed to have made a number of interesting discoveries which further support the notion that the Nahanni Valley has a long history of human habitation. These include flint arrowheads, which she discovered alongside a stream called Moose Creek; a spearhead made of white stone, which she claimed to have found near the Netla River (a tributary of the Liard located about 24 kilometres from the village of Nahanni Butte); an arrowhead at Little Doctor Lake, located just beyond the northeastern slopes of the Nahanni Range; a flint axe head, which she found next to the South Nahanni;

and a number of other artifacts made from chert (a fine-grained sedimentary rock) and sandstone.

* * *

In *Dangerous River*, Raymond Patterson described finding some ancient artifacts of his own inside one of the many caves of the Tlogotsho Mountains, which evidently once served as a crude habitation. "A couple of paces into the cave," he wrote, "and on the left-hand side there was a fireplace- a rough semi-circle of big, flat stones enclosing a little space against the wall in which lay a pile of old charcoal and butt ends, greyed over with a thick layer of dust and grit through long years of eddying winds. The wall and roof of the cave just there were blackened and scarred with the smoke and flames of many fires, and soon the latest one of all in the cave's long history was flickering there, sending up a warm glow of welcome...

"The step of the cave, I noticed, was well worn. An idea struck me, and I got the little axe from beside the fire and started a small excavation with the back of it in the mossy slope below the step and away from the trail. It was as I had expected- bones and then more bones, the midden of the cave. After supper I came back to it, lighting a small fire on the edge of the step in order to see better. But there was nothing, only bones in all stages of decay—gnawed bones, bones smashed for the sake of the marrow in them, feeble old powdery bones, splinters and chips of bone. I was on the point of giving up and was scratching idly amongst the fragments when I came on one piece that seemed harder and sharper than the rest. There were curious toothmarks on it, and I held it up to the firelight and examined it more closely- it was a stone arrowhead. I dropped off to sleep that night by the fire, very snug with the warm rocks of the cave around and above me- and behind me a long line of copper-coloured hunters reaching far back into the darkness of forgotten centuries..."

Perhaps the "copper-coloured hunters" who once inhabited that ancient dwelling place were Naha tribesmen, and perhaps the bones, charcoal, and arrowhead that Patterson unearthed constitute proof that members of this legendary lost tribe once lived within the caves of the Nahanni Valley, as some versions of the legend purport. Whatever the case, Mackenzie Mountain folklore certainly contends that the cave systems which permeate Nahanni Country were, at one time or another, the abode of all manner of extraordinary entities, from the Naha to the Nakani to evil spirits. Throughout the 20th Century, fearless spelunkers put these legends to the test, entering these formations, exploring them, and ultimately emerging to reveal the chilling secrets of what popular literature has styled the Mongol Caves.

The Mongol Caves

"As we watched the famous mists of the Nahanni come drifting down out of the first of the canyons, we could well understand how superstitious natives had built it up into a place of mystery. Wherever we would look up at the canyon's walls you could see one of the so-called 'Mongol caves' dominating every each river... Some were high up on the cliffs and looked as if they would be almost impossible to get to. Some of them were down just along the treetops. With the black mouths of all those caverns staring at us, sometimes we would get a feeling that someone was watching us... The natives used to tell stories about huge hairy men with red eyes who were supposed to inhabit these canyons and carry off any lone hunters or squaws they happened to see... So we made camp on a little beach and decided to see just what was in all the caverns."

- Mel Ross, *Headless Valley*, 1958.

FROM VIRGINIA FALLS to Pulpit Rock, the Nahanni Valley boasts a variety of striking geological formations. Among the most abundant of these are the caves which feature so prominently in the various myths and legends that surround the region. Some said that these caverns were the abode of the Nakani, the hairy, man-eating giants of Dene tradition. Others claimed that they were haunted by ghosts and evil spirits who claimed the lives of any who entered, anxious to recruit more souls for the spectral legion in which they served. Others still believed that the caves once served as the dwelling places of the Naha, the brutal cavemen who disappeared from the Valley long ago. In spite of their differences, all three versions of this legend agree that the caves of the Nahanni Valley were occupied by sinister forces, and that those foolish enough to enter them were seldom seen again.

ED CLAUSEN'S DISCOVERY

Aside from perhaps Raymond Patterson, who claimed to have spent a night inside one of the Nahanni's caves in 1928, one of the first white men to venture into the region's caverns was a hard-bitten trapper named Ed Clausen.

Ed Clausen first came to the Nahanni Valley sometime in the 1920's and established a trap line on the creek which bears his name today[1]. For years, he trapped, fished, and hunted in the heart of Indian territory, often exploring 'haunted' canyons and mountainsides where local red men feared to tread. Sometime in the 1930's, following a hunting excursion deep within Nahanni Country, he emerged from the wilderness with a startling tale, which he told to any who would listen. In the summer of 1938, he related this tale to

---

[1] This is Clausen Creek, which enters the South Nahanni near the Kraus Hot Springs.

Philip Godsell, who included it in his 1944 book *Romance of the Alaska Highway.*

"Them Injuns ain't so crazy as I figured," Clausen is quoted as having said, in reference to the various Dene legends regarding the caves of the Nahanni Valley. "I didn't see no giant cavemen, but I sure did come across some caves all right. I was hunting mountain goats when I ran plumb into one of 'em cut from the rock half-way up the face of a hundred-foot precipice that spans a two-thousand-foot valley. It was about eighteen feet by twelve, with a hole running straight up through the rock, which must have been a sort of chimney. I found two more that had been chiseled from the living rock by human hands. I'd believe almost anything about that country now."

Godsell also chronicled the trapper's story in a much earlier article for the March 11, 1939 issue of the *Toronto Star Weekly*[2], entitled *"Nahanni Caves Reveal Link in Man's Past".* In that piece, Godsell speculated that the cave that Clausen stumbled upon was carved thousands of years ago by the progeny of the first immigrants to the Americas, whose ancestors made the long trek across the Bering Strait land bridge from Siberia. "There's no doubt it was made by human hands in days long past," Clausen assured Godsell. "You can see where primitive tools have bitten into the solid rock...

---

[2] The *Toronto Star Weekly* later shortened to the *Star Weekly* was a weekly periodical published in connection with the *Toronto Star* newspaper.

"It's quite easy to get to from the South Nahanni River," the trapper continued. "It's a beautiful spot, with white-capped peaks rising all around it. I questioned the Indians, and all the whites in the district, but none of them ever saw or heard of such a cave.

"Of course, many of the present-day Indians are scared to go in that country anyway. I also found a lot of old chipped stone arrowheads on a high sand dome surrounded by spruce. I believe they were left there by the early inhabitants that passed through the country during the Ice Age."

Clausen speculated that these "early inhabitants" may have built the aforementioned cave "as a refuge from some enemies," or perhaps from the mammoths and mastodons which "the Indians still find frozen in the glaciers."

Clausen's interview ended with his refusal to disclose the location of his discovery; trapping was apparently quite poor that year, and the woodsman hoped to "make a few dollars guiding... some scientists or tourists" to the cave that he had found.

According to Godsell, the trapper got what he wished for. In the late summer of 1939, following his interview, anthropologist Dr. Wesley L. Bliss of the University of New Mexico hired Clausen to take him and a number of geology students to the mysterious cave. Allegedly, the anthropologist made several important discoveries there which supported the theory that the Nahanni Valley was once home to proto-Dene

Indians, and that these people were migrants who came to the Americas via the Bering Strait land bridge. Bliss also claimed to have discovered proof that mammoths and other prehistoric animals once roamed the region.

Pierre Berton's Rebuttal

The story of Clausen's discovery spread quickly throughout the Canadian North. As is so often the case with oral lore, the tale subtly evolved with every retelling so that, in time, the derivative story bore little resemblance to the original. By the mid-1940's, rumour had it that the caverns of the Nahanni Valley, in the most remote corners of that country, were still inhabited by Stone Age cavemen- perhaps Neanderthals, or relics of the lost Naha tribe.

This rumour was one of the legends that Pierre Berton was tasked with investigation during his Headless Valley expedition in 1946. Although the journalist and his companions never actually entered any of the caves during their visit to the Nahanni, they studied those that dotted the walls of the First Canyon from a distance and observed that they appeared to be "as empty and lifeless as the canyon itself." They also spoke with Jack La Flair on the subject, learning that the cave to which Ed Clausen led Dr. Bliss and his crew was actually located on the slopes of Nahanni Butte- incidentally, an alleged stopping point for Naha raiding parties- and that the anthropologist's discoveries consisted of smoke-blackened walls and "one old flint arrowhead".

Later, in a radio broadcast, Berton disparaged Ed Clausen and the legend that his discovery engendered. "Clausen claimed he had found old kettles, arrows, and a variety of prehistoric knick-knacks in these caves," he said. "He didn't produce any. I will personally give Mr. Clausen a C-note[3] for every prehistoric kettle he can prove he found in the caves of the Nahanni. Mr. Clausen, I learned, had his trapping licence revoked, and I think he wanted a job as a guide."

In other radio broadcasts, Berton related a story told to him by Jack La Flair which, he suggested, illustrated how relatively unremarkable phenomena, like the arrowheads that Clausen and Bliss discovered, could spawn dramatic legends, like that of the Nahanni cavemen. The story goes that LaFlair, while travelling from his trading post to Fort Simpson, noticed a curious rock formation atop Nahanni Butte which, from a certain location on the Liard River, vaguely resembled a Maltese cross.[4] When he finally reached Fort Simpson and paid a visit to the HBC post there, he casually mentioned this observation to the storekeeper. The next summer, when he returned to Fort Simpson to stock up on winter supplies, the new storekeeper told his own story back to him- this time, a tale of mysterious, gargoyle-like

[3] A $100 bill.

[4] The Maltese cross is a stylized, eight-pointed cross associated with the Mediterranean island of Malta, and sometimes with the Knights Hospitaller, a monastic military order founded during the First Crusade.

stone sculptures which stood like sentinels atop the Nahanni's canyons.

DISCOVERIES ON THE NORTH NAHANNI
Billy Clark's Story

Shortly after Ed Clausen's discovery, the North Country was abuzz with talk of ancient caves containing prehistoric artifacts. The media dubbed these formations the 'Mongol caves', apparently espousing the theory that their early inhabitants were Siberian migrants whose ancestors followed large game herds from the steppes of Central Asia to the Bering Strait. Soon, a handful of Nahanni frontiersmen began to learn from their Indian friends that such caverns were said to exist on a tributary-of-a-tributary of the North Nahanni River, a waterway which drains into the Mackenzie River about 70 miles northeast of the Kraus Hot Springs. In no time, Billy Clark, one of the few white men made privy to this information, decided to see for himself if the stories had any merit to them.

According to Clark, legend had it that the entrances to these caves in North Nahanni Country were littered with fragments of ancient pottery which, from their description, evoked canopic jars- burial urns in which the Ancient Egyptians interred the internal organs of their pharaohs while preparing their bodies for mummification. The Indians were afraid of these caves, and avoided the area surrounding them whenever possible.

Upon questioning some of his Dene friends, who seemed reluctant to speak on the subject, Clark learned that one of the men who knew the location of these North Nahanni caves was George Cli, the son of a local Dene chief. Cli, Clark knew, was a well-built hunter in superb physical condition who was renowned in those parts for his skills in bushcraft. Moreover, the Indian was reputedly fearless, and was said to possess an adventurous spirit. Although Cli, like most Dene at that time, was hesitant to discuss taboo topics with white men whom he did not know well, Clark was certain that, if given proper compensation, the hunter would happily lead him to the ancient caves long shunned by his people.

Accordingly, Billy Clark got in touch with George Cli-perhaps through a mutual friend named Julian Hardisty, a Mission-educated Indian from Hay River- and offered him a daily salary of $5 to take him and two of his friends, trapper George Sibbeston and a mining engineer named Dr. Duncan Derry, to the caves of the North Nahanni. Cli, who did not strike Clark as "the type who was out for the money," readily agreed, on the condition that the frontiersman supply his family with enough food to sustain them in his absence. Billy Clark complied with the Indian's request, and in no time, he, Sibbeston, and Dr. Derry were geared up and ready to follow George Cli into the wilderness.

Unfortunately, due to an unforeseen delay, the expedition was cancelled at the last minute. Neither Billy Clark nor his friends ever got around to arranging another expedition to North Nahanni Country, and George Cli ultimately took the secret of the caves' location with him to the grave.

The Tale of Pansy Cameron

At the time of Billy Clark's proposed expedition, there was another native who knew the location of curious caves in North Nahanni Country, and who did not hold the same superstitious aversion to them as most of her Dene counterparts. This woman was Pansy Cameron, the wife of a white trapper named Jack Cameron.

Although Pansy was of aboriginal descent, she was neither Dene nor a native of the Northland; both of her parents were Swampy Cree who hailed from the lake-ridden forests of Northern Manitoba. During the North-West Rebellion, her father, a trapper named Desoto, shouldered his rifle and cartridge belt and headed south to fight under Metis general Gabriel Dumont on the prairies of what is now Central Saskatchewan. In 1885, following the execution of revolutionary leader Louis Riel, Desoto fled northwest with his family, eventually settling in Mackenzie Country.

At the time of Ed Clausen's widely-publicized discovery, Pansy Desoto- now Pansy Cameron- was in her sixties, having spent roughly half a century living in the watersheds of the Mackenzie and Liard Rivers. When she received word of Clausen's find, memories from her youth came flooding back to her. Pansy recalled camping with her family beside a creek in the North Nahanni area when she was about twelve years old. The slopes that fronted this creek were riddled with caves, inside each of which lay large, beautiful, perfectly round stone pots. When she recounted this story to her husband, Jack Cameron, the old trapper refused to believe her, perhaps without justification; according to Billy Clark, Pansy was "Mission-brought-up, and had no reason to lie". Whether or not the two canoe-going government men who interviewed her in the 1940's, having travelled to Nahanni Country from Ottawa in order to investigate Clausen's claim, felt similarly about her story is a matter of conjecture.

One man who did believe Pansy's tale, or was at least sufficiently intrigued by it to pursue it, was Gus Kraus. Sometime in the 1940's, this American trapper, following Pansy's directions, hiked deep into the wilderness and into a particular valley in North Nahanni Country. Sure enough, he came to a spot where the valley's limestone slopes were pockmarked with dozens of shallow caves, inside each of which sat a single stone sphere. Some of these stones were as small as pool balls. Others were the size of bowling balls. Others still were as large as 45-gallon oil drums. All of them, however, were completely spherical and polished to a sheen. "I gave three of them, one time, to Gerald Hansen..." Kraus said in an interview for Parks Canada. "Perfectly round. You could just roll 'em. You couldn't see no wobble in the darn thing."

In the same interview, Kraus speculated that the region's caves were formed millennia ago, when the creek was high enough to cover them, by a peculiar sort of mechanical erosion. Specifically, he believed that the smooth spheres inside them, which he referred to as "pots", were once rough rocks which, by some action of the current, pressed up against the walls of the riverbank and began to rotate, slowly grinding away at the limestone until they carved out small pockets for themselves. Over the centuries, these pockets grew into shallow caves, while the rough rocks were reduced to smooth spheres. Could these spheres, which both Pansy Cameron and Gus Kraus likened to carved stone pots, have some connection with the shattered Egyptian urns which feature in the narrative that captivated Billy Clark?

PETROGLYPHS

One facet of the legend of the Mongol caves has it that the walls of some of these formations are covered with petroglyphs, or cave drawings, carved or painted by the caves' ancient inhabitants. Most references to these alleged cave drawings were quite vague. A few were more specific, and some downright bizarre. For example, according to one newspaper article published in the July 16, 1946 issue of the *Toronto Star*, some archaeologists believed that these Nahanni cave glyphs "indicate possible connections with early Maya civilization."

Mel and Ethel Ross' Discoveries

In 1958, roughly two decades after Ed Clausen's find, Canadian adventurers Mel and Ethel Ross made their trip up the South Nahanni River, which they documented in the homemade film *Headless Valley*. It is possible that this husband-and-wife team, during their 1958 escapade, captured what might be the only tangible evidence of Nahanni cave drawings that we have to date.

While riding their motor-powered scow through the South Nahanni's First Canyon, the couple couldn't help but take notice of the sinister-looking caves that pockmarked the canyon's walls. "Some were high up on the cliffs," Mel narrated, as the camera panned a limestone precipice, "and looked as if they would be almost impossible to get to. Some of them were down just along the treetops. With the black mouths of all those caverns staring at us, sometimes we would get a feeling that someone was watching us. Usually, whenever we got that feeling, we would look around and we would find someone peering at us." At this point, in accordance with the charming, old-fashioned humour that characterizes the film, we are treated to footage of a squirrel glaring defiantly at the camera. "Nothing was going to get past these lookouts; they just stared you straight in the eye."

Later on in the documentary, the Ross couple made camp on a beach and headed up the valley's slopes, determined to explore some of the caverns. "There are dozens and dozens of these so-called 'Mongol caves,'" said Mel. "Some are in the main canyon, but many of them are way back in side-canyons.

"I spent quite a few days poking around back among those canyons. Most of the caves were way up on ledges and pretty hard to get to. We had to be extremely careful because any injury like a broken leg way up here in that country wouldn't leave one much of a chance of getting out.

"Some of the caverns were only twenty to thirty feet deep, and one could see clear to the back by daylight. In others, we had to use a light to get back to the end. And then there were some that were so deep that we didn't ever manage to reach the end of the cave.

"These caverns aren't safe at all. They are in a very shattered formation, and the floors are covered with large blocks of rock which seem to have fallen off the roof very recently. The continual fall of rocks gives the caves that appearance of just having had a load of rock dumped out by some Mongol tenant enlarging his premises... at least, we hoped it was just the rock fall that made them look that way.

"Way back in one cavern, we found a blackened spot on the floor which looked like embers of an old fire and what appeared to be some drawings on the wall. After brushing away the dust of the drawings, we got wood and lit up a fire trying to get enough light to photograph by. But even with the firelight supplementing my lamp, I had to take these shots of the drawings with single-frame time exposures. We began to think that perhaps the natives had some basis for those tales they used to tell about the big hairy men with the red eyes."

After showing grainy footage of these supposed cave drawings, flickering as they did in the light of the fire, Mel went on to describe the physical nature of the caverns that he and Ethel explored:

"The cave entrances all had piles of tremendous boulders... Some of them were so low that you had to crawl in on your hands and knees, but others had rooms that would almost hold a two-story building. Another of the caverns we explored had a high vaulted entrance which led in a long, wide passage going straight back into the mountain. Way back at the end of that passage we found an opening through which we could just manage to crawl into a regular maze of passages at a higher level. We had three hundred feet of nylon ropes with us. We tied one end there at the opening and went back in to the various corridors and rooms. In one of those rooms, we found another blackened spot on the floor and some more of those odd sketches. We paid our three hundred feet of nylon rope in several directions, but it never did get us to the end of the passages. We felt we would be foolish to try to go in any deeper without better equipment, and believe me, it felt good to be back out into the fresh air and sunlight again."

JEAN POIREL'S EXPEDITIONS

Six years after Mel and Ethel's expedition, a French-born, Montreal-based former boxing champion named Jean Poirel arrived in Nahanni Country, determined to test himself against the elements. He was accompanied by three friends: Bertrand Bordet, Claude Bernardin, and Roger Rochat, all of whom planned to descend the South Nahanni River in a circular RCAF dingy, its bottom fortified with truck tires.

On June 29, 1964, the four companions entered the country via bushplane. Bernardin and Rochat were dropped off at a particular point above Virginia Falls, where they set up a base camp. Poirel and Bordet, on the other hand, continued northwest to the headwaters of the river, where they parachuted in their dinghies into the water, air force-style. The two men paddled downriver, rejoined their companions, and proceeded down the South Nahanni together. After portaging around Virginia Falls, they plunged through the river's four rapids-riddled canyons, ultimately arriving at Nahanni Butte wet and weary, yet safe and sound.

Poirel returned to the Nahanni many more times in the ensuing years. He dedicated four of these subsequent expeditions to the exploration of some of the hundred and twenty caves of the First Canyon- all of which were hitherto untouched by man. Using climbing equipment, he and those who accompanied him scaled the canyon's limestone walls and, with headlamps strapped to their helmets, proceeded into the heart of the rock. Nothing could have prepared them for what they found inside.

Grotte Valerie

Of all the caverns that Poirel and his companions explored, among the most impressive is the cave system which Poirel named *"Grotte Valerie"*, after his daughter. "Extending 430 metres north into the canyon wall," wrote canoeist Neil Hartling of the formation in his book *Nahanni: River of Gold, River of Dreams*, "it lies from 40 to 60 metres below the plateau. There are over two kilometres of passages with three entrances."

The Stalactite Gallery

If you enter the westernmost of Grotte Valerie's three entrances and take a left at the first two forks in the tunnel, you will come to a passage known as the Stalactite Gallery. This tunnel contains hundreds of stalactites (calcium carbonate deposits which hang from the roof of the cave like icicles) and a number of stalagmites (reverse stalagmites which jut upward from the cave floor), many of them older than the last Ice Age.

Ice Lake

Beyond the middle of Grotte Valerie's three entrances lies an obstacle called Ice Lake- a frozen passageway bottomed with a slick sheet of ice.

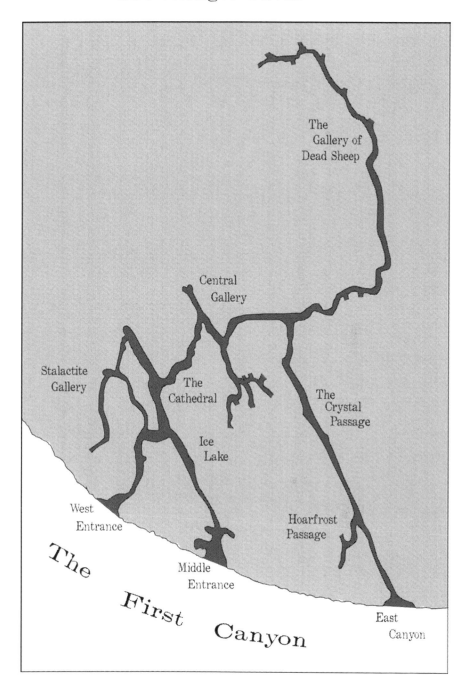

Legends of the Nahanni Valley

The Crystal Passage

Grotte Valerie's third and final eastern entrance is succeeded by a long, visually spectacular tunnel called the Crystal Passage. The walls of this channel are coated with a delicate layer of hoarfrost which glitters in the lamplight like a million crystals. As Peter Jowett explains in his book *Nahanni: The River Guide*, "the large feathery ice crystals that cling to the floor, walls and ceiling" are created by the condensation of "warm, moist air... drawn down into the cave's depths."

The Gallery of Dead Sheep

All three of the main branches of Grotte Valerie are connected by a lofty, transverse tunnel known as the Cathedral. If you follow this tunnel east, beyond the intersection of the Crystal passage, you will come to a sharp, slippery decline succeeded by a long, dark passageway that holds an even darker secret. This tunnel is known as the Gallery of Dead Sheep, so-named for the skeletons of over a hundred Dall sheep which litter its floor.

It appears that these mountain sheep- the bones of some of which have been allegedly carbon dated to the 1st Century B.C.- all wandered into Grotte Valerie for one reason or another, perhaps seeking food, or refuge from a predator. Something compelled them to stumble blindly through the Cathedral and into the tunnel beyond, where they slid down the icefall preceding the passageway in question. Unable to climb back up the slippery slope, they slowly starved to death in that natural oubliette, alone but for the skeletons of the unfortunates that went before them. "It is not uncommon for sheep to seek refuge from a storm in a cave," wrote Peter Jowett, "although it does seem unusual that these sheep wandered in the dark for hundreds of meters," ultimately to their doom.

———•———

Today, geologists know that the caverns of the Nahanni Valley, sometimes collectively referred to as the "Nahanni karstlands," are natural structures formed by a chemical reaction between carbonic acid present in rainwater and the more basic calcium carbonate found in limestone; if any of the Nahanni's caverns are man-made, they are exceptions to the rule. 20th Century journalists dubbed these formations the 'Mongol caves,' believing that they were once inhabited by the Mongoloid ancestors of the First Nations. The Dene, however, long maintained that these caves were home to mysterious creatures of whom they lived in perpetual fear- the wild mountain men known as "Nakani".

The Nakani

"That he had nowhere seen the slightest Indian sign bore out
the redskin reports that the country was taboo and recalled
their superstitions that it was haunted by a race of prehistoric
Troglodytes, or Nakanies, as they called them, with repulsive
gargoyle-like faces who lived in caves cut from the living rock;
creatures reported to be twice the size of ordinary humans, who
never missed a chance to carry off unwary hunters or stray
squaws in their powerful, gorilla-like arms."

- Philip H. Godsell, *The Curse of Dead Man's Valley*, 1950

FROM THE YOWIE OF AUSTRALIA to the Yeren of
China to the Yeti of the Himalayas, huge hairy
wildmen feature in folklore around the world, and
Canada is no exception. Undoubtedly, the Great White
North's most famous wildman is the Sasquatch, the shy,
reclusive giant said to roam the rainforests of the Pacific
Northwest; often colloquially referred to as Bigfoot. Less well-
known are the Sasquatch's coastal counterparts: the
emaciated, long-haired *Bukwus*, or "Wild Man of the Woods",
said to haunt the rivers and streams of Vancouver Island and
the Queen Charlotte Sound; and the huge, dimwitted

Dzunukwa of Kwakiutl and Nootka legend- an old, black-skinned, red-lipped ogress purported to snatch up mischievous children and carry them off in a basket to her forest lair. More obscure wildmen have been reported in other parts of the country, from the Rocky Mountains of Western Alberta to the rocky highlands of Labrador. Perhaps most mysterious of all, however, are the various subhuman hominoids said to inhabit the taiga, tundra, and alpine areas of the Canadian North. Among the most prominent of these are the Nakani.

Long before Alexander Mackenzie dipped his paddle into the *Deh Cho*, Dene tribes from all over the North, from the eastern shores of the Mackenzie River to the forests of Alaska, spoke of mysterious wildmen who harassed them at night, often lurking in the shadows just beyond the light of the campfire. The Dene were terrified of these elusive creatures, who were as vividly real to them as the wolf and the raven, and went to great lengths to avoid crossing paths with them.

One of the first frontiersmen to write about these wildmen was Father Emile Petitot, a 19th Century Oblate missionary who lived among the Slavey and the Sahtu Dene of the North Country's two great lakes. In 1876, Petitot wrote of a fear that spread among the Indians each summer like an epidemic: "They live at times in continual terror... of an imaginary enemy who pursues them without rest and who they believe to see everywhere even though he doesn't exist at all."

According to ethnographer Cornelius B. Osgood, belief in the Nakani was strong among the Slavey, Dogrib, and Sahtu Dene as late as 1929. When they suspected that a Nakani was lurking nearby, entire Dene bands would often abandon their camps and seek shelter on a nearby lake island, secure in the belief that their pursuer, for one reason or another, was unable to cross over to their new campsite from the shore. On other occasions, according to a Hudson's Bay Company trader named John Firth, entire encampments would instead stand their ground and fire their muskets "into the forest at suppositious wanderers in the night."

According to HBC trader B.R. Ross in his 1879 report entitled *Notes on the Tinneh or Chipewyan Indians of British and Russian America*:

"A strange footprint, or any unusual sound in the forest, is quite sufficient to cause great excitement in the camp. At Fort Resolution I have on several occasions caused all the natives encamped around to flock for protection into the fort during the night simply by whistling, hidden in the bushes. My train of hauling dogs also, of a large breed of great hunters, would, in crashing through the branches in pursuit of an unfortunate hare, frighten some women out gathering berries, who would rush in frantic haste to the tents and fearfully relate a horrific account of some strange painted Indians whom they had seen. It was my custom in the spring, during the wild fowl season, to sleep

outside at some distance from the fort. Numerous were the cautions that I received from the natives of my foolhardiness in doing so..."

The names that the Indians applied to their mysterious unseen enemies varied from place to place and from tribe to tribe. To the Slavey, Kaska, and Mountain Indians of Mackenzie Country, they were the *"Nakani"*. The Gwich'in who lived further to the north, in the frozen forests that skirt the Arctic Circle, referred to them as *"Mahoni."* The Koyukon Indians of the Yukon River Valley called these creatures *"Nakentlia,"* or "Sneakers," while the Tanaina of Southwest Alaska referred to them as *"Nant'ina,"* or "Hairy Men". Other appellatives included "Bad Indian," "Bellowing Man," and "Bushman." Although the labels attached to these wildmen were numerous, Indian descriptions of them were eerily consistent across the Northland.

DESCRIPTION
Physical Appearance

Most 19th and 20th Century frontiersmen who wrote about the Nakani in their books and journals were under the impression that the Dene regarded them as hairy cannibalistic giants, vaguely human in appearance, with red eyes and long, muscular arms.

According to English adventurer Michael H. Mason in his 1924 book *The Arctic Forests*, the Gwich'in of Peel

River Country in Northern Yukon described the Nakani (or "Mahoni," as they called them) as "terrible wild men, with red eyes, and of enormous height, completely covered with long hair." Their tremendous size was attested to by the three-foot-long, human-like footprints that they left in their wake, as well as their alleged ability to tear entire birch trees from the earth with their bare hands, roots and all. Similarly, Philip Godsell, who spent much time around the campfires of the Slavey and Kaska during his years as an inspector for the Hudson's Bay Company, described the Nakani as "troglodytes, twice the size of ordinary humans, who went about naked save for a coating of evil-smelling hair..." In some articles, he likened them to gorillas and gargoyles, and commented upon the superhuman strength and speed they were said to possess.

Many frontiersmen wrote about the incredible size of this creature's footprints, which they left behind in the snow and muskeg. Their tracks were purportedly manlike in appearance, yet much longer and narrower. In some accounts, their big toe stood out from the remaining four. Although their footprints never bore any nail marks, some said that the Nakani's fingers were tipped with long, nail-like claws.

By the mid-20th Century, the image of the Nakani as an enormous hairy monster was making its way into books and popular magazines, often in dramatic fashion. For example, an article entitled "Cursed Treasure of Deadman's Valley," published in the June 1968 issue of the magazine

Saga, maintained that the Nakani (or "Naconni," as the author called them), were "hairy demons who stand as high as a Kodiak bear, are as swift as a bird in flight, and... kill all things they can reach by cutting off their heads... Their skin is so tough that a bullet will not penetrate it, and cutting it with a knife is more difficult than cutting stone."

Domain

The Kaska, Slavey, and Mountain Indians of Mackenzie Country long maintained that the Nahanni Valley was the domain of the Nakani, and that these fearsome monsters resided within its foreboding caves and canyons. This belief is attested to by the region's toponymy; according to Dene language expert Allan Adam, *"Na'aahdee"*, an old native word for the South Nahanni River, means "River of Giants."

The Nakani were by no means confined to these remote mountain hideaways. Many of these monsters tirelessly traversed the subarctic forests in search of prey, often travelling extraordinarily long distances without stopping for food or rest, usually alone. Natives all over the Northland, from the coastal regions of Alaska to the forests of the Yukon, lived in almost perpetual fear of them.

Nakani attacks occurred almost exclusively during the spring, summer, and early autumn. The subarctic winter, on the other hand, though dark, miserable, and bitterly cold, was mercifully devoid of these dreaded encounters. Where the Nakani retreated to during the winter months was a mystery to the Dene. Some said that they retired to carefully-concealed burrows that they dug from the permafrost, where they spent the winter hibernating like bears. Others claimed that they migrated south to a place where their kind were more numerous.

Behavior

Like the Nahanni Indians, the Nakani have been blamed for the unusual number of mysterious deaths and disappearances that have plagued Nahanni Country since the days of Willie and Frank McLeod. Legend has it that these monsters did their grisly work at night, prowling about the river valley in the dark and quietly dispatching any campers they happened to encounter, perhaps tearing, twisting, or hacking their victims' heads from their shoulders.

Outside the Mackenzie Mountains, the Nakani hunted travelling Indians, stalking them from concealment in the brush. Oftentimes, a Nakani's intended victims only became aware of its presence when one of their number- perhaps a scout on reconnaissance duty- stumbled upon its strange tracks in the forest, or caught a glimpse of its dark figure out of the corner of his eye, darting noiselessly into the bush. In other instances, the uncanny feeling of being watched might serve as sufficient proof that a Nakani was somewhere nearby.

When a Nakani targeted a particular camp, it took up residence in the trees just beyond the light of the campfire and waited. Sometimes it taunted its intended victims by throwing rocks or sticks at them. It also, on occasion, emitted strange whistling sounds or noises resembling human laughter. Often, it would slip into camp in the middle of the night and steal food- typically fish, either from drying racks or smokehouses- or destroy fish nets and other equipment.

Legend has it that the purpose of the Nakani's visits were twofold. Its primary objective was stealing women; girls who strayed too far from the camp, especially at dawn or dusk, were in serious danger of being abducted and dragged away into the woods, never to be seen again. The other motivation that drew these monsters to Dene camps was sustenance. If afforded the opportunity, Nakani would snatch children and lone hunters and carry them off into the woods, where it would devour them.

On rare occasions, intended victims- most often young women- narrowly escaped the Nakani's clutches and returned to tell the tale. Those who survived such encounters often described a powerful, nauseating odor which preceded the attack. Others reported being beset by an overwhelming, almost petrifying sense of dread, as if the Nakani had exercised some sort of hypnotic power over them.

THEORIES
Wild Indians

Frontiersmen weren't the only white men to document the Nakani phenomena; another category of Caucasian to write about these subarctic wildmen were ethnologists and anthropologists- professional academics who included the tale in their peer-reviewed articles on Dene culture and beliefs. Interestingly, the majority of these scholars extracted an entirely different version of the Nakani legend from the Indians whom they interviewed. In this version, the Nakani are not huge, hairy hominoids, but rather strange-looking bedraggled Indians.

Most academics who wrote on the subject agreed that the Nakani, according to their Dene informants, were Indians who became wild after engaging in murder or cannibalism. As a result of their hard life in the bush and their separation from society, they acquired a frightening, grotesque appearance. Their faces were gaunt and their bodies emaciated on account of malnutrition. Their skin was often caked with filth and grease, their hair unkempt, and their clothing worn and ragged. Oftentimes, their outfits were strange or incomplete. One knife-wielding Nakani, for example, was said to have been seen wearing nothing more than hard-soled shoes made from untanned hide and a headscarf. Others were purported to wear strange boots which could not be purchased at any trading post in the region.

Although the Nakani described by academics were literally wild men bereft of civilization, some of the attributes with which they were ascribed were distinctly inhuman. For example, although Osgood described the Nakani as "a human being, generally an Indian... dressed either in the fashion of an Indian or a white man..." he also maintained that it wore "tremendously large boots which are noted by the tracks he leaves in the mud"- tracks evocative of the long, narrow footprints left by the hairy giant of frontier legend. In a similar vein, anthropologist Richard K. Nelson wrote that the Koyukon Indians of the Yukon River Valley described the Nakani as being among the "large mammals"- a creature that was neither Man nor Beast, but something in between.

Most academics dismissed these inhuman qualities as inevitable distortions added by Dene storytellers who hoped to make their tales more interesting to the listener. The Nakani, they firmly maintained, was nothing more than a man (or, in rare occasions, a woman) who became separated from society, either having been banished for some crime he committed, or isolated through some tragedy such as starvation or revenge warfare which claimed the lives of everyone else in his band. The Dene were afraid of these wild Indians because they considered them crazy and unpredictable, well aware of the deleterious effect of extreme isolation on one's mental state.

A Dene Fairytale

Many of those who have written on the subject have concluded that the Nakani was a boogeyman who served to dissuade women, children, and lone hunters from wandering too far from the safety of the camp. These people maintain that the Nakani legend is probably a relic of bygone times, when the Dene tribes of the Canadian North were in a state of total warfare with one another. During those days, Dene raiding parties would stealthily approach their enemies' camps during the night and, hiding in the brush, would steal any women and children they found alone on the outskirts. As Poole Field put it on one of his letters:

"In trying to run the stories down and by careful investigation I have finally come to the conclusion that it originated from the old days, when practically all the Indians at one time or another used to make raids on each other and would take anything of value found in the camp conquered, killing the men and taking any women or young girls or boys back to their own camp. After Dawson was struck and the civilized portion of the country became policed, it was given up, but still some of the younger men and also some of the older ones would take hunting trips into the country that was claimed by other tribes, and while doing this they would hang around any Indian camp at night in some case they would capture a young girl that some of them had taken a fancy to and take her back to their own tribe. Each tribe if the occasion just came right would give a foreign tribe a good scare any way even if they didn't do any worse. In the tribe that I was travelling with, there was a grandmother that had been stolen as a girl from the Pelly's and another from the Loose Shoe tribe at Peel River and I know several on the Pelly at the time of which I write."

Some believed that the Nakani legend specifically derived from warfare between Dene tribes and the more southerly Cree, who, equipped with HBC muskets that were far superior to traditional Dene weapons, invaded the North

Country in the late 1700's, pressured by their fur trading rivals to the south.

Other Ethnological Explanations

Some ethnographers have argued that that the Nakani legend served a variety of important functions in Dene society in addition to the cautionary capacity mentioned above. Some claimed that it promoted solidarity among members of the tribe, uniting them against a common (if imaginary) enemy.

According to American ethnologist Ellen B. Basso in her 1978 article *The Enemy of Every Tribe: 'Bushman' Images in Northern Athapaskan Narratives,* Nakani tales served to illustrate and reinforce important cultural norms in Dene society. In some stories, victims of the Nakani were doing something wrong at the time of their abduction, or were made vulnerable to such an attack as the result of someone else's moral aberration. "For example," wrote Basso, "it is interesting that in many narratives of bushman encounters, the initial state of isolation in which the victim is placed is caused by a serious violation of some social norm: a child is not properly watched, a hunter is alone in the bush during the spring, or a woman wanders away from her friends picking berries on the muskeg."

Basso also argued that the Nakani displayed certain characteristics which the Dene considered repugnant and unacceptable in polite society. "He screams in rage rather than speaks," she wrote, "grabs food rather than waits to receive it, and shuns the invitation of hunters to warm himself and drink hot tea by the fire, a simple but basic gesture of hospitality." This unkempt, unwashed, antisocial perversion of a human being was the antithesis of the virtuous Dene. It was the metaphorical monster that lurked inside them all.

The Cryptozoological Explanation

One of the most intriguing theories regarding the nature of the Nakani is that this figure is a cryptid, or "hidden animal"- specifically a species of great ape endemic to North America. Some cryptozoologists, as experts in the study of hidden animals are known, suggest that the Nakani might be the same species as the Sasquatch, another suspected North American hominid. Some have theorized that it is a remnant Neanderthal or Denisovan- archaic humans generally believed to have gone extinct about 40,000 years ago. Others believe that it might be a relative of Gigantopithecus, an enormous, possibly bipedal ape that disappeared from the jungles of Southeast Asia around 100,000 years ago. Others still hypothesize that the Nakani is an entirely new species of hominid which has yet to be accepted by the scientific community.

Homo sapiens, or modern humans, are the only species of great ape widely believed to have migrated to the Americas in ancient times, although the ancestors of New World monkeys, as improbable as it sounds, are suspected to have voyaged from Africa to the eastern shores of South America via vegetation rafts sometime during the Paleogene Epoch, preceding Christopher Columbus' first trans-Atlantic voyage by about 50 million years. If archaic humans or some other variety of great ape really travelled to the Americas in prehistoric times, how did they do it?

As was mentioned earlier in this book, most anthropologists believe that the first humans to arrive in the Americas travelled from Siberia to Alaska via an ancient bridge of land and ice, formally referred to as Beringia. The first of these nomads are believed to have followed large game herds across the Bering Strait around 13,000 year ago, near the end of the last ice age. At that time, North America was dominated by two great glaciers: the western Cordilleran ice sheet, and the easterly Laurentian ice sheet, which met at a point just east of the Rocky Mountains. During an event known as the Wisconsin Glacial Episode, these glaciers began to melt, opening up a longitudinal passage that ran down the length of the continent. Seeking greener pastures, many of the nomads followed this passage south. Their descendants multiplied and scattered across North and South America, forming the various nations whose members are collectively known today as Amerindians.

Is it possible that other less-advanced hominids-perhaps the ancestors of the Sasquatch and the Nakani- also crossed from Siberia to the Americas via Beringia? Fossil evidence clearly indicates that both Neanderthals and Denisovans inhabited Northeast Asia around the same time as *Homo sapiens*. And intriguingly, Russian folklore contends that the Altai Mountains of Central Asia and the boreal forests of Siberia are home to hairy subhumans eerily evocative of North American wildmen, known respectively as the *Almas* and the *Chuchunya*.

Although most scientists believe that human beings were the only hominids to make their way to the New World prior to the Age of Exploration, a tantalizing archaeological discovery made near the Gwich'in village of Old Crow, Yukon, in the late 1970's indicates that the Canadian North was occupied by intelligent, tool-wielding animals at least twelve thousand years before the first Paleo-Indian set foot on Alaskan soil. In the Bluefish Caves, located about 110 miles from the shores of the Arctic Ocean, anthropologist Jacques Cinc-Mars discovered a mammoth bone which appeared to have been fashioned into a caribou fleshing tool around 23,000 B.C.

More recently, some archaeologists have argued that a mastodon bone unearthed near San Diego, U.S.A., during a routine highway excavation in the early 1990's- coupled with a handful of primitive stone tools discovered nearby- constitutes proof that some sort of intelligent hominid lived in the Americas as early as 130,000 B.C. The bone in question bore spiral fractures which indicated that someone or something had smashed it with a rock when it was still fresh, presumably in an attempt to gain access to the nutritional marrow within. Flat cobblestones and round stones discovered nearby bore markings which implied their employment as primitive hammers and anvils.

One of the most intriguing pieces of evidence supporting the notion that the Nakani are real, flesh-and-blood cryptids is that the fact that they share a number of peculiar attributes with other supposed wildmen from all over the world. For example, 19th Century Slavey trappers, whose only connection with the Outside was through a handful of missionaries and the HBC traders with whom they haggled, claimed that the Nakani made whistling calls, left behind huge footprints, had a penchant for stone-throwing, and emitted a putrid odour somewhat akin to the smell of rotten flesh- characteristics which the Coast Salish of the Fraser Delta ascribed to the Sasquatch, and Aborigines of the Australian Outback to their own wildman, the Yowie.

The Feral Ape Hypothesis

In his 1973 book *The Headless Valley*, Sir Ranulph Fiennes described an entertaining, if improbable, theory regarding the origin of the Nakani legend, which he and his crew picked up during their Nahanni expedition. "We heard tales of Spanish galleons shipwrecked on the rocky coastline of British Columbia," he wrote, "with 'cargoes of apes'. The theory was that some of these apes escaped ashore and headed inland. The long winters killed off all but a few who, finding hot sulphurous springs somewhere in the Nahanni region, survived over the years and were the cause of the various decapitations."

SIGHTINGS

The Nakani of Old Crow, Yukon

Harrowing stories of encounters with the Nakani have been a staple of Dene campfire conversation for countless generations. Unfortunately, most of these tales have long been lost to history, as is so often the case with oral lore.

One old Dene story which survived to the present day, recorded as it was in 1964 by Northern folklorist Charles J. Keim, tells of Nakani which haunted the woods surrounding Old Crow, Yukon, not far from the Bluefish Caves. According to this narrative, a young girl tasked with gathering spruce branches for her bed wandered a little too far from the camp. The Nakani, who had been watching her from concealment in the trees, "snatched the girl and took her back to his cave." There, he bound her hands with babiche and tethered her to a tree stump situated just outside the cave's mouth so that she could not escape.

After spending several days outside the Nakani's lair, the girl asked the wildman to give her some privacy. The monster obliged and turned his back while she moved behind the tree stump, contenting himself with holding one end her tether in his hand. Somehow, the girl managed to free herself from her bonds when the Nakani was not looking. She stripped naked, dressed the stump with her clothes and bonnet, tied her tether to the stump, and stealthily slipped away into the woods, homeward-bound.

When some time had elapsed, the Nakani, oblivious, called out to the girl to see if she still required privacy. When she failed to answer him, he tugged on her tether and was surprised to find that he could not move her. The wildman began to sing a love song and moved towards what he thought was his prisoner, dancing as he went. "What a surprise he had," wrote Keith, "when he leaped and hugged a stump."

Eliza Andre's Tale

In the 2007 book *The History and Stories of the Gwichya Gwich'in*, Eliza Andre, a Gwich'in elder from the settlement of Tsiigehtchic, NWT, located at the confluence of the Mackenzie and Arctic Red Rivers, related an old local story involving a Nakani:

Once, an old woman and her grandson went out into the bush to snare rabbits. One day, when they were inspecting their traps, the grandson stopped dead in his tracks. "Grandmother," he said, "I hear something."

"What do you hear?" the old woman asked.

"Back past our trail, someone is making noise."

The old woman listened very carefully until she, too, heard the sound. Immediately, she stuffed the rabbits she had snared into a bundle, threw the bundle over her shoulder, and set out for camp as fast as she could, urging her grandson to follow quickly.

When the pair finally reached their tent, the old woman promptly built a fire, hastily skinned the rabbits, and threw their intestines onto the burning wood. Slowly, the intestines began to sizzle.

"By this time," wrote Andre, "they could both hear someone making noise outside their camp; someone was approaching their camp, drawing nearer and nearer." In preparation for their encounter with what could only be a Nakani, the old woman gathered the hot intestines and crouched by the door of the tent, waiting. Sure enough, the intruder, who was indeed a Nakani, poked his head through the tent opening. His ravenous eyes fell upon the old woman and her grandson.

Immediately, the old woman slapped the creature in the face with the hot intestines. The Nakani howled in pain and surprise and reeled back from the tent, clutching his scalded face. With a heavy thump, he landed on the ground and lay still.

"The following morning," Andre continued, "they went out to investigate the incident of the previous night. They found a big bushman stretched outside their camp. They did not bother to do anything to him but instead retired to their tent, never to be bothered again for a long, long time."

John McLeod's Experience

It is possible that the first white men to have a brush with the Nakani were HBC *engage* John McLeod and his crew, during their expedition up the 'West Branch' of the Liard River in the summer of 1831. One night, while resting by the fire after a long day of tracking and portaging, the voyageurs were harassed by an unseen assailant, who hurled stones at them from the shadows. Although McLeod speculated that this marauder was probably a Nahanni Indian, native legend suggests that this stone-throwing provocateur, considering his behavior, may have been a Nakani.

Paul Peters' Sighting

In his 2002 book *Mysterious Creatures: A Guide to Cryptozoology*, author George M. Eberhart related a Nakani encounter had by a native named Paul Peters in August, 1960. While at his fishing camp, located ten miles down the Yukon River from Ruby, Alaska, Peters watched a Nakani make its way along a rocky beach towards his dogs, "which were whining and acting strange." The creature was broad-shouldered and very muscular, and walked on two legs like a man. It was covered in black hair, and was about 6'6" tall. Suddenly, perhaps frightened by the dogs, the Nakani altered its course, climbed a steep hill overlooking the river, and disappeared into the bush.

Patty Nollnar's Account

In 1970, a Koyukon woman named Patty Nollnar, along with six other companions from the village of Nulato, Alaska, may have encountered a Nakani while camping on the shores of the Koyokuk River, about twenty miles north of its confluence with the Yukon River. The Alaskans didn't see the creature, but couldn't help but notice the rocks that it threw at them while they were seated around the campfire.

Bob Angus' Photograph

According to Sir Ranulph Fiennes in *The Headless Valley*, a man named Bob Angus, who was the editor of the *Fort Nelson News* in 1971,[1] received "reports and a photograph of a seven-foot-tall furry creature standing in the forest" of Northeastern British Columbia. Angus had acquired the photo from a trapper, who had seen the wildman on two separate occasions, and in two different locations. Fiennes and his crew "later met the trapper in question, but he refused to be drawn on his experiences."

Poole Field's Story

In one of his letters, Poole Field recorded a dramatic account of his own run-in with a Nakani in the Nahanni Valley. The incident took place in the summer of 1914, following Field and Oskar's adventure with Joe the mad prospector and preceding their discovery of Martin Jorgensen's corpse. After seeing Joe and his companions off, bound as they were for Dawson, Field and Oskar reunited with Chief Jim Pellesea and his band of Mountain Indians.

---

[1] Incidentally, Bob Angus purchased the *Fort Nelson News* from Margaret "Ma" Murray, the wife of George Murray, who, according to Pierre Berton, started the wave of 'Headless Valley' stories that took Canada by storm in 1946.

One night, at a point near the headwaters of the South Nahanni River, the company was visited by a lone Nakani. Hiding in the shadows of the forest, this creature snuck in close and began throwing sticks at the tents pitched on the outskirts of the camp, much to the terror of their female residents. Soon, the dogs picked up the creature's scent and began barking at it. By the time that the band's hunters, rifles in hand, stepped out of their tents to greet their uninvited visitor, the Nakani was long gone.

For several nights in a row, the Nakani repeated this routine, making strange noises and hurling objects at the Mountain Indians' teepees before melting back into the bush. "Oskar and I and two other Indians would sneak out after dark in the hope he would stumble on to us in the dark," wrote Field, "but he seemed to have an uncanny sense and would avoid us."

One night, while Field and Oskar were making their evening rounds, they spotted a strange figure standing on a gravel bar across from the camp. "We both turned loose with our 30-30s," wrote Field. But as quickly as it had appeared, the fleet-footed Nakani vanished into the night.

In the ensuing days, the party worked its way down the South Nahanni River. When the Indians reached a point at which the river was sufficiently wide, they shot twelve moose and constructed an enormous canoe from their hides, similar in design to the Viking-style York boats once favoured by the Hudson's Bay Company. The entire band piled into the watercraft and headed down the South Nahanni, making excellent time. Inexplicably, the Nakani kept pace with them and continued to harass them, easily evading the increasingly-frustrated Mountain Indian sentries who kept watch over the camp at night. Soon, the lone Nakani, as evidenced by tracks discovered in the morning, was joined by five companions who aided him in his nightly endeavours.

"There was a good deal of speculation on who they were and what they wanted," wrote Field. "Most everybody had made a speech in the night inviting whoever it was to come in daylight and he or them would be treated right. We spoke in two or three of the Mackenzie dialects and I gave them one in Pelly, Liard, and Yukon as well as English, but nothing doing. They would not answer."

One morning, the band decided to stock up on meat. Field, accompanied by a party of eight, crossed the South Nahanni and went hunting on the opposite bank.

"We had killed two moose and was having a cup of tea," wrote Field, "when we noticed a big smoke from where our camps were. Shortly after, a number of shots fired quick. We knew this was either a signal for us to return, or that some strangers had arrived. We listened for a few minutes and could hear no answering shots, so I fired two shots. They were answered at once from our main camp, so we knew we were wanted."

Field and his companions returned to the camp as quickly as they could. The entire band was congregated by the time they arrived, and the camp was in a state of total agitation. An eighteen-year-old hunter named Chiboo, they learned, had killed the Nakani that had caused them so much grief. With bated breath, the hunters listened as Chiboo recounted his chilling tale.

"The hunting party had split up shortly after leaving camp," Field expained, "and Chiboo was following up a small creek alone when he heard someone following him. He stopped and waited, but the man also stopped. He started to run, and his follower ran."

The undergrowth was thick, and Chiboo could not see far. With shaking fingers, he slipped a round into the breech of his rifle, slammed the bolt handle forward, and stumbled out into a small opening in the trees. Suddenly, a strange Indian emerged from the opposite side of the clearing.

"Chiboo shot at him and knocked him down," wrote Field. "The wounded man started calling in a strange language, and Chiboo turned and ran the other way and never stopped until he got back to camp. The whole tribe was for getting into their boats and leaving, but after a lot of talking we decided that Oskar and I, Big Foot, and the Chief would go back and investigate."

Nothing would convince Chiboo to guide Field and his party to the site at which he had encountered the Nakani. Big

Foot, however, who was the best tracker in the band, assured Field that he would have no trouble following the young brave's trail back to the clearing.

"So, leaving us with a small canoe that would hold the four of us," continued Field, "we started back in Chiboo's tracks. We had to go very careful when we thought we were nearing the place, for if any of the wounded man's companions were there, they would not hesitate to shoot at us."

When they finally arrived at the clearing, Big Foot entered first. After peering into the underbrush for some time, he concluded that the strange Indians had left the area and signalled that the coast was clear. The four men followed him into the clearing proceeded to scan it for any signs of the fallen Nakani.

They quickly discovered a place where the willows were trampled and the grass stained with blood- evidently the spot where the Nakani had fallen. Signs indicated that the wounded wildman had been joined by two others who hoisted him up and carried him off into the brush. Field and his companions followed their trail for some time, but decided to abandon it after about half a mile, when it was joined by two additional pairs of footprints.

After lighting a signal fire that went unanswered, Field and his fellows returned to their canoe and set off down the South Nahanni. Eventually, they rejoined the remainder of the band, which had already set up camp on the riverbank. As they paddled their canoe over to the shore, Field and his companions saw that the entire band was gathered around a campfire; a ceremony was about to take place.

At that time, "a young wife of eighteen summers" had come down with some mysterious illness that showed no signs of abating. The Dene girl was newly married to a 65-year-old hunter named Dee-Choo, or "Blue Grouse," who guarded her jealously. "She was quite a lively young thing when she was well," wrote Field, "and not beyond casting a few sheep's eyes at some of the younger bucks when her old Lord and Master wasn't around, and had made quite a hit, I thought, with the old Chief's son from the upper Liard that spring. However, now she was sick, and they had to call in the Medicine Man..."- an old shaman named Neretah. With great pomp and ceremony, Neretah began the first step in the Dene healing ritual, which Poole Field explained in great detail in another of his letters:

"Whenever any of the grown people were very sick, either man or woman, the doctor could be assured of a full audience as one of the first acts was the confession of the patient which everybody wanted to hear. It was always held in the open and everybody was invited to a ring side seat, and the only possible chance for the patient's life was to tell everything regardless of what or whom it implicated. There always was some hot arguments and family rows after one of these sessions. But take it all in all they actually did make some startling cures."

The young bride "made quite a job of it and confessed quite a lot," wrote Field, "but Neretah was not satisfied; in fact, he made quite a fuss over it." The old medicine man lamented that he could not cure the girl. She was gravely ill, he moaned, and although he had done his best, he was afraid that she was going to die.

Poole Field watched the display with silent astonishment. The girl did not appear all that ill to him, and he wondered what could possess the medicine man to make such dire declarations. That night, he paid a visit to the shaman and offered him some tobacco. Neretah thanked him for his gift and invited him to sit with him by the fire. While the two smoked, Field shared his thoughts with the old medicine man and voiced his suspicion that there was more to the young bride's situation than met the eye.

"The old man eyed me with a twinkle in his eye," wrote Field. "'My son,' he said, 'you would make a great Medicine Man if you would just put your mind to it. There is something wrong, and if you are around tomorrow night you will hear it.'

"Of course," Field continued, "I was on hand the next night when he started doctoring the young girl. He worked himself up into quite a state, beating his drum, getting up and stamping around, fanning her with an eagle's wing, blowing his breath on her head, singing his medicine song all the time, but calling out, 'No! No! I can't beat it; there is something you haven't confessed. If you don't confess, how can I beat the evil spirit that is in you? How can I drive him out?'"

Finally, the girl broke down and admitted that she had omitted one sin from her confession: earlier that spring, she had engaged in an affair with the son of the Kaska chief from the Upper Liard River. During one of their springtime trysts, the young brave had "vowed to follow her and steal her away, and she was sure it was him who had been hanging round [the camp]. It was his song [they had] heard one night, as he had sung the same song for her at the Ross River one time...

"Old Neretah let an extra whoop out of him," continued Field, "and worked himself up to an awful state. Suddenly stooping, he put his lips on the side of her neck and began sucking, groaning as though in great pain, and finally, with a great gasp, he broke away and threw something into the fire which made a slight sputtering noise. 'There it is. It's out. You're well. Get up at once.' And I will be darned if she didn't get up, and seemed as well as ever, and gave us all a sort of sickly smile, and old Dee-Choo took her home and that night he gave her a whale of a licking."

That night, Poole Field paid another visit to Neretah and congratulated him on his successful ministration. "Yes," said the old medicine man solemnly, "I knew there was something." After staring into the flames of his campfire for some time, he muttered, "Yes, we will pay. If not us, then our children, and who knows who it will be."

It would be some time before Field understood what the old man meant. Several years later, he visited the Kaska of the Upper Liard River and learned that the chief's son, the young bride's paramour, was indeed the 'Nakani' whom Chiboo had shot in the Nahanni Valley. The brave had initially survived his injury and lived through the winter. Unfortunately, he died from complications the following spring.

In those days, most Dene tribes held that the debt incurred by the killing of a human being must be paid in human blood, specifically that of the murderer or one of his kin. Irrespective of the context of the crime, and whether or not the killer was justified in his actions, in the event of a murder, someone else had to die. Accordingly, when the chief's son succumbed to his wound, the Kaska sought retribution and set out to bring Chiboo to justice. When they learned that the young Mountain Indian had already died of natural causes, they seized his brother and "tied [him] up for a witch," subjecting him to a cruel form of execution which Field described in great detail another letter, before burying his corpse in a gravel bar by the Liard River.

Philip H. Godsell's Story

In a response to a letter-to-the-editor of the magazine *Adventure* regarding a Labradorean wildman popularly known as the "Traverspine Gorilla", Philip Godsell, in 1951, recounted a northern 'wildman' story of his own.

The Nakani

In the spring of 1907, Godsell paid a visit to a remote HBC outpost called Pepekwatooce, situated in the heart of Northern Manitoba's Keewatin district. At that time, a number of Cree Indians were camped in the area.

"The Indians had seen a snake in the vicinity of the palisade," wrote Godsell, "and Big Simon, a hoary old Cree veteran, made a special trip over to see me to persuade me to sleep in his wigwam that night 'as the lightning ate snakes' and would be sure to strike in the vicinity. I declined his suggestion and spent the night alone in the one-roomed cabin that constituted the so-called 'Master's House.'"

That night, around midnight, something heavy smashed the side of the cabin and scraped across its walls, making a horrible grating sound that spoke of rending claws. Godsell sprang from his bed and seized an HBC tomahawk, determined to escape through the window if his nocturnal visitor decided to crash through the cabin door. Fortunately, he was not obliged to resort to such desperate measures; although the mysterious visitor battered the cabin's exterior walls at random intervals throughout the night, it departed sometime before dawn.

In the morning, the Cree examined the tracks that encircled the cabin and determined that they were "half-human and half-bear". They concluded that Godsell's nocturnal visitor was some sort of supernatural wildman possessed by the spirit of a vengeful Indian.

Accompanied by Big Simon and two other Cree hunters, Godsell followed the creature's tracks through the brush and muskeg. At around noon, the four men were suddenly attacked by an enormous animal, which they shot to death with their rifles. "It proved to be a huge and very emaciated bear," wrote Godsell, "with nothing in its stomach, but the peculiar thing about it was its coat, for it appeared to be a cross between a polar bear and a black bear. The Indians called it a "medicine bear" and continued to maintain that they had never seen a creature like it, that it had unquestionably owed its origin to the spirit of some 'bad' Indian!"

Godsell went on to reference similar 'wildman' experiences he had amongst the Beaver Indians at Fort St. John and the Ojibwa (a.k.a. Chippewa) of Northern Ontario. He attributed the Indians' persistent belief in the Nakani "to their imagination and to some hereditary subconscious recollection of spring raiding and scalping parties in earlier days."

Recent Eyewitness Accounts

Far from being obsolete phenomena relegated to the 19th and 20th Centuries, Nakani sightings still occur with casual frequency in the wilderness of Northern Canada and Alaska. On July 28, 2016, for example, the CBC (the Canadian Broadcasting Corporation; a major Canadian media company) published an article describing a Nakani encounter reported by Tony Williah, a Dogrib native from the settlement of Whati, NWT.

Earlier that month, while boating from his hometown to the northern tip of Lac La Martre (the third largest lake in the Northwest Territories, situated roughly halfway between the Great Slave and Great Bear Lakes), Williah spied a plastic bag bobbing in the water. Hoping to retrieve the object, he pulled his boat alongside it. While he reached down to grab the bag, a rogue wave tipped his boat over, and Williah found himself immersed in freezing water. After struggling in vain to right his vessel and climb back inside, he decided to swim for the nearest island. Hampered though he was by his waterlogged clothing, he managed to reach the island and crawl onto its rocky shore, exhausted and chilled to the bone.

"All of a sudden," Williah told the CBC, "there was a big man standing beside me. He must have walked away, because I heard some branches break throughout the bushes. I packed up my clothes in a white bag and readied myself to leave."

And leave he did, though not before spending a terrifying 48-hours alone on the beach, certain that the isle's mysterious resident was watching him from concealment. On July 19, 2016, Williah was rescued by an RCMP and Canadian military search party and taken to the Stanton Territorial Hospital in Yellowknife, NWT, where he made a full recovery. He later claimed that he never slept a wink throughout the entire ordeal.

One blogger who commented upon Williard's experience suggested that the Dogrib's Nakani sighting may have been a case of what has been called "Third Man Syndrome"- a phenomenon reported by explorers, outdoor athletes, and disaster survivors in which a mysterious, guardian angel-like figure appears in times of extreme difficulty to offer comfort and assistance. Intriguing though it may be, this explanation cannot account for another potential Nakani sighting reported in the fall of 2012 by two Inuit women from Quebec's northern Nunavik region.

While picking berries near the village of Akulivik, Maggie Cruikshank Qingalik and her friend spotted a strange creature out on the tundra. Initially, the two ladies thought that that the figure was another berry picker. As it got closer, however, they realized that it was covered in long, dark hair.

"We weren't sure what it was at first," said Qingalik in an interview. "It is not a human being, it was really tall, and kept coming towards our direction and we could tell it was not a human." Qingalik estimated that the creature was around three metres tall (9'10"). Its footprints were later found to be 40 centimetres (15.7 inches) long.

OTHER NORTHERN WILDMEN

Over the years, hundreds of wildman sightings have been reported on the Pacific Coast of Alaska, the historic homeland of the Tlingit Indians. Many of these have been diligently documented by Dr. J. Robert Alley in his 2003 book *Raincoast Sasquatch*. Although dozens of eyewitnesses in Alley's book referred to the figure they encountered as a "bushman", evoking the Nakani of Dene lore, some of the descriptions they furnished correspond more closely with the classic portrait of a Sasquatch- a supposed ape-man whose coastal range, some believe, extends from California to as far north as St. Michael, Alaska.

Indeed, the Nakani is not the only wildman said to inhabit the North Country. As Pierre Berton put it in his 1956 book *The Mysterious North*:

"The Mohoni, who flit through the Peel River country in the northern Yukon, are enormous hairy giants with red eyes, who eat human flesh and devour entire birch trees at a gulp. The predatory Sasquatches of British Columbia's mountain caves are eight feet tall and covered with black woolly hair from head to foot. There are others, all akin to these: the terrible Brush Man of the Loucheaux in the upper Mackenzie, with his black face and yellow eyes, preying on women and children; the Weetigo of the Barrens, that horrible, naked cannibal, his face black with frostbite, his lips eaten away to expose his fanglike teeth; the eight-foot head-hunting 'Mountain Men' of the Nahanni; and those imaginary beings of Great Slave Lake whom the Dogrib

Indians simply call 'the Enemy' and fear so greatly that they must always build their homes on islands safe from the shoreline where the Enemy roam."

It is likely that a portion of Pierre Berton's succinct summary of the various wildmen of the Northland derives from Michael H. Mason's aforementioned chapter in *The Arctic Forests*. Mason began this chapter, which more broadly details the "Superstitions" of the Dene Indians, by stating: "It is no easy task to write on the habits and philosophy of these most interesting and attractive people, for their most outstanding characteristic is general inconsistency." After detailing the spiritual philosophy of the 20th Century Dene, which he characterized as a blend of traditional animistic beliefs and Missionary-introduced Christianity, Mason went on to describe the human-like monsters in which these people very much believed.

Tinjih Rui

"Chief among the devils of the [Gwich'in]," wrote Mason, "is the Tinjih Rui[2] or Brushman. He is very tall and thin with a black face and yellow eyes..." Although some authors have lumped the Tinjih Rui in with the Nakani, Mason claimed that the Gwich'in made a distinction between this creature and the "Mahoni" (another name for the Nakani), and that they were far more terrified of the latter.

Na-In

[2] In a footnote, Mason explained that "Tinjih Rui," in the Gwich'in language, translates to "Black Man."

Later on in the chapter, Mason briefly described a hostile, invisible wildman called the "Na-in," of whom "many old men living to-day... are afraid." According to Mason, when a branch broke from a tree and landed on someone, some old Dene men would blame the incident on this mysterious creature.

Kushtaka

No chapter on the wildmen of the North would be complete without a nod to the Kushtaka- the notorious "Land Otter Man" of Tlingit folklore. The Tsimshian of Prince Rupert and Terrace, BC; the Haida of the Queen Charlotte Islands; and the Nootka of western Vancouver Island all have their own versions of this treacherous, semi-supernatural denizen of the Pacific Northwest.

According to Northwest Coast tradition, Kushtaka are small shape-shifters which can take the forms of otters, humans, and human-sized otter men. Considered to be evil trickers, they are said to prey on those who have drowned or become lost in the woods. Sometimes, these creatures 'save' their victims before stealing their souls. On other occasions, they viciously rake at their victims with their sharp claws. Much like the Nakani and the Sasquatch, the Kushtaka is said to emit a high-pitched whistle alternating from low to high.

The Strangest Story Ever Told

In 1953, a mysterious book entitled '*The Strangest Story Ever Told*' was privately published in New York under the name "Harry D. Colp". The book's preface stated that the author had been dead for several years, and that the manuscript he put together was edited and submitted for publication by his daughter, Virginia. This story, ostensibly based on true events, describes a race of hairy wildmen whom some believe might be Kushtaka.

The book is divided into seven chapters, each of them revolving around a particular stretch of wilderness inland of Thomas Bay- a small inlet situated northwest of Wrangell, Alaska, not too far from the mouth of the Stikine River. Locals sometimes referred to Thomas Bay as the 'Bay of Death' on account of a massive landslide which swept through it in 1750, wiping out an entire Tlingit village and killing over five hundred of its inhabitants.

In the first chapter, the narrator claimed that he was one among four bankrupt prospectors who shared a cabin at Wrangell, Alaska, in the early 20th Century. In the spring of 1900, one of the four returned to the cabin with the happy news that he had met an Indian with a chunk of gold-bearing quartz in his possession, and that the Indian had given him directions to the place where he had found it. "He told me to go up to Thomas Bay," the prospector informed his partners, "and camp on Patterson River on the right side, travel upriver for about eight miles and then turn to the high mountains, and after traveling about a mile and a half, I would find a lake shaped like a half moon." It was there that the Indian claimed to have found his prize.

The prospectors decided to pool their money together and secure an outfit for Charlie, the man who had returned home with the good news. Charlie was to head into the wilderness beyond Thomas Bay and see if there was any truth to the Indian's tale.

That May, Charlie set out for the northerly diggings. In the meantime, the narrator and the other two partners found work in a sawmill and began to save up money for a grubstake in the hope that Charlie's preliminary expedition would prove fruitful.

"Things went along until the first part of June," Colp wrote, "when, on a Sunday in the late afternoon, we all being home, and in walks Charlie without a coat or hat and looking as if he'd been through hell. He didn't give us any greeting whatever; just heaved a piece of quartz over into a corner of the room and said, 'Get me something to eat; I'm all in and want to rest.' The fellow looked it, and, after he had eaten, he turned in without telling us a thing about his trip."

The quartz piece that Charlie brought home was heavily streaked with gold, much to his partners' delight. Despite the unbridled enthusiasm that took hold of his colleagues, convinced as they were that they were on the verge of a major strike, Charlie spent the next few days acting very strangely. He seldom spoke, refusing to answer his partners' many questions, and occupied himself with hard manual labour from dawn to dusk.

Finally, Charlie returned to the cabin one day and asked his partners to lend him enough money for a steamboat ticket to Seattle. He was finished with Alaska, he said, and wanted to leave the North Country for good. He agreed to tell his partners about his experience in Thomas Bay, but only if they promised to never remind him of it again. When the prospectors agreed to his condition, Charlie told them his story:

Charlie had reached the shore of Thomas Bay four days after his departure and proceeded up Patterson River, as the Indian had instructed him. He searched everywhere for the lake shaped like a half moon, but only succeeded in locating one in the shape of the letter 'S'.

The area surrounding the lake was curiously lifeless, devoid of even the smallest game. Charlie was beginning to grow weary of the simple frontier fare he had brought with him from Wrangell- namely beans, rice, and bacon- and decided hike over to a ridge about eight miles east of the lake, where he had heard some grouse hooting.

Sure enough, Charlie found a few ptarmigan there and began to hunt them. In doing so, he stumbled upon a ledge of quartz liberally streaked with gold. As he did not have a pickaxe with him, he used the butt end of his rifle to break a break off a chunk of the rock, destroying the wooden stock in the process. The disappointment that Charlie felt over the loss of his rifle was overshadowed by the elation that his discovery

elicited. He thrilled at the prospect of returning to the site
with his partners and striking it rich.

After concealing the quartz ledge with moss and
detritus, Charlie climbed to the top of the ridge in order to
scout for landmarks by which he might relocate his discovery.
"Right there, fellows," he told his partners, "I got the scare of
my life. I hope to God I never see or go through the likes of it
again. Swarming up the ridge toward me from the lake were
the most hideous creatures. I couldn't call them anything but
devils, as they were neither men nor monkeys- yet looked like
both. They were entirely sexless, their bodies covered with
long coarse hair, except where the scabs and running sores
had replaced it. Each one seemed to be reaching out for me
and striving to be the first to get me. The air was full of their
cries and the stench from their sores and bodies made me
faint."

Abandoning his broken gun, Charlie fled for the sea
with the creatures in hot pursuit. He felt their hot breath on
his neck and their sharp claw-like nails scratching at his
back. Reason abandoned him, and later that night, Charlie
found himself adrift in his boat with no clear memory of how
he managed to get there. "Cold, hungry, and crazy for a
drink of water," he started for Wrangell with his piece of
gold-streaked quartz.

The following five chapters of *The Strangest Story
Ever Told* relate the misadventures of Colp, his other
prospecting partners, and three frontiersmen of Norwegian,

Russian, and Japanese descent, who all went into Thomas Bay Country for one reason or another. Aside from the location in which they take place, these stories are united by, as cryptozoology pioneer Ivan T. Sanderson put it in his commentary on the book, "a thread of reference to hairy, stinking humanoids", as well as the temporary insanity which their "overpowering and nauseating stink" appeared to induce in all who encountered them. "This is not just a commonplace," Sanderson continued, "but now an almost invariable concomitant to all reports made by persons all over the world who say they have been in close proximity to one of these creatures."

The seventh and final chapter of *The Strangest Story Ever Told* describes the experience of a frontiersman who established a trapline in the wilderness beyond Thomas Bay. When inspecting his traps, he found that they had all been sprung by a creature which left behind strange footprints, the likes of which he had never seen before. Sometimes, the animal walked on four legs; at other times, it walked on only two. The trapper described the animal's hind tracks as "about seven inches long and looked as if they were a cross between a two-year-old bear's and a small barefooted man's tracks. You could see claw marks at the ends of the toes, toe pads, and heavy heel marks; between toe-pad marks and heel marks was a sort of space where the foot did not bear so heavily on the ground, as if the foot were slightly hollowed or had an instep. The front set looked like a big raccoon's tracks, only larger."

After his dog was abducted and presumably eaten by the strange creature, the trapper returned to civilization, where he related his story to Colp. He eventually overcame his fear of the mysterious animal and returned to his trap line in Thomas Bay Country. The trapper was never seen again.

Some of those who have speculated on the nature of the mysterious 'devils' of Thomas Bay have suggested that they might be Kushtaka- perhaps flesh-and-blood mammals yet unknown to science, or the transmogrified souls of the Tlingit who perished there in 1750.

The Glacial Demon

Based on two separate incidents reported in the late 19th and early 20th Centuries, the author of this book has decided to include another Alaskan monster in this list of northern wildmen, which one U.S. Army officer styled the 'Glacial Demon'.

The first incident took place in 1898, during the Klondike Gold Rush. At that time, rumour had it that an old Russian trail led from the shores of Prince William Sound, an Alaskan inlet situated in the shadow of the vast Valdez Glacier (located about 185 kilometres (115 miles) due east of Anchorage, AK), to the Yukon goldfields, circumventing Canadian customs. Eager to avoid paying duty on their outfits at the Canadian border, about 3,500 American Stampeders disembarked at this remote part of Alaska and set out in search of the trailhead.

As it turned out, there was no secret Russian route to the interior; the only way through the Coast Mountains in that part of Alaska was over the Valdez Glacier. Prospectors who chose this route had to haul their supplies over three hundred yards of sand and six miles of snow to reach the base of the glacier. After that, they had to ascend the icy monolith, hoisting their sleds up with pulleys.

Upon reaching the windy, frozen summit of the Valdez Glacier, Stampeders ventured out onto the icefield one by one. With steel crampons strapped to their feet, they slowly inched their way northwest, picking their way through a minefield of deadly crevasses. It would be several weeks before any of them reached the other side, where an even more dangerous obstacle, the Klutina River, awaited them.

Some of the gold-seekers who hazarded this so-called "all-American" route to the Klondike were buried in avalanches; their bones still lie trapped beneath the snow. Other unfortunates plunged through thin ice and plummeted to their doom, disappearing down bottomless black crevasses. Those who avoided these fates faced a myriad of physical and mental tribulations on their journey over the glacial plain, enduring extreme exposure, severe sleep deprivation, and countless hours immersed in an unearthly white fog. They did most of their travelling at night, when the ice was solid enough to bear their weight. In the day, when they weren't trying to sleep, the sun reflected off the snow and ice, causing many prospectors to go slow blind. Due to the harsh conditions, Stampeders were unable to thoroughly cook their food, and many survived their journey over the Valdez Glacier by subsisting on half-frozen, half-cooked meals. Many who failed to turn back, too stubborn to abandon their folly, slowly descended into insanity.

In the spring of 1899, a man named W.R. Abercrombie- a Captain in the U.S. Army's 2nd Infantry Regiment- was dispatched to the Valdez area and ordered to report his findings to the War Department. That April, the officer reached Port Valdez- a town that had since sprang up on the shores of Prince William Sound (the site of present-day Valdez, Alaska)- where he encountered a ragged band of Stampeders. Suffering from snow blindness, scurvy, and frostbite, these prospectors had just returned from the icefield. After interviewing them, Abercrombie made the following entry in his report:

"I noticed in talking to these people that over seventy per cent of them were more or less mentally deranged. My attention was first directed to this fact by their reference to a 'glacial demon'. One big rawboned Swede, in particular, described to me how this demon had strangled his son on the glacier, his story being that he had just started from Twelve-Mile Plant (a collection of huts just across the Coast Range of Mountains from Valdez) with his son to go to the coast in company with some other prospectors. When halfway up the summit of the glacier, his son, who was ahead of him hauling a sled, while he was behind pushing, called to him, saying that the demon had

attacked him and had his arms around his neck. The father ran to the son's assistance, but as he described it, his son being very strong, soon drove the demon away and they passed on their way up toward the summit of Valdez Glacier. The weather was very cold and the wind blowing very hard, so that it made traveling very difficult in passing over the ice between the huge crevasses through which it was necessary to pick their way to gain the summit. While in the thickest of these crevasses, the demon again appeared. He was said to be a small, heavily-built man and very active. He again sprang on the son's shoulders, this time with such a grasp that, although the father did all he could to release him, the demon finally strangled the son to death. The old man then put the son on a sled and brought him down to Twelve-Mile camp, where the other prospectors helped bury him.

"During the recital of this tale, the old man's eyes would glaze and he would go through all the actions to illustrate how he fought off the imaginary demon. When I heard this story there were some ten or twelve other men in the cabin and at the time it would not have been safe to dispute the theory of the existence of this demon on the Valdez Glacier, as every man in there firmly believed it to be a reality."

Although Captain W.R. Abercrombie suspected that the 'glacial demon' described by the Swedish Stampeder was nothing more than a delusion brought on by scurvy, a fascinating article written by a prospector named Frank E. Howard, which appeared in the March 1909 issue of the

Alaska-Yukon Magazine, suggests that there may have been some truth to his tale.

In the article, Howard described an incident which took place during a prospecting trip that he made in the early 1900's. While camping alone off the shores of Yakutat Bay, located on the Alaskan coast roughly halfway between Port Valdez and Juneau, Howard decided to explore the nearby Malaspina Glacier, the largest piedmont glacier in the world.

Howard ascended the glacier through a crack in the ice and began to make his way over to a distant ridge. On the way, he lost his footing and slid into an open crevasse. Although he did not sustain any major injuries from the fall, which found him wedged between the fissure's narrow walls, Howard was unable to climb out of the slippery chasm and decided to follow it deeper into the ice, hoping that it would lead out into the bay.

"As I kept going ahead," Howard wrote, "I noticed a gradual increase of light, and in a few more steps, I stood in a broad wall of blue light that came down from above and, looking up, I saw there was no clear opening to the surface. But objects were now revealed some distance around.

"Then an object rose slowly out of the glimmer and took form- a spectral thing, with giant form, and lifelike movement. The object rose erect, a Goliath in the shape of a man."

This glacial being had a small head, narrow shoulders, and abnormally wide hips. It growled a challenge, and suddenly Howard was "engulfed in a rank indescribable odor". Petrified, the prospector desperately searched for an escape route, the hairs of his neck standing on end. Before he could make a move, however, the creature slinked away, eying him "with a slantwise glance" as it vanished into the gloom.

His heart hammering in his chest, Howard continued deeper into the crevasse and found an exit about fifty feet away, which opened up onto a timbered beach.

"Since my miraculous encounter and escape," he wrote, "I often attempt to solve the mystery that still enshrouds the apparition of the glacier. Terror might have magnified my imagination. But the apparition was not the imagination of an over-balanced mind. I am thoroughly convinced I saw something. It was not like any animal that I had ever seen before."

Toonijuk

The Inuit of the Far North, from Alaska to the Arctic Archipelago to Greenland, have legends about a race of primitive giants at least twice the size of regular men who once inhabited the lands they occupy today. They called this ancient people "*Toonijuk*", a word with etymological ties to "*tornat*" (an Inuktitut word denoting helpful spirits, mentioned briefly in the chapter on the evil spirit of the Nahanni Valley).

Physically, the Toonijuk were said to be immensely powerful, and could easily carry full-grown bearded seals on their backs. They did not live in igloos, like the Inuit, but rather in circular stone pit-houses roofed with whale ribs and animal skins.

A simple people, the Toonijuk were said to practice a number of revolting customs. They did not usually cook their meat, and preferred to eat it rotten. Toonijuk women would sometimes sit with raw meat tucked between their thighs and belly in the hope that their body heat would hasten the decomposition process. As they did not know how to cure animal skins, bits of rotten meat and rancid fat dangled from the insides of their robes. Sometimes, the Toonijuk would sew their young warriors into maggot-infested seal skins, believing that this would somehow enhance their skills as warriors.

Although the Toonijuk are said to have fought bitterly with one another, they rarely showed aggression towards the Inuit, and seemed to be deathly afraid of their dogs. In addition to their martial prowess, they were excellent hunters who could summon game with their voices.

Eventually, the Inuit began to hunt down the Toonijuk, and, in time, greatly reduced their number. The giants who survived these predations fled to the mountains of the interior, where, some say, their descendants still linger to this very day.

Some suspect that the legend of the Toonijuk derives from interactions between the Thule, or proto-Inuit (the ancestors of the modern Inuit), and their prehistoric counterparts, the more ancient Dorset people. The ancestors of the Dorset are believed to have arrived in the Canadian Arctic around 3200 B.C. When the Thule people spread west from the Bering Strait and onto Dorset territory in the 12th Century A.D., the Dorset were dying out, unable to cope with the climate change which characterized the Medieval Warm Period. By 1500 A.D., the Dorset are believed to have vanished completely.

In 1955, American writer Katharine Scherman and a handful of scientists visited Bylot Island, a polar isle situated just north of Baffin Island (Baffin Island being the largest of its kind the Arctic Archipelago). It was on this island, the Inuit maintained, that a band of Toonijuk once lived in ancient times. Scherman, who described the experience in her 1956 book *Spring on an Arctic Island*, reported finding a cluster of circular mounds, which proved to be large stones half-buried in the permafrost. Some scientists among the group found whale bones and other stones in the vicinity of the structures and concluded that these large stones had once served as the foundations of crude houses- dwelling evocative of the stone pit-houses of the Toonijuk. Scherman and her companions were baffled as to how the ancient builders of these structures managed to haul the huge foundation stones, which were not of local origin, from their source.

Wendigo

An Algonquian legend which made its way to the North Country from the Great Lakes region by way of the Cree, the story of the Wendigo (a.k.a. Weetigo) is another northern tale containing "wildman" elements.

According to some interpretations of the legend, the Wendigo is a ravenous man-eating giant which roams the northern forests in search of human flesh. Ojibwa storyteller Basil H. Johnston included a colourful description of this corporeal version of the Wendigo in *The Manitous*, his masterwork published by the Minnesota Historical Society Press in 2001:

"The Wendigo was gaunt to the point of emaciation, its desiccated skin pulled tightly over its bones. With its bones pushing out against its skin, its complexion the ash gray of death, and its eyes pushed back deep into the sockets, the Wendigo looked like a gaunt skeleton recently disinterred from the grave. What lips it had were tattered and bloody... Unclean and suffering from suppurations of the flesh, the Wendigo gave off a strange and eerie odor of decay and decomposition, of death and corruption."

Another version of the Wendigo legend has it that this entity is not a physical creature, but rather a malevolent spirit associated with the North, the cold, and starvation. During the winter months, it roams throughout the wilderness in search of human hosts.

Indians who engaged in cannibalism made themselves especially vulnerable to Wendigo possession. When a person became possessed by a Wendigo, they gradually developed an insatiable appetite for human flesh which drove them to butcher and eat their fellow tribesmen, even when other food sources were readily available. Philip Godsell described this phenomenon in his introduction to the June 1946 issue of the *Alberta Folklore Quarterly*, saying:

"The weetigo, I might explain, is an evil spirit that enters the body of a sick man converting him, unless he is destroyed, into a cannibal, endangering the lives of every member of the band. Hardly a spring goes by but some wandering band of nomad hunters becomes obsessed with the idea that there is one of these cannibal spirits haunting the outskirts of the camp, anxious to become domiciled within the person of some sick Indian."

One famous case of suspected Wendigo possession occurred in Central Alberta in 1878. That winter, a Plains Cree trapper named Swift Runner slaughtered, cooked, and devoured his wife and six children. When the North West Mounted Police arrested him for his crime, he claimed that he was possessed by the Wendigo and needed to be killed before he caused more damage. The Mounties acquiesced; after trying Swift Runner and finding him guilty on seven counts of first-degree murder, they hanged him at Fort Saskatchewan, Alberta, in 1879.

Nekedzaltara

Another breed of Northern wildman with both physical and supernatural qualities are the *nekedzaltara*, the demonic minions of the Evil Spirit which the Dene believed to inhabit the Nahanni karstlands. According to Father Julius Jette in his article *On the Superstitions of the Ten'a Indians*, these beings were shadowy devils that sometimes invaded Dene camps in the middle of the night. When the presence of these beings was announced by shamans, "a great excitement ensued, during which the whole village was upset, every one losing his head from fright, and a fine occasion was offered to the sorcerers to do any mischief they pleased..."

When a *nekedzaltara* adopts a physical form, it sometimes appears as a creature similar to a dragon or a whale. More often, however, it assumes the form of some sort of "goblin". There are eight different types of goblins into which the *nekedzaltara* can transform, three of which resemble wildmen. The first of these is the **Nenele'in**, a hairy, long-armed creature with claw-like nails which invades camps at night and steals fish from drying racks. Although the appearance of a *Nenele'in* is considered a bad omen for adults, if the creature "happens to stop near a sleeping child and pat its head, the child shall become a shaman."

Another goblin into which the *nekedzaltara* can metamorphose is the **Yes-yu**, or "Ghastly Wolf", a hairy, long-armed, bipedal creature with lupine features, which Jette likened to "the French *loup-garou*", or werewolf.

Finally, there are the *Tsonterotana,* or "Men of the Rocks", a form of *nekedzaltara* which Jette described as "a kind of wild men, but with all the agility of spirits." These monsters inhabited the valley of the Yukon River, and were notorious kidnappers and thieves.

Sasquatch

As was mentioned earlier in this chapter, hundreds of Sasquatch sightings have been reported over the years on the West Coast of Alaska, many of which are described in Dr. J. Robert Alley's book *Raincoast Sasquatch.* Many eyewitness depictions of this creature are disturbingly consistent and, when considered as a whole, paint a vivid portrait of a hairy, human-like giant which inhabits the rainforests of the Pacific Northwest.

The Sasquatches reported on the Alaskan coasts are usually very tall, extremely powerful, and tend to exude a terrible smell akin to rotten flesh or burning garbage. They appear to communicate with each other through grunts and whistles, and can sometimes be heard howling in the night.

Most stories suggest that Sasquatches are friendly. Shy and reclusive, they tend to avoid human settlements. Although they may abduct people from time to time, they rarely harm them.

———◆———

Of all the wildman encounters described in this chapter, the only ones which took place in the Nahanni

Valley were those described by Poole Field, in which a suspected Nakani ultimately proved to be a jealous lover bent on eloping with his paramour.

It would be another fifty years before a similar series of wildman sightings took place in Nahanni Country. This time, however, there were no jealous lovers hiding in the brush. This time, it was for real.

The Nuk-Luk

"The ABSM reported to be in this area is said to be rather short in stature and to be quite strong with a beard and usually wearing simple clothing. The name given this creature is Nuk-luk, or "Man of the Bush", or as told to me, by one old man, "Bushman.""

- Frank Graves, in a letter to Ivan T. Sanderson, 1965

ONE OF THE FIRST SCIENTISTS to seriously address the question of whether or not modern-day wildmen truly exist in the wilderness of Asia and North America was Ivan T. Sanderson, an eccentric Scottish biologist and adventurer. Along with Belgian-French zoologist Bernard Heuvelmans, he is considered by many to be one of the founding fathers of cryptozoology.

Educated in zoology, geology, and botany in England, France, and Switzerland, Ivan Sanderson- already an extremely well-travelled young man with a wealth of adventures under his belt by the time he completed his graduate studies- began his academic career leading specimen-collecting expeditions all over the world on behalf of various British learned societies. In 1932, during once such expedition in the rainforests of Cameroon, he and his hunting partner were attacked by a giant bat which the locals fearfully referred to as *"Olitiau"*. This incident sparked Sanderson's lifelong interest in animals yet unknown to science- creatures begetting the field of study which he coined "cryptozoology".

During WWII, Sanderson worked as a counter-intelligence operative for both the British and American Navies. After the War, he left his old life behind and immigrated to America, where he enjoyed a long career in radio and television, educating and entertaining his audience in his capacity as a naturalist.

Sanderson's interest in unexplained phenomena- which, as mentioned, first began in the jungles of West Africa in 1932- was rekindled in the 1950's, when UFO and monster sightings became more frequent in the United States and Canada. Unlike many of his academic contemporaries, Sanderson refused to dismiss these stories out of hand, risking his professional reputation in order to give them the attention which he believed they deserved. By the late 1950's, he was writing essays on the subject of UFOs, and in 1961, he wrote a book entitled *'Abominable Snowman: Legend Come to Life'*, a Fortean classic which his friend and fellow cryptozoologist Loren Coleman described as "the first book that comprehensively dealt with the folklore, sightings, and context of Sasquatch and Bigfoot in North America". In this book, Sanderson introduced the term "ABSM"- an acronym for "Abominable Snowman", which was a popular denotation for wildmen at that time.

In 1965, Sanderson was approached by a young mechanic from Philadelphia named Frank Graves. Graves had read Sanderson's work, and, having retained a fascination with the Nahanni legends since his days as a junior high school student, wondered if wildmen such as those described in *Abominable Snowman* might have some connection with the mysterious deaths and disappearances for which the Headless Valley was notorious. He decided to find out, and after saving up enough money, convinced four of his friends to accompany him on an expedition to the Nahanni Valley. Prior to the trip, he decided to pay a visit to Sanderson to see if the seasoned adventurer had any advice for him and his companions.

"To make a really rather long story as proverbially short as possible," wrote Sanderson in a commentary on a letter which Graves wrote to him later that year, "let me just say that all Frank's companions dropped out for one valid reason or another- as almost invariably happens in plans such as his- but he joined up with another gang I had been helping, out in Minnesota, led by one Michael Eliseuson and who were also aiming for the Nahanni."

This "other gang" was the self-styled 'American Expeditionary Society', or AES, an academic club comprised of about thirty American university students who hoped to resurrect the dying art of old-fashioned discovery expeditions. Four AES members with a similar interest in the Nahanni Valley, three of them students of Minnesota State University, allowed Graves to accompany them to the North Country. These members included Society leader Michael Eliseuson, who hailed from Grand Rapids, Michigan; George Boyum of Kasson, Minnesota; Wayne Egrebretson of Windom, Minnesota; and Bruce Shorer of North Mankato, Minnesota.

In the summer of 1965, the five men, armed to the teeth, travelled to Fort Simpson, purchased a flat-bottomed scow, and headed up the Liard River towards the South Nahanni. Frank Graves, who was required to have an official scientific objective in order to join the AES, chose to collect samples of lichen, fungi, mosses, liverworts, and other varieties of subarctic vegetation on behalf of Dr. William C. Steere, Director of the New York Botanical Gardens. Accordingly, he carried a good deal of botanical equipment into the North Country, along with a video camera and 5,000 feet of film.[1]

The five companions capsized their scow on the Liard's Beaverdam Rapids, but managed to right their vessel, rescue most of their gear, and arrive at Nahanni Butte in one piece. They proceeded up the Splits to Gus and Mary Kraus' cabin, out of which they conducted their various scientific expeditions over a three week period.

---

[1] This film is believed to have survived the Nahanni expedition, but its whereabouts are currently unknown.

Around the same time, five friends from Fargo, North Dakota- namely Bob Henry, Rollie White, Bruce Tannehille, Marc Wermager, and David Wolfe- started out on a Nahanni expedition of their own. Beginning their journey at the headwaters of the Ross River, they carried their canoe east over the mountain pass to the headwaters of the South Nahanni and paddled downriver. On August 4, 1965, they made the portage around Virginia Falls, at the bottom of which they encountered the five members of the American Expeditionary Society, who were relaxing and taking in the sights.

The five friends from Fargo fraternised with the AES men that night, and set off down the South Nahanni the following morning. Just beyond the mouth of the Flat River, they ran into Albert Faille, who was taking a pair of geologists up the South Nahanni. At Faille's camp, also, were the AES boy. The thirteen men spent the night in conversation and, in the morning, went their separate ways.

The North Dakotans and the AES team met up a third and final time on August 7, whereupon they engaged in a pancake-eating contest of truly epic proportions. According to an entry in David Wolfe's diary, the ten men devoured a total of 308 flapjacks that morning. "The Yukon boys beat us," admitted Michael Eliseuson on an internet chat site, referring to his team's North Dakotan rivals, "and I haven't eaten many pancakes since. The pancakes were not small, either. They were large."

In another letter to Ivan Sanderson, which he wrote later that year, Frank Graves recounted a number of excursions he personally made into the wilderness above Virginia Falls during his three week stint in the Nahanni, accompanied at all times by a local Dene guide.

"We made several successful forays up side valleys and canyons during the days while we moved up river," wrote Graves, referring to a particular excursion made for the sole purpose of acquiring meat, "and we got our food quite fast. But then one misty day we set off up a canyon that the Indian said he did not know personally but which was 'not lucky'. And in truth we did not spot a living thing in three hours; so we started back down to the river. Then suddenly my pal stopped, and pointed down at the soft wet ground in a little clearing and actually gave one of those grunts that movie-makers love to have their 'Red Indians' make. He was a bit rattled and so was I, for there, most clearly marked in the mud, were three footprints of what appeared to be a barefoot man who would have had to take a shoe with an internal measurement of at least sixteen inches! My friend gave this thing a name, but I never really did catch up with that as we went down that valley at no dog-trot, I can tell you."

Did these giant footprints constitute proof that ABSMs haunted the hinterlands of the Nahanni? Frank Graves, a skeptic at heart, certainly considered the possibility. "I didn't want to bring thus up," he confessed to Ivan Sanderson, "but you know it was in a way this business of what you call ABSMs that really started me on that trip; and let me tell you, I never believed one single word of your book, and least of all about the Canadian NWT. But that's the way it happened..."

Graves went on to relate another truly startling discovery which he and his Dene friend made several days later, which will be described in detail in the next chapter.

"I'm going back again- this year, and on my own..." Graves concluded in the final paragraph of his letter. "Here is this fabulous place right in our own backyard and it's full of all the damned 'adventure' anybody could ask- plus a lifetime of wondrous things to look into, and decent people, clean air, and a real chance to discover something worthwhile."

True to his word, Frank Graves made a second trip to the Nahanni Valley in the fall 1965 and indeed discovered something which many people would certainly consider worthwhile. Upon interviewing a number of Dene from Nahanni Butte, he learned that a wildman had been spotted on three separate occasions in 1964- first in Fort Liard, then in Nahanni Butte, and next in Fort Simpson- as if it were making its way up the Liard River towards the Mackenzie. The creature was said to be "rather short in stature," wrote Graves, "and to be quite strong with a beard and usually wearing simple clothing. The name given this creature is Nuk-luk, or 'Man of the Bush', or as told to me, by one old man, 'Bushman.'"

The Nuk-Luk

The first Nuk-luk sighting took place in April, 1964, in the woods near Fort Liard. According to Graves, "an old Amerind named John Baptist," who worked as a janitor and handyman at the local settlement school, along with several trapping companions, "came upon a man-shaped creature who was rather strong and sported a long dark beard. He wasn't wearing any type of clothing and carried no weapons... He was said to be rather shy, for as the band of trapping Amerinds advanced upon him in a friendly manner, he uttered a low growl and fled."

The second sighting took place at Nahanni Butte in May, 1964. One night at dusk, while weaving a birch bark basket, a Dene woman "was made aware of a presence outside of her cabin. When she looked out of the door she saw nothing, but a little later, she looked up at the window, and there, saw a face. This face was identical in every respect to the one seen earlier that month." The woman and two of her children went outside to look for the little creature, but by that time it had retreated into the bush.

Graves did not receive this last report from the witness directly, as her husband forbade her from speaking with him, but rather from a young man whom Graves had "every intention of believing".

"Now," wrote Graves, "we go to my favourite tale. This was told to me by a boy of about 14, whom I knew only as Jerry. He was recommended to me, for my purpose, by the school teacher there. This little boy saw a creature, identical to the previously mentioned one, except for a few exterior differences. This sighting is said to have occurred last fall right outside of Fort Simpson.

"One evening, at about 9:00 P.M., the little fellow's dog began to bark. This event is not unusual for his home is located right on the edge of the city dump, and a dog can pick up the scent of many different night scavengers during the passing of one night, especially in that country.

"On this night, however, the boy and his father went out to the dog to find out what was the matter. When they got out to the dog, it was quiet and standing most still. At first, they detected nothing of unusual interest, but when the father turned on a flashlight for a little extra investigative work, they heard a slight noise. As they turned the light in the direction of this sound, they were surprised to see a rather small, dark creature, answering to the general description of an ABSM.

"This creature is said to have remained where he stood for several moments. At about that time, the dog, again, began to bark.

"With that, the creature departed at speed. The creature is said to have not immediately entered the bush but instead crossed the boy's property and then across the road in front of the house. He was seen by several bystanders who gave slight chase; but, upon their entrance into the picture, the creature quickly headed for the bush. He was not pursued." Then, despite having claimed earlier that the incident took place in the fall of 1964, Graves curiously ended the paragraph with the date "June- 1964". He went on to state that this wildman wore a piece of moose skin about its waist, and was carrying a stone club.

At the end of his letter, Graves included his own sketch of the creature based on the eyewitness accounts. He added various notes and labels to this drawing, remarking that the creature's nose "was said to be small and black", and its fur "light brown". He also indicated, both visually and verbally, that the creature was believed to have four fingers and a thumb, was about five feet tall, and wore rubber boots. The Nuk-luk's head appeared to be slightly pointed in the back and covered in short "dark black" hair.

Beneath the sketch, Graves included illustrations of the two "different types of tracks found near the scene". Both of these, in spite of the rubber boots depicted in the image above, vaguely resemble elongated bear tracks with claw marks at the end of each toe. One of them, labelled "Our Creature", is shown to be four-and-a-half inches wide and of an unknown length, while the second track, labelled "Other Type," is proportionally much thinner, being three inches wide and ten inches long.

Loren Coleman- who is considered today to be one of the world's foremost cryptozoologists- along with fellow Fortean researcher Patrick Huyghe, attempted to scientifically classify the Nuk-luk, along with other types of wildmen, in his 1999 book *The Field Guide to Bigfoot, Yeti, and Other Mysterious Primates Worldwide*. Specifically, Coleman fit the Nakani into a class which he dubbed "*Neandertaloid*"- a class ostensibly related to the Neanderthal.

"Neandertaloids average about 6 feet tall and have a stocky, muscular build," Coleman explained. "Their bodies sport a reddish hair, and males generally have abundant facial hair, often with a fringe beard... All Neandertaloids have heavy browridges and a large, broad nose. Their feet vary from 7 to 15 inches long and are 4 to 8 inches wide. They have five toes, all about the same size and evenly spread, though their big toes angle slightly outward like those in fossil Neanderthal footprints- but not at all like apes."

Coleman went on to explain that Neandertaloids are shy, reclusive, and probably quite intelligent. They are either diurnal or crepuscular, meaning they are primarily active during the day or at twilight, and prefer to live in caves. Other wildmen which Coleman placed under the Neandertaloid umbrella included the *Wudewasa*, or "Wood Being", a hairy, five-foot-tall wildman from Croatia, believed to be the same species as the forest-dwelling Satyr of Ancient Greek mythology; and the Chinese Wildman, a six-foot-tall ape-man from the mountains of Northwestern Hubei, China.

The Nuk-luk resembles the Nakani in many ways, from its name to its reclusive nature to its long, narrow footprints. However, with a height of approximately five feet, it is much smaller than the giant, red-eyed monster of frontier lore. Although the argument could be made that the bearded, muscular wildman that appeared in Nahanni Country in 1964 was a juvenile Nakani, its diminutive stature conjures images another breed of wildman reported in Northern Canada- the Arctic Pygmy.

THE ARCTIC PYGMY
Skraelings

In 960 A.D., a Norse Viking named Thorvald Asvaldsson fled from Norway to northwestern Iceland with his family, having been banished for committing manslaughter. His son, a red-bearded farmer called Erik the Red, was similarly banished from Iceland twenty two years later for a comparable crime. Accompanied by a handful of loyal friends and relatives, Erik the Red left his longhouse and headed out to sea, bound for a mysterious land to the west which had been spotted by Icelandic sailors blown off course.

Erik the Red and his crew spent three years exploring this new land, and discovered that it had areas which were suitable for farming. In 985, the red-bearded explorer returned to Iceland and regaled his fellow Vikings with tales of what he attractively dubbed *"Groenland"*, or "Greenland". Having convinced a number of Norsemen to help him settle this new territory, Erik the Red returned to Greenland that year and established a colony there.

In 999 A.D., one of Erik the Red's sons, called Leif Eriksson, returned to his father's Norwegian homeland, where he converted from Norse paganism to Christianity. Determined to bring the Christian religion to Greenland, he headed out into the North Atlantic. During his westward voyage, he was blown off course, and landed on strange shores where wild grapes grew in abundance. He called this New World *"Vinland"*, or *"Wineland"*, and later returned there to establish a colony of his own. Some historians believe that Leif Eriksson's Vinlandic colony was what we know today as L'Anse aux Meadows, a cluster of Viking ruins discovered on the northern tip of Newfoundland.

For centuries, Icelanders told stories of Erik the Red and Leif Eriksson's New World adventures around smoky longhouse fires. Medieval storytellers eventually put these tales to parchment, writing what are known as the Icelandic Sagas.

Many of the Sagas spoke of natives whom Norse explorers encountered in the New World, in both Vinland and Greenland. The Vikings called these people *"Skraeling"*. According to the 13th Century *Saga of Erik the Red*, the *Skraeling* "were short in height with threatening features and tangled hair on their heads. Their eyes were large and their cheeks broad." Although their relationship with these aboriginals was initially a friendly one, the Vikings eventually engaged in a number of savage skirmishes with these diminutive New World natives.

Many historians believe that the *Skraeling* were the Thule people, the ancestors of the modern Inuit. Indeed, Inuit folklore contains references to bearded, sword-wielding giants called *"Kavdlunait"*, believed by some to be Viking explorers. Others claim that the *Skraeling* were the ancient Dorset people, upon whom some say the legend of the Toonijuk is based. Others still, however, maintain that the Sagas' references to *Skraeling* constitute the first written records describing a lost tribe of Arctic dwarfs, remnants of which, some say, still inhabit the Northland to this very day.

Norwegian-American historian Kirsten A. Seaver, in her article *'Pygmies' of the Far North*, published in the March 2008 edition of the *Journal of World History*, argued that the word *"Skraeling"* was an Old Norse translation of *"*Pygmy*"*- in this context, a race of dwarves from India which feature in Ancient Greek mythology, with which Classically-educated Vikings would have been familiar. Seaver suspected that Dark Age Norse explorers, knowing that the earth was round, believed they had stumbled upon eastern coast of India when they trudged onto the foamy shores of the New World. Much as 15th Century Spanish conquistadors called the natives of the Americas *"indios"*, or *"*Indians*"*, in the mistaken belief that they had reached the Orient, the Vikings, Seaver argued, named the tiny northern natives they encountered after the legendary dwarves said to inhabit the eastern continent.

Seaver's case is bolstered by a footnote which Flemish cartographer Gerardus Mercator included in his 1569 map of the world. On an island near the North Pole, Mercator wrote:

"Pygmae hic habitant 4 ad summum pedes longi,
quaemadmodum illi quos in Gronlandia Screlingers vocant."

This Latin passage, when translated to English, reads:

"Here live the Pygmies, at most 4 feet tall, like unto those they call Skraelings in Greenland."

Captain Luke Foxe's Discovery

Another explorer to uncover potential evidence of a race of pygmies living in the Arctic was Captain Luke Foxe, a 17th Century English adventurer who followed in the footsteps of Martin Frobisher and Henry Hudson, sailing the frigid waters of Northern Canada in search of the Northwest Passage.

Foxe set out on his first and only Arctic expedition in the spring of 1631. Setting out from Kirkwall, Orkney, he and his crew sailed west across the Atlantic to Frobisher Bay, situated near the northern lip of Hudson's Bay. The Englishmen sailed through the Hudson Strait and, after visiting the crew of Welsh Captain Thomas James, who was similarly searching for the Northwest Passage, headed west.

On July 27, 1631, Captain Foxe and his crew disembarked at Southampton Island, a large island located at the northern end of Hudson's Bay. There, they discovered a peculiar above-ground cemetery consisting of a number of little coffins made from wood and stone. Inside these coffins were, as Ivan Sanderson put it in his 1963 article *Traditions of Submen in Arctic and Subarctic North America*, "tiny human skeletons only four feet in length, surrounded by bows, arrows, and bone lances. They were all adults, and there is some implication that not all of them were skeletons, but might have been whole frozen bodies."

The first part of Foxe's report, which he included in his personal journal, went as follows:

"The newes from land was that this Island was a Sepulchre, for the Savages had laid their dead (I cannot say interred), for it is all stone, as they cannot dig therein, but lay the Corpses on the stones, and wall them about with the same, coffining them also by laying the sides of old sleddes about, which have been artificially made. The boards are some 9 or 10 foot long, 9 inches thicke. In what manner the tree they have bin made out of was doven or sawen, it was so smooth that we could not discerne, the burials had been so old.

"And, as in other places in those countries, they bury all their Utensils, as bows, arrows, strings, darts, lances, and other implements carved in bone. The longest Corpses was not above 4 foot long, with their heads laid to the West. It may be that they travell, as the Tartars and the Samoides; for, if they had remained here, there would have been some newer burials. There was one place walled 9 square, and seated within the earth; each side was 9 or 5 yards in length; in the middle was 3 stones, laid one above another, man's height. We tooke this to be some place of Ceremony at the buriall of the dead."

In a footnote, Foxe added, "They seem to be people of small stature. God send me better for my adventures than these."

The Dwarves of the Mackenzie Mountains

When white men began to establish themselves in Mackenzie Country in the 18th and early 19th Centuries, they learned that the local Dene had a strong tradition that the Mackenzie Mountains were home to a race of mystical dwarves. In one of his letters, Poole Field described these creatures as "little men of the Mountain that are supposed to be about four feet high at the most and have fine living places in the heart of the mountain, and are exceptionally strong and wise who come out occasionally and capture their women for wives, in some cases making the father of the girl they have taken a medicine man in return for the girl."

In his book *The Kaska Indians: An Ethnographic Reconstruction* (1964), John J. Honigmann recounted an old Kaska legend about the *"Klunetene"*- literally "Little Men"- "who lived on mice which they secured with small bows and arrows in the fall grass" and sometimes "befriended men. They also enjoyed a reputation for their making fun."

These dwarves, despite their being constantly menaced by wild animals, were said to be a powerful people with shamanic abilities. "In warfare," Honigmann wrote, "these small beings helped to bring up wind and cold that paralyzed the enemy. In size a dwarf reached about the height of a caribou jaw. One such being could pack only about half a pound. Despite the tendency of the dwarfs to steal women, people laughed when they spoke of the antics of the little people."

Although the dwarves were said to have delighted in helping humans, the Attawapiskat Cree of Northern Ontario were purportedly afraid of these little men "who inhabited the rocky cliffs along rivers."

Ed Ferrell's Story

In 1996, northern writer Ed Ferrell published a book called *Strange Stories of Alaska and the Yukon*, a collection of old Northern newspaper articles about ghosts, lost gold mines, forgotten civilizations, and other weird tales of the Northland. Ferrell dedicated one chapter to his book to stories of strange tribes which prospectors and trappers are said to have discovered during the course of their boreal wanderings.

Ferrell found one of these articles, entitled *"Pygmies of the North Pole"*, in the September 13, 1930 issue of *The Stroller's Weekly*, a newspaper based out of Juneau, Alaska. It tells of a party of scientists, one of them named John Weizl, who participated in an Arctic expedition in June, 1911, led by a Russian explorer named Captain Yvolnoff. Inuit guides led the scientists to an impossible location "about 730 miles northwest of the North Pole", where they found tiny footprints in the snow. They followed the footprints to an underground burrow into which they sent one of their dogs. The dog quickly returned to the surface, "seeming not to like what he had discovered."

After some time, a little man came out of the burrow, speaking a language the Inuit did not understand in a shrill, frightened tone. He was about three and a half feet tall and extremely thin, and was estimated to weigh around 35 to 40 pounds. His head, complete with enormous ears, was "almost triangular-shaped, coming to a peak, with a small tuft of hair at the top."

When the scientists pacified the pygmy with soothing words, he called for his kinsmen to come out of the burrow. Slowly, twenty seven people emerged from the hole in the ground, all of them "clad in very fine skins".

The expedition party spent a day with these little natives. They observed that these tiny people lived on small fish, which they caught with their bare hands. For some reason, they only ate the backs of the fish, and threw the rest away.

Anthony Roche's Encounter

As is the case with Nakani encounters, sightings of Arctic dwarves still occur from time to time in the desolate wilds of the Northland. One man who may have come face-to-face with one of these little people is Anthony Roche, the Northern native whose ghostly experiences at Rabbitkettle Lake are detailed earlier in this book.

In August 2017, Roche paid a visit to his girlfriend's grandmother, who lived in a cabin about ten kilometres west of Cambridge Bay, Nunavut. Cambridge Bay is a hamlet of about 1,500 people, located on the southern shore of Victoria

Island.[2] Despite being the second largest island in the Arctic Archipelago, Victoria Island only home to about 1,900 people, making it one of the most sparsely populated places on earth.

During their visit, Roche and his girlfriend stayed in her parents' cabin, which was vacant at the time. This cottage, situated about eighty yards away from the grandmother's cabin, constituted the only other residence in that remote corner of the Artic at the time.

One day, while his girlfriend went for tea at his grandmother's cabin, Roche went out to inspect her parents' fish net. "I got three fish in the net," Roche told this author, "filleted them and hung them to dry". That accomplished, he and his girlfriend, who had returned from her grandmother's cabin, both decided to take a nap in her parents' cabin. Just as they were drifting off to sleep, the couple heard an unexpected sound.

"We both woke up to footsteps on the deck," said Roche. They heard the creaking of the cabin's outer door. Several seconds later, the inside door swung open. Roche, who was lying on the upper level of a bunk bed, glanced over at the open door expecting to see his girlfriend's grandmother, as she was the only other person in the area at the time. There was no one there. Roche craned his neck to get a better view.

---

[2] Not to be confused with Vancouver Island, British Columbia, which is home to Victoria, the provincial capital.

"And there," said Roche, "was the smallest human I've ever seen, wearing a ragged old orange-coloured coat and caribou skin pants." Suddenly, both doors shut in unison, "as if they were one. My girlfriend screamed, 'Someone tried to get in!' I jumped up to see who it was. Looked out every window and didn't see anyone. I walked out the door and didn't see anyone. I thought to myself, 'grandma can't move that fast.' Her cabin is eighty yards away."

Later, Roche and his girlfriend met up with her parents and told them of their experience. "They told us a little person visited us- an '*inuk*', they call them. '*Inuagulik*', in our language... They were supposed to be folk stories for children, and one walked into our cabin."

As was mentioned earlier in this chapter, Loren Coleman hypothesized that the muscular, dwarf-like Nuk-luk that appeared in Nahanni Country in 1964 was some variety of Neanderthal- a robust archaic human which lived alongside and interacted with our ancient ancestors. In 1965, one year after the Nuk-luk sightings, another mysterious creature was reported in the Nahanni Valley- a colossal predator eerily reminiscent of a monster of Inuit myth. Believed by some to be a prehistoric relict, much like its wildman neighbours, this animal is known as the Waheela.

The Waheela

"In due course, Frank heard some noises at the edge of the forest but, thinking it was either the idiot dog or the hunter coming back, he did not- as the saying goes- 'come to the ready'. Thus, when some bushes at the border of the plateau began to move about, and in a manner that could not have been caused either by the little dog or the hunter, he called out, but got no response. Then, suddenly, Frank found himself confronted by what he at first took for the grand-daddy of all wolves."

- Ivan T. Sanderson†, *The Dire Wolf*, 1974.

DURING HIS FIRST TRIP to the Nahanni Valley in the summer of 1965, Frank Graves spent a good deal of time fraternising with the sourdoughs of Nahanni Butte. When they finally decided that he was neither crazy nor a government agent, the locals warmed up to him and began to tell him amusing stories of unfortunate greenhorns who ventured up the South Nahanni without a lick of backcountry experience, only to come crawling back to Nahanni Butte "plain scared of the world up [that] river."

"At first," wrote Graves, in his first letter to Ivan Sanderson, "I took the stories of the old-timers about these scared trappers and prospectors as being nothing much more than the sort of snide accounts that permanent residents of far out of the way places relate about the behavior of outsiders. But this attitude of mine seems to have gotten under the skins of the locals, and the resident Amerinds, and even those other Indians who wander in from the outlands from time to time. It then dawned on me that I was giving offense by not believing what they told me, so I sort of indicated that I did want to believe what they said but that I had thought they had just been pulling my leg as a greenhorn from the outside. That did it."

The locals proceeded to take Graves on a tour of the lower part of the South Nahanni, showing him burned-out cabins, old rusted rifles, and other relics abandoned by woodsmen who lost their taste for this foreboding stretch of Mackenzie Country. Eventually, one of Graves' new acquaintances, a local Dene hunter, agreed to take the young mechanic above Virginia Falls, where he could find unique subarctic vegetation to add to his botanical collection. As was mentioned in the previous chapter, during one such outing, Frank and his guide stumbled upon three 16-inch-long humanlike footprints in the mud of some 'unlucky' vale- perhaps signs of the elusive Nakani.

Several days later, Graves went out in the bush again with his Dene friend, who had brought his dog along with him in case they came across some game that needed flushing out. The trio worked their way up a glen which led from the river and onto a small plateau covered with grass and brush. Sure enough, Graves' native companion spotted some wild fowl in the timber below and, with his dog by his side, ambled down the slope towards them, hoping to bag something for supper. Graves, who was armed with a double-barrelled 12-gauge shotgun loaded with birdshot, opted to stay up on the plateau in case any game appeared in that area in his partner's absence.

"This Indian was a pretty good tracker," wrote Graves of his Dene companion, "and moved without making a sound, but his dog was not a 'hunter'. So, when I heard a noise and saw some brush moving about at the edge of the trees, I thought it was the dog coming back, and I did not raise my gun.

"But then an enormous white thing that I at first thought must be a Polar bear just sort of wandered out of the trees. It wasn't a bear; it looked more like a gigantic dog. It stood straight up on rather long legs, more like a dog or a wolf. I had seen plenty of wolves and some of them are enormous enough up there; but this thing was twenty times the size of any wolf I had ever heard of. By a sort of reflex action I fired at it- and it was less than twenty paces away and only partly screened by little bushes. I hit it with two barrels of ball-shot. It didn't even jump, but turned away from me, and just walked back into the forest. I reloaded and fired again, and I know I hit it in the rear, but it just kept on walking. Shortly afterwards, my Indian friend bobbed up, asking what I had got. I didn't know what to say for a bit but, when I told him, we did another of our famous disappearing acts, and this time we loaded the boats and pushed off up river- real fast."

———————

In an article entitled *"The Dire Wolf"*, published posthumously[1] in the October 1974 issue of the magazine *Pursuit*, Ivan Sanderson revealed a number of interesting details about this incident which Graves did not include in his letter. Presumably in a face-to-face interview, or perhaps in another letter, Graves told Sanderson that the beast he encountered stood about 3'6" at the shoulder, had a very wide head, and wore a coat of "very long, rather shaggy" white fur.

Sanderson also revealed that, following the incident, Graves' Indian companion "loosened up a bit and told him that they had met an animal that is not a wolf", but rather a mysterious creature which may have been responsible for the deaths of Willie and Frank McLeod, Martin Jorgenson, and other headless victims of the Nahanni Valley. The Dene said that these beasts "were much larger than any wolf; were 'loners'; avoided real wolves; had smaller ears and much wider heads, and rather short legs, with splayed feet. Their tails... were very thick and more like those of otters, while they were scavengers rather than predacious animals."

---

[1] Ivan Sanderson died of brain cancer on February 19, 1973.

Frank's companion also told him that these beasts were quite rare, and that most of them lived further to the north, in the tundra. Some of them made annual trips to the Mackenzie Mountains and the Yukon taiga, and a few of them stayed in the Nahanni all year round. The name that Sanderson gave these cryptids[2], for reasons which we will explore later on in this chapter, was "Waheela".

Interestingly, existence of these mysterious animals was verified in a letter written to Ivan Sanderson on July 12, 1971, by a man whose signature this author was unable to decipher. The man claimed that, in October 1970, while visiting the town of Moosenee in Northern Ontario, he met an old Indian named Guh-goh-nah-neh-neish (or simply "Gugo", as the man refers to him later on in the letter) "who claimed to have come from the Nahanni area". The Dene people were terrified of these monsters, Gugo maintained, claiming that they were impossible to kill. Regarding their appearance, the Indian pointed to a huge mongrel that was running round nearby, which the writer described as a "Husky/Alsatian crossbreed, but with the rear of a St. Bernard," and said that the monster looked similar to that dog but much larger. When the writer inquired as to exactly how large the wild dog-creature was, the Indian indicated that it had an 11-foot-long body, a 4-foot-long tail, and stood as tall as his shoulder. "The rear portion of the body apparently slopes away in the manner of a bear," the writer wrote. "The head appears to be

[2] Cryptids are hidden or unknown animals.

low slung and flattened and having a broad muzzle. Colours range from brown to white.

"Its habits are disgusting, if it exists," the letter writer continued. "Part carrion eater, it can take a bear apart, but prefers to live on injured or young animals. Its delight is to snatch the young from the mother whilst she is in the process of giving birth. Also said to attack man on site. Almost invincible, he has but one enemy.

"Now hang on to your hat!

"That enemy is a..."

[TO BE CONTINUED...]

"THE GRAND-DADDY OF ALL WOLVES"

Following the publication of Sanderson's article in 1974, cryptozoologists and Fortean enthusiasts from all over North America began to speculate as to the nature of this mysterious monster which had appeared to Frank Graves in the summer of 1965. Some thought that it might be a new species, or perhaps a survivor from the last Ice Age, while others suggested that it might be some sort of supernatural entity.

Sanderson himself, in the aforementioned article, disclosed that one of Graves' first thoughts upon seeing the creature was that it was "the grand-daddy of all wolves"- in other words, a freakishly large timber wolf. Considering a

number of sightings reported by Nahanni frontiersmen, this
sentiment is not at all unreasonable; over the years, more than
a few lupine behemoths have appeared in the Nahanni Valley.

———————◆———◆———

Nearly every woodsman to comment on the wolves of
the Nahanni area has made some remark on the incredible
size that many of them manage to attain. One of the first to
put such sentiments to paper was Raymond Patterson, who,
in his journal, made several references to the enormity of
various wolf tracks he came across over the course of his
Nahanni adventures. One of these was so large that he could
fit his fist into it "with room to spare", while another,
measuring about six inches in diameter, he likened to "a
pony's foot". Patterson also described coming across "a huge
timberwolf... a great beast, looking much like the colour of an
Airedale[3] through the falling snow", and noted on November
14, 1928, that his partner, Gordon Matthews, saw "two
timberwolves about the size of calves" down by the river.

That same year, Captain Harry "Doc" Oakes flew
Charlie McLeod and the men of the ill-fated NAME
expedition into Landing Lake, in upper Flat River country.
Also associated with Northern Aerial Mineral Explorations
Ltd. were pilots R.D. Adams and W.J. "Jack" McDonough.
On February 10, 1974- a full eight months before the
publication of Sanderson's *Dire Wolf* article- the *Toronto Star*

[3] Airedales are black and light brown terriers originating from Yorkshire,
England.

ran with a story in which McDonough claimed that Charlie McLeod and his crew, during their prospecting misadventure in 1928, saw wolves that were "almost as big as ponies."

Another frontiersman to encounter lupine colossi in Nahanni Country was Gus Kraus, who claimed to have bagged a 155-pound wolf not far from his cabin.[4] Kraus was one-upped by trapper Arthur George, who shot a 160-pound wolf in the Nahanni Valley in 1929. To give these measurements some context: male Mackenzie Valley wolves- the larger gender of the largest subspecies of *Canis lupus* (gray/timber wolf) in the world- have an average weight of 113 pounds. The largest wolf ever officially recorded- killed by trapper Frank Glaser on Alaska's Seventymile River in the summer of 1939- weighed 175 pounds.

In *The Dire Wolf*, Ivan Sanderson mentioned that an old friend of his- a professional cameraman-turned-film director named Tex Zeigler- "made a few points about what he called the 'great white wolf'" of Alaska back in the 1950's, long before Frank Graves' encounter. Before he became involved in the film industry, Zeigler worked as a prospector, then as a trader, and finally as a pilot in the Alaskan wilderness, earning himself the epithet the "Flying Trader". During his days in the North Country, he came across gigantic, solitary white wolves on a number of occasions.

---

[4] Incidentally, Gus' wife, Mary, claimed to have discovered a 4-inch-long tooth on Bluebill Creek, a stream located 14.6 miles from Nahanni Butte. Wolf canine teeth, in comparison, rarely exceed one inch in length.

According to Sanderson, Zeigler expressed the opinion "that these huge loners were just that- i.e. huge, old wolves that lived alone".

Similarly, in a letter-to-the-editor published in Volume 2, No. 1, of the online Fortean magazine *North American BioFortean Review* (2000), a man who identified himself as Paul W., and who worked in the "outdoors industry," described an enormous white wolf which his good friend encountered in the wilderness of Northern Ontario, not far from his hunting lodge. He estimated that this animal, which was feasting on a moose carcass at the time, weighed at least 200 pounds. "He said that it appeared to have a larger and broader than normal head," Paul stated, "and that the front legs were quite long compared to the rear legs. As he put it, 'it just looked real different than any wolf I have seen before, much larger, and more robust than even a big male should be.'" Paul added that he had personally seen and taken photographs of eight-inch-wide wolf tracks in these same forests; normal wolf tracks in the area, he maintained, have a diameter of around four or five inches.

***

In addition to being extremely large, the wolves of Nahanni Country also tend to be unusually aggressive. Although wolves typically avoid humans and very rarely harm them, a startling number of wolf attacks have taken place in the Nahanni Valley over the years. One of these occurred sometime in the late 1930's. The victim in this case was none other than Albert Faille.

Albert Faille's Account

One day in late September, while out hunting moose in the woods above Virginia Falls, Albert Faille heard an unusual sound which he described as something between a growl, a bark, and a howl. He recognized this as a call which wolves make to each other when they want to indicate potential prey. Slowly, this call was taken up by about a dozen other wolves, rising in volume until it reached a chilling, bloodcurdling cacophony; apparently, the pack was all in agreement.

Suddenly, there was dead silence. Faille knew that the wolves had found their dinner and were going in for the kill. Thinking that they had caught the scent of a moose, which he might be able to intercept, he headed in the direction from which the sounds had come.

After hiking for some time, Faille stopped to listen. The forest was quieter than he had expected. Instead of a frantic flurry of hoof beats and the crackling of broken sticks, all he could hear was the distant roar of Virginia Falls. All of a sudden, a new sound arose from the woods- a chorus of soft, high-pitched whines akin to the mewing of kittens. It seemed to come from all around him. When he noticed ghostly gray shadows gliding through the willows out of the corner of his eye, Faille began to realize that *he* was the one the wolves had singled out for the kill; the hunter had become the hunted.

The frontiersman readied his rifle and prepared for the inevitable. Sure enough, a big, grizzled alpha male emerged from the brush and came bounding towards him, loping silently through the snow. Faille felled the beast with a single shot. After firing additional pot shots at the rest of his unseen assailants, hidden as they were in the woods that surrounded him, he quickly retraced his steps to his boat and paddled downriver, denying those fleet-footed monsters of the Mackenzie their latest meal.

———————◆———◆———

Another Nahanni frontiersman to narrowly avoid becoming lupine lunch was Gus Kraus; in the winter of 1935, a pack of about twenty wolves chased him up a tree at the edge of McMillan Lake. Later on, in May 1942, Stan Turner, the brother of Dick Turner, was similarly chased up a birch tree by four slavering black timber wolves whom, he believed, had mistaken him for a caribou. And in March 1948, a trapper named Edwin Lindberg was stalked by four shaggy *degahi*, as the Dene called them, while setting a beaver trap not far from the Liard River; fortunately, he managed to drive the animals away with fire and buckshot.

Gus and Mary Kraus' Encounter

One of the most interesting wolf attacks to occur in the Nahanni Valley, especially in the context of the Waheela, took place sometime in the early 1940's. In this story, Gus and Mary Kraus decided to head up Clausen Creek to hunt for beaver. On the creek bank, at a site located a mere mile and a half from their cabin, they were attacked by two enormous white wolves who were apparently attracted by the scent of fresh blood.

At that time, Gus Kraus was a habitual pipe smoker, and Mary hated the smell of his tobacco. Whenever the two of them set out into the wilderness together, Gus took the lead, usually with a pipe in his mouth. In order to avoid the smoke, Mary trailed far behind him, keeping a distance of up to fifty feet, often grumbling darkly about her husband's odoriferous habit as she trudged along in her moccasins.

That day, when they arrived at a natural mineral lick off Clausen Creek where moose and caribou often came to taste the salt, Gus heard Mary's familiar mutterings some distance behind him. Assuming that his smoking was the cause of her "yammering," as he put it, he paid her no heed and carried on, daydreaming. When he finally detected an edge of frantic urgency in his wife's tone, he looked up, and there on the side of the game trail, no more than five feet away from him, was a black bear. "That's what she was yapping about," Gus explained in an interview.

The bear, who appeared to be just as startled to see Gus as the trapper was to see him, snorted in surprise and started to amble away. "Shoot him!" Mary urged, hoping to use the bear as dog feed.

Gus refused. They were after beaver, after all, and the trapper was in no mood to spend his morning butchering a bear just for dog feed.

Mary, however, was adamant. After arguing with her for some time, the trapper finally acceded to his wife's wishes and fired at the animal, which was now about seventy five feet away. He killed it with a single shot.

The couple proceeded to skin the bear and dress its fat and meat for packing. By the time they had finished processing as much of the animal as they could carry back with them, they were covered in blood.

Gus and Mary continued up Clausen Creek for about three hundred yards until they reached the mouth of a small tributary. They decided to wash the blood off there, and maybe have a cup of tea when they were finished. That done, they could finally scout for some beaver.

Gus placed his rifle in the grass beside him and set about making a fire at the base of a steep cutbank, which he hoped would shield his kindling from a strong south wind that had picked up. "I just set [my rifle] down alongside of me," he said in the interview, "and set raking up a little bit of grass, you know, to get the fire started. And all of a sudden [Mary] said, 'Oh, look at the sheep.' Well, I know there's no sheep down there that low... So I put my hand down on the rifle and... Boy, oh boy! Two wolves! Two white wolves! White as can be... They made big jumps, about seven feet to a jump, one behind the other... they're just a-jumping to beat the band."

It was clear that the wolves- both of which were enormous- were heading straight for them, apparently having caught the scent of the bears' blood on the wind. Gus aimed his rifle and pulled the trigger just as the first wolf leapt over the riverbank. The animal dropped dead a mere metre from Mary's feet. "If I hadn't fired," Gus said, "they'd have had her."

The second wolf wheeled around, startled by the report of the rifle. Gus fired at him and missed. The animal quickly recovered its senses and moved to bound across the creek towards Mary. "Just as he was jumping across the creek," said Gus, "I got him right through, and he dropped in the creek."

A WHITE BEAR

Many have suggested that the monster that Frank Graves came across in 1965 was nothing more than an unusually large white wolf, of which the Nahanni Valley has certainly seen its fair share. Perhaps, some say, it was a genetic freak shunned by its pack for its gigantism. However, there are a few details in Graves' description of the creature which indicate that it may have been another animal entirely.

Graves described the Waheela as having a "very wide head", evoking images of grizzly and black bears, the

Nahanni Valley's only ursine residents.[5] The heads of Mackenzie Valley wolves, on the other hand, are comparatively sleek and slender. Graves' creature also had small ears- another characteristic more commonly ascribed to the ursine than the lupine. And finally, the Waheela was estimated to stand about 3'6" at the shoulder. The average Mackenzie Valley wolf, in comparison, has a shoulder height of between 2'8" and 3'4", while black bears' shoulders typically sit somewhere between two feet to 3'5" from the ground.[6] These attributes suggest that the Waheela that Frank Graves ran into may have been an albino black bear[7]- perhaps something similar to the starving white "medicine bear" which Philip Godsell encountered in Northern Manitoba in the spring of 1907. Graves, however, was adamant that what he saw was neither a bear nor a wolf, but rather something which exhibited characteristics of both.

THE AMPHICYON THEORY

Ivan Sanderson had his own theory regarding the nature of the Waheela. In *The Dire Wolf*, he observed that Graves' description of the animal- coupled with the

---

[5] Polar bears are creatures of the High Arctic, and it would be very unusual to find one in the Nahanni Valley.

[6] Grizzly bears, it must be mentioned, have a much higher average shoulder height of 4'11".

[7] While the words "albino black bear" are suggestive of the Kermode, or 'spirit' bear, briefly mentioned in the chapter on the tropical valley, the Kermode's habitat is believed to extend only from Central British Columbia to BC's coastal northwest.

descriptions given by his Dene acquaintances, who claimed to be familiar with them- corresponded with chilling accuracy to that of a mammal believed to have gone extinct several million years ago- an ancient scavenger known colloquially as the "bear-dog".

"Bears, dogs, and racoons appear to have a common ancestry," Sanderson explained, "but, along the line, a group of animals that are popularly called 'bear-dogs', the *Amphicyonidae* (or 'dogs of doubtful origin'), flourished all around the northern hemisphere. These were neither dogs nor bears, but a number of them were the size of the largest living bears, and some had doglike features. Some of these huge creatures are known to have lived on until the end of what is called the Pliocene Period, and were thus contemporary with some animals that still live, like the muskox and [bison], and they could well have survived into the age of man, called the Pleistocene; and even into the post glacial period on this continent."

Sanderson went on to explain that the *Amphicyonidae* family was comprised of a number of genera, the most interesting of which, in the context of the Waheela, was the genus *Amphicyon*, meaning "Ambiguous Doglike Creature", for which the broader family was named. Sanderson's particular interest in the *Amphicyon* genus stemmed from that fact that several of its species were known to have survived in North America "until at least the end of the Pliocene

Period,"[8] which meant that relict populations of these creatures could potentially still exist in remote corners of the continent like the Nahanni Valley.

As of 2018, there are nine species of *Amphicyon* officially recognized by the scientific community, four of which are known to have lived in North America. Paleontologists have unearthed fossils of these creatures in Nebraska, Colorado, Oregon, California, New Mexico, and Florida, as well as in Central Asia, Europe, and North Africa.

The youngest known species of North American *Amphicyon*, called *A. ingens*, was also the largest. This prehistoric monster is believed to have reached a maximum length of 2.5 metres (8'2") and a shoulder height of around 3'11", and to have weighed anywhere from 200 to 550 kilograms (440-1,212 pounds). It displayed a considerable degree of sexual dimorphism, which means that male *A. ingens* were considerably larger than their female counterparts. This bear-dog had a heavy tail, robust legs, wolf-like teeth, and jaws powerful enough to crush bone. It is believed to have been plantigrade, meaning that it walked with its foot bones flat on the ground like a bear, rather than on its toes like a dog. Due to its supposed solitary hunting and scavenging habits, it is believed to have suffered from

---

[8] Today, it is believed that the last North American Amphicyon species actually died out at the end of the Miocene Period, the geological epoch preceding the Pliocene, although one variety of bear-dog called *Arctamphicyon lydekkeri* which some believe might actually be a type of *Amphicyon* called *A. palaeindicus* is believed to have survived in Central Asia until the early Pliocene.

competition with pack predators like primitive wolves, which ultimately resulted in its extinction around six and a half million years ago.

Is it possible that the Waheela that Frank Graves encountered in 1965, along with Tex Zeigler's "great white wolf" and the mysterious predator of Northern Ontario, was a remnant *Amphicyon* whose prehistoric ancestors took sanctuary in the secluded wilderness of the subarctic? Graves maintained that the beast that he saw had both doglike and bearlike features. The Ontario hunter called his own creature "peculiar"-looking. And all three men described their monsters as solitary animals significantly larger than the average wolf. All of these attributes appear to be consistent with Sanderson's theory that these large, lonely, white wolves of the North Country are bear-dogs- relics of the Northland's prehistoric past.

It must be mentioned that many of those who have commented upon Ivan Sanderson's *Amphicyon* theory have puzzled over his choice of title for the article in which he introduced it, namely *"The Dire Wolf"*. The dire wolf was a Pleistocene canine only distantly related to members of the even more ancient *Amphicyon* genus. Officially classified as *Canis dirus*, it was a larger, older cousin of the modern day timber wolf, and is believed to have died out around 10,000 year ago. Was Sanderson suggesting, by choosing that title, that the dire wolf was another potential candidate for the identity of the Waheela in addition to the bear-dog? The answer to this question becomes clear once one considers the seemingly-inappropriate title with the context of its usage throughout the piece; it seems that the Father of Cryptozoology employed the word "dire wolf" as a generic term for all prehistoric canines, much as he often used "Abominable Snowman"- a once-popular name for the Himalayan Yeti- as a blanket term for all wildmen.

Snoodles

While reading through transcripts of interviews with Nahanni old-timers, the author of this book came across two separate references, each of them furnished by a different interviewee, to a remarkable dog named Snoodles, which was once owned by Gus and Mary Kraus.

Until the advent of the snowmobile, the dog was a mainstay of Northern life, as essential to the sourdough as the horse was to the Western plainsman. Like their westerly equine counterparts, dogs were primarily used for transportation in the North Country, being hitched to sleds in the winter and loaded down with packs during the summer months. They also served as guardians against wild animals, and as much-needed companions during the long spells of lonely isolation which typified life on the Northern frontier. A trapper or prospector could easily get to know a hundred dogs in his lifetime, and thus it struck this author as strange that one particular dog could impress itself so indelibly upon the memories of its sourdough associates as to merit specific mention in two separate interviews. Even more bizarre, however, especially considering Sanderson's *Amphicyon* theory, is the physical description that the sourdoughs gave this creature.

"I don't know what was wrong," said Gus Kraus. "He was a really odd dog. He looked more like a bear than a dog. I don't know what breed you would call him. To look from behind, you'd swear it was a bear. Big, heavy legs, feet, heavy body."

In a completely separate interview, Billy Clark stated that Snoodles was Kraus' "best-looking dog... Squat-looking type. Fur like a black bear and quite big ears, but short and stubby but heavily-built, quite a big chest... You could put fifty, sixty pounds on that dog, in the dog pack- twenty-five pound flour on each side, and some other things- and he'd walk along beside you, or ahead of you, around you all day. Tremendous dog."

To give that second last statement some context, trapper Al Lewis, in *Nahanni Remembered*, wrote that the average dog could handle a pack weighing a total of 20 to 30 pounds.

Snoodles' physical strength, robust build, and especially his resemblance to a black bear seemed to echo Frank Graves' description of the Waheela. It also strongly evoked Sanderson's bear-dog theory. Wondering whether Snoodles might have some sort of connection with the legend of the Waheela, this author searched for more information on him and unearthed an intriguing backstory.

According to Billy Clark, Gus Kraus acquired this dog from George Dalziel, the Flying Trapper- a tough frontiersman who, in the words of Nahanni historian Norm Kagan, was "one of the most daring men to cross the Mackenzies."

George Dalziel first came to the North Country in the winter 1932, making his way northeast from British Columbia and heading straight over the Mackenzie Mountains on foot. The hardened woodsman completed this trek with a barebones outfit, lacking even the Spartan comfort afforded by a canvas tent; incredibly, Dalziel spent every night of his gruelling winter journey in an open siwash camp, with nothing over his head but the falling snow and the northern lights. Al Lewis described the Flying Trapper and his remarkable odyssey thus:

"His ability in the air was in direct proportion to his ability in the bush. This was the man who had snowshoed from Lower Post on the Liard River to Fort Norman on the Mackenzie River. Nearly 400 miles (645 km) as the crow flies. And Dal sure as hell never followed any crow. Through mountains, swamps, river valleys, and plateaus, he made the winter journey with rifle, axe, and two pack dogs."

Dalziel purchased his first bushplane in 1934 and spent the subsequent decades earning himself an almost legendary reputation in the Northland as the Flying Trapper.

"George Dalziel was an astounding woodsman and aviator," Norm Kagan once wrote in a brief biographical summary of the man. "His life would make a great story, particularly if all the facts were known. He ignored the rules-smuggled, trapped, hunted, traded where and when he wanted. He survived dreadful winters and a few crashes, too, expecting the same of others."

It was from this remarkable character that Gus Kraus purchased Snoodles for a handful of martin pelts.

In those days, intrepid frontiersman often attempted to cross-breed their sled dogs with wild wolves in order to obtain offspring that were large, swift, powerful, vigorous, and naturally adapted to the harsh climate of the North. One technique that they sometimes used to achieve this end involved waiting for a female dog to go into heat before leaving it in the wild overnight, tied to some tree located a good distance from the cabin. With luck, the trapper brave enough to attempt this risky operation would return in the morning to find his mutt pregnant with a litter of wolfdogs. On rarer occasions, in the event that they were obliged to shoot the adult members of a resident wolf pack, frontiersmen would sometimes seek out the den of the wolves they killed and raise their orphaned pups as their own.

Considering the Flying Trapper's unorthodox nature, the author of this book conceived the notion that- assuming Sanderson's theory was correct, and that a surviving bear-dog population indeed inhabited the wilderness of the Nahanni Valley- perhaps Snoodles was the product of a union between a sled dog and a wild *Amphicyon,* made possible through the employment of the first technique described above. Even more incredibly, perhaps Snoodles was a full-blooded Waheela himself, acquired by Dalziel through the second technique. Intriguingly, these hypothetical scenarios seemed to be in accordance with Billy Clark's description of Dalziel's dogs:

"His dogs were wild. You just couldn't get near Dalziel's dogs, you know... They were absolutely wild, no kidding."

In his interview, Gus Kraus related a story which shed some light upon Snoodles' temperament. The story takes place on Bennett Creek, where Kraus once staked a mining claim. Every day, the trapper laboured with pick and shovel, digging a shaft to bedrock in the hope of striking gold. In the evenings, after a hard day's work, he would cut Snoodles a slab of frozen moose meat and put it by the stove to thaw.

"He was a funny dog, you know," Kraus said. "Almost human. He'd watch. He'd know when that meat was thawed out- mostly bone, you know, with some meat on. And then he'd come over to me and bump me with his nose," prompting Kraus to hand him the morsel. "He'd go over and take the meat, and he'd go off with it to the door...

"I was sitting there- laying there, rather- on the bunk, and talking to Bill [Clark]. This was just before we'd light the lamp. We were burning candles, of course, and I'd see [Snoodles] going out there... I leaned back and talked to Bill. All at once, alongside of me by the window, I hear something." Kraus mimicked a grinding sound. "Something grinding on a bone."

Kraus rose from the bunk and looked out the window and there, crouched in the dark beside his cabin, was an old, grizzled she-wolf attempting, with the few teeth she had left, to gnaw on a moose bone- the same bone that Snoodles had taken outside. Not far from the she-wolf sat Snoodles himself, who did not seem the least perturbed by her presence.

The she-wolf seemed to sense that she was being watched. She raised her eyes to look at the window and, seeing Kraus staring at her, dropped her bone and bolted for the woods. Baffled, Kraus called Snoodles inside and shut the door.

The following morning, Kraus followed the wolf's tracks along a trail that led from his cabin to a stretch of timber on the other side of Bennett Creek. At the end of the trail was a graveyard of artificially-stunted moose bones, many of them boiled or roasted, which suspiciously resembled those he gave Snoodles to gnaw on every night. Snoodles, apparently, had been sharing his nightly rations with the old-she wolf for at least a month. As Gus Kraus put it, "he was feeding that doggone wolf."

Kraus set a trap and, after several unsuccessful attempts, managed to catch the old wolf and shoot it. "You ought to see that dog," he said. "The look of that dog. Boy, oh boy... You could see that he was so put out at me killing that darn female."

⁂

As it turns out, there are four photographs of Snoodles filed away in the Northwest Territories Archives in Yellowknife, NWT. The oldest of these was taken in 1942, and the youngest in 1958, indicating that Snoodles lived to be at least sixteen years old- a ripe old age for a dog, especially one of his size.

Alas, our Snoodles does not look much like a prehistoric monster, at least to this author, but rather resembles something akin to a Swedish Lapphund with the build of a Bernese Mountain Dog. In all likelihood, Snoodles was a mutt- an intelligent, powerfully-built, plain-old domestic dog- and not some sort of husky-*Amphicyon* hybrid.

Interestingly, one of Snoodles' photographs contains a startling background image particularly relevant to this chapter. In this photo, snapped in 1943, Mary Kraus stands with Snoodles in front of the Kraus family cabin, from the eaves of which hang the pelts of two enormous white wolves- the same wolves from which Gus had saved Mary.

NWT Archives/Gus_Mary Kraus/N-1990-022-0300

THE ORIGIN OF "WAHEELA"

Today, cryptozoologists refer to the bearlike, doglike, bone-crushing cryptid of the Nahanni Valley as the 'Waheela'. This name is not some ancient Dene word, nor does it derive from the North Country. According to Ivan Sanderson, who introduced it to the public in his 1974 article and was the first to apply it to the "great white wolf" of the Nahanni Valley, the word 'Waheela' first appeared in an old historical record as a name for a mysterious, wolf-like creature which once haunted the forests of Northern Michigan. He described this record and the means by which he came across it in *The Dire Wolf.*

In 1965, upon learning of Frank Graves' encounter with the giant white wolf of the Nahanni, Sanderson "wrote to several other friends who have spent time on Amerindian myth, legend, and folklore" and inquired as to whether any of them had come across similar stories of mysterious canids in the mythology of the First Nations and Native American tribes that they studied. The only friend to come up with anything concrete was Loren Coleman- at that time, an eighteen-year-old cryptozoology enthusiast with a demonstrable interest in the mysteries of the Nahanni Valley.[9]

According to Sanderson:

"Coleman came through with an extract from an old historical record in the files of the University of Indiana. This was a report of a group of three trappers, possibly Amerinds, who had a camp on the side of a lake in northern Michigan and, according to an early colonial record, had encountered a 'Waheela'. One retired precipitately to the nearest settlement, the other two following it with their guns. Their mangled remains, surrounded by 'wolf' tracks, were found the next morning."

Loren Coleman has confirmed the existence of this historical record in a number of online articles, adding that

---

[9] On December 29, 1963, sixteen-year-old Loren Coleman wrote a letter to the RCMP detachment at Fort Liard inquiring as to the nature of the mysterious deaths and disappearances that have taken place in the Nahanni Valley over the years. Mountie Constable R.C. Clark sent a reply to Coleman on January 28, 1964, stating that "most of the deaths have been attributed to lack of knowledge of survival in such a desolate and rugged country," before cryptically admitting that "the above information has not come from the Police files, as it is not the policy of the R.C.M. Police to divulge such information from their records."

the extract in question described the 'Waheela' as a "phantom-like giant white wolf" reminiscent of Frank Graves' sighting. Unfortunately, he lost his own copy of this document long ago. In a private correspondence with this author, Coleman specified that the document came either the Indiana University Folklore Collection or the Indiana University Folklore Archives, and that he had acquired it in 1962, when he was fourteen years old, entirely through letters to an IU reference librarian.

As a current Indiana University librarian explained to this author, "the IU Folklore Collection and the IU Folklore Archives are distinct things. The Folklore Collection refers to a large collection of published books and journals in folklore which has been shelved as a separate collection in the IU Libraries in 1965. The Folklore Archives, on the other hand, is a collection of unpublished manuscripts, mostly made by students in folklore classes."

Assuming that Loren Coleman remembered his dates correctly and acquired the document in question in 1962, the librarian who forwarded it to him likely found it either in an old book in some 'Folklore' section of one of the university's libraries or in the IU Folklore Archives.

The origins of the IU Folklore Archives lie in materials assembled by American folklorist Dr. Richard M. Dorson of Michigan State University, and initially consisted of about 1,000 Michigan-area folktales collected by students of Dorson's American Folklore course, which he taught back at

MSU. Dorson took over leadership of Indiana University's Folklore Institute in 1957, bringing his folklore archives to Indiana with him. In 1962, it is likely that the student papers of which his archives were comprised were stored away in filing cabinets in his personal office. Perhaps Coleman's reference librarian acquired the historical record- which, in this case, could only be an allusion to an "old historical record"- from these files.

Alternatively, it is possible that Loren Coleman misremembered his dates and actually acquired the document in question in or after 1965. In this case, it is possible that the librarian who forwarded it to him found it in Indiana University's newly established Folklore Collection.

Whatever the case, the author of this book, through IU university staff, attempted to track down the document in question, perceiving it to be an article of immense significance to the Waheela legend, as it was supposedly the first instance in which the word 'Waheela' was used to describe a mysterious wolflike creature. Librarians Molly Wittenberg, Moira Marsh, and Carrie Schwier of the Indiana University Bloomington, along with their respective graduate students, diligently scoured both the IU Folklore Collection and Archives for the old historical record, but met without success.[10] As is the case with most elements of the Nahanni

---

[10] The IU librarians and their graduate students did learn, however, that 'Waheela' is not an Ojibwa Chippewa word; that 'Waheela' means 'Matron of Honour' in the Oromo language, spoken by the Oromo people of Ethiopia and Kenya; that there is a 'Waheela Drive' in Chattanooga, Tennessee; and that

legends, the origins of the word 'Waheela' remains shrouded in mystery.

It must be mentioned that there is one article in Dorson's Folklore Archives which vaguely resembles the original Waheela story described by Sanderson. This tale was related by Russell Staffeld of Iron Mountain, Michigan, to graduate student Marilyn Dittmar on November 26, 1953. In this story, a band of Chippewa hunters, encamped at the entrance to the "Gap au Diable" in St. Mary's River (which drains Lake Superior into Lake Huron) "were awakened several nights in succession by the loud snarling and barking of a dog." As they had no dogs with them, they followed the sound first thing in the morning, but were unable to catch up with whatever was making it. "For the snarling creature was a Windigo, a monster in human form, who employed every artifice to entice the curious and unwary stranger to his habitation at the foot of the precipice, close to the water's edge, where he killed and ate those unfortunate enough to fall into his hands."

Using this technique, the Windigo managed to entice two of the hunters away from their camp and killed them. The remaining hunter, suspecting that something evil had befallen his friends, roamed the Saint Mary's River in search of them. In doing so, he came upon the Windigo.

there is a road called 'Wahella Way' 'Wahella' being a misspelling of 'Waheela' that appears once in *The Dire Wolf* in Columbia, Tennessee.

"He saw that he was like other men, except that he had behind a long tail like a dog's." The creature, the hunter noted, had taken up a position at the top of the precipice that towered over his home, while his wife remained at the bottom, ready to dispatch any unfortunates her husband threw down to her.

The hunter approached the monster and was welcomed by him. "The Chippewa asked him what he was doing at the top of the hill, barking like a dog. 'I was but exercising my lungs,' said the Windigo, 'in the fresh morning air.'" As he said this, the monster inconspicuously slipped a rock between his body and his bearskin shirt, apparently intending to use it on the hunter. The Chippewa noticed this sly manoeuver and attacked the Windigo, ultimately throwing him off the cliff. The monster's wife, being nearly blind, did not recognize her husband and, assuming that creature that tumbled down the precipice to lie at her feet was one of her husband's victims, promptly "put an end to his existence." The Chippewa then approached the Windigo's widow and clubbed her to death. "Thus were the two horrible Windigos slain by the Chippewa hunter, who proved himself a benefactor to mankind by removing the wretches who had slain so many of his kindred."

The 'Windigo' described this in this story is almost certainly a variation of the Wendigo or Weetigo, the cannibalistic monster described earlier in this book. It seems unlikely that Ivan Sanderson and Loren Coleman, both of them serious folklorists, would have mislabelled this famous character of Algonquin folklore a 'Waheela'. Nevertheless, the story does bear vague resemblance to the old historical record described by Sanderson; perhaps there is some connection between the two stories.

Interestingly, there is another dog-like character in Michigan folklore which has some similarities to the original Waheela from the old historical record, and to the Windigo described in the story above. Dubbed the "Michigan Dogman", this ghoulish creature has been described as a tall, wiry, hair-covered, anthropomorphic canine that walks on two legs. In her books *Hunting the American Werewolf* (2006) and *The Beast of Bray Road* (2003), Wisconsin-based journalist Linda S. Godfrey explored a potential connection between this animal and the skinwalker, another character of Algonquin folklore resembling the European werewolf.

THE SHUNKA WARAK'IN

In several books and online articles, a number of cryptozoologists have suggested a potential connection between the Waheela of the Nahanni Valley and the Shunka Warak'in of the Midwestern United States, a cryptid said to resemble a wolf or a hyena.

The concept of the Shunka Warak'in as a cryptid was first conceived by Lance Foster, an anthropologist of Ioway

Indian[11] descent, who detailed his theory in an online article entitled *Shunka Warak'in: A Mystery in Plain Sight.*

In 1991, Foster began his graduate studies in Anthropology at Iowa State University. His thesis revolved around the traditional Ioway medicine bundle system- a medicine bundle being a skin or cloth package containing items considered lucky or sacred, which was often worn by Plains Indian warriors to ensure success in battle. During the course of his research, Foster came across a passage in ethnologist Alanson B. Skinner's 1926 book *Ethnology of the Ioway Indians,* which described the legend behind a "hyena skin" which was a constituent in a particular Iowayan medicine bundle. The passage read:

"About this time [when the Ioway hero Wanathunje was alive] they killed the animal they called Shonka warawayka (Carrying-off-dogs) and placed its hide in the bundle. This is how it happened:

One time the people began to miss their dogs. Every morning a few were gone, and no one knew the cause. Some thought it the work of an enemy, so the young men got up a war party and hid themselves so as to surprise and kill the nightly visitor. It turned out to be a strange animal, different from anything they had ever seen before. They named it 'Carrying-off-dogs," but it is very like the animal the white people keep in their shows today and call hyena. When it entered the camp, the

---

[11] The Ioway are a Sioux people whose ancestral homelands include Southern Wisconsin and Eastern Iowa.

young warriors attacked it just as if it was a person. Again and again they shot at this creature, and could not kill it, but after following it a day and a half they at last succeeded in putting it to death. When it died, it cried just like a human being. When they heard this, and thought of the hard time they had in killing it, they decided that it must be a creature of great power. So they skinned it, and painted its hide, and later placed the hide in with the other powerful objects in the war bundle, to wear in battle across the shoulder to turn away flying bullets and arrows. But before the hide was put in the bundle, a big dance was held. Immediately afterwards a party set out and were very successful, as they killed a number of enemies, returning with many scalps.

Foster, being familiar with the Iowayan language, considered Skinner's translation of *"Carrying-off-Dogs"* to be slightly inaccurate, and renamed the creature *"Shunka Warak'in"*.

Skinner's story reminded Foster of a book entitled *Just West of Yellowstone: A Travel Sketchbook of the Area West of Yellowstone National Park*, written by a landscape architect named Rae Ellen Moore in 1987. In her book, Moore recalled paying a visit to a small museum in Henry's Lake, Idaho, where a mysterious stuffed canine was on display. Foster, who happened to have a passion for Fortean, was intrigued by this mystery canine and made some phone calls to see if the animal was still on display. To his disappointment, he learned that the museum at Henry's Lake had closed since the publication of Moore's book, and that no one knew where its contents had ended up.

When Foster came across Skinner's entry, he wondered whether the legendary Shunka Warak'in and creature from the Henry's Lake museum might be members of the same mysterious species, and passed on his theory to Loren Coleman, of whom he knew via his interest in Fortean. Using the information that Foster had given him, Coleman unearthed the fascinating backstory behind the stuffed animal from Henry's Lake, which, taking his cue from Foster, he dubbed the "Shunka Warak'in". Coleman included this story in his and cryptozoologist Jerome Clark's 1999 book *Cryptozoology A to Z*.

"The story of the Shunka Warak'in begins in the 1880s," Coleman wrote, "when members of the Hutchins family traveled west by covered wagon to settle in the Madison River Valley, near the West Fork, in the lower part of Montana." The family's patriarch, Israel Ammon Hutchins, established a ranch on his new land, which came to be known as the Sun Ranch. No sooner had he and his family settled into their new routine, however, than their lives were turned upside down by the arrival of a strange and unwanted visitor. Israel's grandson, zoologist Dr. Ross Hutchins, described the incident in his 1977 book *Trails to Nature's Mysteries: The Life of a Working Naturalist*:

"One winter morning my grandfather was aroused by the barking of the dogs. He discovered that a wolflike beast of dark *color was chasing my grandmother's geese. He fired his gun at the animal but missed. It ran off down the river, but several mornings later it was seen again at about dawn. It was seen several more times at the home ranch as well as at other ranches ten or fifteen miles down the valley. Whatever it was, it was a great traveler...*

"Those who got a good look at the beast described it as being nearly black and having high shoulders and a back that sloped downward like a hyena. Then one morning in late January, my grandfather was alerted by the dogs, and this time he was able to kill it. Just what the animal was is still an open question. After being killed, it was donated to a man named Sherwood who kept a combination grocery and museum at Henry Lake in Idaho. It was mounted and displayed there for many years. He called it 'ringdocus'."

Clearly, the ringdocus and the mystery canine described by Rae Ellen Moore were one and the same. In his book, Coleman put forth the theory that this creature might be a relict *Borophagus*, an ancient, bone-crushing, hyena-like dog known to have lived in North America during the Pleistocene. Alternatively, in a commentary on Coleman's article, cryptozoologist Jerome Clark put forth the notion that the animal might be a surviving *Hyaenodon montanus*, a species of carnivorous mammal believed to have gone extinct during the Obliocene Epoch (the geological epoch preceding the Miocene).

In November 2007, the *Bozeman Daily Chronicle* of Bozeman, Montana, ran with a story headlined *Mystery Monster Returns Home after 121 Years.* According to the article, a man named Jack Kirby- another grandson of Israel Ammon Hutchins- had spent years searching for the mysterious canine that his grandfather shot back in the 1880s. His quest took him to the Idaho Museum of Natural History in Pocatello, ID, where, he discovered, the stuffed ringdocus had been languishing for nearly twenty years.

The article contended that the specimen "strongly resembles a wolf, but sports a hyena-like sloping back and an odd-shaped head with a narrow snout. Its coat is dark-brown, almost black, with lighter tan areas and a faint impression of stripes on its side. It measures 48 inches from the tip of its snout to its rump, not including the tail, and stands from 27 to 28 inches high at the shoulder." Intriguingly, the article went on to mention that, according to the memoirs of Israel Hutchin's son, Elliott, the animal made haunting screams at night and, in its death throes, bit through a half-inch rope with a single bite and "exerted his very last strength to reach any one of us", displaying characteristics perfectly congruent with the indomitable, shrieking Shunka Warak'in of Iowayan legend.

Jack Kirby, who repossessed the ringdocus mount in his grandfather's name before donating it to the Madison Valley History Museum in Montana, declined Coleman's suggestion that he submit some of its hair for DNA analysis, preferring that the mystery live on. To date, no such DNA analysis has been conducted.

Relatively recent events suggest that the ringdocus might not be an isolated phenomenon. According to cryptozoologist Mark A. Hall, the 1990's saw numerous reports of "mean-looking, near-wolflike and hyena-like animals" in Alberta, Canada, as well as in the States of Nebraska, Iowa, and Illinois.

Then, in 2005 and 2006, a mysterious wild animal invaded farmers' properties all over Montana, killing a total of 120 sheep and seriously mauling many more. On November 2, 2006, the 106-pound culprit was shot in Garfield County, Montana, by state Wildlife Service agents. The creature's fur had a strange hue that ranged from red to orange to yellow, and appeared to be something other than a gray wolf, the only animal it even remotely resembled. Despite postulations that the animal was a Shunka Warak'in, the Montana Fish, Wildlife, and Parks Department identified it as a four-year-old male wolf with abnormally red fur.

Many prominent cryptozoologists have suggested, in their writings, that the Shunka Warak'in might be the same creature as the Waheela of North. Despite the fact that the ringdocus specimen, at least, is much smaller than the great white wolf reported in the subarctic, and has a completely different physiology, both animals are mysterious canids that appear to be very difficult to kill, and to be endowed with the ability to crush bones.[12]

THE MEDICINE WOLF

In his online article entitled *Witchie Wolves, Medicine Wolves, and the Waheela,* published on February 16, 2011, cryptozoologist Dr. Karl Shuker pointed out that the Waheela that Frank Graves encountered in 1965 bears striking resemblance to a New Mexican cryptid known to the Apache as the "medicine wolf."

"According to cryptozoological investigator Nick Sucik," Shuker wrote, "this is a very large, all-white wolf with long shaggy fur, plus a very large chest, and a somewhat long snout and body." Local Apache Indians long maintained that this creature could only be seen by "certain gifted people". One truck driver apparently endowed with such a gift saw a creature matching the description of the medicine wolf while driving down a road outside of Dulce, New Mexico, one evening in the summer of 1979. "Lit by his truck's headlights," Shuker wrote, "the animal came quickly out of some brush and paused briefly in the middle of the road, before swiftly moving away and vanishing into the darkness on the other side."

---

[12] In addition to the Amphicyon, both the hyena and the ancient *Borophagus*-creatures to which the Shunka Warak'in has been compared- have had jaws powerful enough to crush bones.

The 'Bulletproof Wolf' of Skinwalker Ranch

Another creature resembling the medicine wolf is said to have been seen by the former owners of what is known today as Skinwalker Ranch, a property located about 2 kilometres southeast of Ballard, Utah, were UFO sightings, cattle mutilations, poltergeist activity, and other unexplained phenomena have allegedly taken place for the past fifty years. The story goes that in the mid 1990's, while herding their first load of cattle into a corral located on the property, the ranch's new owners saw an enormous white wolf in a nearby pasture. This creature made its way across the field towards the family and, to their astonishment, approached them with its head down and its tail wagging, as if it were a beloved pet. It sidled up to the children and even allowed them to pet it.

Suddenly, the creature lunged at one of the calves that was pressed up against the side of the corral and locked its jaws onto its snout, apparently attempting to pull it through the bars. The family's patriarch leapt into action and proceeded to beat the animal with a stick. The beating had no effect, and the wolf continued to cling to his calf tenaciously. The rancher then seized a .357 Magnum revolver from his truck and shot the wolf at point-blank range. The animal hardly seemed to notice.

Astounded, the rancher shot the wolf a second time, whereupon it released the calf and looked at him quizzically. After firing two more bullets into the giant canine, which elicited neither blood nor the faintest flicker of distress, the man retrieved a hunting rifle from his truck and shot the beast a fifth time, blowing a chunk of hairy flesh from its shoulder. Incredibly, the wolf remained unfazed. After taking a sixth bullet, the creature appeared to recognize that it was unwanted. Seemingly no worse for wear, the giant white wolf turned tail and trotted off into the distance, creating yet another bizarre parallel between the Nahanni Valley and the American Southwest.

AMAROK

According to Ivan Sanderson in *The Dire Wolf*, the Dene of the Mackenzie Mountains maintained that giant, white, wolfish Waheela were more common in the Arctic, and that most of them only travelled south into subarctic territory once a year. Intriguingly, the Inuit have their own legends of a solitary white lupine colossus which once inhabited the Arctic, which they called the "Amarok". Is it possible that the legends of the Amarok and the Waheela derive from encounters with the same type of mysterious animal?

In *Tales and Traditions of the Eskimo*, written by Danish geologist Dr. Hinrich Johannes Rink in 1875, the Amarok is described as a fabulous wolf of enormous size, bigger than a polar bear yet not as large as an Agshik (another "fabulous monster"). The Amarok has more stamina than a bear, but lacks the ability to swim. It can hold an entire caribou in its jaws and still have enough room in its mouth to roar.

In one traditional Inuit tale recounted in Rink's book, an Amarok took pity on an Inuit boy named Kagsagsuk and helped him attain special powers. Kagsagsuk was an orphan and a weakling, and was treated cruelly by everyone in his band. When he had taken more abuse than he could endure, "he ventured out among the mountains by himself, choosing solitary places, and meditating how to get strength... Once, standing between two high mountains, he cried out: 'Lord of strength, come forth! Lord of strength, come to me!'"

To Kagsagsuk's surprise, an Amarok emerged. Terrified, the Inuit boy started to run for his life, but the Amarok caught him and twisted his tail around him. Using his tail, the Amarok squeezed a number of seal bones from Kagsagsuk's body. The giant wolf informed the bewildered Inuit that these bones had been stunting his growth. "If it be thy wish to become strong and vigorous," the Amarok told him, "thou mayst come every day to me."

Kagsagsuk did as instructed and made daily visits to the Amarok. Every day, he underwent the same procedure, allowing the Amarok to squeeze some more seal bones from his body, and becoming a little stronger every day as a result. Kagsagsuk made an effort to conceal his new strength from his spiteful tribesmen, planning to shame them all once he reached his full potential.

That winter, three polar bears were seen climbing an iceberg not far from the Inuit village. Seal hunting was out of the question at that time of year due to the frozen condition of the sea ice, and the hungry band was in sore need of fat and meat. In spite of this, none of the Inuit hunters dared to approach the three polar bears- members of the most powerful species in the Arctic, aside from monsters like the Amarok and the Agshik.

Kagsagsuk decided to use this opportunity to reveal his newfound strength to his tormenters. Using nothing more than his mukluks and his gloved hands, he climbed the iceberg that the polar bears had ascended. When he reached the top, he wrestled with one of the bears and succeeded in slamming it so hard against the iceberg that it ripped in half. The band members, who had gathered at the foot of the iceberg to watch the spectacle unfold, gazed in astonishment as Kagsagsuk picked up the remaining two polar bears one by one, hoisted them above his head, and hurled them off the iceberg to their deaths. From then on, Kagsagsuk's fellow tribesmen treated him with deference and respect.

The Nahanni Valley is said to be home to a number of mysterious creatures. So far, we have explored the Nakani, which some believe to be type of wildman similar to the Sasquatch; the Nuk-luk, which Loren Coleman proposed might be a Neanderthal; and the Waheela, which Ivan Sanderson suspected might be a bear-dog. All three of these crypids, in the eyes of most cryptozoologists, are anachronisms hailing from bygone eras; living fossils like the coelacanth and the horseshoe crab, defying extinction in the last hidden corners of the globe. As it turns out, these three are not the only prehistoric monsters said to roam the Nahanni Valley, living out their secret lives in the most wild, unexplored alcoves of the Northland. In fact, they are just the tip of the iceberg.

Prehistoric Monsters

"They have tales of enormous animals such as the mammoth,
and spiders as large as a full-sized grizzly bear, and long worms
that are supposed to be alive today and nobody can save them
from these animals but their doctors. Some of the Indians will
tell you they have seen these animals."

- Poole Field, in a letter to John "Jack" Moran, Feb. 8, 1913.

GEOGRAPHERS DESCRIBE THE South Nahanni as an
"antecedent river"- a rare sort of waterway older than
the ancient mountains that surround it. Millions of
years ago, the Tlogotsho, Sunblood, and Ragged Ranges rose
up around the South Nahanni, sheltering it from the
enormous, destructive ice sheets that reshaped the face of
North America throughout the four Ice Ages of the
Pleistocene Epoch. Due to its unique geological makeup, the
Nahanni Valley has remained unaffected by glaciation for at
least 100,000 years.

Over the millennia, all manner of flora and fauna have
taken refuge in this secluded haven in the Mackenzie
Mountains. Some of them have left behind fossil evidence of

their habitation. Raymond Patterson came across some of these fossils in Deadmen Valley at the mouth of the Meilleur Canyon, and in 1963, Canadian paleontologist B.S. Norford, with the help of Albert Faille, discovered the fossils of two new species of Cambrian trilobite near Broken Skull River, which he named *Fieldaspis nahanniensis* and *Kochiella mackenziensis*.

Intriguingly, Indian reports and frontier legend suggest that descendants of some of the prehistoric animals that made their homes in the Nahanni- particularly massive, fearsome Pleistocene monsters- still reside there to this very day.

DINOSAURS

In many of his articles on the Nahanni Valley, Philip Godsell related a story told to him by Frank Beatton, who served as the Chief Factor of Fort St. John, B.C. Beatton had heard this story from a scientific party; whose members had heard it from one of their Indian guides, a Cree named Chequina; who had, in turn, heard the tale from his father.

A great wanderer, Chequina's father once travelled to Upper Liard River Country[1], where he fell in with a

---

[1] Chequina's father travelled to different albeit roughly proximate locations in other versions of the story, including "the Lower Mackenzie," the head of the Peace River, the headwaters of the Sekanni Chief River, and "Athabasca Country".

"primitive tribe[2] armed with bone-shod javelins and clubs
made from the jawbones of the moose. Around their fires,
these Stone Age people had told of a 'medicine valley' to the
north, inhabited by monsters of fearful size and ferocity." One
of the Cree's new Dene acquaintances produced a scrap of
buckskin from his medicine bag on which had been burned the
image of one of these monsters. The Cree managed to acquire
this charm and treasured it for years. He eventually passed
the artifact down to his son, Chequina, who showed it to the
scientific party he was tasked with guiding. The scientists
told an incredulous Beatton that the figure depicted on the
buckskin scrap was a "dinosaur", drawn in flawless
anatomical detail.

At first glance, idea of dinosaurs living in the Nahanni
Valley- presumably the 'medicine valley' referred by to by the
Stone Age tribesmen- appears to hinge upon the tropical
valley legend. Until relatively recently, dinosaurs were
believed to be cold-blooded creatures unable to withstand cold
environments. In fact, one of the most widely-held theories
regarding the mysterious demise of the dinosaurs, known as
the Cretaceous-Paleogene extinction event, holds that these
kings of the Mesozoic died out as a result of global cooling.
Assuming that this is true, dinosaurs could only survive in
the frozen Northland in a warm enclave like the tropical
valley.

---

[2] In most versions, these primitive tribesmen are the Sikanni, while in the
earliest version, they are the "Grand Lac Indians".

As of relatively recently, however, paleontologists have unearthed fossil evidence suggesting that some dinosaurs actually did survive in relatively cold environments, and that they may not have been cold-blooded as previously thought. Tropical valley or not, perhaps the idea of dinosaurs in the Nahanni Valley is not as farfetched as it seems.

MAMMOTHS

Legend has it that a forgotten vale tucked away somewhere in the watershed of the South Nahanni is home to relict populations of woolly mammoths- giant, hairy, elephant-like creatures generally believed to have gone extinct around 4,500 years ago. As Philip Godsell put it in *Romance of the Alaska Highway*, the this ravine said to be "a palm girt oasis that had escaped the impact of the Last Ice Age, where living dinosaurs and mammoths of a forgotten age disported themselves in steaming pools rich with luxuriant vegetation." Godsell, in one of his pieces, went on to speculate that "perhaps these ideas originated form Indian reports brought down from the Lower Mackenzie of frozen mammoths being exposed in the falling away of ice cliffs, leaving their flesh- though millions of years old- still fit, when thawed, for dog feed."

Indeed, the North Country once abounded with stories of trappers and prospectors happening upon frozen mammoth carcasses during their boreal wanderings. For example, the 1935 book *The Golden Grindstone: The Adventures of George*

M. Mitchell relates a tale told by a Yukon prospector named
Angus Graham, who claimed to have come across the remains
of a mammoth ensconced in ice in 1898; unfortunately, the
specimen disintegrated when it was finally exposed to the air.
On October 21, 1937, a mammoth washed up on the shores of
Wrangel Island, situated in the Chukchi Sea north of the
Bering Strait, its frozen flesh in near-perfect condition. And,
during the Gold Rush of '98, Stampeders came across, as
Pierre Berton put it in *The Mysterious North*, "the bones and
skulls and even the flesh of animals that have long since
vanished from the earth- the hairy mammoth, the great
tusked mastodon, and varieties of bison, deer, and horse long
extinct," all of these things embedded in the frozen muck of
the Klondike goldfields.

Frozen corpses aren't the vestiges of the woolly
mammoth to show up in the North Country. On particular
stretches of the Yukon River, and along the shores of
Williston Lake in Peace River Country, one can find ancient
mammoth footprints baked into stone, reminiscent of the
giant three-toed tracks reported by Hank Russell, Jack Lee,
and Frank Perry in their "tropical valley" accounts.
Mammoth tusks are also found in surprising abundance in the
Northland. Frontiersmen would often decorate their cabins
with ancient bones they picked up in the wilderness, and
trinkets fashioned from mammoth ivory were once a staple of
Northern gift shops.

In his book *Son of the North*, Charles Camsell described a room on the upper level of Fort Simpson's 'Big House', the residence of all the senior HBC officers and their families, which the *engages* called the 'Ivory Room'. This room housed "a collection of fossil tusks, bones, and teeth of the mammoth."

Adjacent to the Ivory Room was a recreation room dominated by a billiards table. "I remember one winter," Camsell wrote, "when new balls did not arrive with the years' outfit and the attempt was made by the steamboat engineers to turn balls on a lathe out of mammoth ivory some hundreds or thousands of years old. It was then that I first learned the hell of elliptical billiard balls. This ivory in the form of tusks could be found here and there over the North Country…"

Nu′ uti

Dene mythology is filled with tales of giant, monstrous animals called *yareidi* which roamed the world in ancient times. These creatures typically lived underground, or beneath lakes and rivers, and every once in a while people come across their bones, which are called "*Kctien-Tigna*", or "the bones of the underground game".

Some of these monsters are simply gigantic versions of modern animals. For example, Dene legend has it that ferocious giant beavers once wandered about North Country, terrorizing the natives they met along the way. Three of them lived on Lake Athabasca, in Northwest Alberta and Northeast British Columbia, and drowned people by slapping their huge tails on the water. Another giant beaver built his home on Great Slave Lake at the mouth of the Yellowknife River, while another inhabited Nahanni Butte; the Beaverdam Rapids on the Liard River constitute the remains of one of his lodges.

Interestingly, there is another *yareidi,* a huge, elephant-like monster called *"Nu'uti"*, which is almost certainly based upon the mammoth. In his ethnographic reconstruction of the Kaska Indians, John Honigmann related and old Kaska legend featuring one of these creatures.

The story goes that a Nu'uti once accosted a group of Dene campers. "A Shaman who had six fingers went out to meet the animal and addressed it like a person."

The monster told the shaman that it had been stalking him and his friends for some time, and that it intended to eat them. The shaman returned to the camp and urged his friends to flee for their lives. He himself went back to deal with the monster.

The rest of the band fled about twenty miles over the mountains and made camp on the other side. Eventually, they were rejoined by the shaman, who told them that he had delayed the monster, and that it would arrive at their camp in the morning.

"With daylight," Honigmann wrote, "they heard a howling and saw two bars of light in the mountains. All the people became afraid." Once again, the elephant-like monster appeared and approached the camp, and once again the shaman confronted it. This time, the shaman informed the creature that the two of them were going to make a trip together. With that, the pair disappeared into the forest, leaving the rest of the band behind.

The shaman returned to the band after ten days "reeking so strongly that the people could smell him a mile off. He explained that when he had reached the monster, the latter had swallowed him. 'I went all through the guts and came out the other end. That's why I smell so strong.' He then directed the people to smoke him in a fire of rotten wood." After circling the fire and singing, the shaman was made pure again.

This particular story, along with the concept of the Nu'uti in general, seems to imply a strong cultural recollection of living mammoths. In other words, the evidence suggests that the Dene, or perhaps their nomadic ancestors, lived alongside mammoths and dramatized their interactions with them in their oral history. However, this is not the only way in which pre-contact Dene might have developed the notion of giant elephantine monsters.

On the southern bank of the Yukon River, about thirty miles downstream from the mouth of the Tanana, is a considerable deposit of petrified mammoth bones, buried long ago when a section of the riverbank caved in. The local Tanana Indians referred to this place as "*Na-Radenilna-Katlona*", or "The Cutbank of the Spirit Land", believing that disembodied human souls hunt *yareidi* on their way to *Na-radenilna-ta* (the "transitional paradise" that they dwell in before being reincarnated), and that the fossils on the riverbank are the bones of their giant prey- leavings from their ghostly journey.

Ed Farrell's Stories

In the late 19th and early 20th Centuries, frontiersmen returned from the wilderness of Alaska, Yukon, and the Northwest Territories with tales of mammoths and mastodons[3] that still inhabited the most desolate reaches of the Northland. Some of these tales found their way into newspapers and magazines, and a few of these made it into Ed Ferrell's book *Strange Stories of Alaska and the Yukon.*

Ferrell began his chapter on relict mammoths with an article first published on May 5, 1889, in the *Philadelphia Press*. In this article, the writer, a fur trader named Cola F. Fowler, described a story that he heard in 1887.

That summer, Fowler left Kodiak Island, Alaska, and travelled to the headwaters of the Snake River, a waterway which empties into the Bering Sea at Nome, Alaska. There, he met with the chief of a local Inuit band and proceeded to inspect some of the ivory tusks that the natives had collected in the wilderness. "I subjected the ivory to a rigid inspection,"

---

[3] Mastodons were relatives of the mammoth which are believed to have disappeared around 10,000 years ago, at the end of the Pleistocene.

Fowler wrote, "and upon two of the largest tusks, I found fresh blood traces and decomposed flesh."

After the trader pointed this out to the chief, the Inuit informed him that, three months earlier, he and a handful of young men had encountered a small mammoth herd about fifty miles north of their present location, and managed to kill an old bull and a cow with their large-caliber muskets.

At Fowler's insistence, the Inuit drew his impression of the creature on the soft clay of the riverbank using a stick. The animal- which, he maintained, made loud, shrill, trumpet-like calls- resembled a woolly mammoth, albeit with smaller ears, bigger eyes, and a longer, more slender trunk. Interestingly, the creature had four 4-foot tusks in addition to two curved 15-footers.

In a commentary at the end of the article, Ferrell observed that the monster that the Inuit drew is consistent in appearance with a Eubelodon, or "four tusker"- an ancient relative of the woolly mammoth which lived during the Miocene Epoch, and which was unknown to science at that time.

Farrell included several more stories of living subarctic mammoths in his book, including a story in which a man named Dr. J.P. Frizzell found fresh mammoth tracks in the snow of Unimak Island, one of the Aleutian Islands situated off the Pacific Coast of Alaska, in 1903; the account of a Tahltan hunter's 1892 brush with a woolly mammoth in the valley of the Stikine River; and an incredible tale, later proven to be a hoax, describing a successful mammoth hunt in the Alaskan wilderness in the early 1890's.

MOOSE, BEARS, AND PORCUPINES

Many old magazine and newspaper articles maintain that some of the moose that live in the Nahanni Valley are twice as big as elsewhere. In the early 1970's, an RCMP officer-turned-television host named Tommy Tompkins caught one of these legendary creatures on film and showcased it in an episode of his TV show *This Land*, entitled *"Nahani"*. Tompkins estimated that the antlers that the massive bull sported were a whopping twelve feet from end to end- double the antler spread of the average moose. When considered alongside some of the theories purported to explain other faunal freaks reported in the area, the legend of the giant moose of the Nahanni evokes the Irish elk, an Old World cervid which lived during the Pleistocene Epoch, and the largest deer that ever lived.

In addition to giant moose, there have been many reports of colossal grizzly bears in the Nahanni Valley. In *Dangerous River*, for example, Raymond Patterson described seeing a "very large grizzly in Deadmen Valley" which Gordon Matthews named "Slim Jim". This creature was said to be "enormous as a boxcar, and as timid as a deer".

Both Gus Kraus and Nazar Zinchuk, in their Parks Canada interviews, spoke of giant grizzlies in the Nahanni.

Kraus recalled a "monster" grizzly "the size of a two-year-old moose" that obliterated a trail near Bennett Creek. Zinchuk, on the other hand, described coming across a 12-foot-tall grizzly in the wilderness. According to the Alaska Department of Fish and Game, Kodiak bears- the largest subspecies of grizzly bear- seldom exceed a height of 10 feet.

In Sir Ranulph Fiennes' book *The Headless Valley*, an Oblate missionary named Father Mary recalled finding grizzly paw prints in the show which dwarfed the tracks that he made with his size eleven overshoes. Similarly, Frank Graves, in a letter to Ivan Sanderson, described coming across a "real horror" during his Nahanni Valley excursion in 1965. "These were definitely bear tracks," he wrote, "but if I told you their size- and I measured them with my collecting tape- you would just laugh at me. They were bear tracks all right, and the Indian said that they were made by giant brown bears that, as far as I could make out from his pacing things off between the trees, would make any Kodiak Brown look like a Black Bear cub."

One man to see one of these bruin behemoths with his own eyes was adventure writer D.H. Koester, who paddled the South Nahanni with his 12-year-old stepson Mark in the 1970's. In his 2015 book *Canoe on the Nahanni*, Koester described how he and his stepson capsized their canoe on the Cache Rapids just upstream from the First Canyon. Mark managed to pull himself up onto a rock ledge alongside the river, while Koester crawled onto a gravel bar downstream.

That night, while trying to keep warm on the gravel bar, Koester saw a massive grizzly emerge from the forest on the other side of the river, wade through the current to an island in the middle of the South Nahanni, and set about demolishing the trees there. He was "the size of an Abrams tank..." Koester maintained, "bigger even than any polar or Kodiak. He must have stood 12 feet tall, taller than the trees he was busy swatting down- and massive- his arms were the size of tree trunks and his paws twice as big."

These enormous Nahanni grizzlies, in the context of the other giant animals detailed in this chapter, evoke the *Arctodus simus*, or the short-faced bear, one of the largest land-dwelling mammals to ever live. This monstrous animal, believed to have disappeared from North America about 11,000 years ago, could reach a height of twelve feet. Interestingly, in his book *The Beasts that Hide from Man*, British cryptozoologist Dr. Karl Shuker mentioned that extremely large, snow-white bears, known to local Chukchi hunters as "*irkuiem*", have been reported in Russia's Kamchatka peninsula (sandwiched between the Sea of Okhotsk and the Bering Sea), and that Russian zoologist Professor Nikolah Vereschagin opined that they might be modern-day representatives of the short-faced bear.

John and Joanne Moore, the namesakes of Moore's Hot Springs, saw neither the short-faced bear nor the Irish elk during their year in the Nahanni Valley in the late 1970's, although they did see a number of average-sized bears, wolves, wolverines, moose, and caribou. They did, however, also see an enormous porcupine which they initially mistook for a small black bear.

THE NAHANNI LION

In his letter to Ivan Sanderson, the anonymous letter-writer mentioned in the previous chapter learned from his Dene informant, Gugo, that the Waheela was "almost invincible, but he has one enemy.

"Now hang on to your hat!

"That enemy is a LION!

"I thought he meant Puma, which I wouldn't have believed anyway, but no he meant a lion... The lion is itself a giant, at least as big as the bloody dog, and apparently afraid of nothing. Very hairy, with a large woolly [mane] extending nearly all over its body. The lions kill everything when in the mood, including the bears, moose, and what would appear to be mammoths. The latter being described as creatures bigger than all the others, with long noses. I assume that this was what was meant by the description, as Gugo didn't have a name for it and the interpreters seemed rather amazed."

In keeping with the pattern we have been following in this chapter, this enormous lion of the Nahanni Valley conjures up images of not only the famous *Smilodon*, or sabre-toothed tiger, but also the North American cave lion, an extinct subspecies of lion that lived in North America during the Pleistocene Epoch. The North American cave lion is believed to have measured 1.6-2.5 metres (5'3"-8'2") from nose to the base of its tail. With a shoulder height of 1.2 metres (3'11"), it is believed to be one of the largest felines to ever live.

Epilogue

"To me, the Nahanni is a great example of folklore in the making. Trappers and Indians and prospectors and writers like myself have all been spreading these tales and laying them on a little thicker as each year goes by. That's the way fairy tales grow, you know."

- Pierre Berton, circa 1947

IN AUGUST 1970, CANADIAN Prime Minister Pierre Elliott Trudeau flew into Nahanni country by bush plane and travelled down a section of the South Nahanni in a motor boat. Upon his return to Ottawa, he was convinced that the region ought to be preserved as a national park, and tasked his Minister of Indian and Northern Affairs- future Prime Minister Jean Chrétien- with carrying out his vision. Two years later, the Nahanni National Park Reserve was established. Six years after that, the area was named a UNESCO World Heritage Site- the very first of its kind.

The Nahanni Valley would likely never have been made into a Canadian National Park were it not for the mystique it had garnered over the years, and it would probably never have acquired its mystique were it not for the colourful characters whose exploits formed the foundations of the legends for which it became famous. It is almost grotesquely ironic that, in immortalizing this stretch of the Mackenzie Mountains so near and dear to their hearts, these characters innocently and inadvertently destroyed many of the things that they loved best about it. No longer are Dene men like Big Charlie and Diamond See free to hunt moose and mountain sheep in the Nahanni Valley, nor prospectors like Poole Field and Albert Faille allowed to stake claims on Bennett Creek. Trappers like Raymond Patterson and Gordon Matthews are forbidden to build cabins in Deadmen Valley, and the entrance to *Grotte Valerie* is sealed from explorers like Jean Poirel with an iron gate. Nevertheless, hard-core outdoor adventurers still make summer pilgrimages to the national park to tackle the world-renowned rapids of the South Nahanni, and to climb the sheer granite peaks near Rabbitkettle Lake, called the Cirque of the Unclimbables.

In spite of this modest traffic, the Nahanni remains to this day one of Canada's most remote regions, accessible only by boat or canoe. In this wild stretch of the Northwest Territories, on days when the fog rolls in to permeate the valley with an aura of mystery and romance, it's easy to entertain the notion that perhaps somewhere high up in the mist-shrouded crags of the Mackenzie, or somewhere in the deepest corners of the taiga, a land of lost gold, Indian curses, and creatures long consigned to the realm of myth and legend lurks in concealment, just waiting to be discovered.

Note from the Author

Dear Reader,

Thank you for reading *Legends of the Nahanni Valley*! I hope you enjoyed reading it as much as I enjoyed putting it together.

If you have any questions, comments, or concerns about this book, or would just like to get in touch, please feel free to shoot me an email at:

Hammerson@HammersonPeters.com

All the best,

Hammerson Peters

Bibliography

GARY MANGIACOPRA'S ARCHIVE

Courtesy of Mr. Gary S. Mangiacopra

- *Cursed Treasure of Deadman's Valley,* in June 1968 issue of magazine *Saga,* by Brad Williams and Choral Pepper

- *Fortean Expedition,* in what is probably a 1948 issue of *Doubt: The Fortean Society Magazine*

- *Information You Can't Get Elsewhere,* December 1948 issue of magazine *Adventure,* by Philip H. Godsell

- *Hunting the Hudson's Bay Barren Lands,* March 1948 issue of magazine *Adventure,* by Philip H. Godsell

- *Canadian North: Rabbit for Supper, Bears in Yard,* in July 16, 1986 issue of *The New York Times,* by Christopher S. Wren

- *Northwest Territories: No Shangri-La,* in February 24, 1947 issue of *Time* magazine

- *Don't Lose Your Head Over the Waheela!,* in *The Beasts that Hide from Man* 2003 , Dr. Karl P.N. Shuker

- *Three Expeditions to Explore 'Head Hunter Valley' in Canada,* in January 6, 1947 issue of *The Washington Post*

- *The Mystery of Headless Valley,* in fall 1974 issue of *Gold!* Magazine, by Tom Browne

- *The Camp-Fire,* in October 1949 issue of *Adventure* magazine, by Philip H. Godsell

- *The Camp-Fire,* in May 1952 issue of *Adventure* magazine, by Philip H. Godsell

- *Ask Adventure,* in February 1948 issue of *Adventure* magazine, by Philip H. Godsell

- *Ask Adventure,* in November 1951 issue of *Adventure* magazine, by Philip H. Godsell

- *Ask Adventure,* in December 1949 issue of magazine *Adventure*, by Philip H. Godsell

- *The Curse of Dead Man's Valley,* in August 1950 issue of *Adventure* magazine, by Philip H. Godsell

- *The Camp-Fire,* in August 1950 issue of *Adventure* magazine, by Philip H. Godsell

- *4 Start Flight to Prove 'Headless' Valley Myth,* in February 3, 1947 issue of *New York Mirror,* by Pierre Berton

- *'Headless Valley' Trek,* in February 4, 1947 issue of *New York Mirror,* by Pierre Berton

- *Headless Valley Plane Frozen In at 37 Below,* in February 5, 1947 issue of *New York Mirror,* by Pierre Berton

- *...Headless Valley Party,* in February 6, 1947 issue of *New York Mirror,* by Pierre Berton

- *Braves 70-Below Cold,* in February 7, 1947 issue of *New York Mirror,* by Pierre Berton

- *Lost Valley Trek Halted by 'Luck',* in February 9, 1947 issue of *New York Mirror,* by Pierre Berton

Bibliography

- *Headless Valley Plane Beats Stork in Wilds,* in February 10, 1947 issue of *New York Mirror,* by Pierre Berton

- *Air Expedition Within Sight of Lost Valley,* in February 11, 1947 issue of *New York Mirror,* by Pierre Berton

- *'Valley' Plane in 2d Mercy Flight,* in February 12, 1947 issue of *New York Mirror,* by Pierre Berton

- *No Tropic Isle in Headless Valley,* in February 13, 1947 issue of *New York Mirror,* by Pierre Berton

- *Fliers Roam 'Headless' Valley, Spike Legends,* in February 14, 1947 issue of *New York Mirror,* by Pierre Berton

- *Find Headless Valley Ghosts Very Much Alive,* in February 15, 1947 issue of *New York Mirror,* by Pierre Berton

- *Yukon Expedition Finds 3 U.S. Bombers 'Bones',* in February 16, 1947 issue of *New York Mirror,* by Pierre Berton

- *Gold Find Reported By Headless Valley Party,* in February 19, 1947 issue of *New York Mirror,* by Pierre Berton

- *Canada's Superstition Mountains- Strange Story of Gold in the Valley of Vanishing Men,* in August 1986 issue of *Treasure* magazine, by Howard Duffy

- *Canada's New Gold Boom,* in January 1946 issue of T*he Saturday Evening Post,* by Gordon Carroll

- *Of Triumph and Failure,* in November 18, 1954 issue of *The New York Times,* by Stuart Keate

- *The Wilderness Was Home,* in December 17, 1961 issue of *The New York Times,* by Stuart Keate

- *General,* in November 25, 1961 issue of *The New Yorker*

- *General,* in December 11, 1954 issue of *The New Yorker*

- *http: marina.fortunecity.com reach 361 calgary.htm,* September 27, 2004, by Calgary Visitor

- *http: marina.fortunecity.com reach 361 ferry.htm,* September 27, 2004, by Ferry Verwijk

- http: marina.fortunecity.com reach 361 eliseuson.htm, September 27, 2004, by Mike Eliseuson

- Discourse with reader from Prince George, B.C., http: marina.fortunecity.com reach 361 axel friedrich.ht m, September 27, 2004, by Axel Friedrich

- Book Review: R.M. Patterson- A Life of Great Adventure from Petroleum History Society Archives, October 2003, D.W. Axford

- http: marina.fortunecity.com reach 361 dave wolfe.htm, September 27, 2004, by Dave Wolfe

- *The Fate of Frank and Willie McLeod,* from http: marina.fortunecity.com reach 361 mcleods.htm

- *Ask Adventure Experts,* in January 1953 issue of *Adventure* magazine, by Philip H. Godsell

- *Ask Adventure Experts,* in June 1950 issue of *Adventure* magazine, by Philip H. Godsell

- *The Camp-Fire,* in February 1948 issue of *Adventure* magazine, by Philip H. Godsell

- *Ask Adventure,* in May 1952 issue of *Adventure* magazine, Philip H. Godsell

- *McCloud's Missing Millions,* in August 1972 issue of *Treasure* magazine

- *The Camp-Fire,* in June 1949 issue of *Adventure* magazine, by Philip H. Godsell

- *The Camp-Fire,* in November 1947 issue of *Adventure* magazine, by Philip H. Godsell

- *Ask Adventure Experts,* in March 1948 issue of *Adventure* magazine, by Philip H. Godsell

- *Ask Adventure Experts,* in July 1947 issue of *Adventure* magazine, by Philip H. Godsell

- *Ask Adventure Experts,* in July 1947 issue of *Adventure* magazine, by Philip H. Godsell

SOCIETY FOR THE INVESTIGATION OF THE UNEXPLAINED S.I.T.U. ARCHIVES

I.e. Ivan T. Sanderson's archives; courtesy of Dr. Michael Swords and Mr. Will Matthews

- *Alaskan A.B.S.M.'s?,* in May 1984 issue of Info journal, by Scott DeLancey

- *2 26* -b

- *Additional Nahanni,* October 17, 2012, by Fanari Lloyd

- *Canada's Lost World,* by Gordon Cooper

- *Letter to Loren Coleman,* January 28, 1964, by Constable R.C. Clarke of the Liard Detachment of the R.C.M.P.

- *Proto-Historic Period- Mackenzie Drainage Indians*

- *Nakani,* from *Mysterious Creatures: A Guide to Cryptozoology;* 2002 by George M. Eberhart

- *Loren Coleman Piece with Myth References*

- *Letter to Ivan T. Sanderson,* October 7, 1971, by John A. Nicol Director of National and Historic Parks Branch

- *Letter to Ivan T. Sanderson,* circa 1965, by Frank Graves

- *Prehistoric Animals: A Letter to Ivan T. Sanderson*

- *British Explorer Group Unravels Yukon's Mysteries, in the* Thursday, January 20, 1972 issue of *The New York Times.*

- *Some Preliminary Notes on Traditions of Submen in Arctic and Subarctic North America,* by Ivan T. Sanderson

- *Letter to the Department of Indian Affairs and Northern Development,* August 17, 1971, by Ivan T. Sanderson

- *Into Death Valley- Four Men in a Boat,* April 6, 1971

- *Undated Adventure Magazine Article,* by Philip H. Godsell

- *Wonders of the Canadian North: British TV Viewers to Glimpse*

- *Winnipeg Free Press,* August 13, 1963

- *Wonders of the Canadian North: British TV Viewers to Glimpse,* by Kevin Doyle

PERSONAL JOURNALS AND LETTERS

- The journal of David Wolfe, 1965

- The Journal of Captain James Foxe, 1631-1632

- *The Hargrave Correspondence,* 1821-1843, James Hargrave courtesy of the Champlain Society

- *Two Journals of Robert Campbell,* 1808-1853

- *Private Correspondence between Hammerson Peters and Anthony Roche,* 2017

Bibliography

ACADEMIC ARTICLES

- *Kutchin Legends from Old Crow, Yukon Territory*, in 1964 issue of *Anthropological Papers of the University of Alaska*, edited by Charles J. Keim

- *Some Social Functions of Kutchin Anxiety* 1960 , Cornell University, by Richard Slobodin

- *On the Superstitions of the Ten'a Indians*, in 1911 issue of *Anthropos Institut*, by Rev. Father Julius Jette

- *Inuit Knowledge and Perceptions of the Land-Water Interface* May 2007 , PhD thesis, by Scott Heyes

- *The Enemy of Every Tribe: 'Bushman' Images in Northern Athpaskan Narratives*, in November 1978 issue of *American Ethnologist*, by Ellen B. Basso

- *Mammal Investigations on the Canol Road, Yukon and Northwest Territories, 1944*, for the National Museum of Canada's *Bulletin No. 99*, by A.I. Rand

- *Mammals of the Yukon Territory*, in the 1975 issue of the National Museum of Natural Sciences' *Publications in Zoology, No. 10*, by Phillip M. Youngman

- *Range Extensions of Some Mammals from Northwestern Canada*, in April, 1964 issue of National Museum of Canada's *Natural History Papers*, by Phillip M. Youngman

- *Intercontinental Migration of Large Mammalian Carnivores: Earliest Occurrence of the Old World Beardog Amphicyon Carnivora, Amphicyonidae in North America*, in 2003 *Bulletin of the American Museum of Natural History*, by Robert M. Hunt, Jr.

- *The South Nahanni River Region 1820-1972 : Patterns of Socio-Economic Transition in the Canadian North*, thesis submitted to the University of Manitoba's History Department in September 1980, by Kerry M. Abel

- *A Preliminary Archaeological Assessment of Nahanni National Park and Vicinity: Stage 2, 1978* 1979 , by Charles W. Amsden

- *Are There Nahani Indians?* in 1956 issue of the Canadian Anthropology Society's magazine *Anthropologica*, by John J. Honigmann

- *Vegetation and Environment Patterns of Liard River Hot Springs Provincial Park, British Columbia,* Masters' thesis submitted to Simon Fraser University's Department of Biological Sciences, by Terry Charles Reid

- *Mary Gibson Henry Expeditions,* for the Royal B.C. Museum, by Ross Peck

- *The Kaska Indians: An Ethnographic Reconstruction* 1964 , by John J. Honigmann

- *The Ethnography of the Great Bear Lake Indians* 1933 , by C.B. Osgood

- *Mountain Indians,* in *Handbook of North American Indians: Volume 6, Subarctic* 1981 , by Beryl C. Gillespie

- *Nahani,* in *Handbook of North American Indians: Volume 6, Subarctic* 1981 , by Beryl C. Gillespie

- *'Pygmies' of the Far North,* in the March 2008 issue of *Journal of World History,* by Kirsten A. Seaver

MAGAZINE ARTICLES

- *Nahanni Caves Reveal Link in Man's Past,* in March 11, 1939 issue of *The Star Weekly,* by Philip H. Godsell

- *Mary Gibson Henry, Plantswoman Extraordinaire,* in 2000 issue of Harvard University's Arnold Arboretum's magazine *Arnoldia*

- *The Dire Wolf,* in October 1974 issue of the Society for the Investigation of the Unexplained S.I.T.U. magazine *Pursuit,* by Ivan T. Sanderson

Bibliography

- *Traditions of Submen in Subarctic and Arctic North America: Part 1,* in First Quarter 1983 issue of *Pursuit,* by Ivan T. Sanderson

- *Traditions of Submen in Subarctic and Arctic North America: Part 2,* in First Quarter 1983 issue of *Pursuit,* by Ivan T. Sanderson

- *Dead Men's Gold,* in the 1937 issue of the R.N.W.M.P. Veterans' Association's magazine *Scarlet & Gold* magazine courtesy of University of British Columbia's Wallace B. Chung and Madeline H. Chung Collection , by Philip H. Godsell

- *The Nahany Lands,* in the Summer 1961 issue of *The Beaver,* by Raymond M. Patterson

- *Introduction* to the June 1946 issue of the *Alberta Folklore Quarterly,* by Philip H. Godsell

NEWSPAPER ARTICLES

- *13 Died,* in July 17, 1946 issue of the *Chicago Tribune,* by one of the members of the Murray family

- *Penetrate Far North in Search of Gold,* October 12, 1912 issue of *The Lethbridge Daily Herald*

- *Double Tragedy of the Far North: Skeletons of Frank and Willie McLeod Found on the Banks of the Nahanni River,* in January 13, 1909 issue of the *Manitoba Free Press*

- *Ill-Repute of Nahanni Tribe Exaggerated, Veteran Says,* in December 24, 1929 issue of the *Toronto Daily Star*

- *Prospector Vanishes in Dead Man's Valley,* in September 26, 1933 issue of *Toronto Daily Star*

- *Follow 28-Year-Old Trail to Seek Slain Men's Lode,* in January 17, 1934 issue of the *Toronto Daily Star*

- *Dream Identifies Old Mine Left When Brothers Slain,* in January 18, 1934 issue of the *Toronto Daily Star*

- *Air Pilot Returns from Nahanni Area,* in January 26, 1934 issue of the *Toronto Daily Star*

- *Staking Extensive on McLeod Claims,* February 19, 1934 issue of the *Toronto Daily Star*

- *Don't Quote Me: Gossip for the Gullible,* in March 10, 1934 issue of the *Toronto Daily Star*

- *Great Bear Lake Co. Cash is Increased,* in June 14, 1934 issue of the *Toronto Daily Star*

- *Two Trappers Missing,* in June 16, 1936 issue of the *Toronto Daily Star*

- *1,000-Foot Cross of Snow Guards Blood-Red Valley,* in October 9, 1937 issue of the *Toronto Daily Star*

- *Forbidding Caves Tell Man's Story,* in March 9, 1939 issue of the *Toronto Daily Star*

- *Valley of Dead Claims 13 Lives in Gold Search,* in July 16, 1946 issue of the *Toronto Daily Star*

- *Fear Prospector is 14th Headless Valley Victim,* in October 12, 1946 issue of the *Toronto Daily Star*

- *Claims Semi-Tropical Valley Found in 72-Below-Zero Land,* in October 15, 1946 issue of the *Toronto Daily Star*

- *Headless Valley 'Heaven' But No Place For Any Man,* in January 7, 1947 issue of the *Toronto Daily Star*

- *Pair Poised for Trip to 'Headless Valley',* in January 11, 1947 issue of the *Toronto Daily Star*

- *Death in Headless Valley But No Gold, Major Warns,* in January 27, 1947 issue of the *Toronto Daily Star*

- *Headless Valley Big Myth No Head Hunter- Prospector,* in February 7, 1947 issue of the *Toronto Daily Star*

Bibliography

- *'Headless' Death Toll 'Is Stupidity'- Pilot,* in February 10, 1947 issue of the *Toronto Daily Star*

- *Police Records Tell of Tragedy in the Far North,* in August 23, 1922 issue of the *Edmonton Bulletin*

- *The Mysterious Nahanni,* in August 5, 1922 issue of the *Edmonton Bulletin*

- *Motherlode of Yukon Believed Found: Rich Strike is Made on the Nahanni River,* in March 10, 1922 issue of the *Edmonton Bulletin*

- *Headless Valley Myths Dispelled,* in February 15, 1947 issue of *The Desert News,* by Pierre Berton

- *Tropical Valley Myth,* in February 19, 1936 issue of the *Ottawa Journal*

- *Headless Valley Remains Mystery,* in September 26, 1946 issue of the *Winnipeg Tribune*

ONLINE ARTICLES

- *Ancient Navajo and Native Americans Migrations,* http: navajopeople.org blog ancient-navajo-and-native-americas-migrations , May 23, 2012, by Harold Carey Jr.

- *Discovery of the Athabascan Origin of the Apache and Navajo Languages,* http: www.sjsu.edu faculty watkins navajo.htm, San Jose State University, by Thayer Watkins

- *The Hero of the Dene,* http: uphere.ca articles hero-dene, April 1, 2015, by Daniel Campbell

- *Hachoghe Fights Three Giant Beavers,* www.ntwexhibits.ca yamoria documents Yamoria-Legends.pdf, Adapted from a story told by Madeline Mouse to Robert G. Williamson on the Liard River

- *Sasquatch Sighting by Nunavik Berry Pickers*, in October 4, 2012 issue of CBC News, http: cbc.ca news canada north sasquatch-sighting-by-nanavik-berry-pickers

- *N.W.T. man tells of encounter with nahga- the Tlicho sasquatch- following boat accident*, in July 28, 2016 issue of CBC News, by Hilary Bird, www.cbc.ca news canada north whati-man-nahga-bushmen-encounter

- *Yamoria Virtual Companion Exhibit*, www.nwtexhibits.ca yamoria

- *Dire Wolves, Sunka Warak'ins, and Waheelas*, on October 11, 2010, CryptoMundo.com, by Loren Coleman

- *History*, www.BlueStoneAdventures.com

- *Shunka Warak'in Taxidermy Specimen Found!* on November 15, 2007, CryptoMundo.com, by Loren Coleman

- Shunka Warak'in: A Mystery in Plain Sight, March 3, 2009, http: paranormalmontana.blogspot.ca 2009 03 shunka-warakin.html, by Lance Foster

- http: nosleepparanormal.tumblr.com post 82161427772 the-history-of-cryptids-can-be-traced-over

- *Was it a Shunka Warak'in?* on December 10, 2006, http: cryptomundo.com cryptozoo-news mccone-shunka , by Loren Coleman

- *Waheela Watching*, on August 22, 2011, http: cfz-canada.blogspot.ca 2011 08 waheela-watching.html

- *Did Denisovan-Neanderthal-Human Interbreeding Result in the Headless Valley's Nakani?* November 1, 2011, http: www.cryptozoonews.com nakani , Loren Coleman

- http: canadianparks.com northwest nahninp page2.htm, by Herb Norwegian

- http: www.jeanguillemot.com En offres Expedition Nah anni Chronologie.htm

- *Nahanni: Heads and Tales on the River of Gold,* http: www.canoe.ca che-mun 102nahanni.html

STRANGEARK.COM
Courtesy of Mr. Chad Arment

- *Unidentified Canids in North America,* in December 2002 issue of *North American BioFortean Review,* by Nick Sucik

- *The Valley Without a Head,* in October 2004 issue of *North American BioFortean Review,* by Frank Graves and Ivan T. Sanderson

- *Canada's Headless Valley Revisited: Troglodytes, Bigfoot, Mystery Bears, and Dire Wolves,* in January 2006 issue of *North American BioFortean Review,* by Gary S. Mangiacopra and Dwight G. Smith

- *Giant White Wolves in Canada,* in 2000 issue of *North American BioFortean Review,* by Paul W.

- *Literature from the Past,* Katharine Scherman, 1956, reprinted in very first issue of the *North American BioFortean Review*

PARKS CANADA INTERVIEWS

- Interview of Nazar Zinchuk 1-4 , 1979, by William D. Addison & Associates courtesy of NWT archives

- *Nahanni National Park Historical Resources Inventory: Volume I* interviews with Raymond M. Patterson and Willy McLeod, plus appended documents , 1975-1976, by W.D. Addison & Associates

- *Nahanni National Park Historical Resources Inventory: Volume II* interviews with Gus Kraus and Billy Clark, plus appended documents , 1975-1976, by W.D. Addison & Associates

LYNN HANDCOCK FONDS

Courtesy of Ms. Lynn Handcock

- *Northern Women: Interview with Mary Kraus,* conducted by Addison & Associates of Parks Canada on August, 2, 1973

- *Northern Women: Interview with Mary Kraus,* conducted by Addison & Associates of Parks Canada on August 7, 1973

- *Northern Women: Interview with Mary Kraus,* conducted by Addison & Associates of Parks Canada on August 9, 1973

- *Northern Women: Interview with Mary Kraus,* conducted by Lynn Handcock on November 4, 1994

- *Northern Women: Interview with Mary Kraus,* conducted by Lynn Handcock on December 5, 1992

- *Northern Women: Interview with Mary Kraus,* conducted by Lynn Handcock on December 6, 1992

PHILIP H. GODSELL FONDS

Courtesy of the Glenbow Museum

- *Dead Men's Gold,* by Philip H. Godsell

- *Copy of Poole Field's Letter to John "Jack" Moran,* dated July 14, 1939

- *The Curse of Dead Men's Valley,* in *Harding's Magazine: Fur-Fish-Game,* by Philip H. Godsell

PIERRE BERTON FONDS

Courtesy of McMaster University

- *Box 160- Headless Valley Articles, Speeches, and Scripts,* by Pierre Berton

- *Box 160- Headless Valley: Original Series of Articles for the Vancouver Sun,* by Pierre Berton

- *Box 161- North to the Nahanni Series,* by Pierre Berton

- *Box 163- Nahanni Letters, Telegrams, INS Articles,* by Pierre Berton

- *Box 163- Headless Valley Nahanni Valley Expedition,* by Pierre Berton, F1, and F2

- *Box 163: Mysterious North Trip,* F1, F2, and F3

UNIVERSITY OF INDIANA FOLKLORE ARCHIVES

- *Box 9- Michigan Lore* entire box

- *Box 10- Michigan Lore* entire box

- *Box 13- Indian Folklore* entire box

- *Box 21- Legends: Various Monsters* entire box

POOLE FIELD FONDS

Courtesy of the Northwest Territories Archives

- *Poole Field Memorial* 1992 , Norm Kagan

- *Letter from Poole Field to John "Jack" Moran,* dated February 8, 1913

- *Letter from Poole Field to John "Jack" Moran,* dated June 27, 1939

- *Letter from Poole Field to John "Jack" Moran,* dated July 14, 1939

- *Letter from Poole Field to John "Jack" Moran,* dated July 17, 1939

NORM KAGAN FONDS

Courtesy of the Athabasca Archives

- *Poole Field Memorial,* by Norm Kagan

- *Albert Faille and the Dangerous River,* for the 1991 issue of the Minnesota Canoe Association's magazine *HUT!,* by Norm Kagan

- *Nahanni Gold,* by Kerry Abel

- *Letter from Norm Kagan to Ms. Marilyn Mol,* dated December 6, 1995

- *Letter from Marilyn Mol to Norm Kagan,* dated November 23, 1995

- *Letter from Norm Kagan to Ms. Marilyn Mol,* dated October 23, 1995

- *Letter from Marilyn Mol to Norm Kagan,* dated September 12, 1995

- *Letter from Norm Kagan to Ms. Marilyn Mol,* dated July 20, 1995

BOOKS

- *The History and Stories of the Gwichya Gwich'in* 2007 , by Michael Heine, Alestrine Andre, Ingrid Kritsch and Alma Cardinal

- *Cryptozoology A to Z: The Encyclopedia of Loch Monsters, Sasquatch, Chupacabras, and Other Authentic*

Bibliography

Mysteries of Nature 1999 , by Jerome Clark and Loren Coleman

- Canoe on the Nahanni 2015 , by D.H. Koester

- Klondike: The Last Great Gold Rush, 1896-1899 1972 , by Pierre Berton

- Of Wolves and Men 1978 , by Barry Lopez

- The Beasts that Hide from Man: Seeking the World's Last Undiscovered Animals 2003 , by Karl P.N. Shuker

- The Bigfoot Book: The Encyclopedia of Sasquatch, Yeti, and Cryptid Primates 2015 , by Nick Redfern

- The Dangerous River: Adventure on the Nahanni 1954 , by Raymond M. Patterson

- Tales and Traditions of the Eskimo 1875 , by Henry Rink

- The Mad Trapper of Rat River: A True Story of Canada's Biggest Manhunt 2003 , by Dick North

- Amazing Flights and Flyers 2010 , by Shirlee Smith Matheson

- Pierre Berton: A Biography 2008 , by A.B. McKillop

- The Beast of Bray Road: Tailing Wisconsin's Werewolf 2003 , by Linda S. Godfrey

- Sasquatch: Legend Meets Science 2006 , by Dr. Jeff Muldrum

- The Mysterious North: Encounters with the Canadian Frontier, 1947-1954 1956 , by Pierre Berton

- Nahanni 1975 , by Dick Turner

- Nahanni Journals: R.M. Patterson's 192-1929 Journals, edited by Richard C. Davis

- The Headless Valley 1973 , by Sir Ranulph Fiennes

- *Nahanni: The River Guide* 1993 , by Peter Jowett

- *The Field Guide to Bigfoot, Yeti, and Other Mystery Primates Worldwide* 1999 , by Loren Coleman and Patrick Huyghe

- *Tales from the Dena: Indian Stories from the Tanana, Koyukuk, & Yukon Rivers* 1995 , by Frederica de Laguna and Dale DeArmond

- *Romance of the Alaska Highway* 1944 , by Philip H. Godsell

- *The Arctic Forests* 1924 , by Michael H. Mason

- *Hunting the American Werewolf* 2006 , by Linda S. Godfrey

- *Drum Songs: Glimpses of Dene History* 1993 , by Kerry Abel

- *Nahanni Remembered* 1997 , by A.C. Lewis

- *Nahanni: River of Gold... River of Dreams* 1993 , by Neil Hartling

- *Ten Rivers: Adventure Stories from the Arctic* 2005 , by Ed Struzik

- *Scenic Wonders of Canada: An Illustrated Guide to Our Natural Splendors* 1979 , by Reader's Digest

- *Son of the North* 1954 , by Charles Camsell

- *Lost Bonanazas of Western Canada: 13 True Stories of Lost Mines, Buried Treasure, or Outlaw Loot from British Columbia, Alberta, and the Northwest Territories* 1983 , by Garnet Basque

- *Hotsprings of Western Canada: A Complete Guide* 1978 , by Jim McDonald, with Donna Pollack and Bob MacDermot

Bibliography

- *Fur Trade and Exploration: Opening the Far Northwest, 1821-1852* 1983 , by Theodore J. Karamanski

- *Starting Out, 1920-1947* 1987 , by Pierre Berton

- *Wings of the North* 1980 , by Dick Turner

- *Mike Krutko's Amazing Adventures* 2004 , by Mike Krutko

- *Strange Stories of Alaska and the Yukon* 1996 , by Ed Farrell

- *Raincoast Sasquatch: The Bigfoot Sasquatch Records of Southeast Alaska, Coastal British Columbia & Northwest Washington from Puget Sound to Yakutat* 2003 , by Robert Alley

- *Nahanni Trailhead: A Year in the Northern Wilderness* 1980 , by Joanne Ronan Moore

- *The Sasquatch and Other Unknown Hominoids* 1984 , by Vladamir Markotic and Grover Krantz

- *Mysteries Creatures: A Guide to Cryptozoology, Volumes I and II* 2002 , by George M. Eberhart

- *In Search of Prehistoric Survivors: Do Giant 'Extinct' Creatures Still Exist?* 1995 , by Karl Shuker

FILM

- *Nahanni,* 2013, by Stephanie Huc and Jean Guillemot

- *Nahanni,* 1962, National Film Board of Canada, by Donald Wilder

- *Headless Valley,* 1958, by Mel and Ethel Ross

OTHER SOURCES

- *The Trail of '35: An Address by Charles Camsell to the Members of the Empire Club,* on March 13, 1936

- *Documenting and Interpreting the History and Significance of the North West Mounted Police Peace-Yukon Historic Trails,* June 11, 2008, report prepared for the Northern Interior Region Inter-Agency Management Committee, the North Peace Historical Society, and the Halfway River First Nation; by David Mills

- *Commentary on Loren Coleman's 1996 article 'On the Trail: Hunting Hyenas in the U.S.,* 1999, Jerome Clark

- *Our 'tropical' Arctic,* James F. Bassinger

The *Oak Island Encyclopedia*, coming to Mysteries of Canada this summer. To learn more, please check out our Facebook page:

www.Facebook.com CanadianHistory

Printed in Great Britain
by Amazon